"Drinks hard, and swears much"

White Maryland Runaways,

1770-1774

Compiled by

Joseph Lee Boyle

CLEARFIELD

Copyright © 2010 by Joseph Lee Boyle
All Rights Reserved

Printed for
Clearfield Company by
Genealogical Publishing Company
Baltimore, Maryland
2010

ISBN 978-0-8063-5503-0

Made in the United States of America

INTRODUCTION

One of the many neglected episodes of American history is that of the many thousands of white Europeans did not come to the colonies as free men and women. Instead they came as indentured servants, political exiles, or transported convicts. White servitude was a major institution of the social and economic fabric of colonial British America. Bound whites preceded the used of black slaves in every colony. It is estimated that from 350,000 to 500,000 servants were imported through 1775. Though by the start of the eighteenth century the importation of black slaves increased dramatically in the Chesapeake and southern colonies, white bound labor remained significant.

There were thousands of white people who wanted to leave their home countries, but were unable or unwilling to pay the cost of their passage, so they became servants for a period of years to a colonial master who purchased them. Others were convicts or exiles. More than half the whites who came to the colonies south of New England were servants. Those who came voluntarily hoped for a better life. Most indentures were from four to seven years, though this varied.

Some were kidnapped to the colonies, as made famous in Robert Louis Stevenson's *Kidnapped*, but many are likely to have made the claim to escape the terms of their indenture. Others may have runaway from home to leave their families, debt, or other personal problems.

Of course the numbers of both free and indentured immigrants depended on economics. For example, the Irish came in a wave in 1770-1775 due to the collapse of the linen industry. Crop failures, wars, and economic disruptions in general added to the level of immigrants.

Underwriting of transportation was sometimes assumed by the planter, or more often by English merchants specializing in the sale of indentured servants. Recruiting agents called "crimps" hired drummers to recruit, sometimes making extravagant promises about the good life in the colonies. Illiterates were likely the most easily taken advantage of.

Though convicts were sent to the colonies before, the Transportation Act of 1718 opened the floodgates for exiled criminals, those convicted of minor crimes could be sent to the colonies for seven year terms. Capital crimes meant terms of fourteen years. After serving their time, they were eligible for royal mercy, and could return to England, but returning early was a capital offense. Convicts were attractive as they were relatively cheap, their sales prices were about one-third that of African slaves, and female felons sold for only two-thirds the price of males. From 1718 to 1773, some 50,000 convicts from all parts of Europe were sent to America.

Importation of servants into Maryland reached its height in the middle of the eighteenth century, while convicts arrived in ever-increasing numbers. In Maryland there was always a market for "His Majesty's Seven-Years Passengers" despite prejudice against them. The perceived evils of the consignment of convicts to Maryland and Virginia, resulting in those colonies passing laws by 1723. But the Lords Proprietor rejected this. Maryland passed a number of other acts to regulate the convict trade, such as imposing duties on each one imported.

After arrival in America, "soul drivers" sometimes drove coffles of convicts from town to town, selling them as they progressed into the interior of a colony drove coffles of convicts from town to town, selling them as they progressed into the interior of a colony. This was not without risks to the drivers. In 1774 a Baltimore merchant purchased a parcel of convicts, most of which he sold, except four men before he reached Frederick. One complained that he was too tired to go on, and they rested by a tree, the driver then insisted they go on, but they refused, threw him over a tree, dragged him into the woods, and cut his throat from ear to ear. All four were hanged for their crime.

Benjamin Franklin noted convicts that "must be ruled with a Rod of Iron" and considered "emptying their jails into our settlements is an insult and contempt, the cruellest, that ever one people offered to another." While the colonists were incensed about receiving so many convicts, surviving court records do not show that they committed an inordinate number of crimes. Perhaps the lack of large towns, commercial activity, and general lack of opulence did not lend themselves to crimes the way the cities of England did, nor was there an existing criminal subculture.

There were also "redemptioners," initially German, and then British. They promised to pay ship captains on their arrival in America. If they could not pay, or find a relative or countryman to do so, the captain was free to dispose of them for a number of years, (usually two to seven) to defray the cost of their passage. For many this must have been a distress sale, as they could not return to Europe. Coming in family or large groups, they sold their own, or their children's labor for the cost of passage. The redemptioners were often called "free-willers."

These potential immigrants had the opportunity to negotiate the cost before they embarked. The time involved varied, depending on the amount owed. Upon arrival the immigrant usually had up to fourteen days to negotiate a sale of his services. If he could not do so, the shipper recovered his costs by selling the indenture to the highest bidder.

The Chesapeake colonies received the highest number of servants, followed by Pennsylvania. So many Irish Catholics came to Maryland, that the Protestants became alarmed and a duty was imposed on them, while Protestant servants came in free. The Irish were more likely to come than the English as they were not bound to their parishes by the Poor Laws, and provided with a meager sustenance.

There was money to be made at multiple levels. The contractor who arranged the transportation profited, the ship owner and captain profited, and if the transport involved convicts, the county sheriff in England or Ireland had his palm out to facilitate the process. At one time Irish sheriffs received five pounds a head for convicts sentenced to transportation, but paid out only three pounds to the merchant transporters. Subject to supply and demand at the ports, agents would sometimes keep servants on shipboard or in houses until a sale at a good price could be arranged. Once in America, if the servant ran away, local officials were eager to earn rewards for their capture.

There were risks at all levels of the investment. Some absconded before boarding the ship. While ship captains wanted to make as much as possible from transportation the servants, the less they paid for food, the more they made. Though high shipboard mortality was regrettable, some always occurred after six to eight weeks at sea. While convict cargoes were generally chained, there were cases of uprisings with the ship's crew being overpowered.

Ship arrivals in the colonies tended to be seasonal, with the fall preferred, so that ships could take cured tobacco back to Europe, and new arrivals would have cooler weather to adjust to their new environment. The term "seasoning" was applied to newcomers, whose death rate varied, but was rarely less than ten percent, and as high as forty percent. Malaria in particular was a chronic problem in the Chesapeake area.

Masters purchased their labor, not their bodies, but it was a risky investment. Death, injuries, chronic maladies, running away, or a shirking worker could mean loss of income. But cheap labor was more important than quality labor.

While the terms of indentures varied a great deal, the master was usually required to provide his servants with "sufficient meat, Drink, Apparell, Washing and Lodging." Of course what was "sufficient" from the master's view, was often not deemed such by the servant. White servants had the right to go appeal their treatment to the courts. Maryland courts often took masters to task for the denial of rest, sleep, food, drink, and lodging. A third offense by a master was grounds to set a servant free.

On the other hand, colonial courts could impose servitude, usually for larceny or debt, if restitution could not be made, and fines and court costs paid. A 1692 Maryland law provided that a white woman who married a Negro would become a servant for seven years, if the Negro were free, he was to become a servant for the rest of his life. These individuals, as well as apprentices are included in this collection.

If servitude was to be a significant source of reliable labor, runaways could not be permitted to go free with impunity. As might be expected most runaways departed April through October, staying closer to home during winter weather. Non-English speakers might have runway less, whereas the Irish might have runaway more, due to the general anti-Irish feelings of the time. The not infrequent references to iron collars in these ads, show that running away was common. The collars were intended to make an example of the truants and to make identification easier.

Passes were required for those more than a certain distance away from home. Those who appeared to be suspicious characters, or could not give satisfactory accounts of themselves were committed to jail and held temporarily. Even if no master appeared to pay the costs of the man being held, he still might be remanded to servitude.

Unsuccessful flight also added to the time of servitude. In Maryland, a law was passed in 1661 that added ten days service for every day away. This was done partly as punishment, and partly to compensate for the costs of capture, reward and return. On the other hand bad or abusive masters were sometimes punished by the judicial system with the shortening or cancelling of indentures.

All forms of servitude were an important factor in the development of a landed aristocracy in the Chesapeake colonies. They were also vital in the nascent American industrial scene. Many of the runaways left from iron forges or furnaces.

For those fulfilled the terms of their indentures "well and faithfully [in] such employments as the master may assign" for a set period of time, the average man had a better chance of attaining a decent standard of living than he did in Europe. The master had paid for passage to the colonies, and for food, drink, clothing and shelter during the time of the indenture, and depending on the individual transaction, some form of "freedom dues," which could be money, land, tools, livestock, etc.

For the ambitious servant, the term of servitude was a time of preparation. He was used to the climate and ways of the new land. He learned farming or another skill as practiced in the New World. He made contacts in the area he lived, and if an artisan, might have a ready list of customers when on his own. Abbott Emerson Smith estimated that one in ten would take up land and become prosperous, and that one in ten would become an artisan. The other eight died in servitude, returned to England, and or became "poor whites."

The American Revolution stopped the transport of convicts and regular migration. Though regular immigration resumed, and limited indentured servitude resumed after the war, convicts were not permitted. Botany Bay in Australia became the dumping ground for those undesirables beginning in 1786.

The runaway ads provide a first-hand view of history, as well as valuable demographic information with the age, sex, height, place of origin, clothing, occupation, speech, as well as physical imperfections, etc. They often display attitudes of the owners, and personality traits of the runaway, such as a common affection for alcohol. Some ads give extensive vignettes of individuals with their perceived idiosyncrasies. They provide a bonanza of information for the social historian. Those interested in tracking their ancestors will also find a goldmine of details

It is impossible to know how many runaways there really were. Escapees of low value or close to the end of their terms may not have been advertised. Given that so many of the servants appear to be scapegraces, one wonders why their masters spent money to advertise for them, let alone pay a reward for their return. Those who were useful workers with lots of time remaining were likely to be the most sought after. Masters were likely to ignore those who left for a few days of dissipation, particularly planters during the slow season.

Some masters may have not wanted to pay the cost of the ads. Those masters whose servants absconded from the lower Eastern and Western shores of Maryland, and the farther western parts of the colony may not have bothered to advertise in papers printed in distant Annapolis and Baltimore. One wonders why John Moore bothered to advertise for John Harris who had been gone for three years and "drinks hard, and swears much, and used to have a sore leg."

The reader will note that many of those who appear only in Pennsylvania newspapers were from Cecil County, Maryland. Relative proximity to Philadelphia was part of the reason, but the barrier of the Susquehanna river was another. Ferrymen would demand passes, and supplementing their incomes with rewards was always appealing

All of the legible ads for runaways appearing in the two Maryland newspapers are included. These include fugitives from Delaware, New Jersey, Pennsylvania, and Virginia. Maryland, Pennsylvania and New York newspapers are represented, with one runaway, Sarah Wilson, appearing only in New England papers. The *Virginia Gazette* was not included in this compilation as it is online. I have retained the original spelling, punctuation, and capitalization of the ads. Illegible words or letters are indicated by brackets.

This compilation lists only white men and women. In the Maryland newspapers ads, wherein whites and blacks are listed together, I list the names of the blacks without any details. For blacks the reader is referred to: Lathan A. Windley, *Runaway Slave Advertisements: A Documentary History from the 1730s to 1790, Volume 2, Maryland* (Westport, Conn.: Greenwood Press, 1983).

Sometimes the ads in different papers are very similar and only the ad which occurs first in time is included, with references to the later ones. Minor differences in the advertisements are considered to be capitalization, spelling such as trousers/trowsers and 7/seven. If the ads are substantially different, each appears at the time it is first run. The three ads for James Dickson/Edward Rogers illustrate the differences as well as the use of aliases by runaways. Advertisements that are largely illegible are not included.

It will be noticed that far more men were runaways than women. In part this was due to the imbalance in the ratio of those who were indentured. A 1755 census in Maryland showed that of 1,981 transported convicts that year, almost 80 percent were men.

The reader may wonder was John Roberson really only four feet tall? Did a man named Cullen have the first name of Joan? There are a number of variations in names such as Legh Master/Masters. John R. Holliday, John Robert Holliday, and John Robert Hooliday are doubtless the same individual based on the context of the ads. When the same runaway appears in different ads, the relevant ads are referenced.

For further reading:

Blumenthal, Walter Hart. *Brides From Bridewell: Female Felons Sent to Colonial America* (1962, reprint, Westport, Conn.: Greenwood Press, 1973).

Coldham, Peter Wilson. *Emigrants in Chains: A Social History of Forced Emigration to the Americas of Felons, Destitute Children, Political and Religious Non-Conformists, Vagabonds, Beggars and Other Undesirables, 1607-1776* (Baltimore: Genealogical Publishing Company, 1992).

Ekirch, A. Roger. *Bound for America: The Transportation of British Convicts to the Colonies, 1775-1778* (Oxford: Clarendon Press, 1987)

Fogleman, Aaron S. "From Slaves, Convicts, and Servants to Free Passengers: The Transformation of Immigration in the Era of the American Revolution," *The Journal of American History* 85 (1998), 43-76.

Galenson, David W. *White Servitude in Colonial America: An Economic Analysis* (Cambridge: Cambridge University Press, 1981)

Kellow, Margaret M. R. "Indentured Servitude in Eighteenth-Century Maryland," *Histoire Sociale — Social History* 17 (November 1984), 229-255.

Lancaster, R. Kent. "Almost Chattel: The Lives of Indentured Servants at Hampton-Northampton, Baltimore County," *Maryland Historical Magazine* 94 (1999), 340-362.

McCormac, E. I. *White Servitude in Maryland, 1634-1820* (Johns Hopkins University Studies in Historical and Political Science, Series XXII, Baltimore, 1904).

Meaders, Daniel. *Dead or Alive: Fugitive Slaves and White Indentured Servants Before 1830* (New York: Garland Publishing, 1993).

Menard, Russell R. "From Servants to Slaves: The Transformation of the Chesapeake Labor System," *Southern Studies*, 16 (1977), 355-388.

Miller, William. "The Effects of the American Revolution on Indentured Servitude." *Pennsylvania History* 7, 3 (July, 1940), 131-41.

Morgan, Kenneth. "Convict Runaways in Maryland, 1745-1775," *Journal of American Studies* 23 (August 1989), 253-68.

Morgan, Kenneth. "The Organization of the Convict Trade to Maryland: Stevenson, Randolph and Cheston, 1768-1775," *The William and Mary Quarterly* third series 42, (April 1985), 201-227.

Prude, Jonathan. "To Look Upon the "Lower Sort": Runaway Ads and the Appearance of Unfree Laborers in America, 1750-1800," *The Journal of American History* 78 1 (June, 1991), 124-159.

Semmes, Raphael. *Crime and Punishment in Early Maryland* (Baltimore: The Johns Hopkins University Press, 1938, reprint 1996.

Sollers, Basil. "Transported Convict Laborers in Maryland During the Colonial Period," *Maryland Historical Magazine* 2 (1907), 17-47.

Smith, Abbot Emerson. *Colonists in Bondage: White Servitude and Convict Labor in America, 1607-1776* (1947; reprint; Gloucester, Mass.: Peter Smith, 1965)

Tomlins, Christopher L. *Reconsidering Indentured Servitude: European Migration and the Early American Labor Force, 1600-1775.* American Bar Foundation Working Paper #9920 American Bar Association, 1999.

NEWSPAPERS CONSULTED

It should be noted that many of these newspapers did not have a complete run for the period. For example, *The Maryland Journal, and the Baltimore Advertiser*, did not begin publication until August 1773. Also there were no newspapers published in Delaware or New Jersey for the entire period.

Boston Evening Post
The Boston Gazette, and Country Journal
The Boston News-Letter
Boston Post Boy
Connecticut Courant
Connecticut Gazette
Connecticut Journal
Dunlap's Pennsylvania Packet or, the General Advertiser
Essex Gazette
Essex Journal
The Maryland Gazette
The Maryland Journal, and the Baltimore Advertiser
The Massachusetts Spy Or, Thomas's Boston Journal
The New-Hampshire Gazette
The New-Hampshire Gazette, and Historical Chronicle
The New-London Gazette
The New-York Gazette; and the Weekly Mercury
The New-York Journal; or, The General Advertiser
The Norwich Packet and the Connecticut, Massachusetts, New-Hampshire and Rhode-Island Weekly Advertiser
The Pennsylvania Chronicle, and Universal Advertiser
The Pennsylvania Gazette
The Pennsylvania Packet; and the General Advertiser
The Providence Gazette; And Country Journal
Rivington's New-York Gazetteer
Der Wöchentliche Pennsylvanische Staatsbote, (Philadelphia),

1770

Lancashire Furnace, *Baltimore* County, *Dec.* 4.
RAN away last Night, from the Subscriber, a Convict Servant, named EDWARD HOOPER, about Twenty-four Years of Age, fair Complexion, about 5 Feet 3 or 4 Inches high, wears his own dark brown Hair: Had on, and took with him, an Osnabrig Shirt and Trousers, an old Fearnought Jacket, and Cotton Breeches. This fellow has on an Iron Collar when he went away, being under a Prosecution for Housebreaking.

Ran away from his Bail, at the same Time, JOHN BISHOP, by Trade a Collier, about Thirty Years of Age, 5 Feet 6 or 7 Inches high, wears his own lank dark brown Hair, is a thin Fellow, speaks in the *Shropshire* Dialect, and has a remarkable Scar on his left Hand: Had on, and took with him, a Copper coloured Suit of Cloaths, a drab lappelled Waistcoat, new blue Cloth Breeches, old blue Coat, and a close bodied Great Coat. It is supposed he is a great Villain, and has inveigled away the said Servant, who, it's supposed, he will be in company with, and possibly will spare him some of his Cloaths; as likewise a Woman, who passeth for his Wife, and a Child, about Two Years old; the Woman is about Twenty-one, or Twenty two Years of Age, about 5 Feet 1 or 2 Inches high, fair Complexion, and brown Hair; she had on a dark coloured Shalloon Gown, red Petticoat, and black Silk Hat; she strolled some Time ago from *Queen-Anne's* County, on the Eastern Shore. Her maiden name was *Ann Hand*. Whoever apprehends said Runaways, so that they may be had again, and gives Notice to the Subscriber, shall have Forty Shillings Reward for *Edward Hooper*, and Three Pounds for *John Bishop*, with reasonable Charges, if brought home.
GEORGE RANDELL.
The Maryland Gazette, January 4, 1770; January 11, 1770; January 18, 1770.

RAN away from the Subscriber, at *Marsh* Creek, an indented Servant Man, named THOMAS WHITE, a Carpenter by Trade, about Five Feet Six Inches high, thin Visage, red Hair, wears it sometimes tied, and he formerly liv'd with Mr. *Roberts* in *Annapolis*: Had on, when he went away, a blue patch'd Coat and Jacket, and Leather Breeches.—Whoever takes up said Servant, and secures him in any Jail, shall have Fifty Shillings Reward, and reasonable Charges if brought home, paid by
ROBERT BIGHAM.
The Maryland Gazette, January 4, 1770.

January 12, 1770.
RAN away last Night from *Piscataway*, a white Servant Boy, named JAMES TAYLOR, belonging to the Rev. Mr. *Boucher*, of *Virginia*, He is about 16 Years of Age, pretty lusty, has short light colour'd Hair, and is of a ruddy Complexion: Had on and took with him when he went away, a black Velvet Cap, blue Duffil Great-Coat, Drab Frize Coat, with Cape and Sleeves, with plain Silver Buttons, plain blue Broadcloth Waistcoat, with a like Button, Leather Breeches, and Boots and Shoes. Whoever apprehends the said Servant, and brings him to his Master, shall be rewarded for his Trouble. JOHN BAYNES.

The Maryland Gazette, January 18, 1770; January 25, 1770; February 1, 1770; February 15, 1770; February 22, 1770; March 1, 1770.

RUN away from the subscriber, living on Elkridge, in Ann Arundel county, Maryland an Irish convict servant man, named John Fowler; he is a tanner by trade, about 30 years of age, 5 feet 10 inches high, a lusty down looking fellow, and much pitted with the small-pox, has long black hair, not tied; he had on and took with him, a Carolina felt hat, newly dressed, a blue surtout coat, a black broadcloth coat, a pair of brown cloth breeches, a pair coarse country knit stockings, coarse shoes, and check shirt. Whoever takes up said servant, and brings him to the subscriber, shall have, if taken 10 miles from home, TWENTY SHILLINGS, and if out of the province, FIVE POUNDS reward, paid by GEORGE SCOTT.

N.B. It is supposed that said servant has papers of Jacob Hoolbrooke's.

The Pennsylvania Gazette, January 18, 1770.

RUN away from the subscriber, living at Patapsco Ferry, Maryland, on the 14th of this instant December, a convict servant man, named JOHN PRAT, about 6 feet high, with red hair, and a down look, he appears of be about 25 years of age; had on, when he went away, a long blue jacket, with leather buttons, a white flannel under jacket, bound round with black, an ozenbrigs shirt, long ozenbrigs trowsers, with white flannel drawers under them, blue ribbed stockings, and country made shoes, with buckles; had on a sailor's cap; he complains of a weakness in his back, and wears a broad duck belt next to his shirt, he passes for a sailor, and possibly may change his name and clothes, and I imagine he has a forged pass. Whoever takes up said servant, and secures him, so that the owner may have him again, shall have Two Pounds reward, if taken in the province, if out of the province, THREE POUNDS, paid by FLORA DORSEY.

The Pennsylvania Gazette, January 18, 1770.

Virginia, December 30, 1769.

RAN away from the Subscribers, on the 26th of this Instant, living in *Loudon* County, the following Convict Servants, *viz*.

CHARLES DAYLY, an Irishman, about 21 Years of Age, of a middle Size, well set, speaks fierce, and walks nimble, wears his own black Hair, not tied: Had on, an old Felt Hat, Cotton Jacket, Crocus Shirt, Cotton Breeches, plaid Hoes, [*sic*] and a Pair of Shoes, nail'd all round.

JOHN NEAVERS, about 5 Feet 10 Inches high, well set, has very large Wrists and Hands: Had on, a very fine Hat, with Hooks and Eyes instead of Loops, with a black Ribbond round the Crown, and a blue Sailers Waistcoat.—Whoever takes up, the said Servants, and secures them, so that the Subscribers gets them again, shall have Five Pounds Reward, and if out of the Colony, Eight Pounds, paid by
THOMAS BLINCOE, & HARDAGE LANE.

N. B. 'Tis imagined they will change their Dress, as they took otehr Cloaths with them.

The Maryland Gazette, January 25, 1770.

RUN away from the subscribers, living in Dorchester county, Maryland, on the first day of January instant, a servant man, named CHARLES EAST, born in England, about 5 feet 5 inches high, of a dark complexion, black hair and beard, and dark eyes; he has lately been fighting, and bruised in his face about the eyes; had on, when he went away, a blue duffle coat, striped linen shirt and jacket, a pair of blue everlasting breeches, old shoes and stockings. Whoever takes up and secures the said servant in any goal, so that the owners do get him again, shall have Three Pounds reward, and if brought home Four Pounds, and reasonable charges, paid by ISAAC NICOLLS, and RISDON MOORE.

The Pennsylvania Gazette, January 25, 1770. See *The Pennsylvania Gazette*, March 1, 1770 and October 31, 1771.

RUN away from on board the Snow *Friendly Adventure*, whereof I am Commander, and now lying at *Annapolis*, the following Persons, who came Passengers in said Snow, liable to a certain Redemption, as specified in their several Agreements, *viz*. *John Goodwin, Edward Murphy, Edward Loney, James M'Carty,* and *William Niness*: They are gone towards *Baltimore*, and pretend that they have complied with their Engagements to me, which not being the Case, they are still answerable for the same; and, I'm informed, by the Laws of this Province, may be taken and secured, as if they were Indented Servants, until they comply with their Engagements. I therefore promise a Reward of Twenty Shillings Currency for each of the

abovementioned Persons, besides what the Law allows, to have them, or any of them secured in any public Jail in *Maryland*, or brought to me at *Annapolis*, where the Reward will be paid by Messieurs *James Dick* and *Stewart*; or, if secured in any Jail, and the abovementioned Gentlemen being acquainted therewith, the Reward will be duely paid.
WILLIAM SNOW.

John Goodwin, about 5 Feet 7 Inches high, a brown Complexion, wears his own Hair, and wore a white Jacket and Trousers.

Edward Murphy, about 5 Feet 8 Inches high, a dark Complexion, wears a brown Coat and Waistcoat, a Native of *Ireland*.

Edward Loney, about 5 Feet 7 and an Half Inches high, a dark Complexion, wore a white Coat turned up with blue.

James M'Carty, about 5 Feet 6 Inches high, a brown Complexion, wore a blue Coat and red Waistcoat, a Native of Ireland.

William Niness, about 5 Feet 8 Inches high, wore a brown Coat and Waistcoat, and a Wig, a Native of *England*.

The Maryland Gazette, February 1, 1770; February 15, 1770; March 1, 1770; March 15, 1770; March 29, 1770; April 5, 1770; *The Pennsylvania Chronicle, and Universal* Advertiser, From Monday, February 5, to Monday, February 12, 1770; From Monday, February 12, to Monday, February 19, 1770. The *Chronicle* ads have *Annapolis, Feb. 1, 1770.*" at the bottom. Minor differences between the papers.

TWENTY DOLLARS REWARD.

Dorchester County, *January* 1770.
BROKE Jail the following Persons, *viz*, THOMAS DILLING, alias EDWARD MURRAY, (by which Name he was committed for Felony:) He is a slender Fellow, about 5 Feet 9 or 10 Inches high, and has a thin Countenance: Had on when he went away, an old Fustian Coat, Shirt and Trousers, neither Shoes nor Stockings, and says he was born in *St. Mary's* County. EDWARD HARMON, a short thick made Fellow, and wears his own Hair: Had on an old gray Cloth Coat and Breeches, old Shoes and Stockings, and had a Sore on his left Arm. CHARLES CORNISH, a Free Mulatto....Whoever secures and brings back the aforesaid Prisoners, shall have the above Reward, or Fifty Shillings for each, besides reasonable Charges, paid by   ROBERT HARRISON, Sheriff.

The Maryland Gazette, February 8, 1770; February 15, 1770; February 22, 1770; March 1, 1770; March 15, 1770; March 22, 1770; March 29, 1770; April 5, 1770; April 12, 1770; April 19, 1770; April 26, 1770; May 3, 1770; May 10, 1770; May 17, 1770; May 24, 1770.

Baltimore, January 30, 1770.
COMMITTED to my Custody as Runaway Servants the following Persons, *viz*. WILLIAM SANDFORD, a Lad of about 20 Years of Age, about 5 Feet 6 Inches high, smooth Face, with dark brown Hair. THOMAS BURRELL, a *Welshman*, and says he is Father-in-Law to the above Lad, a well set Man, wears a Matchcoat Blanket Coat, with a blue Inside Jacket, and has a Sort of Musical Harp with him, The above two were taken up together, and say they came from *North-Castle, West-Chester* County, in *New-York* Government, and work'd as Labourers for *Benjamin Kipp*, Esq; a Magistrate in that County. JOHN M'FALL, about 5 Feet 6 Inches high, supposed to be 25 Years of Age, and has black Hair that curls naturally: Has on a gray Bearskin double-breasted Jacket, and Breeches of the same. JANE BURNEY, an *Englishwoman*, who says she is a Servant to *Thomas Gibbons*; she seems about 35 Years of Age, and is in a most ragged Condition.

Any Person having a proper Claim to any of the above Servants, are desired to fetch them away, or they will be sold out to pay their Fees, by DANIEL CHAMIER, Sheriff.

The Maryland Gazette, February 8, 1770; February 15, 1770; February 22, 1770; March 1, 1770.

Maryland, February 3, 1770.
RAN away on the 29th of last Month, a certain MORRIS RAGON, by Trade a Cooper, about 5 Feet 8 or 10 Inches high, and of a fair Complexion: Had on when he went away, a new Castor Hat, Claret colour'd Coat, red Frize Jacket, Buckskin Breeches, Two Pair of Hose, one of which was blue ribb'd. He is supposed to have stole a small black Horse about 12 or 13 Hands high, short Tail and Mane, one of his hind Feet white, shod before and branded in the near Shoulder and Buttock (|). Whoever secures the said *Morris Ragon* and Horse, so as he may be brought to Justice, shall have a reward of Five Pounds, or Forty Shillings for the Horse, paid by the Subscriber, living near *Baltimore-Town*.
JOHN CONDON.

The Maryland Gazette, February 8, 1770; February 15, 1770.

Philadelphia, February 27, 1770.
THERE is now in the goal of this city, three runaway servants, viz.....Risdon Moore, of Dorchester county, Maryland....The owners of the above servants, are desired to come, pay charges, and take them away....
JEHU JONES, *Goaler.*

The Pennsylvania Gazette, March 1, 1770; March 8, 1770. See *The Pennsylvania Gazette,* January 25, 1770 and October 31, 1771.

RAN away from *Newington* Rope-Walk near *Annapolis,* on Monday the 5th Instant, a Convict Servant Man, named JOHN DENNIS, about 5 Feet 6 Inches high, wears his own short dark Hair, had a thin sharp Face, and pale Complexion: Had on when he went away, a Flannel, a Bearskin, a light colour'd Jacket, blue Breeches, speckled Stockings, a Pair of Country made Shoes, and a Felt Hat.—Whoever takes up the said Runaway, and brings him to *Annapolis,* or secures him in any Jail in the Province, shall have Forty Shillings Reward, besides what the Law allows, paid by
JAMES DICK and STEWART.
The Maryland Gazette, March 8, 1770.

RUN away from the subscriber, in Sassafras Neck, Cecil County, Maryland, a servant man named Joseph Edwards. He was born in England, and pretends to have been bred up to the care of horses, and to understand the management and breaking of colts, is a talkative impertinent fellow, about 20 years of age, well set, swarthy complexion, little or no beard, and much pitted with the small-pox. He wears a brown wig, leather breeches, loose blue great coat, with a brown or blue close-bodied under coat, boots, &c. and has a variety of other good cloaths, which he may change. He has taken with him a small bright bay half-blooded curricle horse, with a small star, a bushy switch tail, is at least 12 years old, paces a slow travel, and is remarkable for a fine light easy gallop. Whoever takes up and secures the said servant and horse, so that the subscriber may have them again, shall receive a reward of FIVE POUNDS, Pennsylvania currency, or in proportion for either.
9th March 1770.   HENRY WARD PEARCE.
N. B. He has also an old saddle and bridle; and has money.
The Pennsylvania Chronicle, and Universal Advertiser, From Monday, March 5, to Monday, March 12, 1770; From Monday, March 12, to Monday, March 19, 1770; From Monday, April 9, to Monday, April 16, 1770.

RAN away from the Subscriber, living in *Annapolis,* Two Convict Men, *viz.* JOHN BENTLY, about 5 Feet 4 or 5 Inches high, full faced and well made: Had on, when he went away, a blue Coat, Osnabrig Shirt, old striped Flannel Jacket, Leather Breeches, old Hat, old Country made Stockings, and new Shoes.

THOMAS TOOL, 5 Feet 4 or 5 Inches high, of a Sandy Complexion, a little pitted with the Small-Pox, has a Cut over his left Eye, and is very impertinent: Had on, when he went away, a Check striped Cotton Handkerchief round his Neck, a Jacket with blue Half-Thick Foreparts and brown Backs, with white Metal Buttons, a white Cotton Coat, old Leather Breeches, black Stockings, pretty good Shoes, and had an Iron Collar on.

Whoever takes up the said Servants, and secures them in any Jail, shall have Forty Shillings Reward for each, including what the Law allows, and reasonable Charges if brought Home, paid by
JOHN JEVINS.
The Maryland Gazette, March 22, 1770.

COMMITTED to *Prince-George's* County Jail, a Convict Servant Woman, named *Sarah Webb*, of a pretty fair Complexion, has light coloured Hair, is about 5 Feet high, and says she belongs to *John Wiseman*, living in *Charles* County.

Her Owner is desired to take her away and pay Charges.
JOHN ADDISON, Sheriff.
The Maryland Gazette, March 22, 1770.

COMMITTED to *Anne-Arundel* County Jail as a Runaway, *John Smith*, who says he is a Servant to *John Meeke*. His Master is desired to take him away and pay charges.
JOHN CLAPHAM, Sheriff.
The Maryland Gazette, March 29, 1770.

COMMITTED to *Anne-Arundel* County Jail as a Runaway, a certain *William Finley*, who appears to be about 16 Years of Age; he says he is not a Servant, but came in last Year in Capt. *Frost*, and was by him discharge from the Ship on Account of his ill State of Health. His Master, if he has one, is desired to take him away and pay Charges.
JOHN CLAPHAM, Sheriff.
The Maryland Gazette, March 29, 1770.

March 20, 1770.
FOUR POUNDS REWARD.
RAN away from the Subscriber in *Chester-Town, Kent* County, on Monday the 19th Day of *March*, Two Convict Servant *Englishmen, viz.*

JOHN MERRY TANDY, about Thirty Years of Age, Five Feet Ten Inches high, pitted with the Small-Pox, fair Complexion, grey Eyes, he pretends to be a Wheelwright, Carpenter and Sawyer, but is Master of neither: Had on and took with him, when he went away, a Strawberry colour'd Broad-Cloth Coat, a Crimson Plush Jacket, and striped Cotton ditto, black *Manchester* Velvet Breeches, Worsted rib'd Stockings, good Shoes almost new, Steel Buckles plated, had on a striped Cotton Shirt much wore, a new beaver Hat, and a coarse Felt, the Beaver Hat he might have sold, as it was stole by them.

THOMAS WEAVER, a Butcher by Trade, about Five Feet Six Inches high, fair Complexion, grey Eyes, red Beard, light brown Hair: Had on, and took with him, when he went away, a blue Surtout Drab, a Coat and Jacket of purple Claret colour'd Broad-Cloth, Leather Breeches, black and white mixt Stockings, new Shoes, Brass Buckles not Fellows, one brown Sheeting Shirt, and one white Shirt patch'd Racoon Hat half wore.

Whoever takes them shall have the above Reward for both, or Forty Shillings for each separately, paid by
WILLIAM COLLINGS.

The Maryland Gazette, March 29, 1770; April 5, 1770.

March 31, 1770.
SIX POUNDS REWARD.

RAN away the Twenty-sixth Instant from the Subscriber, living in *Baltimore* County, near *Deer-Creek, Maryland*, the Two following convicted *Irish* Servant Men. JOHN REILY, about 35 Years of Age, 5 Feet 9 Inches high, of a dark Complexion, one of his upper fore Teeth stands above the rest: Had on and took with him, a new Felt Hat, brown cut Wig, Fearnought Jacket, strip'd under ditto, a Pair of Fearnought Breeches, Two coarse Country Linen Shirts, a Pair of Stockings, and a Pair of old Country made Shoes.—JAMES REYNOLDS, about 26 Years of Age, 5 Feet 8 Inches high, dark Complexion, and short dark Hair: Had on and took with him, a Felt Hat half-worn, a new Coat, Jacket and Breeches, of coarse Country Cloth, of a lightish Colour, a new Bearskin Coat, a Pair of lightish blue Country Cloth Breeches, and a Pair of new Shoes, with white Metal Buckles.—Whoever secures the said Servants, so that their Masters may have them again, shall have the above Reward, or Three Pounds for either of them, paid by
BERNARD PRESTON,   JOHN BULL.

N. B. It is supposed that *Reynolds* took the Bearskin Coat and blueish Breeches for *John Reily*.

The Maryland Gazette, April 12, 1770. See *The Pennsylvania Gazette*, April 12, 1770.

SIX POUNDS REWARD.

RUN away the 26th of March last, from the subscriber, living near Deer-Creek, in Baltimore county, Maryland, two convict Irish servant men. JOHN REILY, about 35 years of age, 5 feet 9 inches high, of a dark complexion, one of his upper fore teeth stands above the rest; had on, and took with him, a new felt hat, brown cut wig, fearnought jacket and breeches, a striped under jacket, two coarse country linen shirts, a pair of stockings, and old country made shoes. The other, named JAMES REYNOLDS, about 26 years of age, 5 feet 8 inches high, a dark complexion, and short dark hair; had on, and took with him, a half-worn felt hat, a new coat, jacket and breeches, of coarse country cloth, of a lightish colour; a new bearskin coat, a pair of lightish blue country cloth breeches, two coarse shirts, a pair of black and white yarn stockings, and new shoes, with white metal buckles. It is supposed that Reynolds took the bearskin coat and blue breeches for John Reily. Whoever secures the said servants, so that their masters may have them again, shall have the above reward, or three pounds for either of them, paid by
BERNARD PRESTON, JOHN BULL.

The Pennsylvania Gazette, April 12, 1770. See *The Maryland Gazette*, April 12, 1770.

FIFTEEN POUNDS Reward.

RUN away from his Bail, living in Baltimore-Town, in Maryland, the 8th Day of February, 1770, a certain BARSEL FRANCIS, a Watch-maker by Trade, very remarkable in his Walk, both of his Ancles being very crooked; his Apparel is one brown Suit, with Gold Basket Buttons, a blue Surtout Coat, and a blue Suit of Clothes; he stole several Watches, the Quantity unknown. Whoever takes up the said Francis, and commits him to any of his Majesty's Goals, shall receive the above Reward, if brought to Baltimore Town, and all reasonable Charges, besides, paid by
VOLARIUS DUKEMART.

The Pennsylvania Gazette, April 12, 1770.

TEN POUNDS REWARD.

Maryland, Dorsey's *Forge, April 17,* 1770.
RAN away from the Subscriber, a Convict Servant Man named JOHN AIKENS, about 40 Years of Age, near 5 Feet 5 Inches high, has brown Hair, Hazel Eyes, and is pitted with the Small-Pox; he is a coarse rustic Fellow, of a brown Complexion, is very aukward, in his Address, and speaks in the West Country Dialect: He has been for some Years employed

in driving a Team, and went off in his Working Cloaths, *viz.* a Cotton Jacket and Breeches, an old Felt Hat, and coarse Shoes and Stockings.—Whoever apprehends the said Runaway, and brings him home, shall have, if taken Ten Miles from said Forge, Forty Shillings, if Twenty Miles, Three Pounds, if Forty Miles, Five Pounds, and if out of the Province Ten Pounds Reward (including what the Law allows) paid by
CALEB DORSEY.
It is supposed he has other Cloaths, and may have a forged pass.
The Maryland Gazette, April 19, 1770; May 3, 1770; May 10, 1770.

April 7, 1770.
RAN away last Night, from the Subscriber, living in *Baltimore-Town,* a Convict Servant Man, named PATRICK CLEARY, an *Irishman,* about 19 Years of Age, 5 Feet high; he is thick and well set, has a fresh Complexion, blue Eyes, and dark brown Hair tied behind: Had on and took with him, an old dark brown Coat with plain Twill Buttons, torn and mended in several Places, a blue Jacket, a red ditto, a Pair of greasy Buckskin Breeches, a Pair of old white Worsted Stockings, a Pair of unbleached Thread ditto, a Pair of blue Worsted ditto, a Pair of coarse Yarn ditto, a Matchcoat Blanket, an old town Dowlas Sheet. He generally wore a blue and white Cotton Handkerchief about his Jaws, which are a little swelled with the Venereal Disorder; and speaks much on the *Irish* Accent.—Whoever takes up the said Servant, and secures him, so that his Master may have him again, shall have Three Pounds Reward, besides what the Law allows, paid by
JOHN MACNABB.
The Maryland Gazette, April 19, 1770; May 3, 1770.

April 18, 1770.
RAN away from the Subscriber, in *Kent* County, *Maryland,* on Monday the 16th Instant, a Convict Lad, named GEORGE HALL, *alias* ATTIX, about 18 or 19 Years of Age, 5 Feet 3 Inches high, well set, has a Scar on one of his Legs, occasioned by a Scald, wears his own short brown Hair, and he has been used to go by Water, all Masters of Vessels are forewarned carrying him off at their Peril: Had on when he went away, a Pair of old Leather Breeches, brown Kersey or Plains Jacket, blue Broad-Cloth Under ditto, white Linen Shirt, a Pair of white Yarn Stockings, a Pair of Shoes, and a Felt Hat half worn. Whoever takes up and secures him in any Jail, so that his Master may have him again, shall receive a Reward of Forty Shillings besides what the Law allows, paid by
JOHN GRANT.
The Maryland Gazette, April 26, 1770; May 10, 1770; May 30, 1770.

RAN away from the Subscribers, living in *Caecil* County, *Maryland*, Two Servant Men, *viz.* DANIEL DORROVAN, an *Irishman*, about 25 Years of Age, near 6 Feet high, has dark Hair, fair Complexion, and used to Country Work: Had on when he went away, a good Felt Hat, gray colour'd double-breasted Jacket, black Cloth Under ditto, gray colour'd Breeches, all old and patch'd, wide Trousers, and old Shoes and Stockings. JOHN TAYLOR, an *Englishman*, about 30 Years of Age, 5 Feet 6 Inches high, has black Hair, fair Complexion, and by Trade a Blacksmith: Had on when he went away, a Felt Hat, old brown Coat, strip'd Linen Jacket, good Homespun Shirt, Osnabrig Trousers, and old Shoes and Stockings. Whoever takes up and secures the said Servants, so that their Masters may have them again, shall have Four Pounds Reward, paid by
JOHN COX,
BENJAMIN ETHERINGTON.
The Maryland Gazette, April 26, 1770; May 10, 1770; May 17, 1770; May 24, 1770; May 30, 1770; June 7, 1770; June 14, 1770; June 21, 1779; June 28, 1770; July 12, 1770.

COMMITTED to *Anne-Arundel* County Jail as Runaways, WILLIAM THOMPSON, and GEORGE WILLIAMS, who say they belong to *Edward Norwood*. They had a small Boat with about 3 Fathom of Rope in her. Their Master is desired to take them away and pay charges.
JOHN CLAPHAM, Sheriff.
The Maryland Gazette, April 26, 1770.

April 30, 1770.
RAN away from the Subscriber, the 17th Inst. living in *Charles* County, *Lower-Cedar-Point*, a Convict Servant Man, named THOMAS SAPLETON, 25 Years of Age, slender made, about 5 Feet 10 Inches high, Sandy colour'd Hair, and a down look: Had on and took with him, when he went away, a Fearnought Jacket, Osnabrig Shirt, a Pair of Broad-Cloth Breeches much wore, old Shoes and Stockings, an old Felt Hat, and one Check Shirt.
Whoever takes up said Runaway, and brings him to the Subscriber, shall receive Thirty Shillings Reward and reasonable Charges, paid by
STEPHEN COMPTON.
The Maryland Gazette, May 10, 1770; May 17, 1770; May 24, 1770; May 31, 1770; June 7, 1770.

Baltimore Town, May 1, 1770.
THIRTY DOLLARS REWARD.

RAN away from the subscriber, an indented servant man, named JOHN GREEN, a shoemaker by trade, born in Ireland; about 24 *years of age,* 5 *feet* 9 *inches high, a likely well made man, has a good countenance, wears his own dark brown hair, smooth faced, and has but little beard, has a scar near his mouth, speaks good English, and can talk in the native Irish dialect, says he served several years on the Earl of Drogheda's regiment of light dragoons; took with him a blue cloth coat above half worn, a hole in one of the skirts, eaten by the rats, one check shirt, one white do. wore a black handkerchief, one white diaper jacket, one thickset do. of an olive colour, a castor hat half worn, a new pair of buckskin breeches a little soiled and some shoemakers wax on them, one pair of blue worsted stockings, one pair of yarn do. a pair of ozenbrigs trowsers, a leather apron, a set of shoemakers tools, a pair of new turned pumps, and a pair of pinchbeck buckles; he is a good workman and a good fiddler. Whoever takes up the aforesaid servant, if in the province, shall have Seven Pounds Ten Shillings, if out of the province, the above reward if brought home or laid in any of his Majesty's gaols on the continent, paid by me*
JOSEPH HAYWARD.

N. B. He writes a very good hand, and possibly may forge a pass.

The Pennsylvania Chronicle, and Universal Advertiser, From Monday, May 7, to Monday, May 14, 1770. See *The Pennsylvania Chronicle,* From Monday, September 23, to Monday, September 30, 1771.

SIXTEEN DOLLARS REWARD.

May 8, 1770.

RAN away last Night from the Subscriber, living in *Charles-Town,* Two Servant Men, *viz,* JOSEPH MILLER, by Trade a Cooper, has lost one of his fore Teeth: Had on and took with him, a light colour'd Broad-Cloth Coat half worn, a Snuff colour'd Jacket, Two shirts, the one Check, the other Country Linen, a new Felt, [sic] One Pair of Shoes, and plated Buckles. JOHN FOSSETT, about 4 Feet 10 Inches high, middle aged: Had on and took with him, Two Jackets, the one Fearnought, the other Lincey, Two Country Linen Shirts, Two Pair of Trousers, a Pair of Shoes half soled, and an old Felt Hat. He has been on board a Man of War, but is by Trade a Shoemaker.

Whoever takes up the aforesaid Servants, shall have the above Reward, or Eight Dollars for either of them, and reasonable Charges, paid by JOHN RANKIN.

N. B. 'Tis supposed they went off in a Boat with one Sail.

The Maryland Gazette, May 17, 1770; May 31, 1770; Jun 7, 1770.

TEN POUNDS REWARD.

May 16, 1770.

RAN away last Night from the Subscribers, living in *Baltimore-Town*, Two Convict Servant Men, *viz.* JOHN HUMPHRIES, about 25 Years of Age, 5 Feet 10 Inches high, fresh colour'd, brown Complexion, and his Face is very full of Pimples: Had on when he went away, an old Beaver Hat cropt round the Edge, brown Coat, with a few brass Buttons, spotted Flannel Waistcoat, old Check Shirt, a Pair of old brown Thickset Breeches, gray mill'd Stockings, and is a very bold quarrelsome Fellow. THOMAS LACY, about 19 or 20 Years of Age, 5 Feet 6 Inches high, near the same Complexion as the other, and is an easy quiet sort of Fellow: Had on when he went away, an old Felt Hat bound round the Brim with a Piece of another, strip'd Linsey Jacket, Osnabrig Shirt and Trousers, and a Pair of Shoes shod with Iron.

Whoever takes up the said Runaway and secures them in any Jail, so as their Masters may have them again, shall have for each, if taken in the Province Three Pounds, if out of the Province Five Pounds, and reasonable Charges if brought home, paid by
GEORGE BACKSTER, & PHILIP LIDICK.

The Maryland Gazette, May 24, 1770; May 31, 1770; June 7, 1770; June 21, 1770; June 28, 1770.

Virginia, *Loudoun* County, *April* 28, 1770.

RAN away from the Subscriber living in *Loudoun* County, near *Cub* Run, on the 10th Instant, and *English* Convict Servant Man, named JOHN MILLER, a Blacksmith by Trade, is a short thick Fellow, about 5 Feet 2 or 3 Inches high, 28 Years of Age, has short light colour'd Hair and Eye-Brows, a Scar on his Forehead, tho' likely his Hat may keep it undiscovered, speaks good *English*, and has a bold impudent Look: Had on when he went off, a spotted lappell'd Cotton Jacket, with an Under ditto, of plain Cotton, which Laces, a Pair brown Cloth Breeches, a Pair of Cotton Boots, the same of the Under Jacket, an Osnabrig Shirt, old Shoes and Stockings, and an old Hat. It's supposed he went in Company with one *Betty Moody*, (by some called *Betty Tuff)* a Freewoman, very meanly dress'd; she is a very small Woman, and hard favour'd.

Whoever takes up the said Fellow, and brings him to Capt. *William Carr Lane's* Store, shall receive Ten Dollars Reward, from
JOHN HENDERSON.

The Maryland Gazette, May 24, 1770; May 31, 1770; June 7, 1770.

EIGHT POUNDS REWARD.

RAN away from the Subscriber living near *Elk-Ridge* Church, in *Anne-Arundel* County, on the 30th Day of *April* 1770, Four Servant Men. Two are the Property of *Charles Hammond*, Junr. *viz*, JOAN [sic] CULLEN, a young Man about 5 Feet 10 Inches high: Had on when he went away, an old blue Coat, and sundry other Wearing Apparel, not known. PATRICK RILEY, middle aged, and narrow fac'd: Had on when he went away, a Felt Hat, Yarn Stockings, a Worsted Cap, and sundry other Cloaths, not known.

The other Two are the Property of Dr. *Ephraim Howard, viz*. HUGH LACY, about 5 Feet 10 Inches high, and Pock mark'd: Had on when he went away, an old brown Cloth Coat, striped Woollen Jacket, blue Yarn Stockings, Check Shirt, striped Breeches, and a Pair of old Shoes. He says he is a Farmer. JOHN HUGHS, about 5 Feet 8 or 9 Inches high, full faced, well set, and of a middle Age: When he went away he was dress'd much in the same Manner as the old Man, and likewise calls himself a Farmer. They are all *Irish*, and have been but a few Days from on board the Ship, and all have a peculiar Smell incident to all Servants just coming from Ships. It's supposed that the old Man has been in the Country before, and make no doubt but every Artifice will be used to pass, especially that of changing their Cloaths and Names.

Whoever takes up and brings the said Fellows to their Masters, shall have Thirty Shillings for each, and if out of the Province Forty Shillings Currency, paid by
CHARLES HAMMOND, Junr.
EHPRAIM HOWARD, Son of *Henry*.

The Maryland Gazette, May 24, 1770; May 31, 1770. See *The Maryland Gazette*, October 11, 1770.

RUN away from the Subscriber, on the 30th Day of March last, living near Elk-Ridge, in Maryland, a Convict Servant Man, named SAMUEL ALLSWORTH, about 5 Feet 6 or 7 Inches high, about 22 Years of Age, by Trade a Gun-stocker, has short curled brown Hair, brown Complexion, and walks with his Toes much out: Had on, and took with him a brown Cotton Jacket and Breeches, Ozenbrigs Shirt, Yarn Stockings, old Shoes, Half worn Felt Hat, and two Pair old Ozenbrigs Trowsers. He is well acquainted about MacCallister's Town, and it is supposed he will change his Name and Cloathing. He went while there by the Name *JOHN WILLIAMS*. Whoever takes up the said Servant, and brings him to me, shall receive TWENTY DOLLARS Reward, paid by
SAMUEL POOLE.

The Pennsylvania Gazette, May 31, 1770; June 14, 1770.

June 1, 1770.

RAN away, on Tuesday last, from the subscriber, living in Newtown, Kent county, Maryland, a servant men, named Henry Flemings, a west country Englishman, about 5 feet, 10 or 11 inches high, 35 years of age, wears his own short black hair, has a large scar over his right eye, a little pock-pitted and freckled, and has lost the fore-finger off one of his hands: Had on when he went away, a half worn felt hat, half worn brown kersey coat, a striped jacket, old buckskin breeches, white shirt, yarn stockings of a mixed colour, half worn shoes, with yellow metal buckles. Whoever takes up the said servant, and secures him in any gaol, so that his master may get him again, shall have Three Pounds reward, and reasonable charges, paid by
WILLIAM WELES.

The Pennsylvania Chronicle, and Universal Advertiser, From Monday, May 28, to Monday, June 4, 1770; From Monday, June 11, to Monday, June 18, 1770.

SIX POUNDS REWARD.

Elk-Ridge, June 6, 1770.

RAN away from the Subscriber, on the 25th of *April*, a Convict Servant Lad, named *William Dickerson*, of a thin Visage, 5 Feet 6 or 9 Inches high, about 18 or 19 Years old: Had on and took with him a new Castor Hat, a half worn Felt ditto, two white Country Cloth Jackets half worn, an old Pair of Country made Shoes newly soled and nailed, and three new Osnabrig Shirts. He has a remarkable Lump on one Side of his under Jaw, and took Three Pounds Cash with him.

Whoever secures the said Servant, so that I may get him again, shall receive the above Reward, and all reasonable Charges paid if brought Home, by me   JAMES HOWARD.

The Maryland Gazette, June 14, 1770; June 21, 1770; June 28, 1770; July 5, 1770.

WENT away from the Subscriber, on Monday the 5th Instant, BENJAMIN DANIEL, an Indented Servant, by Profession a Gardener; he is an *Englishman*, remarkably stout and well set, about 5 Feet 9 Inches high, round faced, with his own Hair, not tied: He had on, when he went away, a blue Cloth Coat, with yellow Buttons and a red Cape, a striped Linen Waistcoat, green Serge Breeches, and a Pair of Osnabrig Trousers.—It is believed he went away in Company with one *Drury*, a Carpenter by Trade, an *Irishman*, and Free. The said *Drury* is a strait well made Man, about 6 Feet high.

Whoever will bring the abovementioned *Benjamin Daniel* to the Subscriber, in *Annapolis*, or to *Charles Carroll*, Esq; Sen. on *Elk-Ridge*, may receive Three Pounds Reward, if taken in the Province, or Five Pounds, if taken in any other.
CHARLES CARROLL, of *Carrollton*.
The Maryland Gazette, June 14, 1770; June 21, 1770; June 28, 1770; July 12, 1770.

Talbot County, *June* 4, 1770.
RAN away from the Subscriber, living in *Bay-Side Neck*, near the Church, on *Sunday* Night, Four Servant Men, *viz*. CHARLES DODD, being about Six Feet One Inch high, of a brown Complexion, with short black Hair tied behind, and has a Wound in his left Leg, occasioned by a Cannon Ball. JOHN JOHNSON, being about Five Feet Eight or Nine Inches high, of a brown Complexion, with black Hair tied down his Back; he has a great Scar on his Face, owing to a Scald. WILLIAM ROBINSON, being about Five Feet Six or Seven Inches high, round shouldered, with short brown Hair, and has lately had a great many Ringworms on his Face. WILLIAM INKLEY, being about Five Feet Eight Inches high, of a swarthy Complexion, with short brown Hair inclined to sandy, blind in his left eye, but not perceivable without nicely looked into, is nock-kneed, has one of his Legs much swolen, is a West Countryman, talks very broad, and is lately come into the Country.

Whoever takes up or secures the said Runaways, or either of them, shall receive Forty Shillings Reward for each Man, if taken out of the Province, or, if taken in the Province, Twenty Shillings, besides what the Law allows.
ROBERT RICHARDSON for PHILIP WEATHERALL.
The Maryland Gazette, June 14, 1770; June 21, 1770; June 28, 1770.

NINE POUNDS REWARD,
RAN away from the Subscriber, living in *Charles* County, on Sunday the 3d Instant, the following Servant Men, *viz*, PETER GOLDING, a Convict, by Profession a Gardener, born in *England*, and came into the Country in the Year 1766; has short brown Hair, is about 45 Years of Age, 5 Feet 6 or 7 Inches high, and has several large Lumps on the Calf of his right Leg: Had on and took with him a light coloured Cloth Coat, a Pair of Buckskin Breeches, a double breasted white Flannel Waistcoat, a Silk Handkerchief, One Old and One new Osnabrig Shirt, a Pair of Shoes, Three Pair of white Thread Stockings, Two Pair of Hempen-Roll Trousers, and a new Felt Hat. WILLIAM PLAIN, an Indented Servant, by Profession a Gardener, was

born in *England*, and came into the Country last Year; is about 25 Years of Age, 5 Feet 8 or 9 Inches high, has dark brown Hair, and a Blemish or Cast in his left Eye, which he seldom opens so wide as his right: He had on and took with him a very short Frize Frock Coat, with a small Collar lined with red Velvet, a Pair of old Leather Breeches, a white Linen Waistcoat, One new Osnabrig and Two old white Shirts, a Pair of Shoes, One Pair of Worsted and One Pair of Thread Stockings, Two Cambrick or Muslin Neckcloths, and an old Hat. WILLIAM HARRISON, an Indented Servant, can shave and dress Hair very well; he is about Thirty Years of Age, 5 Feet 7 or 8 Inches high, the middle Finger of his left Hand cut off at the second Joint, and has short brown Hair, which curls naturally; he was born at *York* in *England*, but appears more like an *Irishman*, and came into the Country last Fall, and has served as a Waiter with Mr. *Middleton* in *Annapolis* some Months, and is very apt to get drunk: He had on and took with him a Drab coloured broad Cloth Coat, a red Waistcoat, a Pair of Buckskin Breeches, 8 white Shirts, Two Pair of white Thread, One Pair of white raw Silk, and One Pair of black Worsted Stockings, an old Castor Hat, a Pair of Shoes, a red and white Silk Handkerchief, a Bristol Stone Stock-Buckle set in Silver, and sundry other Things. He is supposed to have with him 10 or 12 Pounds Sterling, in Gold, Silver, and Paper.

Whoever takes up the said Servants, or either of them, and brings them to the Subscriber, or secures them so that he may get them, or either of them again, shall receive Three Pounds Inspection Currency for each, and all reasonable Charges paid by
PHILIP R. FENDALL.

The Maryland Gazette, June 14, 1770; June 21, 1770; June 28, 1770; July 5, 1770.

RUN away, the 30th of this inst. May, at night, from the subscriber, living in Cecil County, Milford Hundred, a native Irish servant man, named Cornelius Crowley, came in last fall from Cork, a butcher by trade, about 5 feet 9 inches high, well made, wears his own fair short hair, has a down look, of a pale complexion, talks very short and thick, and has some cuts on his head; had on, and took with him, a blue broadcloth coat, with white lining, gilt buttons, redish coloured velvet jacket and breeches, a good deal faded, a pair of tow trowsers, which he carries by way of a wallet, a stampt linen jacket, light blue worsted stockings, black grained pumps, Pinchbeck buckles, and a beaver hat, almost new, maker's name John Clark. Whoever takes up said servant, and secures him in any of his Majesty's goals, so that his master may have him again, shall have FOUR DOLLARS, reward, and reasonable charges, paid by   SAMUEL THOMPSON.

The Pennsylvania Gazette, June 14, 1770.

Baltimore county, June 6, 1770.
RUN away from the subscriber, the 4th instant, a convict servant man, named ROGER McEVOY, about 5 feet 8 or 9 inches high; had on, when he went away, a white cotton jacket, ozenbrigs shirt, a pair of new shoes, nailed on the soals, a pair of tow linen trowsers, and felt hat; he had a scar on the right side of his face. Whoever takes up the said fellow so that his master may get him again, shall have Thirty Shillings reward, paid by HUMPHREY BROOKS.

The Maryland Gazette, June 14, 1770; *The Pennsylvania Gazette*, June 14, 1770.

SIX POUNDS REWARD.
RAN away from the Subscriber, living in *Anne-Arundel* County, the 18th of *June* Instant, Two Indented Servants; *viz* JOHN WHITE, by Trade a Gardener, about 30 Years of Age, 5 Feet 7 Inches high, has dark brown Hair tied behind, a pretty good Complexion, is pitted with the Small-Pox, and born in *Scotland*: Had on and took with him a grey half-thick Jacket, Dowlas Shirts, Osnabrig Trousers, a dark coloured Cloth Coat much mended about the Arms, a light coloured Cloth Waistcoat, Country made Shoes, and a remarkably short Gun, Maker's Name *Barber, London*, marked on the Cock and Barrel. HENRY JOSEPH, a short punch Lad, about 18 Years of Age, has short brown Hair, and a Scar on his Forehead, occasioned by the Kick of a Horse, was born in *England*, and says he has been a Post-Chaise Boy in London They went off in a Yawl, 14 Feet in the Keel, with a Pair of Oars Whoever secures the said Servants, or either of them, shall receive Three Pounds for each, and all reasonable Charges paid. And Masters of Vessels are forewarned not to harbour or carry them away at their Peril.   SAMUEL GALLOWAY.

The Maryland Gazette, June 21, 1770; June 28, 1770; July 5, 1770; July 19, 1770; July 26, 1770; August 2, 1770; August 9, 1770; August 16, 1770; August 23, 1770. See *The Maryland Journal, and the Baltimore Advertiser*, From Saturday, October 9, to Saturday, October 16, 1773, for White.

Caecil County, *May* 4, 1770.
COMMITTED to my Custody, as Runaways, THOMAS COULSON, who says he was born in *England*, about 5 Feet 5 Inches high; has on a blue upper Jacket, a black under ditto, white Cloth Breeches, blue Stockings,

pretty good Shoes and Buckles. He has got a Scar upon the fore Finger of the left Hand, and is supposed to be about 50 Years of Age. COLLIN PORTER, a *Scotchman*, about 5 Feet 7 Inches high; has on a blue Coat, Linsey-woolsey Jacket, blue Breeches, grey Worsted Stockings, Shoes and Brass Buckles; says he served his Time with *John Robinson*, in the Barrens of *Baltimore* County: He is about Forty Years of Age. The Owners are desired to come and pay Charges, and take them away.
RICHARD THOMAS, Sheriff.
The Maryland Gazette, June 21, 1770; June 28, 1770.

Kent County, *June* 14, 1770.
RAN away from the Subscriber, to Day, a Servant Lad, named JOSEPH MARSHALL, about 16 Years old, Five Feet high; Had on and took with him a new Osnabrig Shirt, One Check ditto, and a Pair of Oznabrig Trousers. He has a down Look and white Complexion, and went off in a Canoe to the Western Shore. Whoever secures the said Servant, so that his Master may have him again, shall receive Forty Shillings Reward.
GEORGE HANSON.
The Maryland Gazette, June 21, 1770.

RUN away, on Tuesday last, from the Subscriber, living in Baltimore County, Maryland, a Convict Servant Man, named Michael Kelly, born in Dublin, about 5 Feet 8 Inches high, of a sandy Complexion, wears his own fair Hair, has a Scar on one Side of his Neck, and says he got a Hurt on the lower Part of his Belly, which occasions him, at Times, to wear a Belt: Had on, an old Broadcloth lapelled greyish Coat, coarse yellow Flannel under Jacket, tow Shirt and Trowsers, old Shoes, with Nails in the Heels; and it is supposed he will go towards Philadelphia. He ran away last Fall, and was taken up towards Lancaster, and chiefly discovered by the Scar on his Neck. He is about 24 Years of Age, and by all Accounts a great Rogue, as he has, by his own Confession, followed Shop-lifting and Pilfering in his own Country. It is possible he will break Spring-houses; and steal Clothes, in order to change his Dress. Whoever takes up said Servant, and secures him, so that his Master may get him again, shall have Forty Shillings Reward, if taken within 20 Miles from home, and Three Pounds if further, and reasonable Charges, if brought home, paid by
 June 8, 1770.   JAMES HUTCHINSON.
N. B. All Masters of Vessels are forbid to carry him off at their Peril.
The Pennsylvania Gazette, June 21, 1770.

TWENTY DOLLARS REWARD.

June 20, 1770.

RAN away from the Subscriber, living near the Head of *Wiccomoco* River, on the Eastern Shore, the 4th Instant, an Indented Servant Man, named THOMAS KELLY, born in *Ireland*, and came from *Dublin* last *August*, is a strong lusty Fellow, about 5 Feet 10 or 11 Inches high, with short black Hair and Eyebrows, has been scalded on the Instep of his right Foot by hot Water, the mark of which is very plain to be seen; he pretends to be a great Ditcher, Mower, and Reaper: Had on, when he went away, an old Pea Jacket, a Check Shirt and Trousers, new Shoes with long Quarters, an old Hat, bound round with yellow Tape; but it is supposed he will change his Dress, as he has Money with him, which he stole the Night before he went off. Whoever takes up said Servant, and brings him to his Master, shall receive the above Reward, or if secured in any Jail, and Notice thereof given, so that he may be had again, shall have Five Pounds, paid by
JAMES NEVIN.

The Maryland Gazette, June 28, 1770; July 12, 1770; July 19, 1770; July 26, 1770; August 2, 1770; August 9, 1770.

FOUR DOLLARS REWARD.

Annapolis, June 26, 1770.

RAN away from the subscriber, on Sunday last, an Indented Servant Man, named JOSEPH MOOR, alias JOSEPH SIMON; about 5 Feet 5 Inches high, a thin Visage and swarthy Complexion, has a very down Look, and wears his own short brown Hair: Had on when he went away a blue Cloth Coat, Linsey-woolsey striped Jacket with Sleeves, old Leather Breeches, Worsted Stockings, a Check Shirt, a Neckcloth, and a Pair of Shoes almost new; he stammers in his Speech and seems very simple, is Country born, and about 25 Years of Age: He has served some Time to the Carpenters Trade. All Masters of Vessels and others are hereby warned from carrying away or harbouring him at their Peril.

Whoever takes up or secures said Runaway, so that the Subscriber may have him again, shall be entitled to a Reward of Twenty Shillings, or if out of the Province the above Reward, to be paid by
WILLIAM HEWITT.

The Maryland Gazette, June 28, 1770; July 12, 1770; July 19, 1770.

TWENTY DOLLARS REWARD.

RAN away last Night from the Subscribers, living near *Soldiers Delight*, in *Baltimore* County, about Twelve Miles from *Baltimore-Town, Maryland*, a Servant Man, named THOMAS AGER, an *Englishman*, about 23 Years of

Age, a Schoolmaster, a short well set Fellow, about 5 Feet 4 Inches high, has a long Visage, and a remarkable long Chin, greyish Eyes, and a pert Countenance, with dark long Hair tied. He took with him, a Castor Hat, a brown mixt Cloth Coat, with high round yellow Metal Buttons, a brown Bearskin Coat, with Mohair Buttons, a blue grey Cloth Pair of Breeches, One Pair of light grey Worsted Stockings, a Pair Thread ditto, a Pair of black grained Shoes, and a Sair [sic] of carved Steel Buckles, One Holland Shirt, a Pheeting [sic] ditto, and One Osnabrig ditto, a Pair of Osnabrig Trousers, a Saddle pretty much worn, the Stirrups with Swivels, and is much worn in the Middle, a Saddle-Cloth with red Binding, and a Snaffle Bridle; it is supposed he will steal a Horse; he is a good Scholar, and no Doubt but he will forge a Discharge and Pass, and change his Name; he has been in the *West Indies*, and has travelled towards the Northward. Whoever takes up the said Servant, and brings him home, shall have 40 Shillings; if 20 Miles from home, 4 Pounds; and if 40 Miles, the above Reward, paid by
ALEXANDER WELLS,
CHARLES HOWARD,
THOMAS OWINGS.

The Maryland Gazette, June 28, 1770; July 12, 1770. See *The Pennsylvania Chronicle, and Universal Advertiser*, From Monday, June 25, to Monday, July 2, 1770.

June 6, 1770.
RAN away from the Subscriber living near *Soldiers Delight*, in *Baltimore* County, *Maryland*, a Convict Servant Man, named JACOB DUFFIELD, born in *Essex*, in *England*, has been in the Country about Nine Months, was brought in the Ship *Douglass*, Capt. *Breckenridge*, he is a Blacksmith by Trade, well set, about Five Feet Five Inches high, short brown Hair: Had on when he went away, a Felt Hat, black Silk Handkerchief, Osnabrig Shirt and Trousers, double soaled Shoes, Whoever takes up the said Servant, and secures him in any Jail, so that his Master may have him again, shall receive, if taken Ten Miles from home, Twenty Shillings; if Twenty Miles, Forty Shillings; and if Forty Miles, Three Pounds, and reasonable Charges if brought home, paid by.
SAMUEL MUMMY.
N. B. All Masters of Vessels are forbid to carry him off at thir Perril. [sic]

The Maryland Gazette, June 28, 1770; July 5, 1770; July 12, 1770; *The Pennsylvania Chronicle,* From Monday, July 16, to Monday, July 23, 1770; From Monday, July 30, to Monday, August 1770; From Monday, August 6, to Monday, August 13, 1770. Minor differences between the papers. *The Chronicle* shows his hair as "curl'd" and adds Duffield is "about 23 years of age".

June 19, 1770
TWENTY DOLLARS REWARD.
RAN away last Night from the subscriber, living near Soldier's Delight, in Baltimore county, about 12 miles from Baltimore-Town, Maryland, a servant man, named THOMAS AGER, an Englishman, about 23 years of age, a school-master; a short well set fellow, about 5 feet 4 inches high, long visage, greyish Eyes, pert countenance, and has dark long hair tied behind; he took with him a castor hat, a brown mixed cloth coat, with high round yellow metal buttons, a brown bearskin coat, with mohair buttons, a blue grey cloth pair of breeches, a pair of light grey worsted stockings, a pair of thread ditto, a pair of black grained shoes and a carved steel buckles; one holland shirt, one sheeting ditto, and one osnabrigs ditto, and a pair of osnabrigs trousers; a saddle pretty much worn, the stirrups with swivels in the middle much worn, a cloth likewise much worn, and a snaffle bridle. It is supposed he will steal a horse; he is a good scholar, and no doubt but he will forge a discharge and pass, and change his name; he has been in the West-Indies, and has travelled towards the northward. Whoever takes up the said servant, and brings him home, shall have Forty Shillings reward; if twenty miles from home Four Pounds and if forty miles the above reward, paid by Alexander Wells, Charles Howard, and Thomas Owings.

The Pennsylvania Chronicle, and Universal Advertiser, From Monday, June 25, to Monday, July 2, 1770; From Monday, July 9, to Monday, July 16, 1770; *The New-York Journal, or, the General Advertiser*, July 5, 1770; July 12, 1770; July 19, 1770. Minor differences between the papers. See *The Maryland Gazette*, June 28, 1770.

EIGHT POUNDS REWARD.
Anne-Arundel County, *June* 30, 1770.
RAN away from the Subscriber, living at the Head of *South River*, EDWARD SIMMINS, a Convict Servant Man, by Trade a Shoemaker; a slim Fellow, about Five Feet Nine Inches high, short red Hair, and red Complexion; but as he is an artful Fellow and a good Scholar, it is likely he has cut off his Hair and forged a Pass. Had on and took with him, a blue Cloth Coat and Breeches, Shoes, several Pair of Thread Stockings, Two Swanskin Jackets, Three white shirts, several Osnabrig Shirts, and some other old Cloaths, Leather Bags, some Shoemakers Tools, and Two Silver Tea-spoons. It is supposed he has taken a Horse, as there is a black one missing with a white Face, near fore Leg white, and several blotch'd Brands

something like this r. Whoever brings the said Servant or the Horse to the Subscriber, shall receive Five Pounds for the Man and Three for the Horse. WILLIAM IIAMS.
The Maryland Gazette, July 5, 1770; July 12, 1770.

Baltimore County, *July* 2, 1770.
RAN away from the Subscriber, living in *Gunpowder Forest*, about Ten Miles from *Baltimore* Town, a Convict Servant Man, named GEORGE ADAMS, about 37 Years of Age, a lusty stout well looking Fellow, Five Feet Ten or Eleven Inches high, of a good Countenance, black Beard and Hair, almost bald on the Crown of his Head, full faced, smiles when he talks, has a Scar on the right Side of his Chin, and his Breast is very hairy. Nobody would take him for a Servant but by his Apparel. Had on when he went away an old brown Wig and a striped Worsted Cap, an Iron Collar, and all round his Neck very red and a little sore, and full of small Pimples; a blue gray Fearnought Sailor's Jacket, Two Osnabrig Shirts with very long Sleeves, a pair of hempen Roll long Trousers very black and coarse, a Pair of black greasy Leather Breeches, an old Pair of Shoes patched behind, a Pair of black Yarn Stockings, an old Hat trimmed round the Brim: He is a very good Scholar and probably will forge a Pass; it is expected he will make for some Vessel or Boat; he is an excellent Farmer, and can turn his Hand to any sort of Business. All Masters of Vessels and others are forewarned not to take him out of the Province at their Peril. Whoever takes up the said Servant, and secures him so that his Master may get him again, shall have Forty Shillings if within the County, if out of the County Three Pounds, and if out of the Province Five Pounds, and reasonable Charges paid by   NICHOLAS BRITTON.
The Maryland Gazette, July 5, 1770; July 12, 1770. See *The Pennsylvania Chronicle,* From Monday, September 10, to Monday, September 17, 1770.

RUN away, on the 30th of March last, from the subscriber, living in Caecil county, Maryland, an indented servant man, named Barney M'Caddem, about 5 feet 4 or 5 inches high, about 22 years of age, by trade a flax hackler, has short brown hair, sandy complexion, is flat footed, knock-kneed, has a long nose; had on, and took with him, a white cloth jacket, a blue ditto, without sleeves, old leather breeches, and linen ditto, one white shirt, some coarse ditto, and tow trowsers, and a new wool hat; he has a forged pass, and says he got it from Charles Brookins, of Maryland. Whoever takes up said servant, and secures him in any of his Majesty's

goals, shall receive Forty Shillings reward, and reasonable charges, paid by me   WILLIAM CATHER.
The Pennsylvania Gazette, July 5, 1770.

Philadelphia Goal, June 20, 1770.
WHEREAS I DENNIS KEAINE, a currier by trade, was committed to the gaol of this city, on Thursday the 7th of this inst. June, on suspicion of running away from my bail, from Dorchester county in Maryland; this is therefore to give public notice to any person or persons whatsoever, who have any demands against me, to come and prove their demands against me, otherwise I shall be discharged, according to the law, in three weeks from the date hereof.
DENNIS KEAINE.
The Pennsylvania Chronicle, and Universal Advertiser, From Monday, July 2, to Monday, July 9, 1770.

Alexandria, July 2, 1770.
RAN away from the Subscriber, living in *Alexandria*, a young Servant Man, named JAMES HOLAWAY, about 5 Feet 4 or 5 Inches high, he has a sore Leg, but by some Means that he has taken it is something better: Had on, when he went away, a dark Broad Cloth Coat, red Waistcoat, long striped Trousers, a course Shirt, and old Shoes, but in all Probability he may change his Dress. I imagine he has got my Indenture. All Persons or Masters of Vessels are forewarned harbouring or carrying him off at their Peril.

Whoever takes up, and secures the said Servant, so as his Master gets him again, shall have Thirty Shillings Reward, besides what the Law allows, paid by
EDWARD RIGDEN.
The Maryland Gazette, July 12, 1770.

July 2, 1770.
RAN away from the Subscriber, near *Annapolis*, a Convict Servant Man, named JOHN STILLIN, is very slim made, about 5 Feet 8 or 9 Inches high, wears his own Hair, which is of a light Colour, and is a little mark'd with the Small-Pox: Had on, and took with him, a coarse Felt Hat, light coloured Fearnought Jacket, Two Osnabrig Shirts, One Check ditto, a Pair of Osnabrig Trousers, a Pair of brown Roll ditto, a Pair of old Fall Shoes, and an old Match Coat Blanket, but as he is an artful Rogue, it is probable he may change his Name and Dress, as he did once before when he ran away.

Whoever takes up, and secures the above Servant, so as his Master may have him again, shall receive a Reward of Forty Shillings, if taken in the Province, and if out of the Province, Four Pounds, including what the Law allows, paid by
THOMAS RUTLAND.
The Maryland Gazette, July 12, 1770; July 26, 1770; August 2, 1770; August 9, 1770.

RAN away from John Forwood, living on Deer Creek, in Baltimore county, in Maryland, on the 8th day of July, 1770, an Irish servant man, aged about 25 years, about five feet eight inches high, of a fair complexion, short dark hair, had nothing on him but an old felt hat, a good white linen shirt and trowsers, old shoes with one steel buckle, and one brass buckle having the rim broke; after he left home, it is thought he got by the way a light purple-coloured coat, and sundry other clothes, as also Ten Dollars in silver, and some paper money: He will undoubtedly change his name and pass by the name of William Barnet. Whosoever takes up said servant, if taken up in Baltimore county, and secured so that his master gets him again, shall have Twenty Shillings, and if taken up out of Baltimore county and brought home, shall have Five Pounds, paid by me
JOHN FORWOOD.
The Pennsylvania Chronicle, and Universal Advertiser, From Monday, July 9, to Monday, July 16, 1770; From Monday, July 16, to Monday, July 23, 1770. See *The Pennsylvania Gazette,* July 19, 1770.

Chester County, July 12, 1770.
THIS day was committed to my custody, a certain *George Adamson*, who says he is a runaway servant of *Mary Kinnard*, of Newtown, on Chester River, in Maryland. His mistress is desired to come, pay charges, and take him away, or he will be discharged in four weeks from the date hereof.
JOSEPH THOMAS, Goaler.
The Pennsylvania Gazette, July 19, 1770.

FIVE POUNDS Reward.
WHEREAS a certain James Moore, on the 7th day of July instant, sold to the subscriber, at his house, a servant, whom he called William Welsh, who entered into an indenture to serve his father James Moore, in the Kingdom of Ireland, and was brought over to America to him the said James Moore, and landed, on the 20th of June last, at New Castle, and brought to him by one Small (who came over in the same vessel) as a present from his said

father, as the said James Moore, at the time of the said sale, informed the subscriber; and whereas the said person, so sold as a servant, immediately after the said sale run away, and the subscriber upon the last enquiry he can make into the matter, has reason to believe that he has been most egregiously imposed upon, as no such person as William Welsh came over a servant in the said vessel with the said Small, nor was delivered to the said James Moore, by the said Small; and it is supposed that a certain William Barnett (who absconded about that time) signed the said indenture by the name of William Welsh; the said William Barnett resembling the man so sold as a servant, and immediately absconded as aforesaid. The said William Welsh, alias Barnett, is about 24 years of age, 5 feet 8 or 9 inches high, of a fair complexion, short dark hair; had on, when he went away, an old felt hat, good shirt and trowsers, of this country made linen, old shoes, with one brass, the other a street buckle, and may appear in other clothes, as he purchased, since he run away, a mixed light coloured cloth coat, with double gilt brass buttons, a diaper wrought linen jacket, the chain brown, and filling white, a pair of buckskin breeches, almost new, and sundry other clothes. Whoever shall take up the said William Welsh, alias Barnett, and bring him home, or secures him, so that the subscriber, living at Deer Creek, Baltimore county, in Maryland, may get him again, shall have the above reward, paid by
JOHN FORWOOD.

The Pennsylvania Gazette, July 19, 1770. See *The Pennsylvania Chronicle, and Universal* Advertiser, From Monday, July 9, to Monday, July 16, 1770.

Baltimore Town, July 11, 1770.
RUN away from on board the ship lying at Fell's Point, two convict servant men; one named *William Reeves,* about 27 years of age, about 5 feet 5 inches high, brown complexion, has short black hair, and wears a wig over it; had on a brown coat and jacket, new buckskin breeches, white worsted stockings, half-worn English shoes, with silver buckles; has two castor hats, one new, the other old and Plenty of money with him. The other named *John Jarvis,* about 25 or 26 years of age, about 5 feet 7 inches high, of a fair complexion, grey eyes, dark hair, speaks very good English, and had on a blue coat, and striped jacket, his other apparel unknown. Whoever takes up the said servants, and secures them in any jail so that their masters may have them again, shall receive, if taken in the county, *Thirty Shillings* for each, if out of the county, Three Pounds, and reasonable charges, if brought home, paid by the Subscriber, living in Baltimore county, on Carroll's Manor, near the Church.
THOMAS TREVERS, PETER BUTLER.

The Maryland Gazette, July 19, 1770; *The Pennsylvania Gazette,* November 22, 1770; December 13, 1770; December 20, 1770. Minor differences between the papers. See *The Pennsylvania Gazette,* August 23, 1770.

TEN POUNDS Reward.

RUN away from the subscriber, living in Baltimore county, near Charles Ridgely's iron works, the 9th of July Instant, an English servant man, named Thomas Hewitt, by trade a Bookbinder, a lusty well set fellow, about 5 feet 6 inches high, dark brown curled hair, and is about 27 years of age; had on, and took with him, a felt hat, check shirt, blue plush breeches, old shoes, yarn shockings [sic], a blue pea jacket, a striped flannel ditto, ozenbrigs shirt and trowsers; it is supposed he has forged a pass, and changed his name. Whoever takes up and secures the said servant, so that his master may have him again, shall have, if 10 miles from home, Three Pounds; if out of the county, Five Pounds; if 100 miles, Seven Pounds; and if 200 miles, the above reward, and reasonable charges, if brought home, paid by   ROBERT WILLMOTT.

The Pennsylvania Gazette, July 19, 1770.

FIVE POUNDS REWARD.

RAN away from the Subscriber, living in *Baltimore* County, in the Forks of *Gunpowder,* in the *Long Green,* on Tuesday the 10th of July, an *English* convict Servant Man, named WILLIAM BLAKE, a Shoemaker by Trade: Had on, and took with him, a brown Fustian Fly-Coat, Osnabrig Shirt, Check Shirt, and a Country homespun ditto, a Pair of light coloured Kersey Breeches, white Thread Stockings, black grained Pumps, and an old Felt Hat; he is about 5 Feet 10 Inches high, about 40 Years of Age, has gray Hair, speaks thick and fast, very often gets drunk: He has taken Part of his Tools with him.

Whoever takes up and secures said Servant, so that his Master may have him again, shall have Three Pounds, if take out of the County; and if out of County; and if out of the Province, the above Reward, and reasonable Charges, paid by   PETER HUNTER.

The Maryland Gazette, July 26, 1770; *The Pennsylvania Gazette,* July 26, 1770; August 16, 1770. Minor differences between the papers.

July 21, 1770.

RAN away from the Subscriber, living on the Eastern Neck Island, in *Kent* County, an indented Servant Man, named HENRY BALL, about 21 Years

of Age; he is marked with the Small-Pox, and is very much freckled. Also a Negro Wench, named SARAH.... It is supposed they were carried off by one *John Jones*, a Tailor, he is a short likely Fellow, and has brown Hair, which curls: Had on, when he went away, a Claret coloured Coat, Linen Vest and Breeches. Whoever takes up and secures said Servant and Negro, so that they may be had again, shall have Three Pounds Reward for each, and Five Pounds for JOHN JONES, paid by
NATH. HYNSON.
The Maryland Gazette, July 26, 1770.

FIVE PISTOLES Reward.

RUN away last night, from Mount Royal Forge, near Baltimore-Town, in Baltimore county, Maryland, an English convict servant man, named JOHN CARR, born in Cheshire, and speaks in that dialect, by trade a bricklayer, about 45 years of age, about 5 feet 10 inches high, spare made, and has bow legs, wears short black curled hair, which is turning grey; had on, and took with him, an old felt hat, 2 old black handkerchiefs, old brown coat, new blue pea jacket, 2 old ozenbrigs shirts, 1 check ditto, 2 old coarse white linen ditto, 1 pair of old leather breeches, patched on the seat, and daubed with tar in several places, 1 pair of new long ozenbrigs trowsers, 1 pair of old country sacking ditto, 2 pair of old grey worsted stockings, 2 pair of old black leather shoes, and 2 odd buckles, which are rusty; he has also a coarse linen bag, in which are several things I cannot describe. Whoever secures said servant, so that he may be had again, shall have, if taken in the county, Two Pistoles, and if out of the province, the above reward, and reasonable charges, if brought home.
July 17, 1770. *JAMES FRANKLIN.*
N.B. He came into this country about two weeks ago, in the ship Friendship, Captain Parker, master, and has taken with him two bricklayer's trowels, and an old lathing hammer.
The Pennsylvania Gazette, July 25, 1770. See *The Pennsylvania Gazette*, June 6, 1771.

FIVE POUNDS Reward.

RUN away, on the 10th day of July instant, from the subscribers, living in Queen-Anne's county, Maryland, near the Horse Head, two convict servant men, viz. JOHN ROSS, a tall slim fellow, about 6 feet 4 inches high, very much pock marked, he has a cast with his left eye, very red short hair; had on, when he went away, a tow linen shirt and trowsers, an old red coat, with the skirts cut off, and sleeves taken off, the buttons have number 12 on every one of them; but it is expected he will change his clothes, as his

companion has stole some of his master's; the above servant belongs to Wm. Brown. The other, belonging to William Jones, named THOMAS COLLERD, about 5 feet 7 or 8 inches high; had on, when he went away, a tow linen shirt and trowsers, a good felt hat, a striped jacket, with the stripes round the body, and a pair of blue and white striped trowsers. Whoever takes up the said servants, and secures them, so that their masters may have them again, shall have Three Pounds reward for *Ross*, and Forty Shillings for *Collerd*, and reasonable charges, paid by
WILLIAM BROWN and WILLIAM JONES.
The Pennsylvania Gazette, July 26, 1770; August 16, 1770; August 30, 1770.

FIVE POUNDS REWARD.

July 24, 1770.

RAN away on the 10th Instant, from the Subscribers, living in *Queen-Anne's* County, the following convict Servant Men, *viz.*

JOHN ROSS, a tall slim Fellow, about 6 Feet 4 Inches high, very much marked with the Small-Pox; he has a Cast with his left Eye, and very red short Hair: Had on, when he went away, a Tow Linen Shirt and Trousers, a striped Jacket, with the Stripes round him; but it is supposed he will change his Cloaths, as his Companion stole some from his Master.

THOMAS COLLERD, about 5 Feet 7 or 8 Inches high: Had on, when he went away, a Tow Linen Shirt and Trousers, a good Felt Hat, and a Pair of blue and white striped Trousers.

Whoever takes up said Servants, and secures them, so that their Masters may have them again, shall have Three Pounds for *Ross*, and Forty Shillings for *Collerd*, with reasonable Charges, paid by
WILLIAM BROWN,
WILLIAM JONES.
The Maryland Gazette, July 26, 1770; August 9, 1770; August 16, 1770; August 23, 1770. See below.

FIVE POUNDS Reward.

RUN away, on the 10th day of July instant, from the subscribers, living in Queen-Anne's county, Maryland, near the Horse Head, two convict servant men, viz. JOHN ROSS, a tall slim fellow, about 6 feet 4 inches high, very much pock marked, he has a cast with his left eye, very red short hair; had on, when he went away, a tow linen shirt and trowsers, an old red coat, with the skirts cut off, and sleeves taken off, the buttons have number 12 on every one of them; but it is expected he will change his clothes, as his companion has stole some of his master's; the above servant belongs to

Wm. Brown. The other, belonging to William Jones, named THOMAS COLLERD, about 5 feet 7 or 8 inches high; had on, when he went away, a tow linen shirt and trowsers, a good felt hat, a striped jacket, with the stripes round the body, and a pair of blue and white striped trowsers. Whoever takes up the said servants, and secures them, so that their masters may have them again, shall have Three Pounds reward for *Ross*, and Forty Shillings for *Collerd*, and reasonable charges, paid by
WILLIAM BROWN and WILLIAM JONES.

The Pennsylvania Gazette, July 26, 1770; August 16, 1770; August 30, 1770. See above.

July 23, 1770.
RAN away from the Subscribers, living on *Rock-Creek*, in *Frederick* County, the following Persons, viz.

ANDREW KEITH, about 30 Years old, and about 5 Feet 10 Inches high: Had on, and took with him, a blue close bodied Coat and Jacket, a Pair of Leather Breeches, a Pair of Trousers of Rolls, and several *Irish* Linen Shirts.

DANIEL MACDONALD, a young Lad, about 18 Years old: Had on, when he went away, an old Cotton Coat, Osnabrig Shirt and Trousers of Rolls.

BELL RILEY, supposed to be in company with the above Servant Men: Had on, when she went away, a green short Gown, Country Cloth Petticoat, and blue Cardinal. Whoever takes up the said Servants, and brings them home, shall receive Three Pounds Reward for each, paid by
JOHN LACLAND,
ALLEN BOWIE, Jun.

N. B. Several Servants in the Neighbourhood went off at the same Time, and are supposed to be all together.

The Maryland Gazette, July 26, 1770; August 2, 1770; August 9, 1770; August 16, 1770; August 23, 1770; August 30, 1770; September 6, 1770; September 13, 1770; September 20, 1770; October 4, 1770; October 18, 1770; October 25, 1770; November 1, 1770; November 8, 1770.

Kent-Island, July 30, 1770.
RAN away from the Subscriber, living in *Queen-Anne's* County, on the 19th of *June* last, a convict Servant Man, named GEORGE BOWLLS, born in the West of *England*, about 20 Years of Age, 6 Feet high, and has dark brown Hair: Had on, and took with him, a new Country Linen Shirt, an old ditto, and Trousers of the same, an old black and white striped Country

Kersey Jacket, with Sleeves of another Sort, a Felt Hat, an old small Drab coloured great Coat, no Shoes or Stockings, has some very large Scars on one of his Legs, and stoops in his Walking. Whoever takes up said Servant, and secures him, so that his Master may have him again, shall have Thirty Shillings if taken in the County, if our of the County, Forty Shillings, and if out of the Province, Three Pounds Reward, besides what the Law allows, paid by   WILLIAM HORN.

The Maryland Gazette, August 2, 1770; August 9, 1770; August 23, 1770; August 30, 1770; September 6, 1770; September 13, 1770; September 20, 1770; October 4, 1770; October 18, 1770; November 1, 1770; November 8, 1770; November 15, 1770; November 22, 1770; December 6, 1770; December 20, 1770; January 3, 1771; January 10, 1770; January 17, 1771; January 24, 1771; January 31, 1771; February 7, 1771; February 14, 1771.

Charles County, *July* 22, 1770.
RAN away from the Subscriber, on Tuesday the 17th Instant, an *Irish* indented Servant Man, named JOHN MURDOCK, about 5 Feet 4 Inches high, of a ruddy Complexion, very red Hair, Beard, and Eyebrows, stutters much, especially when drunk, and is very crooked in the Shoulders: Had on when he went away, an Osnabrig Coat, Jacket, and Breeches, an old Beaver Hat, striped Linen Shirt, brown Thread Stockings, a Pair Boot Leggings, and Campaign Shoes, with Brass Buckles; he also took with him, a Horse, Saddle and Bridle. The Horse was a Bay, about Fourteen and an Half Hands high, has a Bob Tail, ridged Mane, and his Foretop cut off, has a Star in his Forehead, trots and gallops, with a high Carriage. His Brand forgot. Any Person bringing the said Servant, and Horse, to the Subscriber, or Mr. *Frederick Stone*, in *Port-Tobacco*, shall receive Four Pounds Currency.
T. STONE.
N. B. The above Servant had a Pass from me to *Annapolis*, but was ordered back after he had gone Part of the Way, and the Pass omitted to be taken from him; this perhaps he may alter, or forge a new one, as he writes tolerably well.
The Maryland Gazette, August 2, 1770.

COMMITTED to *Anne-Arundel* County Jail, as a Runaway, *Thomas Newton*, who says he is a Servant to *William Hodges*.
His Master is desired to take him away and pay Charges.
JOHN CLAPHAM, Sheriff.
The Maryland Gazette, August 2, 1770.

Port-Tobacco, July 23, 1770.
RAN away from the Subscriber, a convict Servant Man, named JOHN NORTON, by Trade a Tailor, about 26 Years of Age, 5 Feet 4 or 5 Inches high: Had on when he went away, a dark brown Frize Coat, trimmed with black, a white Dimity Jacket, a Pair of blue knit Breeches, a Pair of white Stockings, and good Shoes. He probably will change his Name, and forge a Pass. Whoever takes up the said Servant, and secures him, so that he may be had again, shall have Three Pounds if taken within the Province, and if out of the Province, Five Pounds, and reasonable Charges, of brought home, paid by   PATRICK GRAHAME.

The Maryland Gazette, August 2, 1770; August 9, 1770; August 23, 1770; August 30, 1770.

RAN away from the Subscriber's Plantation, on the North Side of *Severn* River, on the 29th of *July*, a convict Servant Man, named JOHN HICKEY, about 22 Years of Age, and about 5 Feet 6 Inches high, has short black Hair, blue Eyes, and a very impudent Look: Had on, when he went away, a good Felt Hat, with a broad black Ribbon round the Crown, Osnabrig Shirt and Trousers, and old Shoes. He is very fond of Drink. Whoever takes up, and secures said Servant, so that his Master may have him again, shall receive Four Dollars Reward, paid by
DENTON HAMMOND.

The Maryland Gazette, August 2, 1770; August 9, 1770; August 16, 1770. See *The Maryland Gazette*, April 25, 1771.

Annapolis, July 30, 1770.
RAN away from the Subscriber, a convict Servant Man, named THOMAS WILLIS, he is about 30 Years of Age, 6 Feet high, of a fair Complexion, and a down Look: Had on, and took with him, when he went away, One red Waistcoat, Two Osnabrig Shirts, and One white ditto, One Pair of long Crocus Trousers, and One Pair of light coloured Cloth Breeches, speaks much in the West Country Dialect, and appears to be a very simple and undesigning Fellow.

Whoever secures said Servant, so that his Master may have him again, shall receive a Reward of Twenty Shillings.
WALTER DULANY.

The Maryland Gazette, August 2, 1770.

RAN away from the Subscriber, living in *Charles* County, on the 23d of *July*, a convict Servant Lad, named GEORGE OAKLY, about 5 Feet high, and about 16 Years of Age; he is a thick bluff Fellow, of a pale yellow

Complexion: Had on when he went away, an Osnabrig Shirt and Trousers, a Cloth Jacket, with one of the fore Skirts burnt much, and a coarse Hat with a very narrow Brim. Whoever takes up the said Servant, and brings him home, or secures him, so that the Owner may have him again, shall have a Reward of Two Dollars, if in the County, if out of the County, Three Dollars, and if out of the Province, Six Dollars, paid by
JOHN COOKSEY.
The Maryland Gazette, August 2, 1770; August 9, 1770.

RAN away from the Subscriber, living on *Elk-Ridge, Maryland*, near *Snowdens* Iron-Works, on the 27th *June* last, a convict Servant Lad, named JOSEPH DOBBINS, about 19 Years of Age, of a fair Complexion, a little Freckled, stoops in his Shoulders, about 5 Feet 3 or 4 Inches high, a very pleasant Countenance, speaks mild, and has brown curled Hair: Had on when he went away, a Felt Hat stitched round the Brim, Osnabrig Shirt and Trousers, white Fearnought Jacket, and old Country made Shoes. Whoever takes up the said Servant, and secures him any Jail, so that he may be had again, shall receive a Reward of Forty Shillings, and if brought home, Three Pounds, paid by   SETH WARFIELD.
The Maryland Gazette, August 2, 1770; August 9, 1770; August 16, 1770; August 23, 1770; August 30, 1770.

July 16, 1770.
RAN away from the subscriber, an English convict servant man, about 36 years of age, named John Green, with short black curled hair, has a large sore on the left side of his nose, he wears a handkerchief over it to hide it, he has lost the first joint of his right hand fore-finger; had on when he went away, a linen frock-fashion coat, a blue jacket, a pair of homespun trowsers, a pair of buckskin breeches, two white shirts, two coarse ditto, three pair of worsted stockings, a pair of shoes, a pair of plaited buckles, a coarse hat half worn, brown complexion, pitted with the small-pox. The above runaway is suspected to have taken two fifty pound bonds, and one thirty pound bond, payable from Thomas Poteet, to John Logan, and one eight pound note, payable from Arthur O'Hara to said Logan, and one bond of performance of 200 acres of lease land, from Robert Jewel, to John Logan; the first fifty pound bond is payable the first day of April 1771, the second the first of April next ensuing, the third the first of April next ensuing, and the note will become payable the beginning of February 1771.—He likewise took two Holland shirts, and two silk handkerchiefs, and one pair of thread stockings. I forewarn all persons from buying said bonds, or note. I do suppose he will make use of them as a pass. Whoever takes up said

servant, and secures him in any gaol, or brings him home, shall have Thirty Shillings reward; if taken out of the county, Three Pounds, paid by me, WILLIAM M'COMOS, living near Deer-Creek, in Baltimore county.

The Pennsylvania Chronicle, and Universal Advertiser, From Monday, July 30, to Monday, August 6, 1770.

July 22, 1770.

RAN away from the Subscriber, living near *Frederick-Town*, in *Frederick* County, Two Convict Servant Men, viz.

JAMES CATLING, a short well set Fellow, of a very swarthy Complexion, short black curl'd Hair: Had on, when he went away, an old Castor Hat, a red Seaman's Jacket, an old blue under do. Osnabrig Shirt, Sailor's Trousers, old Worsted Stockings, and old Shoes. He has followed the Sea, and was born in London.

ROBERT LIFE, a West Country Man, about 5 Feet 6 Inches high, is hard of Hearing, of a fair Complexion, down Look, has a Cast in One of his Eyes, and a Scar under his right Jaw: Had on, when he went away, an old Cotton Jacket, a spotted Swanskin ditto, a new Tow Linen Shirt, Sailors Trousers, old Stockings and Shoes.

Whoever takes up, and secures the said Servants, so that their Master may have them again, shall, if taken 30 Miles from home, have Four Pounds, if taken out of the Province, Five Pounds, and if brought home reasonable Charges, paid by   JOHN EASON.

The Maryland Gazette, August 9, 1770.

SIX POUNDS REWARD.

RAN away from Subscriber's Plantation, in *Frederick* County, on *Linganore*, Two Convict Servant Men, viz.

THOMAS TIPPING, about 40 Years of Age, 5 Feet 7 or 8 Inches high, his Apparel unknown: He was lately imported in the *Thornton*, Captain *M'Dougall*. He may strive to pass as a Sailor

JOHN LAWRENCE, about 19 Years of Age, 5 Feet 9 or 10 Inches high, very dark Complexion, black Eyes, and short black Hair: Had on when he went away, an Osnabrig Shirt and Trousers, old Fearnought Jacket, One spotted Swanskin ditto without Sleeves, and an old Felt Hat.

Whoever takes up said Servants and brings them to the Subscriber at *Elk-Ridge* Landing, shall have, if taken Ten Miles from home, Twenty Shillings; if Thirty Miles, Forty Shillings; and if out of the Province, Three Pounds Reward for each, including what the Law allows, paid by BENJAMIN DORSEY.

The Maryland Gazette, August 9, 1770; August 16, 1770; August 23, 1770. See *The Pennsylvania Gazette,* September 20, 1770.

July 30, 1770.
RAN away last Night from the Subscriber, living near the Head of *South-River,* an Indented Servant Lad, named ARTHUR EVANS, about 19 Years of Age, 5 Feet 2 or 3 Inches high, wears his own Hair, cut short upon the Top of his Head: Had on, and took with him, a new Osnabrig Shirt, a Pair of ditto Trousers, an old Check Shirt, an Osnabrig Jacket without Sleeves, a short skirted Frize Coat, a Pair of old Shoes and Buckles. He likewise took with him, a small gray Horse, with a small Saddle, and an old Snaffle Bridge; the Horse was branded on the near Buttock **AD** joined together.

Whoever takes up the said Runaway, with the Horse and Saddle, and secures them so as the Subscriber may get them again, shall receive if taken in the Province, Thirty Shillings, and if out of the Province Three Pounds Currency, paid by　　　　CORNELIUS DUVALL.
N. B. All Masters of Vessels are forbid to carry him off at their Peril.
C. D.

The Maryland Gazette, August 9, 1770; August 16; August 23, 1770; August 30, 1770.

August 7, 1770.
RAN away from the Subscriber, in *Baltimore-Town,* on the 8th Instant, an indented Servant Man, named HUGH GERMAN, by Trade a Tailor, about 28 Years of Age, 5 Feet high, of a dark Complexion, and dark Hair, tied behind, but it is supposed he will cut it off and get a Wig; he chews, smokes, takes Snuff, and loves Liquor very well: He took with him a green Coat, a light blue ditto, a black ditto, and a brown Cloth ditto, with Two brown Waistcoats, and a white Holland ditto, Twice stitched round the Edges, a Pair of Nankeen Breeches, a Pair of black Serge ditto, and a Pair of light mixt Cloth Breeches. Two white Holland Shirts, and Two coarse Linen ditto, One Pair of white Stockings, One Pair of coarse brown ditto, and One Pair of blue and white ditto; good Shoes, and Buckles plated with Silver. It is supposed he went away with one *Ullas,* a *Dutchman,* a Tailor, who lately came from *London;* he had on a brown Wig; his Cloaths are uncertain, as he has different Changes, and speaks very bad *English.* Whoever takes up said Servant, and secures him in any Jail, so that his Master may have him again, shall have Five Pounds Reward, and reasonable Charges, paid by
HUGH FRASER.

The Maryland Gazette, August 16, 1770; August 23, 1770; August 30, *1770; September 6, 1770; September 13, 1770; September 20, 1770;* October 4, 1770; October 11, 1770.

FIVE POUNDS REWARD.

August 1, 1770.

RAN away from the Subscriber, living in *Augusta* County, *Virginia*, on Sunday the 8th Day of July last, a convict Servant Man, named WILLIAM WATTS, a *Scotsman*, but does not speak in that Dialect, about 25 Years of Age, 5 Feet 10 Inches high, well set, thin faced, swarthy Complexion, something pitted with the Small-Pox, and has brown Hair tied behind: Had on, when he went away, a Half worn Felt Hat, Blanket Coat, bound with brown Linen, striped Lincey Jacket, coarse Country Linen Shirt and Trousers, and Shoes and Stockings. It is supposed he will forge a Pass, as he is a good Scholar. Whoever takes up and secures said Servant, so as his Master may have him again, shall have the above Reward, paid by
DAVID BELL.

N. B. All Masters of Vessels are forbid carrying him off at their Peril.
The Maryland Gazette, August 16, 1770.

RAN away from the Subscriber, an *Irish* Servant Man, named JOHN DOWNS, about 23 Years of Age, 5 Feet 7 Inches high, has short curled Hair, remarkably pitted with the Small-Pox, is very talkative, and will endeavour to pass for a Sailor: Had on, and took with him, and Osnabrig Shirt and Trousers, and a Pair of old Shoes. Whoever will secure said Servant, so that his Master may have him again, shall receive a Reward of 30s. paid by
SAMUEL HARRIS.

N. B. All Masters of Vessels are forewarned carrying him off at their Peril.
The Maryland Gazette, August 16, 1770.

Caecil County, *August* 6, 1770.

COMMITTED to my Custody, as a Runaway, *Henry Kennedy*, who says he came from *Sommerset* County, in *Maryland*; he is about 5 Feet 8 or 9 Inches high, and well made; he has with him some Check Shirts and Trousers. The Owner is desired to come and pay Charges, and take him away.   RICHARD THOMAS, Sheriff.

N. B. He came away in a Schooner belonging to *Edward Parker*.

The Maryland Gazette, August 16, 1770; August 23, 1770; August 30, 1770; September 6, 1770; September 13, 1770; September 20, 1770; October 4, 1770; October 18, 1770; October 25, 1770; November 8, 1770; November 15, 1770; November 22, 1770; December 20, 1770; January 3, 1771.

Annapolis, August 14, 1770.
WENT away from the Subscriber, on Sunday the 12th Instant, DANIEL SQUIRES, an indented Servant, by Trade a Polisher, or Stone Mason, aged about 24 Years, 5 Feet 9 Inches high, stout and well made, of a sandy Complexion, and short sandy Hair: He took with him, when he went away, a blue Cloth Body Coat, a white Flannel Waistcoat, black Leather Breeches, and a gray Surtout Coat. It is thought he went over the Bay in a Canoe, in Company with Two indented Servants of *Edmond Maw's*; the one named *Richard Warren,* the other *Mansfield Lewis Gwynn.* Whoever will secure the above *Daniel Squires,* so as he may be brought to the Subscriber, may receive Three Pounds, if taken in the Province, or Five Pounds, if taken out if it.   CHARLES CARROLL, of *Carrollton.*
The Maryland Gazette, August 16, 1770; August 23, 1770. See below.

Annapolis, August 14, 1770.
Went away from the Subscriber, on Sunday the 12th Instant, Two indented Servants, Carpenters by Trade, *viz.*
RICHARD WARREN, about 5 Feet 7 Inches high, 22 Years of Age, and thin made, much pitted with the Small-Pox: Had on, when he went away, a light coloured German Serge Coat, bound, a white Linen Waistcoat, a Pair of Buckskin Breeches, blue Stockings, turned Pumps, and a fine Hat; he also took with him a blue Shirt.
MANSFIELD LEWIS GWYNN, about 24 Years of Age, 5 Feet 5 Inches high, smooth faced, with short black Hair, curled: Had on, when he went away, a blue Coat with yellow Buttons, light coloured Cloth Breeches, and light coloured Worsted Stockings. Their Shirts are marked in the Bosom with the initial Letters of their Names, *viz.* R. W. M. G. It is supposed they went over the Bay in a Canoe, in Company with one *Daniel Squires,* an indented Servant belonging to *Charles Carroll,* Esq; of *Carrollton.* Whoever will secure said Servants, or either of them, so as they may be had again, may receive Three Pounds Reward for each of them, if taken in the Province, or Five Pounds for each of them, if taken out of it.
EDMOND MAW.
The Maryland Gazette, August 16, 1770; August 23, 1770. See above and *The Maryland Gazette,* September 6, 1770.

Baltimore Town, Maryland, August 7, 1770.
RUN away from the subscriber, in Baltimore Town, on the 5th instant, at night, an Irish servant man, named DENNIS ROYNANE, middle size, full face, ruddy complexion, thick lips, marked with the small-pox, and speaks much in the Irish dialect: Had on, and took with him a blue sailor jacket, old hat, a short cut wig, one check, and one ozenbrigs shirt, ozenbrigs trowsers, shoes and stockings, and some other clothes, not known. It is likely he will pretend to pass for a sailor. Whoever takes up said servant, and secures him in any goal, so that his master may have him again, shall have THREE POUNDS *reward, and if brought home* FIVE POUNDS, *including what the law allows, paid by*
MARK ALEXANDER.
The Pennsylvania Gazette, August 16, 1770; August 30, 1770; January 10, 1771.

RUN away on Sunday night, the 5th of this inst. August, from the subscribers, living in Baltimore county, Maryland, two servant men, viz. DANIEL HERKINS, an Irishman, but speaks good English, about 25 years of age, about 5 feet 8 or 9 inches high, very lusty and fat, wears his own short dark coloured hair; had on a check shirt, and this country linen trowsers, a country made hat, about half worn, and very greasy, good shoes, and buckles. The other, named WILLIAM REDFORD, an Englishman, about the same age of Herkins, near 5 feet 7 inches high, of a swarthy complexion, a good deal pitted with the small-pox, wears his own short yellow hair, is a brazen looking fellow, and a shoemaker by trade; had on, and took with him, two pair of ozenbrigs trowsers, and two shirts of the same, a new felt hat, black silk handkerchief, country made shoes, and good buckles. It is supposed he took several ruffled shirts with him also. Whoever takes up said servants, and secures them so that their master may get them again, shall have FIVE POUNDS, reward, or Fifty Shillings for either, and reasonable charges, paid by ABRAHAM WHITAKER, and JACOB WHEELER.
N. B. Said *Herkins* is a ship carpenter, and lately indentured himself a servant for 4 years in the city of Philadelphia.
The Pennsylvania Gazette, August 16, 1770; August 30, 1770.

Caecil county, Maryland, July 23, 1770.
RUN away from the subscriber, living near the head of Bohemia, two servants; one an Irishman, born in Cork, aged about 25 years, about 5 feet 4 or 5 inches high; had on, when he went away, a red and white spotted swanskin jacket, an old homespun shirt, coarse tow trowsers, one a half

worn felt hat; has short light brown hair, and a small blemish on one of his eyes. The other a Negroe man....they had neither shoes nor stockings. Whoever takes up said servants, and secures them, so that their master may have them again, shall have FORTY SHILLINGS reward, or Twenty Shillings for each, paid by me
WILLIAM WEATHERS.

The Pennsylvania Gazette, August 16, 1770; August 30, 1770.

RAN away on Friday the 20th of *July* last, a Convict Servant Man, named PHILIP CALENDER, Five Feet Seven or Eight Inches high, wears his own Hair, which is of a sandy Colour, and has a remarkable large Foot: Had on, when he went away, an Osnabrig Shirt and Crocus Trousers; took with him, an old Cloth Snuff Coloured Coat, with Mohair Buttons, about half worn, a Pair of Osnabrig Trousers, an Osnabrig Shirt, a Felt Hat, and a small Prayer-Book, in which it is believed his Name is wrote. Whoever takes up said Servant, and delivers him to the Subscriber, shall have, if taken within this Province, Four Dollars, if taken out of the Province, and delivered to the Subscriber, Three Pounds Reward, paid by
HOWARD DUVALL.

The Maryland Gazette, August 23, 1770; August 30, 1770; September 13, 1770; September 20, 1770; September 27, 1770; October 11, 1770; October 18, 1770; October 25, 1770; November 1, 1770.

August 15, 1770.

RAN away from the Subscriber, living on *Swan-Creek*, in *Kent* County, *Maryland*, Two Convict Servant Men, *viz.*

WILLIAM POWEL, a Fellow with One Eye, much Pock marked in his Face, born in *Bristol*, he is about 25 Years of Age, 5 Feet 7 Inches high, a Shoemaker by Trade, he has been as a Hand in the *Rock-Hall* Packet.

WILLIAM CASWELL, he has a thin Visage, about 5 Feet 10 Inches high, a Weaver by Trade. Their wearing Aparrel I cannot describe, as they have taken a Trunk of Cloaths out of the House; they have Three Watches with them. They went off in a small Pettiaugre.

Whoever takes up said Servants, and secures them, so that their Master may have them again, shall receive if taken in the Province, 20 Shillings for each (besides what the Law allows) and reasonable Charges if brought home, paid by   ABRAHAM AYRES.

The Maryland Gazette, August 23, 1770.

Head of Wye River, in Talbot County, August 13, 1770.
RUN away from the subscriber, on Monday, the 30th of July, an Irish servant man, called THOMAS AGNEW, a weaver by trade, about 30 years of age, of a pale complexion, about 5 feet 10 inches high; had on, when he went away, a coarse tow linen shirt, and trowsers, much worn, an old grey jacket, much worn, with cuffs on the sleeves; he has exceeding bad sore legs, ulcerated and swelled, two sores on the left leg; he has very little hair on his head, and is very much bald, it is thought he has a wig on, and a hat; he is a subtle fellow, was born in the west of Ireland, and brags much of his trade. Whoever bring back said servant to his master, or secures him so as he may be had again, shall have Forty Shillings reward, paid by
FRANCES HUMPHREYS.
The Pennsylvania Gazette, August 23, 1770; August 30, 1770; September 20, 1770.

RUN away, on the 30th of July, 1769, from the subscriber, living in Carroll's manor, Baltimore county, Maryland, a convict servant man, born in Yorkshire, in England, and speaks much upon that dialect, named Amburst Clemmisson, but since has changed it to George Bell, he is about 5 feet 6 inches high, of a fair complexion, sandy hair; had on, when he went away, a brown coat, with wrought brass buttons, a red jacket, without sleeves, and a pair of home made trowsers. He went away, with another servant, but that other servant was since taken up at Philadelphia, and gives an account, that the said Amburst was taken up at Stoney creek, over the Allegany Mountains about September last, by three men, and the subscriber has not heard of him since. Whoever takes up the said servant, and brings him to his master, shall receive TEN POUNDS, Pennsylvania currency, and reasonable charges, paid by me
EDWARD BOSMAN.
The Pennsylvania Gazette, August 23, 1770; August 30, 1770; September 20, 1770.

Baltimore county, Maryland, August 20, 1770.
RAN away, on the 15th instant, from the subscribers, living in Carroll's manor, on the Forks of Gunpowder, two English convict servant men; one named JOHN JARVIS, but may change his name, 24 years of age, about 5 feet 6 and an half inches high, pale complexion, grey eyed, short black hair; had on and took with him, when he went away, two very good hats, a new brown fly coat, red and white striped jacket, black thickset breeches, two pair of white thread stockings, pretty good English shoes, with brass

buckles, blue pea-jacket, two shirts, one dowlas the other holland, very much worn, ozenbrigs trowsers, and three silk handkerchiefs; has got a pass, by forging Mr. Plowman's hand writing to it, and it is imagined he will go by the name of Thomas Kees, and has money pretty plenty. The other name WILLIAM BARKER, about 40 years of age, 5 feet 8 inches high, a lusty man, short brown hair, brown complexion, very much pitted with the small-pox; had on, when he went away, an old felt hat, old lightish coloured coat, patched with cotton patches, with broad white metal buttons, short cotton jacket, without sleeves, coarse shirt and trowsers, old shoes, with brass buckles; but it is likely he may wear some of the clothes the other took with him, as they are both gone together. Whoever takes up said servants, and secures them, so that their masters may have them again, shall have, if taken within said county, TWENTY SHILLINGS for each, besides what the law allows; and if taken out of the county, THIRTY SHILLINGS for each, beside what the law allows, paid by
PETER BUTLER, and EDWARD BOSMAN.

    N.B. It is possible they may both forge passes.—The person or persons that takes up said servants, are requested to notify it in the Pennsylvania Chronicle.
    The Pennsylvania Gazette, August 23, 1770; August 30, 1770; September 6, 1770; September 20, 1770. See The Pennsylvania Gazette, July 19, 1770, and November 22, 1770.

COMMITTED to *Anne-Arundel* County Jail as Runaways, *John Inch* and *John Street*, who say they are Servants to *James Walker*, on *Elk-Ridge*. Negro *Abram*....Negro *Ned*....
    Their Masters are desired to take them away and pay Charges.
JOHN CLAPHAM, Sheriff.
The Maryland Gazette, August 30, 1770.

                              Annapolis, September 2, 1770.
RAN away from the Subscriber, on Sunday the 12th of last Month, an indented Servant Man, named MANSFIELD LEWIS GWYNN, who professes to be either a Carpenter, Painter, or Cabinet-maker by Trade, he is about 24 Years of Age, 5 Feet 5 Inches high, smooth faced, with short black curled Hair, has a Scar under One of his Eyes: Had on, when he went away, a blue Cloth Coat, with yellow Buttons, a Pair light coloured Cloth Breeches, a brown great Coat, a light coloured Pair of Rib'd Worsted Stockings, red striped Linen Waistcoat, his Shirt marked in the Bosom with the initial Letters of his Name, *viz.* M. G. He went over the Bay in a Canoe, in Company with 2 other Servants, who were Runaways, but are since taken, and confessed they left the said *Mansfield Lewis Gwynn* sick, near *Queens-Town*.

Whoever will secure said Servant, so as his Master may have him again, may receive Three Pounds Reward, if taken in the Province, or Five Pounds if taken out of it, paid by
EDMOND MAW.
The Maryland Gazette, September 6, 1770; September 13, 1770. See *The Maryland Gazette*, August 16, 1770.

Lancaster Goal, August 22, 1770.
THIS day was committed to my custody, on suspicion of being runaway servants, James Lusby, and William Hewes, as they call themselves, and, on both their own confessions, say, that they are servants to Mr. Charles Ridgely, living opposite the market-house, in Baltimore Town, Maryland. Also was committed to my custody, as a runaway, on the 24th of this instant August, a certain Martin Long, as he calls himself, and on seeing some printed advertisements, of Twelve Dollars reward, for the taking up of the said Martin Long, he is the same person; and, on his own confession, says, that he is a servant to Mr. Daniel M'Farland, pot ash maker, at Mouth holly, in East New Jersey, which said name is to the advertisement of the said Martin Long. The masters of the above servants, are desired to come and pay their said servants charges, and take them away, otherwise they will be sold out for their fees, in 2 or 3 weeks from the date hereof, by
GEORGE EBERLY, Goaler.
The Pennsylvania Gazette, September 6, 1770; September 20, 1770.

Kent county, Maryland, August 30, 1770.
FIVE POUNDS Reward.
RUN away from the subscriber, a servant lad, about three years ago, but has been often seen in Philadelphia lately, and it is said that he lives in the Jerseys, near Gloucester, at a place called Woodbury, he may have changed his name, but his right name is John Harris, born in England, and was convicted to Maryland, and served his time out, and became a servant again; he drinks hard, and swears much, and used to have a sore leg. Whoever takes up said servant, and brings him to his master, or secures him in any goal, so that his master may have him again, shall receive the above reward, from me   JOHN MOORE.
The Pennsylvania Gazette, September 6, 1770.

FOUR DOLLARS Reward.
RUN away, on the 17th of August, 1770, from the subscriber, living in Queen-Anne's county, near Queen's-Town, Maryland, an English servant

woman, named Catherine Marsh, of a middle size, much pock-marked, has yellowish hair, aged about 22 years, or thereabouts; had on, when she went away, a striped linsey quilted petticoat, a home made linen short gown, with pale stripes, a home-made linen shift, and a small black silk hat, much wore. The above servant arrived in Philadelphia on Friday, the 24th of August, late in the evening and was taken up on the 28th in the morning, but was rescued on Market-street wharff, by some fellows unknown, and is supposed to be about that city or suburbs yet. Whoever takes up said servant, and brings her to me, or secures her, shall have the above reward, and reasonable charges, paid by me
PETER DENNY.
    N.B. All masters of vessels, and others, are forewarned not to harbour or carry off said servant, at their peril.
    The Pennsylvania Gazette, September 6, 1770; September 20, 1770.

Stratford, August 8, 1770.
RAN away the 26th of July last, an indented Servant Man, named THOMAS BENTLEY, born and bound in *England* for Four Years: Had on, when he went away, an osnabrig Coat, Jacket and Breeches, the Coat Cuffs lined with red: Carried with him, white and brown Thread Stockings, Two Pair of Shoes, One Pair *English*, the other *Virginia*, a Sailor's Hat, bound with black Worsted Ferrit, Two Shirts, and sundry other Cloaths. He is pale faced, wears his own Hair, which is light brown, is about 6 Feet high, has an impudent Way of Talking, and is by Profession a Coachman. Whoever will take him up, and bring him to me, if taken near my House, or joining *Westmoreland*, shall have Thirty Shillings; if further, or in any Province on the Continent, Three Pounds, besides what the Law allows.
PHILIP LUDWELL LEE.
    The Maryland Gazette, September 13, 1770; September 20, 1770; September 27, 1770.

TWENTY DOLLARS REWARD.

RAN away from the Subscriber, living in *Anne-Arundel* County, in the Province of *Maryland*, and the 13th of *August* last, a convicted Servant Man, named JOHN SHIELDS, alias JOHN WILSON, a *Scotchman*, and Thirty Years of Age, Five Feet Eight or Nine Inches high, round shouldered, of a dark Complexion, has a black Beard and short black Hair, is bald on the Top of his Head, but wears some Hair tied on with a String, in order to conceal it; he talks very broad *Scotch*: Had on and took with him a blue Cloth Coat, striped Waistcoat, Osnabrig and white Shirts, Country made Shoes, Worsted Stockings and Felt Hat. It is probable he will change his Dress and forge a Pass. Whoever apprehends the said Servant, and secures him in any Jail, that I may get him again, shall receive Five Pounds Reward, if taken in the Province of *Maryland*, and Twenty Dollars if out of the Province.   JOHN DORSEY.

The Maryland Gazette, September 13, 1770; September 20, 1770; September 27, 1770; October 11, 1770; October 18, 1770; October 25, 1770; November 1, 1770; November 8, 1770; November 15, 1770; November 29, 1770; December 6, 1770; December 20, 1770; January 3, 1771; January 10, 1770; January 17, 1771; January 24, 1771; January 31, 1771; February 7, 1771; February 14, 1771; *The Pennsylvania Gazette*, September 13, 1770; September 27, 1770. Minor differences between the papers. *The Pennsylvania Gazette* has the date September 6, 1770 at the bottom of the ad.

September 3, 1770.
RAN away last Night from the Subscriber, living on *Elk-Ridge*, in *Anne-Arundel* County, *Maryland*, Two convict Servant Men, viz.

ANTHONY JACKSON, an *Englishman*, born in *Yorkshire*, and speaks a little in the West-Country Dialect, a likely well made Fellow, about 19 or 20 Years of Age, 5 Feet 8 Inches high, stoops in his Shoulders, a fresh looking Fellow, has short dark Hair, and a thin dark Beard: Had on, and took with him, Two Osnabrig Shirts, Hempen Roll Trousers, new white Kersey Jacket, new Felt Hat, old *English* Shoes, a white Cotton Blanket, and an old Flannel Jacket, with black Stocking Sleeves.

WILLIAM WARRIKER, an *Englishman*, about 25 Years of Age, about 5 Feet 3 Inches high, a likely well set Fellow, but of a sullen Temper, dark Complexion, with dark Hair and Beard, is a little bald pated, and much pitted with the Small-Pox: Had on, and took with him, One Osnabrig Shirt, One striped ditto, coarse Country Linen Trousers, a new white Cotton Jacket, Country made Shoes, an old Flannel Jacket, with gray Stocking Sleeves, an old small Hat, with a Patch on one Side, and an old brown curled Wig.

Whoever takes up said Servants, or either of them, and secures them in any Jail, so that the Subscribers may get them again, shall have, for each, if taken Twenty Miles from home, Forty Shillings, and if Thirty Miles, Three Pounds, and if out of the Province, Five Pounds, including what the Law allows, and reasonable Charges, if brought home,
JOHN HOOD, JOHN HOOD, Jun.

N. B. They were imported in the *Thornton*, Capt. M'Dougall. All Masters of Vessels are forbid from carrying them off at their Peril.

The Maryland Gazette, September 13, 1770; September 20, 1770; September 27, 1770; October 11, 1770; October 18, 1770. See *The*

Pennsylvania Gazette, September 20, 1770, *The Maryland Gazette,* May 27, 1773, and *The Pennsylvania Chronicle,* From Monday, June 14, to Monday, June 21, 1773, for Jackson.

St. Mary's County, *Sept.* 4, 1770.
COMMITTED to *St. Mary's* County Jail, as a Runaway, RICHARD WELCH, who says he belongs to *William Crandell,* of *Anne-Arundel* County; is about 5 Feet 2 Inches high, and about 18 or 19 Years of Age: Had on, and with him, One Osnabrig Shirt, One Check ditto, a Pair of Osnabrig Trousers, a Crocus Frock, and a Pair of Trousers of the same. His Master is desired to take him away, and pay Charges.
ROBERT WATTS, Sheriff.

The Maryland Gazette, September 13, 1770; September 20, 1770; September 27, 1770; October 4, 1770; October 18, 1770; October 25, 1770; November 1, 1770; November 8, 1770; January 10, 1771.

RUN away, on the night of the 21st of August, 1770, from the ship Thornton, Captain M'Dougall, lying in the Ferry-branch of Patapsco, in Maryland, two convict men, viz. WILLIAM SYMONDS, *by trade a Barber, about 25 years of age, 5 feet 5 inches high, wears his own short light coloured hair, and is very fond of tobacco, has a down look when spoke to, or taxed with any thing amiss.* JOHN HILL, *by trade a Glass-blower, about* 2[5] *years of age, fair complexion and pitted with the small-pox, wore an old brown cut wig, is about 5 feet 4 inches high, and is a talkative sensible fellow. We cannot describe their clothes particularly, but from the best information the Captain can give us, they both have it in their power to dress genteely, and it is very probable they will pass for master and man. Whoever takes up the said servants, and brings them to us, shall receive a reward of Forty Shillings for each, if taken in the province; if out of the province, FOUR POUNDS for each, besides reasonable charges, and the reward allowed by law.*
WILLIAM RUSSELL, *and* MATTHEW RIDLEY.
   N. B. All masters of vessels are forewarned from harbouring or carrying off either of them.
   The Pennsylvania Gazette, September 13, 1770.

Baltimore county, September 3, 1770.
FIVE POUNDS REWARD.
RUN away from the subscriber living Baltimore county, about ten miles from Baltimore-Town, in Maryland, an English servant MAN, named

GEORGE ADAMS, about 35 years of age, about 5 feet 10 inches high, pitted with the small-pox, has black hair and beard, a scar on his upper lip, and is remarkably pleasant and smiles when talking; had on when he went away, an old felt hat, a brown great coat without a cape, with metal buttons, a blue-grey fearnought jacket without sleeves, oznabrigs shirt and trowsers. He likewise took away with him a bay HORSE, with a blaze face, about 14 hands high, has a standing mane, a natural pacer and shod before. Whoever takes up said man and horse, and secures them so that their master may get them again, shall have, if in the county, Forty Shillings, if out of the county Three Pounds, and in proportion for either, with reasonable charges if brought home, paid by   NICHOLAS BRITTON.

The Pennsylvania Gazette, September 13, 1770; *The Pennsylvania Chronicle,* From Monday, September 10, to Monday, September 17, 1770. See *The Maryland Gazette*, July 5, 1770. Minor differences between the papers.

Frederick County, Maryland, September 2, 1770.
RAN away from the Subscriber, living on *Bennet's Creek*, a Convict Servant Woman, named ANN INCH, about 40 Years of Age: Had on a brown Camblet Gown, Two Check Linen Aprons, Two old white Shifts, old coarse Shoes, a black Hat.—Any Person bringing said Servant home, shall receive 20 Shillings Reward, besides what the Law allows, paid by
THOMAS KIRK, Senior
The Maryland Gazette, September 20, 1770.

Annapolis, August 31, 1770.
RAN away from the Subscriber, on the 29th Instant, a Convict Servant Man, named JOHN JONES, by Trade a Bricklayer, Plasterer, and Stucco-worker; he has a Cut on his Forehead, and One down his Nose, is about 5 Feet 7 Inches high, 28 Years of Age, and wears his own short black Hair: Had on, when he went away, a black Hair Stock, lined with red, a blue Cloth Coat, red Jacket, a Pair of Black Buckskin Breeches, mingled Worsted Hose, a Pair of *English* Shoes, and large Brass Buckles, on which is, *May Trade revive,* Wilkes *and Liberty, Number* 45. Whoever takes up, or secures said Servant, so that his Master may have him again, shall receive, if Thirty Miles from home, Thirty Shillings, if Forty Miles, Forty Shillings; and if out of the Province, Five Pounds.
JOHN UNSWORTH.
The Maryland Gazette, September 20, 1770; September 27, 1770; October 4, 1770; October 18, 1770; October 25, 1770; November 1,

1770; November 8, 1770; November 15, 1770; November 22, 1770; December 20, 1770.

SEVEN POUNDS REWARD.

RUN away from subscriber's plantation, on Linganore, in Frederick county, Maryland, a convict servant man, named *Thomas Tipping*, a Welchman, about 5 feet 7 or 8 inches high, 40 years of age; his apparel unknown: He was lately imported in the Thornton, Captain M'Dougall. Whoever takes up said servant, and delivers him to the subscriber, at Elk-Ridge Landing, receive the above reward, and reasonable charges, paid by
BENJAMIN DORSEY.   *August*, 1770.
Pennsylvania Gazette, September 20, 1770. See *The Maryland Gazette*, August 9, 1770.

TWENTY POUNDS Reward.

RUN away last night, from the subscribers, living on Elk Ridge, in Anne-Arundel county, Maryland, two English convict servant men, viz. *Anthony Jackson*, born in Yorkshire, a likely well made fellow, stoops a little in his shoulders, fresh colour, dark thin beard, and short dark hair, about 20 years of age, and about 5 feet 8 inches high; had on and took with him, an ozenbrigs shirt, a pair of new hempen roll trowsers, a new white kersey jacket, an old flannel ditto, with black stocking sleeves, new felt hat, old English shoes, with old buckles and a white cotton blanket. *William Warricker*, a likely well set fellow, about 25 years of age, about 5 feet 3 inches high, of a sullen temper, dark complexion, with short dark hair and beard, a little bald pated, much pitted with the small-pox; had on and took with him, one ozenbrigs shirt, one striped ditto, coarse country linen trowsers, a new white cotton jacket, an old flannel ditto, with grey stockings sleeves, good country made shoes, old brown curled wig, and an old small hat, with a patch on one side: They were both imported in the Thornton, Captain M'Dougall, in July last. Whoever takes up the said servants, or either of them, and secures them in any goal, so that the subscriber may get them again, shall receive for each, if taken 20 miles from home, Forty Shillings; if 30 miles, Three Pounds; and if out of the province, Ten Pounds, including what the law allows; and reasonable charges, if brought home paid by JOHN HOOD, and JOHN HOOD, jun.
N.B. All masters of vessels are forbid carrying them off, at their peril.
September 3, 1770.
The Pennsylvania Gazette, September 20, 1770. See *The Maryland Gazette*, September 13, 1770; *The Maryland Gazette*, May 27, 1773,

and *The Pennsylvania Chronicle,* From Monday, June 14, to Monday, June 21, 1773, for Jackson.

September 14, 1770.
RAN away, the 26th of *August* last, from the Subscriber, living near the Head of *Rock Creek, Frederick* County, *Maryland,* an *Irish* Servant Man, named ISAIAH THOMSON; about 38 Years of Age, 5 Feet 8 Inches high, a broad well set Fellow, short brown curled Hair, has had the Small Pox, is slow of Speech, and will endeavour to pass for a Sailor or Soldier: Had on and took with him, Two Check Shirts, brown Roll Trousers, old Shoes, One Pair of Leather Breeches, One blue Pea Jacket, One striped Flannel ditto, and One old Castor Hat. It is supposed he will endeavour to pass to *Philadelphia.* He has said that he is Proprietor of 100 Acres of Land in *Pennsylvania* Government, and has Two Brothers living there. Whoever will secure said Servant, so that his Master may have him again, shall receive a Reward of Three Pounds current Money, and is pursued, and taken out of this Province, Twenty Dollars, paid by
RECTOR MAGRUDER.

The Maryland Gazette, September 27, 1770; October 4, 1770; October 11, 1770; *The Pennsylvania Chronicle,* From Monday, October 8, to Monday, October 15, 1770; From Monday, October 22, to Monday, October 29, 1770. Minor differences between the papers. The *Chronicle* shows the last name of the runaway as "Thompson" and the county he escaped from as "Fredericksburgh."

Caecil County, *September* 24, 1770.
SIXTEEN DOLLARS REWARD.
Caecil County, September 24, 1770.
BROKE out of *Caecil* County Jail, on Saturday Night the 22d Inst. Two Servant Men, *viz. Henry Kennelly,* and *Cornelius Crowly; Kennelly* is about 5 Feet 7 Inches high, well made: Had on, a brown Coat, Check Shirt, and Linen Trousers. *Crowly* is about 5 Feet 6 Inches high, well Made: Had on, a blue Coat, Linen Shirt, and Buckskin Breeches. Whoever takes up the said Runaways, and brings them to the Subscriber in *Charles-Town,* shall have the above Reward, or Eight Dollars for each, and reasonable Charges, paid by RICHARD THOMAS, Sheriff.
*Crowly took with him, Two Pair of New Shoes.

The Maryland Gazette, September 27, 1770; October 4, 1770; October 11, 1770; October 18, 1770; October 25, 1770; November 8, 1770; November 15, 1775; November 22, 1770; December 20, 1770; January 10, 1771; January 17, 1771; January 24, 1770. See *The Pennsylvania Gazette,* June 14, 1770.

THREE POUNDS REWARD.

September 24, 1770.

RAN away Yesterday from the Subscribers, living near *Annapolis*, an *Irish* indented Servant Man, named PATRICK DOWLING, a Shoemaker by Trade, 25 Years old, about 5 Feet 6 Inches high, well made, of a brown Complexion,, has black Hair, large Beard, pitted with the Small Pox, and is marked in his right Arm with Gunpowder, PD IS, with some other Marks which cannot be described: Had on, a new Felt Hat, old Bearskin Coat, Osnabrig Shirt and Trousers, and it is supposed he has a Pair of old Shoes, and a large Knife.—Whoever takes up, and secures said Servant, so that his Masters get him again, shall receive, if taken above Ten Miles from home, Forty Shillings, and if out of the Province, the above Reward, and reasonable Charges, if brought home, paid by
CALEB BURGESS, JOHN WORTHINGTON, junr.

The Maryland Gazette, September 27, 1770; October 4, 1770; October 11, 1770; October 18, 1770; November 1, 1770; November 8, 1770; November 15, 1770; November 22, 1770.

Lancaster Goal, September 19, 1770.

ON the 31st day of October, 1769, was committed to my custody, a certain Thomas Pugh, as he calls himself, and is by trade a taylor; and whereas the said Thomas remained in my custody until the month of July last, without any knowledge, or his own confession, that he, the said Thomas, was a servant to any person or persons whatever; at which time a certain Solomon Duffey, of Bridgetown, in Kent county, Maryland, came and claimed the said Thomas as his servant, he being a runaway from him; this is therefore to give notice to said Solomon Duffey, to come and pay his said servantcharges and cost, and take him away, otherwise he will be sold out for his fees, in 3 weeks from the date hereof, by
GEORGE EBERLY, Goaler.

The Pennsylvania Gazette, September 27, 1770.

TWENTY DOLLARS REWARD.

RAN away from the subscribers, living in Garrison Forrest, in Baltimore county, Two English convict servant men, THOMAS PRICE, a taylor by trade, about 30 years of age, 5 feet 10 inches high, a talkative fellow, of a yellowish complexion, short black hair; had on, and took with him, a blue cloth coat, black cloth jacket, one callico ditto, a check shirt, one white ditto, three pair ozenbrigs trowsers, a new felt hat, old shoes, a large pair of taylor's shears; he has a large scar on his right leg.

JAMES BORDMAN, about 40 years of age, 5 feet 4 inches high, a well-set fellow, short brown Hair, has one leg shorter than the other, which makes him walk lame; had on an old brown cloth coat with white metal buttons, old leather breeches, ozenbrigs shirt, light coloured yarn stockings, half boots and felt hat. Whoever takes up said servants, and secures them in any gaol, so as their masters may have them again, shall have the above reward, including what the law allows, and reasonable charges, if brought home, paid by
      BENJAMIN WELLS, and LARKIN RANDALL.
The Pennsylvania Chronicle, From Monday, October 1, to October 8, 1770; From Monday, October 22, to October 29, 1770.

RAN away from the Subscriber living near *Elk-Ridge* Church, in *Anne-Arundel* County, on the 20th of *September*, Two Convict Servant Men, both *Irish*. HUGH LACY, about 50 Years of Age, and of a dark Complexion: Had on, when he went away, a Pair of coarse, Country-made Linen Trousers, as also a Shirt, a strip'd Jacket, an old Pair of Shoes, bluish Yarn Stockings, and an old brown Wig.
      JOHN HUGHS, about 30 Years of Age, full faced, well set; Had on the same Kind of Cloaths as the other, with a white Wig. They have taken with them, a Country Cloth Coat, of a brown Colour, doubled [sic] breasted, lined with green, and the Lining very much tore, also Two old brown Cloth Coats, daubed with Tar. Whoever takes up the said Servants, and brings them home, if within the Province, shall receive Fifty Shillings for each, if out of the Province, Three Pounds, paid by
EHPRAIM HOWARD, Son of *Henry.*
The Maryland Gazette, October 11, 1770; October 18, 1770; October 25, 1770. See *The Maryland Gazette,* May 24, 1770.

RAN away from the Subscriber near *Upper-Marlborough,* on the 9th of *September* last, a Servant Man, named WILLIAM JACKSON, about Seven or Eight and Twenty Years of Age, wore short black Hair, has a down Look, black Eyes, and Yellow Complexion: Had on, when he went away, a light coloured Bearskin Coat, about half worn, Osnabrig Shirt, brown Roll Trousers, and an old Castor Hat. He served part of his time with the late Mr. *John Scott,* in *Upper-Marlborough.*
      Whoever takes up and secures the said Servant, so that his Master may get him again, shall receive, if taken in the County, 20 Shillings, if out of the County, 30 Shillings, and reasonable Charges if brought home, paid by NINIAN WILLETT, junior.

The Maryland Gazette, October 11, 1770; October 18, 1770; October 25, 1770; November 8, 1770; November 15, 1770.

Baltimore County, *Sept.* 9, 1770.
THREE POUNDS REWARD.
RAN away from the Subscriber, living in *Garrison-Forest*, about Ten Miles from *Baltimore Town*, an indented Servant Man, named LAURENCE CRAVAN, by Trade a Painter, about 5 Feet 6 Inches high, wears his own short brown Hair, has black Eyes, a Scar on one of his Cheeks, and pitted with the Small Pox, a bold looking Man, and has a good Education; he served Two Years on *Baltimore-Town*, and is well known there, is about 30 Years of Age, and very fond of Liquor: Had on, a short blue Jacket with Sleeves, Osnabrig Shirt and Trousers, a Pair of good Shoes, white Metal Buckles, a Felt Hat, about Half worn, cocked round, and marked with Paint. Whoever takes up said Servant, and secures him, so that he may be had again, shall receive, if 10 Miles from home, Twenty Shillings, if 20 Miles, Forty Shillings, and if out of the Province the above Reward, with reasonable Charges, if brought home.
JOHN COCKEY.
The Maryland Gazette, October 11, 1770.

Reading Goal, October 2, 1770.
ON the 15th day of September last, was committed to my custody, a certain William M'Dougall, as he calls himself, and says he is a servant to Johannes Gleen, near Salsborough town, in Maryland, about 5 miles from George-Town. This is therefore to give notice to said Johannes Gleen, to come and pay, his said servantcharges and cost, and taken him away, otherwise he will be sold out for his fees, in six weeks from the date hereof,
by GEORGE NAGEL, Goaler.
The Pennsylvania Gazette, October 11, 1770.

WAS committed to the Work-house of Philadelphia, as a runaway, September 14, 1770, a little man, he says his name is Thomas Jones, and came in with Captain McDougall, to the Ferry Branch of Patapsco, in Maryland, and was sold to John Dobbs, not far from that place; he is about 5 feet high, bow legged, limps in his walk, and has red hair, tied behind. HIs master is desired to come or send for him, or he will be let out, by JAMES WHITEHEAD, keeper of the Work-house, in six weeks from this 10th day of October, 1770.
The Pennsylvania Gazette, October 11, 1770.

Fredericksburg, October 9, 1770.

RAN away from the Subscriber, last Saturday Night, an Indented Servant Man, named JOHN FLETCHER, he is an *Englishman* born, by Trade a Tanner, about Six Feet Two Inches high, Twenty-five Years of Age, wears his own dark brown Hair; his left Leg is very sore, which may easily be discovered by the Stain of the Sore through his Trousers, and occasions a bad smell when close to him: His Apparel is, a light coloured Frize Coat, blue Frize Jacket, Check Shirt, Osnabrig Trousers much stained with Tan, new Country made Shoes, a Pair of Buckskin Breeches, when he commonly wears under his Trousers, and a Felt Hat. He came in with Captain *Anderson* about Eighteen Months ago.

Whoever will apprehend the said Servant, and deliver him to me in *Fredericksburg*, shall have Three Pounds Reward, paid by
WILLIAM HOUSTON.

The Maryland Gazette, October 18, 1770; October 25, 1770; November 1, 1770; November 8, 1770.

October 10, 1770.

RAN away from the Subscriber, at Deer-Creek, an English Convict Servant Man, named DANIEL DUNN, 5 Feet 6 Inches high, about 35 Years of Age, wears his own light Hair, gray Beard, with more gray on the left Side of his Chin than the right, he talks in the West of *England* Dialect: Had on, and took with him, a good Felt Hat, black Silk Handkerchief, dark gray Cloth Coat, with a velvet Cape, a Jacket with dark gray fore Parts, hind Parts blue Damask, another dark gray Jacket, with light gray Sleeves, Two Osnabrig Shirts, and One Ten Hundred Linen ditto, Two Pair of Leather Breeches, Two Pair of Trousers, Two Pair of ribbed Stockings, One of which is dark gray, the other light, half worn Shoes, with Steel Buckles—Whoever takes up, and secures said Servant, so that his Master may have him again, shall have if taken in the County, Forty Shillings, if out of the County, Three Pounds, including what the Law allows, paid by
JOHN FORWOOD.

The Maryland Gazette, October 18, 1770. See *The Pennsylvania Gazette*, October 18, 1770.

RUN away, on the 10th of October instant, from the subscriber, living at Deer Creek, in Baltimore county, an English convict servant man, named Daniel Dunn, about 5 feet 7 inches high, about 35 years of age, has light hair, a grey beard, more grey on the left side of his chin than the right,

speaks on the west country dialect, and is a nailer by trade; had on, and took with him, a good felt hat, black silk handkerchief, dark grey cloth coat, with a velvet cape, a jacket, with dark grey fore-parts, the hind parts blue damask, another dark grey jacket, with light grey sleeves, two Ozenbrigs shirts, and one ten hundred linen ditto, two pair of leather breeches, a pair of trowsers, 2 pair of ribbed stockings, one pair dark grey, they other light, and half-worn shoes, with steel buckles. Whoever takes up and secures said servant, so as his master may have him again, shall have, if taken in the county, Forty Shillings, and if out of the county, three Pounds, reward, (including what the law allows) paid by
JOHN FORWOOD.
N.B. It is supposed he went away in company with one Thomas M'Cann, a servant belonging to John Harris, Esq; of the same place.
The Pennsylvania Gazette, October 18, 1770. See *The Maryland Gazette*, October 18, 1770 and *The Pennsylvania Gazette*, December 6, 1770.

RUN away, on Monday night, the 9th of last July, from Guest's tavern, about 13 miles from Baltimore, 3 convict servant men, viz. *Edward Holder*, about 6 feet high, of a dark complexion, and dark brown curled hair, about 40 years of age; had on, a brown great coat, check shirt, and a pair of dirty trowsers; took with him 2 small bags, containing check shirts, green sailor's jackets, 1 white swanskin ditto, bound with black, and also a brown cut wig with him. *Henry Dew*, about 5 feet 6 inches, of a black complexion, and black hair, about 30 years of age; had on, a waistcoat, without sleeves, a pair of drawers and took with him a leather bag, containing 1 pair of black silk breeches, some shirts, and a brown cut wig. *John Blackall*, 6 feet, of a light complexion, brown hair, about 26 years of age; had on a white flannel waistcoat, and leather breeches; had 1 small white bag, containing white shirts, &c. The above 3 servants arrived at Baltimore in the Friendship Captain Parker, from London; they were all born in England and *Holder* has been in the country before as a convict. If taken and secured in any goal, Twenty Shillings for each to be paid and all reasonable charges, by Mr. RICHARD FOOTMAN, of Philadelphia.
The Pennsylvania Gazette, October 18, 1770.

FIVE POUNDS Reward.
RUN away from the subscriber, living at the Baltimore Iron-works, in Maryland, about the middle of last June, an English convict servant man, named RICHARD PARKS, he is a lusty well-set fellow, of a fair complexion, has red hair, and a wooden leg, he came from towards the

north of England; where he spent most of his time about Iron-works, and is by trade a Basket-maker, at which he is very useful. He went away in company with one JOHN ROBESON, a small elderly man, who came in the country with PARKS, he is by trade a Butcher, and followed that business in Baltimore-Town, for about twelve months. I expect they are still together, and about some Iron-works. PARKS is a very drunken fellow. Whoever takes up and secures the said servant, so that his master may have him again, shall have the above reward, paid by
October 12, 1770.   JOHN WELSH.

If the runaway above mentioned should be taken up by this advertisement, the taker up is desired to acquaint Mr. JOHN WELLS, of Philadelphia, as soon as possible.
The Pennsylvania Gazette, October 18, 1770.

RUN away last night from the subscriber, living near the Head of Elk, in Caecil county, Maryland, a servant man, named PETER HUGHES; had on, when he went away, a blue coat, red waistcoat, black breeches, black stockings, new shoes, with large brass buckles; lately from Ireland, and speaks pretty good English. Whoever takes up said servant, and secures him, so as his master may have him again, shall have Thirty Shillings reward, and reasonable charges, paid by
October 2, 1770. ANDREW FRAZER.
The Pennsylvania Gazette, October 18, 1770; October 25, 1770. See *The Pennsylvania Gazette*, January 17, 1771.

RUN away from the Subscribers, living in Baltimore County, in the Fork of Gunpowder, the 14*th of this instant October, two native Irish servant Men, one convict, the other indented; the Convict is about* 30 *Years of Age,* 5 *Feet* 5 *Inches high, black Hair, grey Eyes, a down ill Look, good Truth, dark Complexion, stoops a little in his Walk, and goes by the Name of* Thomas Hanway, *alias* Conway, *alias* M'Gowen; *the other named* William David, *about* 21 *Years of Age,* 5 *Feet* 4 *Inches high, short black Hair, grey eyes, well made Fellow, pitted with the Small-pox; had on, and took with them* 2 *old Felt Hats,* 4 *Jackets,* 1 *double and twist green and white double breasted, the other,* 1 *short about, another striped, both blue and white, and* 1 *white Fearnought, with Sleeves, old light coloured Cloth Coat, with round Brass Buttons, brown Shag and old Fustian Breeches,* 2 *Pair of Trowsers, old pumps, grafted, Country made Shoes, with Strings. It is supposed they will change their Names and Apparel; and it is likely they have Passes. Whoever secures said Servants in any Goal, shall have Thirty Shillings for*

each if in the County, if out of the County Fifty Shillings for each, and reasonable Charges, if brought home, paid by
WILLIAM PARRISH, *jun.*   HENRY HOUSHOLDER.
The Pennsylvania Gazette, October 25, 1770.

RAN away from the subscriber, living in Baltimore county, near the Lower ferry, on Susquehannah, on the seventh day of October, a servant man, named Edward Murphy, by trade a weaver, about five feet four inches high, much pock marked, has a f[ ]sh mark on the side of his nose, which disfigures him somewhat, black hair and beard; had on when he went away a felt hat, a duffil coat, light colour, a linsey jacket, a pair of trowsers, and two shirts, all homespun, a pair of thread stockings, a good pair of pumps, with old buckles in them: Whoever takes up the said servant, and secures him so that his master may get him again, shall have forty shillings reward, paid by me   ABRAHAM ROBINSON.
The Pennsylvania Chronicle, From Monday, October 22, to October 29, 1770.

October 25, 1770.
RAN away from the Subscriber, living in *Chester-Town, Kent* County, *Maryland,* on Tuesday the 23d of *October,* a Convict Servant Man, named PHILLIP GRIFFITH, about Twenty-one Years of Age, Five Feet Nine or Ten Inches high, a Tailor by Trade, of a remarkable pale Countenance, has short dark Hair, gray Eyes, and a very large Nose: Had on, and took with him, a short dark coloured fly Frize Coat much worn, a Cinnamon coloured Waistcoat, a Pair of old blue knit Breeches, a Pair of light brown Worsted ribbed Stockings, a coarse Felt Hat half worn.

Whoever takes up and secures the said Servant, so that the Owner may have him again, shall have Fifty Shillings Reward, and all reasonable Charges, paid by   TOBIAS ASHMORE.

N. B. It is supposed the said Servant went off in an Oister-Boat belonging to *Little-Choptank.*
The Maryland Gazette, November 1, 1770.

October 9, 1770.
FIFTY DOLLARS REWARD.
RAN away from the Subscriber, living in *Garrison-Forest, Baltimore* County, about Twelve Miles from *Baltimore,* an *English* Convict Servant Man, named THOMAS PRICE, by Trade a Tailor, about 30 Years of Age, 5 Feet 10 Inches high, a talkative Fellow, of a yellow Complexion, short black Hair: Had on, and took with him, a blue Surtout-Coat, a blue Close bodied ditto, Calico Jacket, Two Check Shirts, Linen Breeches, light

coloured Yarn Stockings, Two Pair of Shoes, One Pair of Osnabrig Trousers, old black Wig, Felt Hat, has a large Steel Collar, and a Spur on his left Leg.

Likewise ran away from the Subscriber, on the 13th of *October*, an *Irish* Servant Man, named DANIEL HEAVEY, a Whitesmith by Trade, but has worked for some Time past at the Blacksmiths Business, about 26 Years of Age, 5 Feet 8 or 9 Inches high, pale Complexion, short yellowish Hair, Crocus Trousers, new Shoes, and a new felt Hat: He went away in Company with a likely young Mulatto Woman, about 22 Years of Age.'

Whoever takes up the said Servants, and secures them, so that their Master gets them again, shall receive if Fifty Miles from home, Ten Dollars for each of the Men, and Five Dollars for the Woman; if One Hundred Miles Twenty Dollars for each Man, and Ten for the Woman (including what the Law allows) paid by
LARKIN RANDALL.

The Maryland Gazette, November 8, 1770; November 15, 1770; November 22, 1770. See *The Pennsylvania Chronicle*, From Monday, October 1, to October 8, 1770, *The Pennsylvania Gazette*, November 8, 1770, and *The Maryland Gazette*, January 10, 1771.

FIFTY DOLLARS Reward.

RUN away from the subscriber, living in the Garrison Forrest, Baltimore County, about 12 miles from Baltimore, an English convict servant man, named Thomas Price, by trade a taylor, about 30 years of age, 5 feet 10 inches high, a talkative fellow, of a yellow complexion, short black hair; had on and took with him a blue surtout coat, and one blue close bodied ditto, calicoe jacket, 2 check shirts, linen breeches, light coloured yarn stockings, 2 pair of shoes, 1 pair ozenbrigs trowsers, old black wig, felt hat, a large steel collar, and a spur on his left leg. Likewise run from the subscriber the 13th of October, an Irish servant man, named Daniel Heavey, a white-smith by trade, but has worked for some time past at the black-smith's business, about 26 years of age, 5 feet 8 or 9 inches high, pale complexion, short yellowish hair, a down look when spoke to; had on a kersey jacket, ozenbrigs shirt, crocus trowsers, new shoes, and new felt hat: He went away in company with a likely young mulattoe woman, about 22 years of age. Whoever takes up the said servants, and secures them, so that their master gets them again, shall receive, if 50 miles from home, Ten Dollars for each of the men, and Five Dollars for the woman, if 100 miles, Twenty Dollars for each man, and Ten for the woman (including what the law allows) paid by LARKIN RANDALL.

The Pennsylvania Gazette, November 8, 1770; November 22, 1770; December 20, 1770. See *The Pennsylvania Chronicle*, From Monday,

October 1, to October 8, 1770, *The Maryland Gazette*, November 8, 1770, and *The Maryland Gazette*, January 10, 1771.

COMMITTED to *Anne-Arundel* County Jail, as a Runaway, a Servant Woman named RACHEL EVANS, says she belongs to *John Dorsey*, on *Linganore*. Her Master is desired to take her away and pay Charges.
JOHN CLAPHAM
The Maryland Gazette, November 29, 1770.

COMMITTED to *Charles* County Jail, a Servant Man, who calls himself STEPHEN SMITH, by Trade a Shoemaker, says he belongs to JOHN BALLANDINE, of *Virginia*. The owner is desired to takes legally away the aforesaid Servant.
RICHARD LEE, Jun. Sheriff.
The Maryland Gazette, November 29, 1770.

RUN away last night, from the subscriber, living at Bladensburg, in Prince-George'scounty, Maryland, an indented servant man, named Thomas Bevan, about 5 feet 4 or 5 inches high, and about 25 years of age, wears his own hair, which is rather short, of a dark colour, and inclinable to curl, is of a pale complexion, and a little pitted with the small-pox; had on and took with him, a suit of mixed colour broadcloth cloaths, trimmed with basket buttons, a light coloured bearskin coat, with flat metal buttons, a lead coloured drugget jacket and breeches (the jacket short and double breasted) dark blue silk knit breeches, lined with brown holland, a striped jacket of silk damascus, a new castor hat, a pair of single channelled boots, with silver boot buckles, and a pair of plated spurs, and sundry other wearing apparel, not particularly known.—He also took with him a small bay horse, branded on the near shoulder **B**; he was seen riding into Philadelphia about the 20th inst. Whoever takes up the said servant, or secures him, so that he and the horse may be had again, shall receive Three Pounds reward, by applying to John Ross, or James Maccubbin, Merchants, in Philadelphia.
JAMES MILLER
N. B. All masters of vessels are forewarned taking him off at their peril.
The Pennsylvania Gazette, November 29, 1770; December 20, 1770; January 3, 1771. See *The New-York Gazette; and the Weekly Mercury*, December 10, 1770.

RAN away last night, from the subscriber's plantation, in the fork of Gunpowder, a convict servant man, named CHARLES CAMPBELL, about 24 years of age, 5 feet 8 or 9 inches high, fresh colour'd, gray eyes, brown hair, cut off on the top of his head; had on a felt hat, old bearskin coat with a collar, short cotton jacket with sleeves, old oznabrigs shirt, crocus trowsers, country shoes nailed in the feels, and tied with strings. He had on an iron collar, and a spur on one of his legs. Whoever takes up said servant, and secures him so that his master may have him again, shall have, if 20 miles from home, THIRTY SHILLINGS, FORTY SHILLINGS if out of the county, and THREE POUNDS if out of the province, (including what the law allows) and reasonable charges if brought home, paid by
Sept. 4, 1770. CHARLES RIDGELY, jun.

    N. B. He was put in Lancaster gaol some time ago, and would not for some time confess his master. It is thought he is now in some goal, and conceals his master's name.

    The Pennsylvania Chronicle, From Monday, November 26, to Monday, December 3, 1770; From Monday, December 3, to Monday, December 10, 1770; From Monday, December 24, to Monday, December 31, 1770; From Monday, December 31, to Monday, January 7, 1770; From Monday, February 18, to Monday, February, 25, 1770. The Pennsylvania Gazette, December 6, 1770; December 13, 1770; December 20, 1770. Minor differences between the papers.

SIX DOLLARS Reward.

RUN away last night, from the subscriber, living near the Head of Bush-River, in Baltimore county, Maryland, an Irish servant man, named THOMAS M'CANN, about 25 years of age, 5 feet 8 or 9 inches high, dark complexion, short black hair, pitted with the small-pox; had on a good castor hat, old claret-coloured coat, two jackets, one an old red one, the other a cloth-coloured broadcloth, with white flannel back-parts, two pair of country-made coarse linen trowsers; he is a very talkative fellow, pretends to be a scholar, writes a good hand, and it is likely may forge a pass. Whoever takes up and secures said servant, so that his master may have him again, shall have the above reward, and reasonable charges, paid by
    JOHN HARRIS. Oct. 11, 1770.

    The Pennsylvania Gazette, December 6, 1770. See The Pennsylvania Gazette, October 18, 1770.

Philadelphia, November 16, 1770.

Ran away last night from the subscriber, living in Bladensburgh, Prince George county, Maryland, an indented servant man, named THOMAS BEVAN, about 5 feet 4 or 5 inches high, and about 25 years of age, wears his own hair of a dark colour, which is rather short, and a little pited with the small pox: Had on and took with him, a suit of mixed broadcloth clothes, trimmed with basket buttons, a light colour'd bearskin coat, with flat metal buttons, a lead colour'd drugget (short double breasted jacket) and breeches, a pair of dark blue silk knit breaches,[sic] lined with brown holland, and a striped jacket of silk damascus, a new castor hat, a pair of single channel boots, with silver boot buckles, and a pair of plated spurs, sundry other wearing apparel not particularly known; he also took with him a small bay horse, branded on the shoulder **B.** and he was seen to ride into Philadelphia about the 20th instant. Whoever takes up the said servant, or secures him so that he and the horse may be had again, shall receive Three Pounds *reward, by applying to Messieurs John Ross, or James M'Cubbin, Merchants, in Philadelphia.* JAMES MILLER.

The New-York Gazette; and the Weekly Mercury, December 10, 1770.
See *The Pennsylvania* Gazette, November 29, 1770.

FIVE POUNDS REWARD.

RAN away on the 11th Instant, from the Subscriber, living at *St. Catharine's*, near *Killam's*, by *George's* Creek, *Allegany* Mountain, an *Irish* Convict Servant Man, named THOMAS BURN, alias BRYAN, about 26 Years of Age, 5 Feet 6 Inches high, blind of the left Eye, wears his own Hair, and is by Trade a Mason: Had on and took with him a Blanket Coat, Two Osnabrig Shirts, Two Pair of Trousers, a Surtout Coat, and Felt Hat. Whoever secures the said Servant, so that his Master gets him again, shall receive the above Reward, and reasonable Charges if brought home, paid by THOMAS FRENCH.

N. B. He is remarkably cut on the Buttocks by a Flogging he received from a former Master, and it is probable he may change his Name.

The Maryland Gazette, December 13, 1770; December 20, 1770; January 3, 1771; January 10, 1771.

Burlington, December 3, 1770.
THIS Day was committed to the Goal of this City, a certain Thomas Gearn, upon Suspicion of being a runaway Servant; he says he belongs to William Withers, living in Caecil County, Maryland, and that he left his said Master about 14 or 15 Weeks ago. Said Servant is about 20 Years of Age, and says, when he left his Master, he had an Iron Collar on his Neck, but soon got it off. Whoever owns the said Thomas Gearn, is desired to come or send, pay Charges, immediately and take him away.

The Pennsylvania Gazette, December 13, 1770.

December 18, 1770.
FORTY SHILLINGS REWARD.
RAN away last night after dark, from the subscriber, living in Cecil county, Maryland, an Irish servant man, named JOHN CROWLY, about 5 feet 3 or 4 inches high, 33 years of age, has grey hair, almost white, well-set: Had on, and took with him, a broadcloth coat and jacket, with a small cape to the coat, home-made cloth breeches, a country cloth jacket, two shirts, one made of flax, and the other of tow linen, a pair of old, and a pair of new shoes, a wool hat, bound with canvas, Whoever takes up the said servant, so that his master may have him again shall have the above reward, and reasonable charges paid by me.
SAMUEL MILLER.
> *The Pennsylvania Chronicle,* From Monday, December 17, to Monday, December 24, 1770; From Monday, December 24, to Monday, December 31, 1770; From Monday, January 7, to Monday, January 14, 1771. See *The Pennsylvania Gazette,* January 3, 1771.

THREE POUNDS REWARD.
RAN away the 9th of this inst. from the subscriber, living in Cecil county, Maryland, about 3 miles from Elisha Hughes, two servant MEN, one named JOHN QUELCH, about 5 feet, 6 or 7 inches high, 19 years of age, of a dark complexion, wears his black hair, has a large nose, and is an ill-looking fellow: Had one when he went away, a blue surtout coat, with mohair buttons, buckskin breeches, short lapelled buckskin jacket, Russia sheeting shirt, blue and white cotton stockings, good shoes, with buckles not Fellows, and a half worn beaver hat; he is a leather dresser and breeches maker by trade. The other, named JOHN MEAHAN, by trade a leather dresser, about 21 years of age, 5 feet 7 or 8 inches high, smooth faced, wears his black hair, and well limbed: Had on when he went away, a dark grey short coat, with two pieces in the back of it, lined with striped linsey, an old whiteish jacket, Russia sheeting shirt, good buckskin breeches, with strings in the knees, coarse dark grey stockings, soaled shoes, one of them ripped in the side of the quarter, an old wool hat, with one cock in it stitched with thread. Whoever takes up said servants and secures them, so that their master may get them again, shall have TWENTY SHILLINGS for each, if taken within 20 miles of home, or the above reward if 40 miles, and reasonable charges paid by
Dec. 11.   JACOB LEMMON.
> *The Pennsylvania Chronicle,* From Monday, December 17, to Monday, December 24, 1770; From Monday, December 31, to Monday, January 7, 1771; *The Pennsylvania Gazette,* December 20,

1770; January 3, 1771. Minor differences between the papers. The *Gazette* does not have the date at the bottom.

1771

December 5, 1770.
TEN POUNDS REWARD.

STOLEN last Night from *Mount-Royal* Forge, near *Baltimore-Town*, a dark bay Gelding, of the *English* running-breed, is a round made Horse, and shews but little of the Blood, about 7 Years old, 14 Hands and an Half high, branded on the near Shoulder **I. F.** with the mark of a Heart on the Top: He has some gray Hairs in his Forehead, a hanging Mane and switch Tail, shod all round, gallops, trots, and paces, has some white on the inside of One of his hind Feet.

Whoever brings said Horse to the Subscriber, and secures the Thief, so that he may be brought to Justice, shall have the above Reward, or Eight Dollars for the Horse. JAMES FRANKLIN.

N. B. It is supposed the Horse was stole by *Thomas Grant*, an *Englishman*, about 28 Years of Age, 5 Feet 8 Inches high, fresh Colour, wears brown Hair tied behind: Had on, an old Bearskin surtout Coat, *German* Serge Jacket and Breeches, of a redish Colour, Felt Hat, Country Shoes, and yellow Buckles. He served his Time at the *Baltimore* Iron-Works on *Patapsco*, in *Maryland*, and had a Discharge from *Clement Brooke* in *July* last.

The Maryland Gazette, January 3, 1771; January 10, 1771; January 17, 1771; January 24, 1771; January 31, 1771; February 7, 1771; February 14, 1771.

FORTY SHILLINGS Reward.

RUN away from the subscriber, living in Caecil county, Maryland, the 18th of December 1770, an Irish servant man named JOHN CROWLEY, born in Cork; he is a check weaver by trade, and can weave linen, but is not perfect in that business, is about 33 years of age, 5 feet 3 or 4 inches high, a little pitted with the small-pox, something bald on the forehead, and is remarkably grey for a person of that age, is a well set fellow; had on a broadcloth coat, a jacket of a light colour, above half-worn, a new country cloth ditto, country cloth breeches, have been seated, light coloured yarn stockings, two pair of shoes, one pair new, a half worn wool hat, bound round the edge; likely he will sell some of his clothes, as he has no money, and no doubt change his name. Whoever takes up said servant, and secures him, so that his master may have him again, shall have the above reward, paid by me. SAMUEL MILLER.

The Pennsylvania Gazette, January 3, 1771; February 28, 1771; May 2, 1771; May 9, 1771; June 20, 1771; July 4, 1771: July 15, 1771; August 22, 1771. See *The Pennsylvania Chronicle,* From Monday, December 17, to Monday, December 24, 1770.

Baltimore, December 29, 1770.
TEN POUNDS REWARD
RAN away, last night, from the subscriber, living in Baltimore-town, an English convict servant-man, named JACOB SILCOCKE, by trade a collar and harness-maker, is about 20 years of age, about 5 feet 7 Inches high, remarkable broad shoulders, and strong limb'd; with short dark curled hair, mixed at the sides with greys, with a broad forehead, and full face, dark brown eyes, a thick, broad nose, and walks pretty upright, he is very talkative when in company, and can talk a little broken Dutch, but when he stoops, has a stiffness in the small of his back, he is a great player on the violin; and writes a tolerable good hand. Had on when he went away, a light grey double-breasted jacket, with metal buttons, the jacket is bound round the edges; likewise a pair of good buckskin breeches, much soiled, a white fine shirt, with sundry other clothes unknown, and may probably change his dress. Whoever takes up the said servant man, within 20 miles from town, shall receive FIFTY SHILLINGS, but if out of the province, shall receive the above reward, paid by me
JACOB MYERS.

N. B. All masters of vessels, or others, are forbid to carry him off at their peril.

The Pennsylvania Chronicle, From Monday, December 31, to Monday, January 7, 1771. See *The Maryland Gazette,* January 10, 1771; *The Pennsylvania Gazette,* March 14, 1771.

EIGHT POUNDS REWARD.
Anne-Arundel County, *January* 4, 1771.
RAN away from the Subscriber, living on *Elk-Ridge,* a Servant Man named PETER KELLY, he is young, much pitted with the Small-Pox, about Five Feet high: He took with him a Parcel of good Cloaths, among which there is a blue Coat, a spotted Swanskin Jacket, *German* Serge ditto, a Pair of *German* Serge Breeches, Two white Shirts, and several Pair of Stockings, he has likewise with him a Discharge signed by *Richard Green.* He went away with an *Irishman* named *Thomas Hall,* a Weaver by Trade, who has a Pass with him signed by the Subscriber.

Whoever secures the said *Peter Kelly*, so that the Subscriber gets him again, shall receive the above Reward, and reasonable Charges paid if he is brought home.   HENRY HOWARD.

The Maryland Gazette, January 10, 1771; January 17, 1771; January 24, 1771.

TWENTY DOLLARS REWARD.

September 3, 1770.

RAN away from the Subscriber, living in *Garrison-Forrest*, in *Baltimore* County, Two *English* Convict Servant Men, *viz.*

THOMAS PRICE, a Tailor by Trade, about 30 Years of Age, 5 Feet 10 Inches high, a talkative Fellow, of a yellow Complexion, short black Hair: Had on, and took with him, a blue Cloth Coat, black Cloth Jacket, One Calico ditto, a Check Shirt, One white ditto, Three Pair of Osnabrig Trousers, a new Felt Hat, old Shoes, and One large Pair of Tailors Sheers, and has a large Scar on his right Leg.

JAMES BOARDMAN, about 40 Years of Age, 5 Feet 4 inches high, a well set Fellow, short brown Hair, has One Leg shorter than the other, which makes him walk lame: Had on, an old brown Cloth Coat with white Metal Buttons, old Leather Breeches, Osnabrig Shirt, light coloured Yarn Sockings, [*sic*] Half Boots and Felt Hat.

Whoever takes up the said Servants, and secures them in any Jail, so as their Masters may have them again, shall have the above Reward, including what the Law allows, and reasonable Charges, if brought home, paid by   BENJAMIN WELLS, & LARKIN RANDALL.

The Maryland Gazette, January 10, 1771; January 17, 1771. See *The Pennsylvania Chronicle,* From Monday, October 1, to October 8, 1770, *The Maryland Gazette*, November 8, 1770, and *The Pennsylvania Gazette*, November 8, 1771.

TEN POUNDS REWARD

December 29, 1770.

RAN away last Night from the Subscriber, living in *Baltimore-Town*, an *English* Convict Servant Man, named JACOB SILCOCKE, by Trade a Collar and Harness-maker, he is about 20 Years of Age, about 5 Feet 7 Inches high, remarkable broad Shoulders, and strong limbed with short dark curled Hair, mixed at the Sides with gray Hairs, with a broad Forehead, and full Face, dark brown Eyes, a thick broad Nose, and walks pretty upright, but when he stoops has a Stiffness in the small of his Back; he is very talkative when in Company, and can talk a little broken Dutch, plays pretty well on the Violin, and writes a good Hand: Had on, when he went away, a light gray double breasted Jacket, with Metal Buttons, bound round the Edges, likewise a Pair of good Buckskin Breeches, much soiled, a fine Shirt, with sundry other Cloaths unknown, and may probably change his Dress.

Whoever takes up the said Servant, and brings him to his Master, shall receive, if taken in the Province, Three Pounds, and if out of the Province, the above Reward, and reasonable Charges, paid by
JACOB MYERS.

N. B. All Masters of Vessels, or others, are forbid to carry him off at their Peril.

The Maryland Gazette, January 10, 1771; January 17, 1771; January 24, 1771. See *The Pennsylvania Chronicle,* From Monday, December 31, to Monday, January 7, 1771; *The Pennsylvana Gazette*, March 14, 1771.

Baltimore, January 7, 1771.
THERE is now in my Custody, committed as Runaways to the late Sheriff of this County, who has by Indenture assigned them over to me.

JOHN WILLIAMS, about 56 Years of Age, with a sandy Beard and Hair, says he belongs to Mr. *William Tucker*, of *St. Mary's*.

WILLIAM LANGLEY, of a pale Complexion, light brown Hair, about 5 Feet 7, but will not tell to whom he belongs.

NEGRO MOSES.... NEGRO JOAS....NEGRO HARRY....NEGRO JEM....

Their Masters are desired to fetch them away, paying their Fees and Reward due, to
JOHN ROBERT HOLLIDAY,   Sheriff of Baltimore County.

The Maryland Gazette, January 10, 1771; January 17, 1771; January 24, 1771; January 31, 1771; February 7, 1771; February 14, 1771. See *The Maryland Gazette*, July 11, 1771, October 17, 1771, December 5, 1771, and *The Pennsylvania Gazette*, June 27, 1771.

RUN away from the subscriber, living in Baltimore, near the Forks of Gunpowder, on the 29th of December last, two English convict servant men, viz. JOHN BURNES, about 5 feet 6 inches high, well set, and has light coloured hair, tied behind; had on, when he went away, a light coloured frieze jacket, the sleeves of two different colours, the lower part yellow, a blue double-breasted ditto, a pair of cotton breeches, the knees tied with blue strings, an ozenbrigs shirt, felt hat, country made shoes, tied with strings, and light-blue ribbed worsted stockings. The other, named JOHN JOHNSTON, about 5 feet 5 inches high, much pitted with the smallpox, thin visage, and short black hair; had on, when he went away, a blue

surtout coat, a red regimental jacket, with yellow facings, one blue under jacket, a pair of old shoes, old worsted stockings, old leather breeches, much daubed with tar and grease. Whoever takes up and secures the said servants, so as their masters may have them again, shall have SIX POUNDS reward, paid by
HERCULES KAMP, and CHARLES BAKER, junior.
The Pennsylvania Gazette, January 10, 1771; January 17, 1771.

Baltimore county, January 3, 1771.
SEVEN POUNDS Reward.
RUN away last night, from the subscriber, living in Bond's Forrest, Baltimore county, two convict servant men, viz. *John Brown*, about 26 years of age, about 5 feet 7 inches high, has black hair, large temples, narrow chin, and thick lips, used to the sea, and a great swearer: Had on, when he went away, a brown pea jacket, cotton breeches, and ozenbrigs shirt.

Abraham Peters, about 24 or 25 years of age, about 5 feet 9 inches high: Had on, when he went away, a fearnought jacket, country cloth breeches, ozenbrigs shirt, and says he is a Jew, both swarthy complexion. They took with them two mares, two mens saddles, and sundry wearing Apparel, viz. One dark bay mare, 14 hands and 2 inches high, branded on the near buttock with a blotch. The other a strawberry roan, 13 hands and 3 inches high, branded on the near buttock or shoulder with a single **B**, one double breasted bearskin coat, one double breasted red jacket, 5 or 6 white shirts, a parcel of womens cloaths, half a dozen silver tea spoons, one country cloth great coat, with metal buttons, the cape lined with yellow shalloon, and a pair of brown country cloth breeches. Whoever takes up and secures the said runaways, shall receive, if taken in the county, Fifty Shillings for each, and if out of the county, Three Pounds Ten Shillings for each, and Forty Shillings for the mares, paid by BUCKLER BOND.

N. B. All masters of vessels, or others, are forbid to carry them off, at their peril.

The Pennsylvania Gazette, January 10, 1771; February 7, 1771; February 21, 1771; March 7, 1771; April 4, 1771. See *The Maryland Journal, and the Baltimore Advertiser*, From Saturday, June 11 to Saturday, June 18, 1774, and *The Pennsylvania Gazette*, May 3, 1775, for Brown.

COMMITTED to *Caecil* County Jail, as a Runaway, a Man who calls himself WILLIAM JOHNSON, about Five Feet Six Inches high, black curled Hair, an *Englishman* born, says he served some Part of his Time with

Mr. SAMUEL YOUNG, of *Baltimore* County, and the rest with JAMES LYNCH, and LEVIN ROBERTS.

His Master (if any) is desired to pay Charges, and take him away.

RICHARD THOMAS, Sheriff.

The Maryland Gazette, January 17, 1771; January 24, 1771. See *The Maryland Gazette*, January 31, 1771; *The Pennsylvania Gazette*, March 14, 1771; *The Pennsylvania Gazette*, February 21, 1771, *The Pennsylvania Chronicle,* From Monday, February 25, to Monday, March 4, 1771; and *The Pennsylvania* Gazette, August 8, 1771.

Johnson also went by the name Samuel Deale/Dale.

EIGHT DOLLARS Reward.

RUN away from the subscriber, living near the Head of Elk, in Caecil county, Maryland, on the 10th of October last, an Irish servant man, named PETER HUGHES, about 5 feet 6 or 7 inches high, straight black hair, was scalped before, but now grown about an inch long, with a small scar on his forehead, walks very smart, and speaks tolerable good English; had on, when he went away, a small wool hat, bound with tape, a blue jacket, without sleeves, the back parts lighter than the fore-parts, coarse tow breeches trowsers, two shorts, one check, the other white, old shoes, but no buckles; he is very much addicted to steal, and may possibly have got more clothes; he came into the country about the last of September, with Captain M'Causland, in the Wallworth, and this is the second time he has run away; he was seen in Philadelphia, and is supposed to be gone to New-Jersey; he is very apt to get drunk, and, when drunk, very quarrelsome; he pretends to be a weaver by trade, but knows very little about that business; he will probably change his name. Whoever secures said servant in any of his Majesty's goals, shall have the above reward, and reasonable charges, paid by   ANDREW FRAZER.

The Pennsylvania Gazette, January 17, 1771. See *The Pennsylvania Gazette*, October 18, 1770.

January 15, 1771.

BROKE out of *Caecil* County Jail, a Man who was committed by the Name of *William Johnson*, and the Time of his Commitment was advertised in the last *Maryland* Gazette, since which he has owned his Name to be *Samuel Dale*, and said he was a Servant to Mr. *Mark Alexander,* of *Baltimore-Town.*

The same Day was committed to my Custody, a Man who calls himself *Philip Laughley*, about 5 Feet 6 or 7 Inches high, black Hair, Beard, and Eyes: Has on, a white Woollen Jacket, white Woollen Trousers, much darned with blue Yarn, good Shoes and Stockings; has in One Shoe, a white Metal carved Buckles, the other tied with a String.

Whoever apprehends the Person that made his Escape, or secures him so that I may get him again, shall have a Reward of Thirty Shillings and reasonable Charges, and the Master (if any) of *Philip Laughley*, is desired to come, pay Charges, and take him away.

RICHARD THOMAS, Sheriff.

The Maryland Gazette, January 31, 1771; February 14, 1771; February 21, 1771; February 28, 1771; March 21, 1771; March 28, 1771; April 4, 1771; April 11, 1771. See *The Maryland Gazette*, January 17, 1771; *The Pennsylvania Gazette*, March 14, 1771; and *The Pennsylvania* Gazette, August 8, 1771.

Annapolis, February 4, 1771.

RAN away last Night from the Subscriber, a Convict Servant Lad, named JOHN BAKER, about 19 Years of Age, a Tailor by Trade, born in the West of *England*, but may easily pass for an *Irishman*, and a Sailor, having, as I am informed, a forged Discharge from a Captain of a Ship. He is about 5 Feet 4 Inches high, has a down Look, short straight brown Hair, with Features that denote the Villain: Had on, a short red Pea Jacket, Cloth Breeches, Yarn Stockings, good Shoes, and plated Buckles.

Whoever takes up said Servant, and secures him so that his Master may have him again, shall have Four Dollars if taken in this County, if out of the County, Three Pounds, and if out of the Province, Five Pounds, and reasonable Charges if brought home.

ROBERT PINKNEY.

The Maryland Gazette, February 7, 1771; February 14, 1771.

Baltimore County, near *Northampton-Works*, January 31, 1771.

RAN from his Bail, a thick well set Man, named SAMUEL AMBLER, about 25 Years of Age, lightish Hair, tied behind, swarthy Complexion: Had on, a dark brown Coat, with Mohair Buttons, but may perhaps change his Cloaths: He is a Shoemaker by Trade, and is hurt in his right Hip, which makes him walk much upon his Toes.

Whoever secures the said Man, so that his Bail shall have him again, shall have, if taken in the County, Three Pounds, and if out of the County, Five Pounds, and all reasonable Charges, paid by

RICHARD GOTT.

The Maryland Gazette, February 7, 1771; February 14, 1771.

July 20, 1770.
RAN away from the Subscriber, living near *Frederick-Town, Frederick* County, *Maryland*, on *Monockasay*, an indented Servant Man, passing for an *Englishman*, named ADAM STANTON, a short thick Fellow, about 5 Feet 3 Inches high, of a very dark Complexion, so that some People think he is a Mulatto, a Brick-maker by Trade, wears a Cap and his Head shaved, aged about 50 Years, a little pitted with the Small-Pox: Had on, and took with him, one old light coloured Cloth or German Serge Coat, one Jacket of a Kind of Cloth, partly of the same colour, double breasted, Two Pair of Osnabrig Trousers, Two Osnabrig Shirts, and one Pair of old Shoes.

Whoever takes up the said Servant, and secures him, so that the Subscriber may get him again, shall have Three Pounds Reward, and reasonable Charges if brought home, paid by
WILLIAM HARBETT.

The said Servant has a Wife which is supposed is gone with him, she is tall and slender, and commonly wears a green Stuff Gown, with red and white Flowers, by Trade a Breeches-maker and Tailorist. [*sic*]

The Maryland Gazette, February 7, 1771; February 14, 1771; February 21, 1771; February 28, 1771; March 14, 1771; March 28, 1771; April 4, 1771; April 11, 1771.

Dorchester County, *January* 14, 1771.
RAN away from the Subscribers, a Servant Man, named *William Henry Bawden*, he is a slim made Man, about 24 Years of Age, and has followed the Occupation of a School-Master: Had on, when he went away, a blue Coat, Country made Jacket, with Lappels, Snuff coloured Velvet Breeches, and wears his own Hair, which is black and straight: It is supposed he took a small bay Mare away with him, the Mare has Two white Feet, and her Mane hangs on the rising Side; there was a good Saddle on the Mare, and a Pair of blue Housing Bands, with Leather and Surcingle to the Saddle.

Whoever takes up the Man and Mare, and secures them, so as the Owners shall get them again, shall have Five Pounds paid them, if taken out of the County, and if taken in the County, Satisfaction for their Trouble, paid by the Subscriber
WINLOCK RUPUM, JEREMIAH CARTER.

N. B. The above Servant was born in England, he is a great Talker, and loves gaming.

The Maryland Gazette, February 7, 1771; February 14, 1771; February 21, 1771; February 28, 1771; March 7, 1771; March 14, 1771.

Cecil County, Maryland, Feb. 3, 1771.
Committed to my custody as a runaway, a certain person who calls himself William Collins, and answers the description of a man who is advertised by Benjamin Insheek by the name of William Wilson, alias William M'Cullen. His master, if any, is desired to come, pay charges and take him away.
RICHARD THOMAS, Sheriff of Cecil County.
N. B. Benjamin Insheek lives near Cooper's ferry, the Jerseys.
The Pennsylvania Chronicle, From Monday, February 4, to Monday, February 11, 1771. See *The Pennsylvania Chronicle,* From Monday, February 25, to Monday, March 4, 1771, also *The Pennsylvania Chronicle,* From Monday, July 1, to Monday, July 8, 1771.

Chester-Town, January 29, 1771.
RAN away from the Subscriber, a Convict Servant Man named THOMAS WOOD, 25 Years of Age, about 5 Feet 10 Inches high, of a very dark Complexion, and may be taken for a Mulatto, has short dark curled Hair: Had on, and took with him, a Country Kersey Jacket and Breeches, Osnabrig Shirts, and a white Shirt, a Pair of Buckskin Breeches, white Fustian Coat and Jacket, a Pair of Country made Shoes and Stockings, with other things unknown.
Whoever takes up, and secures the said Runaway, so that they [sic] may be had again, shall have for the Convict Three Pounds Reward, and reasonable Charges if brought home to
EMORY SUDLER.
The Maryland Gazette, February 14, 1771.

Lancaster, February 12, 1771.
COMMITTED to my custody, September 25, 1770, a certain JAMES HOGAN, 23 years of age, 5 feet 9 inches high, a shoemaker by trade; he says he belongs to RICHARD LONG, in Anne-Arundel county, and province of Maryland; his said master is required to come, in three Weeks after the sate hereof, and pay his charges, or he will be sold out for the same, by   GEORGE EBERLY, Goaler.
The Pennsylvania Gazette, February 21, 1771.

Cecil County, Maryland, Feb. 1, 1771.
Committed to my custody as a runaway, a man who calls himself WILLIAM COLLINS; but has since acknowledged himself to be the person advertised by Benjamin Inskeep. His master is desired pay charges, and take him away.

RICHARD THOMAS, Sheriff.
The Pennsylvania Chronicle, From Monday, February 25, to Monday, March 4, 1771; From Monday, March 4, to Monday, March 11, 1771. See *The Pennsylvania Chronicle,* From Monday, February 4, to Monday, February 11, 1771, also *The Pennsylvania Chronicle,* From Monday, July 1, to Monday, July 8, 1771.

Caecil County, January 15, 1771.
COMMITTED to my custody, as a runaway, JOHN LAUGHLEY, about 30 years of age, 5 feet 6 or 7 inches high, black hair and beard; has on; an old felt hat, a short white jacket, and an old pair of trowsers. His master, if any, is desired to pay charges, and take him away.
RICHARD THOMAS, Sheriff.
N. B. He says he has worked about Christiana Bridge, and that Mr. Samuel Patterson, knows him.
The Pennsylvania Gazette, February 21, 1771; *The Pennsylvania Chronicle,* From Monday, February 25, to Monday, March 4, 1771; From Monday, March 4, to Monday, March 11, 1771. See *The Maryland Gazette,* January 31, 1771.

January 15, 1771
RAN away from the Subscriber, living in *Frederick* County, *Maryland*, an indented Servant Man, named JOHN GORMAN, born on the *Eastern-Shore*, he is about Six Feet high, strong made, his Age about 45, has a down Look, and his Hair is dark coloured: Had on when he went away, an old dark coloured Cloth Jacket, a Pair of Kersey Breeches; he has worked at the Carpenters Trade, and is well acquainted with the Country. He is a palavering plausible spoken Fellow, but is a great Rogue, and excessively fond of Drink. The last Place when he was heard of, was upon *Elk-Ridge*, but it is very probable that he will make it across the *Bay* to the *Eastern-Shore*.
Whoever brings the said *Gorman* to Mr. *John Macnabb*, Merchant in Baltimore-Town, or to Jail in *Frederick-Town*, shall receive Five Pounds Reward.   NORMAND BRUCE.
The Maryland Gazette, March 7, 1771; March 14, 1771; March 21, 1771.

Annapolis, March 4, 1771.
RAN away last Night from the Subscriber. a Convict Servant Man, named *Charles Burgess*, a Carpenter by Trade, about Five Feet Eight Inches high,

born in the West of *England*, and talks in that Country Dialect; is about 25 or 26 Years of Age: He is of a fair Complexion, light brown Hair, much pitted with the Small-Pox, has a down Look, and is round shouldered: Had on, and took with him, a brown Frize Coat, bound round with Binding of the same Colour, black Everlasting Waistcoat with Diamond Figures, a green Flannel ditto, Buckskin Breeches, coarse white Linen Shirt, dark brown Worsted Stockings, and half worn Shoes. He likewise took with him, Two Surtout Coats, the one blue the other an Orange Colour; and as there is a Saddle missing, in all Probability he will borrow the first Horse he meets with.

Whoever takes up and secures said Servant, so that his Master may have him again, shall have Forty Shillings if taken in this County, Three Pounds if out of the County, and Five Pounds if out of the Province, with reasonable Charges if brought home.
WILLIAM REYNOLDS.

RAN away at the same Time from *Samuel Howard*, near *Annapolis*, a Convict Servant Man, named *George Bartham*: He is an *Englishman*, and was brought up to Farming; about Five Feet Four Inches high, with short black Hair, a square well set Fellow, with a down Look: Had on, a white Country Cloth Jacket with Sleeves, a black and white under ditto, Buckskin Breeches, Country black and white yarn Stockings lately footed, Country made Shoes almost new, with One Steel and One Copper Buckle.

Whoever takes up and secures said Servant, so that his Master may have him again, shall receive the same Reward, with reasonable Charges, as offered above by Mr. Reynolds. Paid by
SAMUEL HOWARD.
The Maryland Gazette, March 7, 1771.

Dorchester County, *February* 11, 1771.
RAN away from the Subscriber between the 26th and 29th of last Month, an indented Servant Man, called *John Glanding*, aged 26 or 27 Years, about 5 Feet 6 or 7 Inches high, by Trade a House Carpenter, can make Shoes, and pretends to be a Weaver: Had on, when he went away, a light coloured Cloth Coat about half worn, a brown Cloth Waistcoat about half worn, a Pair of Leather Breeches almost new, a Pair of ribbed Stockings, and a Pair of Shoes; he has a lump on his left Leg below his Knee, occasioned by a Cut with an Ax; he chews Tobacco, and is fond of Liquor; as he can write it's likely he will change his Name and forge a Pass; he ran away in Company with a certain *James Dawson*.

Whoever takes up and secures the said *Glanding* in any Jail, shall if taken in the County have Three Pounds, if out of the County Six Pounds, and if out of the Province Twelve Pounds Reward, paid by
JAMES SHAW.
The Maryland Gazette, March 14, 1771; March 21, 1771; March 28, 1771; April 4, 1771.

Baltimore-Town, February 20, 1771.
TWENTY DOLLARS Reward.
RUN away last night, from the subscriber, an Irish servant man, named WILLIAM M'CABE, about 21 years of age, fair hair, a little sandy, and fresh complexioned; had on, and took with him, a good dark grey surtout coat, something too large, a light grey bearksin coat, with yellow gilt buttons, one ditto, with mohair buttons, a red double-breasted bearskin jacket, and old buckskin breeches. He went away in company with a certain GEORGE WILLIAMS, a Dutchman, a short set fellow, who has lived some time in the Jerseys, to which place it is supposed they are gone; *Williams* probably may have a pass, as he is a freeman, and may have forged one for his companion, as they can both write. Whoever secures said servant, so that his master may have him again, shall have Ten Dollars reward; and *Ten Dollars* for apprehending *Williams*, so that he may be brought to justice, paid by   WILLIAM SMITH.
The Pennsylvania Gazette, March 14, 1771.

RUN away from the subscriber, living in Talbot county, on the 26th day of February last, an English servant man, named RICHARD GOLDEN, about 5 feet 10 inches high, pale face, down look, short curled hair, and is a miller by trade; had on a white hat, an old lappelled bearskin coat, broke under the arms, a blue jacket, a coarse tow shirt, old leather breeches, old white stockings, and new shoes. The above servant served 4 years in New York, and it is supposed will make for that place. Whoever takes up said servant, and secures him in any of his Majesty's goals, so that the owner may get him again, shall receive Forty Shillings reward, and all reasonable charges, paid by me   MARTHA HUMPHRIES.
The Pennsylvania Gazette, March 14, 1771.

FIVE POUNDS Reward.
RUN away from the subscriber, living in Baltimore-Town, an English convict servant man, named JACOB SILCOCKE, by trade a collar and harness maker, is about 21 years of age, about 5 feet 7 inches high,

remarkable broad shoulders, and strong limbed, with short dark curled hair, mixed at the sides with grey hairs, a broad forehead, and full face, dark brown eyes, a think broad back, he is very talkative when in company, and can talk a little broken Dutch, plays pretty well on the violin, and writes a tolerable good hand; had on, when he went away, a light grey double breasted jacket, with metal buttons, bound round he edges; likewise a pair of good buckskin breeches, a pair of light coloured stockings, a fine shirt, with sundry other clothes, unknown; and may probably change his dress. Whoever takes up the said servant, and brings him to his master, shall receive, if taken in the province, Three Pounds; and, if out of the province, the above reward, and reasonable charges, paid by
March 5, 1771.   JACOB MYERS.
   N.B. All masters of vessels, or others, are forbid to carry him off, at their peril.
   The Pennsylvania Gazette, March 14, 1771 See *The Pennsylvania Chronicle,* From Monday, December 31, to Monday, January 7, 1771; *The Maryland Gazette*, January 10, 1771;

SIX POUNDS REWARD.
RAN away on the 17th of December, 1770, from the subscriber, living in Baltimore Town, Maryland, a servant man named *Samuel Deale*, an Englishman, about 24 years of age, 5 feet 6 or 7 inches high, slender made, brownish bushy hair, pale complexion, down look, pretends to be a Doctor, and a great horse farrier, and will pretend to any thing, is handy in a kitchen, and is a low, artful insinuating fellow, much addicted to lying; he can write, and will probably forge a pass. Took with him one half worn brown sagatthy coat, his other clothes not known. He was taken, and committed to Cecil county gaol by the name of *William Johnson*, and was there some time before he would own his master; he broke gaol, and made his escape, and it is probable he will change his name. Whoever takes up said servant, and secures him in any gaol, so as his master may have him again, shall have *Three Pounds*, and if brought home, the above reward, including what the law allows, paid by
MARK ALEXANDER.
   The Pennsylvania Gazette, March 14, 1771; *The Pennsylvania Chronicle,* From Monday, March 11, to Monday, March 18, 1771; From Monday, March 18, to Monday, March 25, 1771; From Monday, March 25, to Monday, April 1, 1771; From Monday, April 1, to Monday, April 8, 1771; From Monday, April 22, to Monday, April 29, 1771. See *The Maryland Gazette*, January 17, 1771; *The Maryland Gazette*, January 31, 1771; and *The Pennsylvania* Gazette, August 8, 1771.

RUN away, from the subscriber, living in Baltimore county, near Deer Creek, Upper Cross-roads, a convict servant Man, named JOSEPH POOL, who wants his left hand from his wrist, and wears a leather socket up to his elbow, with a ring skrewed in the end, about five feet four or six inches high, a good deal pock marked, a large scar in his upper lip, has been about six months from England, and writes a good hand, and calls himself a limner; had on when he went away, a black old waistcoat, half worn lightish coloured great coat, half worn leather breeches, country stockings lately footed, and good country made shoes: Whoever takes up said servant, and secures him, if in the county, shall have Forty Shillings, and if out of the county, Three Pounds, and reasonable charges if secured, or sent home, paid by me.
March 1, 1771. THOMAS BLEANY.
The Pennsylvania Chronicle, From Monday, March 18, to Monday, March 25, 1771; From Monday, March 25, to Monday, April 1, 1771; From Monday, April 1, to Monday, April 8, 1771. See *The Pennsylvania Gazette,* May 30, 1771.

March 6, 1771.
RUN away last night from the subscriber, living near the Bald-frier Ferry, Sasquehanna, Baltimore county, Maryland, an Irish servant man, named JOSEPH ALDWORTH, *about 19 years of age, about 5 feet 8 or 9 inches high, a likely fellow, a little pock-marked, fair hair; had on, and took with him, a grey napt surtout coat, pretty much worn, with two rows of hair buttons on the breast, an old blue jacket, much patched with white patches, a pair of old leather breeches, patched on the right knee, one tow linen shirt, one flaxen ditto, a red and white striped silk handkerchief, a pair of shoes half soaled, with nails across the soals, a pair of grey yarn stockings, much darned, and a felt hat, half worn. Whoever takes up the said servant, and secures him, so that his mistress may have him again, shall receive, if taken in the county, Twenty Shillings, if out of the county, Forty Shillings, and if out of the province, Three Pounds, and reasonable charges, paid by* LYDIA MORGAN.
The Pennsylvania Gazette, March 28, 1771.

On the 23d of March last, a certain THOMAS RUCKMAN, of Maryland, and lives within a few miles of Ball Fryer's ferry on Susquehannah, came to the house of the subscriber, in the township of Montgomery, in the county of Philadelphia, and borrowed a bay Mare, about 14 hands high, paces and

trots, and as he wanted to go about 3 miles, and had formerly been an acquaintance, I supposed the same to be true; but he has not since returned, and I have reason to think he don't intend to return the Mare—Whosoever will apprehend the said Thomas Ruckman, and deliver him in the gaol of Philadelphia, shall receive a reward of FIVE POUNDS, and upon securing the Mare, and delivering her to me, they shall receive the further reward of FIVE POUNDS, and reasonable charges, paid by me
April 6, 1771.   CHRISOPHER WELLS.
The Pennsylvania Chronicle, From Monday, April 1, to Monday, April 8, 1771.

Annapolis, March 27, 1771.
RAN away last Night from the Subscriber, a Convict Servant Man, named *Richard Crouch*, about Twenty-five Years of Age; Five Feet Four Inches high, dark Complexion, and much pitted with the Small-Pox; is something low in his Speech: Had on and took with him, a brown Suit of Cloaths, a light coloured Frize Coat and Jacket, with other Things unknown.

Whoever takes up said Servant, so that I may get him again, shall receive, if taken in the County, 20 Shillings, if out of the County, 40 Shillings, besides what the Law allows, paid by me,
ANNE MIDDLETON.

It is supposed he is gone off in my Yawl, along with Two Sailors, belonging to the Brigantine *Venus, Moses Rankin Cail* Master; One of their Names *Benjamin Hays,* middle sized, about Thirty Years of Age, brown Complexion, and wears his own black Hair. The other named *Edward West*, short of Stature, wears his own brown Hair, and is about Twenty-Five Years of Age: Had on, when he went away, an old Graego.

Whoever takes them up, and brings them to *Annapolis*, shall have 20 Shillings Reward for each of them, and all reasonable Charges, paid by
JOHN CATTELL.
The Maryland Gazette, March 28, 1771; April 4, 1771; April 11, 1771; April 25, 1771; May 9, 1771.

Langford's Bay, *Kent* County, *Maryland, March* 25, 1771.
RAN away last Night, Two *English* Convict Servant Men, viz.THOMAS DYER, about Twenty-one Years of Age, came into the Country last August, with Captain *John Maine,* from *Bristol*; he is about Five Feet Six Inches high, pretty well set, fair Complexion, wears his Hair: Had on and took with him, a large Fearnought Jacket, a Linen Vest, a light coloured Wilton Vest and Breeches, Two Osnabrig Shirts, One Pair of blue Yarn

Hose, One Pair of coarse white ditto, Three Pair of Shoes new and old, a small Felt Hat; he has a Scar on the inside of One of his Legs, which was cut with an Ax, and is cured; he is the Property of *Richard Hymon*, of *Kent* County, in *Maryland*.

WILLIAM HARPER has been in the Country about Nine Months, he is about Five Feet Four Inches high, about Forty five Years of Age, and it is supposed he has a good deal of Money, he is of a swarthy Complexion, wears his Hair, talks much in the West-Country Dialect: Had on and took with him, a white Coat, lined with pale blue, brown Vest, with Stocking Sleeves, and Breeches of the same, Osnabrig Shirts, One Pair of Black Yarn Hose, One Pair of Half worn Shoes, One Pair of Brass Buckles, One Pair of Boots; the Property of *Charles Morgan*, of the County and Province aforesaid.

Whoever tales up the said Convicts, or either of them, and secures them in any Jail, so as the Owners may get them again, shall have Twenty Shillings besides what the Law allows, and Forty Shillings if brought home for each of them.

The Maryland Gazette, March 28, 1771. See *The Pennsylvania* Gazette, April 4, 1771 and The *Maryland Gazette*, June 27, 1771.

Ran away from the Ship *Johnson,* Capt. *Wilson*, on Sunday the 24th of March, a Convict Servant Man, named James Donovan, about 32 Years of Age, 5 Feet 9 Inches high, has short curled Hair of a Flaxen Colour, and is much pitted with the Small-Pox: Had on a dark brown Coat with plain Metal Buttons, a red or blue flowered Damask Waistcoat, and Cloth Breeches the same as his Coat; he has a Scar over one of his Eyes. He will probably change his Name, and endeavour to get on board some Vessel outward bound, as he has been used to the Sea.

Whoever takes up the said Servant, and secures him in any Jail, or brings him to the Ship *Johnson*, now lying in *Patapsco*, shall have Forty Shillings Reward if taken in the Province, and Three Pounds if at a greater Distance, paid by   JOHN ASHBURNER.

The Maryland Gazette, March 28, 1771; April 4, 1771; April 11, 1771; April 25, 1771.

March 24, 1771.

WENT away last Night from *Legh* Furnace, *Little Pipe Creek, Thomas Quiegly*, a free Man: Had on, a blue Coat, red Jacket, Leather Breeches, and Caroline Hat, thin Visage, marked with the Small-Pox, bow legged, wears his own Hair, about Thirty Years old, about Five Feet Seven Inches high. Likewise took away with him in the dead of the Night, *Sarah Richardson*, a

Servant Girl, whom he pretends to have married, belonging to *Legh Masters*, Esq: Had on and took with her, a black Gown and Petticoat, with a Cotton ditto, Two black Hats, One trimmed with Lace Kind of Linen, a dark striped coloured Jacket and Petticoat, a black Cloak with a Hood, Eight Shifts, some ruffled, marked with the Small-Pox, about Twenty-seven Years old, about Five Feet Six Inches high.

Whoever takes up or secures said *Quiegly*, or said *Sarah Richardson*, shall have Ten Pounds Reward for both if brought home, paid by me,
LEGH MASTER.
The Maryland Gazette, March 28, 1771.

THREE POUNDS REWARD.

April 3, 1771.

RAN away from the Subscriber, living near *Annapolis*, an *English* indented Servant Lad, named *James Hall*, 16 Years old, about 5 Feet 2 Inches high, of a fair Complexion, smooth faced, and has short brown Hair: Had on an old Castor Hat, Cotton Jacket, old light coloured Sagothy ditto without Sleeves, Cotton Breeches, Osnabrig Shirt, white Yarn Stockings, and good Shoes with Copper Buckles.

Whoever takes up and secures the said Servant, so that his Master gets him again, shall receive, if taken above Ten Miles from Home, Forty Shillings, and if out of the Province the above Reward, and reasonable Charges if brought Home, paid by
BRICE T. B. WORTHINGTON.
The Maryland Gazette, April 4, 1770.

TWENTY DOLLARS Reward.

RUN away, on the night of the 23d of March last, from Mount-Royal Forge, near Baltimore-Town, Maryland, a convict servant man, named JOHN READ, he is a well made man, about 25 years of age, about 5 feet 8 or 9 inches high, born in Yorkshire, and speaks in that dialect, is a sly artful fellow, and has a smooth way of talking, has a large high nose, wears light brown hair, tied with black ribbon; he understands farming and dressing flax; had on, when he went away, a coarse hat, white kersey lappelled jacket, with metal buttons, cotton jacket and breeches, 2 ozenbrigs shirts, cotton or linen spotted handkerchief, coarse yarn stockings, and old country shoes. Whoever secures said servant, so that he may be had again, shall have, if taken in the county, Forty Shillings, and if out of the province, the above reward, and reasonable charges, if brought home.
JAMES FRANKLIN.

N. B. He understands farming, and dressing flax, is a grand rogue, and should he be taken, will make his escape the first opportunity, was at Pittsburg about 18 months ago, and was taken in Philadelphia.

The Pennsylvania Gazette, April 4, 1771; June 6, 1771; June 13, 1771; June 20, 1771; July 4, 1771; July 25, 1771; August 22, 1771. All but the first ad show the reward as "Twenty Pistoles." The lines from N. B. on do not appear in the first ad.

Langford Bay, Kent County, Maryland, March 23, 1771.
RUN away last night, two English convict servant men, viz. *Thomas Dyer*, about 21 years of age, fair complexion (came in the country last August, with Capt. John Main, from Bristol) he is about 5 feet 6 inches high, pretty well set, and wears his hair; had on, and took with him, a large fearnought jacket, a linen vest, a light coloured Wilton vest and breeches, 2 ozenbrigs shirts, 1 pair yarn hose, 1 pair coarse white yard ditto, 3 pair of shoes, new and old, and a small felt hat; he has a scar on the inside of one of his legs, which was cut with an ax, and is just healed up: He is the property of RICHARD HINSON. The other, named *William Harper*, about 21 years of age, swarthy complexion (has been in the country about 9 months) is about 5 feet 4 inches high, wears his hair, and talks much on the West-country dialect; had on, and took with him, a white coat, lined with pale blue, a brown vest, with stocking sleeves, and breeches of the same, ozenbrigs shirt, black yarn hose, half-worn shoes, brass buckles, and a pair of boots; he has a good deal of money with him: He is the property of CHARLES MORGAN. Whoever takes up the said convicts, or either of them, and secures them in any goal, so as the owners may get them again, shall have Twenty Shillings reward, besides what the law allows, and Forty Shillings if brought home, for each of them.

The Pennsylvania Gazette, April 4, 1771 *The Maryland Gazette*, March 28, 1771. See and The *Maryland Gazette*, June 27, 1771.

RUN away, last night, from the subscriber, living in Caecil county, near Charles-Town, Maryland, an English servant man, named Richard Parson, about 22 years of age, 5 feet 7 inches high, has a down look, thin visage, much pitted with the small-pox, his eyes remarkably grey, and is near sighted, wears his own lightish coloured hair, and is apt to drink too much strong liquor; had on, and took with him, a good beaver hat, new redish coloured coarse Bath jacket, lined with lead coloured tammy, two white shirts, half worn, leather breeches, blue yarn stockings, half worn shoes, and buckles not fellows; it is probable he will offer one of his shorts to sale, as it is supposed he has no money. Whoever takes up and secures said

servant, so that his master may have him again, shall have THREE POUNDS, *or, of brought home,* FIVE POUNDS *reward, paid by* CHARLES WHITELOCK.
N.B. All masters of vessels, and others, are forbid to take him off at their peril. March 27, 1771.
The Pennsylvania Gazette, April 4, 1770.

George-Town, Frederick County, *April* 3, 1771.
RAN away from the Subscriber, Two Convict Servants, *viz.* JOHN KELLY, an *Irishman,* about 5 Feet 8 or 9 Inches high, a likely rudy Complexion, and an artful deceitful Fellow: His Cloathing is uncertain, as he has many, and some that are very good, and believe he hath Cash. I do not know that he Professes any Branch of Trade, and is very handy in or out of Doors. He will probably forge a Pass, in the Name of *Andrew Heugh.*

The other named ANNE BAILEY, a small likely Huzzy: Her Apparel at home was a check'd Stuff Gown, but its supposed she has taken some others.

Whoever takes up and delivers them to the Subscriber, shall receive for the Man Fifty Shillings, and for the Woman Thirty, paid by
JOHN ORME.
The Maryland Gazette, April 11, 1771; April 18, 1771; May 2, 1771.

YORK Goal, March 29, 1771.
COMMITTED into my custody, on the 28th instant, a man, who calls himself Joseph Johnson, who, on suspicion of being a servant, was committed, and having feloniously stolen a dark bay gelding, with a snip and a star, supposed to be branded on the near shoulder and buttock, paces, trots and hand gallops; the owner is desired to come, take him away, and pay charges. There is also another man committed into my custody, who calls himself John Crawley, he is about 5 feet 4 inches high; had on him a pair of white cloth breeches, patched on the knees; about 30 years of age, and has remarkable grey hairs on his head; he says his master's name is Samuel Miller, and lives in Caecil county, within 6 miles of the Lower Ferry, and 4 miles from Mr. Johnson's Ferry. The master, and owner, is desired to come, pay charges, and take him away from
JACOB GRAYBILL, Goaler.
The Pennsylvania Gazette, April 11, 1771.

MADE his escape, from the subscriber, Constable in Elk River Neck, Cecil County, Maryland, as he was taking him to gaol, a fellow who calls himself

JOHN WILLSON, a native of Old England, about 5 feet 8 or 9 inches high, 28 or 29 years of age, a slim smart fellow, and pretty good scholar, wears his own short hair, of a dark colour, has a small scar on the upper part of his nose, near his eye-brows, lived some time ago near Warwick, near the head of Bohemia, where it is said his wife lives now. Had on, and took with him, a reddish colour'd surtout, one jacket of the same, a dark brown broadcloth coat, a scarlet jacket, all of them new; the coat remarkably long, Russia linen drawers, old shoes and stockings; but may get new as he has some money. He rode away a dark brown trotting waggon horse, and an old saddle, the fore part and hind part of the seat covered with brass; the horses hair much worn off with drawing, supposed to be a stolen horse, as he was committed for stealing, and on suspicion of being a horse thief and runaway. It is likely he will change his name and horse, as jockies of that sort often do. He aimed to cross Susquehannah, when he was taken, but may alter his course now. Whoever takes up the said Willson, so that he may be brought to justice, shall have FIVE DOLLARS reward, and reasonable charges paid by
WILLIAM CANTER, Constable.   *April* 9, 1770.
   The Pennsylvania Chronicle, From Monday, April 8, to Monday, April 15, 1771; From Monday, April 15, to Monday, April 22, 1771.

COMMITTED to my Custody as a Runaway, a Man who calls himself *Joseph Bennett*, says he was born in the North of *Ireland,* is a thick well set Fellow, appears to be about 35 or 40 Years of Age, 5 Feet 6 or 7 Inches high, has short black curled Hair, double Chin and wrinkled Face. His Master is desired to pay Charges and take him away.
   N. B. He is supposed to be the same Person advertised by Mr. *William Holmes,* in Messiers *Hall's* and *Seller's* Gazette of Feb. 28.
RICHARD THOMAS, Sheriff of Caecil County.
   The Maryland Gazette, April 18, 1771; May 2, 1771; May 9, 1771; May 16, 1771; May 23, 1771; May 30, 1771.

RAN away from the Subscriber's Plantation, on the North Side of *Severn* River, on the 21st of *April,* a convict Servant Man, named JOHN HICKEY, about 22 Years of Age, about 5 Feet 6 Inches high, has short black Hair, blue Eyes, and a very impudent Look: Had on, when he went away, an old Cotton Jacket and Breeches, an Osnabrig Shirt, Country made Shoes and Stockings, and an old Felt Hat. Whoever takes up and secures said the Servant, so that his Master my [sic] have him again, shall receive Four Dollars Reward, paid by   DENTON HAMMOND.

The Maryland Gazette, April 25, 1771. See *The Maryland Gazette*, August 2, 1770.

Baltimore, April 13, 1771.
TWENTY POUNDS REWARD.
WHEREAS I lately received Two threatening Letters, demanding a Sum of Money to be deposited in a certain Place, which Letters, there is good Reason to Believe, were written by Order of *George Baxter* of this Town, Drayman, who was taken up on Suspicion of the same, and has since escaped from the Custody of the Constable. The said *George Baxter* is a square well set Man, about 5 Feet 8 Inches high, round shouldered, about 35 or 40 Years of Age, pitted a good deal with the Small-Pox, very fair Eye-Brows, wants two of his fore Teeth, and wears his own pale Hair pretty short. He is a Fellow well known to many People, having lived several Years as a Labourer about my Distillery. I do hereby offer the above Reward of Twenty Pounds Pennsylvania Currency to any Person who will apprehend the said George Baxter and deliver him into the Custody of the Sheriff of Baltimore County.
SAMUEL PURVIANCE, Jun.
The Maryland Gazette, April 25, 1771; May 2, 1771.

COMMITTED to *Anne-Arundel* County Jail, as Runaways, the Three following Persons, *viz. William Lee*, an *Englishman*, says he is a free Man, and going to *North-Carolina.*
Peter M'Carty and *Timothy Carter*, both *Irishmen*, and has much of the Brogue.
Their Masters are requested to take them away and pay Charges.
JOHN CLAPHAM, Sheriff.
The Maryland Gazette, April 25, 1771. See *The Maryland Gazette*, May 9, 1771.

Prince-George's County, *April* 3, 1771.
COMMITTED to Jail, as a Runaway, on the 5th Instant, an *Irishman*, named *Thomas Dunn*, who says he belongs to *Stephen Gatrill*, living near *Elk-Ridge* Landing. His Master is desired to take him away and pay Charges.
JOHN ADDISON, Sheriff.
The Maryland Gazette, April 25, 1771.

Charlestown, Cecil-County, Maryland, April 9, 1771.
SIX DOLLARS REWARD.
RUN-AWAY, and indented servant man named Anthony Kelso, about 5 feet 7 inches high, and about 30 years of age; he hath a sore on his nose where he formerly had got a cut, short black hair: Had on and took with him a felt hat, brown or claret colour'd coat, brown and green stuff jacket, a good linen shirt, buckskin breeches, blue yarn stockings, good shoes, carried a silver mounted whip with him, is gone towards New-York. Whoever takes up said servant and brings him to Mr. Thomas Irvin, merchant, in Third-street, between Walnut and Market street, Philadelphia, or to me in Charlestown, shall have the above reward, and all reasonable charges; and if secured in any of his Majesty's goals, four dollars, so that I may have him again. Said servants father lives seven miles from Wilmington, came from Ireland last fall in the ship Phoenix. Paid per me,
JOHN M'DONALD.

The New-York Gazette; and the Weekly Mercury, April 28, 1771.

SIXTEEN DOLLARS REWARD.
RAN away from the subscriber, living in Baltimore, two indented servant men, viz. ANGUS M'COY, a Scotchman, speaks much in that dialect, by trade a taylor, about 5 feet 6 inches high, black hair—Had on when he went away, a red coat and breeches, black lapelled jacket, and a black neckcloth. The other named THOMAS MOORE, an Englishman, by trade a taylor, about 5 feet 8 inches high, dark brown hair, and middling long nose, pitted with the small-pox, and a blemish in one of his eyes—Had on when he went away, a light-coloured sagathy coat, brown holland jacket, and light cloth breeches; he is a very talkative fellow. Whoever takes up the said servants and brings them to the subscriber, or secures them in any gaol, so that he may get them again, shall have a reward (if 20 miles from home) of THIRTY SHILLINGS for each, (and if 40 miles) THREE POUNDS for each, and reasonable charges paid, by
JAMES COX.

The Pennsylvania Chronicle, From Monday, April 22, to Monday, April 29, 1771; From Monday, April 29, to Monday, May 6, 1771.

RUN away from the subscriber, living at Church-hill, in Queen Anne's county, Maryland, on the 16th instant, an indented English servant lad, named THOMAS SMITH, about 17 years of age, about 5 feet 2 inches high, well featured, fair complexion, fair hair, very thin, is stoop shouldered, bow legged, with big ancles, and large feet, he will drink no spirits, he says he learned the weaver's trade in England, he lived with

James Thompson, shopkeeper, in Philadelphia, and it is supposed he will make for that place; had on, when he went away, a blue frize jacket, black everlasting breeches, about half worn, good shoes, square white metal buckles, and an old felt hat; the rest of his clothes were unknown; he has not been brought up to any country business; being a shop boy, neither is he a scholar. Whoever takes up and secures said servant in any of his Majesty's goals, so that his master may have him again, shall receive FORTY SHILLINGS reward, and reasonable charges, if brought home, paid by   HUMPHREY CARSON.
April 27, 1771.
All masters of vessels are forbid to carry him off at their peril.
   The Pennsylvania Gazette, May 2, 1771.

MADE his escape from the subscriber, a deputised Sheriff, on the 19th of March, Inst. a certain PATRICK MAGERGY—He is about 24 years of age, [ ] feet 9 or 10 inches high, well set, pock-marked, and [r]ound visaged— He had on a blue surtout, a light-coloured coat, and a red jacket—His other clothes are green, but it is probable he will change them—He went off with horses to sell, and is supposed to be in Baltimore County. Whoever apprehends the said Patrick Magergy, and delivers him to me, or secures him in any of his Majesty's gaols, shall have EIGHT DOLLARS reward, and reasonable charges paid by
March—1771.   CHARLES KNIGHT.
   The Pennsylvania Chronicle, From Monday, April 29, to Monday, May 6, 1771.

Baltimore, April 21.
TEN DOLLARS REWARD.
RAN away, from the subscribers, living in Baltimore County, about 10 miles from Baltimore, in Garrison Forrest, a convict servant man, viz. JOHN CRAIN, an Irishman, by trade a barber, about 30 years of age, 5 feet 9 or 10 inches high, of a brown complexion, brown curled hair, and pitted with the small-pox; had on when he went away, a felt hat, oznabrigs shirt, brown Russia drab coat, blue jacket and breeches, light blue yarn stockings, and a pair of new pumps; he also had on an iron collar, and is a little deaf.
   GEORGE CARR, an Yorkshireman, a well set strong fellow, about 35 years of age, 5 feet 8 or 9 inches high, brown complexion, and has short black hair; had on and took with him when he went away, a felt hat, bound with black worsted binding, and a yellow band round the crown, fastened with wires, 2 oznabrigs shirts, one striped holland ditto, a brown fulled country cloth coat, half worn, black jacket, a pair of greasy leather

breeches, white thread stockings, country made shoes, and a pair of round plain iron buckles. Whoever takes up the said servants, and secures them so that their masters get them again, shall have, if in the country, FOUR POUNDS, if out of the county, SIX POUNDS, and if out of the province, the above reward, with reasonable charges if brought home, or in proportion for either, paid by
WILLIAM RANDALL.   BALE RANDALL.
The Pennsylvania Chronicle, From Monday, April 29, to Monday, May 6, 1771; From Monday, May 13, to Monday, May 20, 1771.

May 7, 1771.
RAN away last Night from the Subscriber, living near *Patapsco* Ferry, in *Anne-Arundel* County, a Convict Servant Man, named *Thomas Williams*, about Twenty-two Years of Age, Five Feet Five Inches high, square made: Had on, when he went away, a Felt Hat, Cotton Cap, an Iron Collar, Osnabrig Shirt, a blue Cloth Coat, and Green Jacket, both Coat and Jacket trimmed with white Metal Buttons, Leather Breeches, old coarse Yarn Stockings, and Negro Shoes.

Whoever takes up and secures the said Runaway, so that his Master gets him again, shall have Twenty Shillings Reward, paid by
JOSEPH JACOBS.
The Maryland Gazette, May 9, 1771; May 30, 1771.

Annapolis, May 5, 1771.
BROKE out of *Anne-Arundel* County Jail, the Six following Persons, viz.

Robert Taylor, by Trade a Joiner, about 25 Years of Age, 6 Feet high, is a well looking Fellow, and has short black Hair tied behind: Had on, an old brown Coat, green Jacket, and *Russia* Drab Breeches.

Thomas Plovey and *Samuel Berkley*, who were both tried this present Provincial Court, the former for Burglary, the latter for Horse-stealing, and found Guilty. *Plovey* is about 5 Feet 10 Inches high, has short black Hair, a little pitted with the Small Pox, and is a very ill-looking Fellow: Had on, a dirty dyed Cotton Jacket, and his other Apparel very mean. *Berkley* is about 5 Feet 8 Inches high, fair Complexion, has a good Countenance, and wears his Hair, which is of a light brown: Had on, a brown Coat, with dirty Leather Breeches.

Nathaniel Read, a Felon left in my Custody by the Sheriff of *Caecil* County, about 20 Years of Age, 5 Feet 10 Inches high, tawny Complexion, and his Apparel excessive mean.

Peter M'Carty, about the same Age and Height, has a Mark over his right Eye, and wears a Cap, is a well set Fellow: Had on, a black Coat and Breeches, and light coloured Waistcoat.

Timothy Carter, about 20 Years of Age, has a healthy Countenance, is a little pitted with the Small-Pox, wears short brown Hair: Had on, an old blue Coat and Leather Breeches.

Whoever secures the abovementioned Persons, and delivers them to the Subscriber, shall have Five Pounds each, for *Taylor, Plovey,* and *Berkley*; Forty Shillings for *Read*, and Twenty Shillings each for the others. JOHN CLAPHAM, Sheriff.

The Maryland Gazette, May 9, 1771; May 16, 1771; May 23, 1771; May 30, 1771; June 6, 1771. See *The Maryland Gazette*, April 25, 1771.

FORTY SHILLINGS Reward.

RUN away from the subscriber, living in Kent county, Maryland, on the 29th of April last, a servant man, named PHILIP GRIFFIS, born in Wales, a straight well shaped man, about 5 feet 7 or 8 inches high, of a fair complexion, and wears his own hair; had on, when he went away, a small brimmed English hat, a deep blue German serge jacket, a little mixt with white, the sleeves of the same colour, but of another kind of cloth, a country linen ditto, lappelled, half-worn broadcloth breeches, of a light colour, one fine shirt, one coarse ditto, the rest of his clothes uncertain. Whoever takes up said servant, and secures him any goal, so that his master may have him again, shall have the above reward, and of brought home reasonable charges, paid by me   ANDREW HICKMAN.

The Pennsylvania Gazette, May 9, 1771.

RUN away from the subscriber, living in Baltimore county, Maryland, the 23d of April last, a convict servant man, named GEORGE LUCAS, an Englishman, about 26 years of age, about 5 feet 6 inches high, fresh coloured, speaks lively and coarse, has black curled hair tied, talks much about jockeying and horse-riding; had on, when he went away, a sky-blue cloth coat and jacket, half worn, with brown buttons, a castor hat, old shirt, of country linen, old brown stockings, old shoes, and odd buckles, buckskin breeches, with horn buttons, very large iron knee-buckles; he has a parcel of brass counterfeit guineas, has a red pocket-book, with a parcel of papers, and an original writ, with the King's seal to it. Whoever takes up the said servant, and secures him, so that his master may have him again, shall have, if in the county, Thirty Shillings, and if out of the county Forty Shillings, and reasonable charges, paid by

GEORGE LYTLE.
The Pennsylvania Gazette, May 16, 1771.

Baltimore County, May 9, 1771.
RUN away, last night from the subscriber's plantation, near Northampton Iron-works, two convict servant men, viz. JOHN PELL, about 5 feet 10 inches high, a well made fellow, has black hair, grey eyes, and a down look; had on and took with him, a fearnought jacket, cotton under ditto, oznabrigs shirt, hempen role trowsers, old shoes, and old felt hat. JOHN MARSH, about 5 feet 5 inches high, a well set fellow, has black hair, dark eyes, and is very talkative; had on, when he went away, a fearnought jacket, cotton under ditto, crocus trowsers, oznabrigs shirts, old shoes, and felt hat.—They also took with them a castor hat about half worn, and a pair of buckskin breeches. Whoever takes up said servants, and secures them in any gaol, so that their master may have them again, shall have, if taken above 10 miles from home, Twenty Shillings for each, if 20 miles Forty Shillings, if out of the province, Three Pounds for each, and if brought home, reasonable charges paid paid by   JOHN ROBERT HOLLIDAY.
The Pennsylvania Chronicle, From Monday, May 13, to Monday, May 20, 1771; From Monday, May 27, to Monday, June 3, 1771; *The Pennsylvania Gazette,* August 15, 1771; August 22, 1771. Minor differences between the papers. See *The Maryland Gazette,* June 6, 1771.

Queen-Anne's county, Maryland, May 6, 1771.
RUN away from the subscriber, a convict servant man, named FRANCIS COWELL, a short square fellow, about 40 years of age, with short hair, a very bald pate, about 5 feet 4 or 5 inches high, carried away with them, 2 outer jackets, one red, the other country kersey, and a blue under jacket, a new country linen shirt, and old trowsers, a pair of country kersey breeches, milled stockings, and old shoes. Whoever secures the said servant, so that his master may have him again, shall receive Thirty Shillings reward, from JOHN WALKER.
The Pennsylvania Gazette, May 23, 1771; June 6, 1771; June 20, 1771.

RUN *away, the* 1*st day of March last, from the subscriber, living in Baltimore county, Maryland, near Deer-creek, a convict servant man, named* Joseph Pool, *but has changed his name to* John *or* Joseph Ensey *since he went away; he is about* 35 *years of age, about* 5 *feet* 4 *inches high,*

a good deal pockmarked, has thin brown hair, wants his left hand from his wrist, has a large scar in his upper lip, writes a good hand, and calls himself a painter and limner, but served his time to the hatter's trade in London; had on, a lightish coloured half worn great coat, and waistcoat of the same, half worn leather breeches, and an old felt hat. Whoever takes up the said servant, and secures him, so as his master may have him again, shall have THREE POUNDS *Reward, if out of the county, or* FORTY SHILLINGS, *if in the county, and reasonable charges,*
paid by THOMAS BLEANY.

The Pennsylvania Gazette, May 30, 1771. See *The Pennsylvania Chronicle,* From Monday, March 18, to Monday, March 25, 1771.

THREE POUNDS REWARD.
RAN away, last night, from the subscriber, living in Cecil county, Maryland, a native Irish servant man, named JOHN MARA, about 5 feet 8 inches high, about 20 years of age, wears his own light-coloured hair, of a ruddy complexion, and speaks pretty good English, can write a tolerable good hand, it's probable will forge a pass. He had on, when he went away, a reddish mixed coloured coat, an old light coloured cloth jacket with metal buttons, and a blue ditto, old leather breeches, middling good shoes and buckles, old grey yarn stockings, new felt hat, and one or two country-made linen shirts. Whoever takes up said servant, and secures him in any gaol, so that his master may have him again, shall have the above reward, and reasonable charges, if brought home, paid by   SAMUEL GILPIN.
N. B. It is suspected that said servant, has changed his coat.
May 30, 1771.

The Pennsylvania Chronicle; From Monday, May 27, to Monday, June 3, 1771; From Monday, June 10, to Monday, June 17, 1771; *The Pennsylvania Gazette,* June 6, 1771. Minor differences between the papers. See *The Pennsylvania Gazette,* July 4, 1771.

Prince-George's County, May 9, 1771.
COMMITTED to my Custody as a Runaway, an *Irishman,* who calls himself *John Linch;* Has on, a black Coat and Breeches, is a short well made Fellow, of a dark Complexion, his Master is desired to pay Charges and take him away.

N. B. He is supposed to be One of the Men advertised by *Hubbard Prince,* in the *Maryland* Gazette of *April* the 17th, 1771.

The Maryland Gazette, June 6, 1771.

FORTY DOLLARS REWARD.

May 9, 1771.

RAN away last Night from the Subscriber's Plantation, near *Northampton* Iron-Works, *Baltimore* County, *Maryland*, Two Convict Servant Men, viz.

JOHN PELL, about 5 Feet 10 Inches high, a well made Fellow, black Hair, grey Eyes, and a down look: Had on, and took with him, a Fearnought Jacket, Cotton under ditto, Osnabrig Shirt, Hempen Role Trousers, old Shoes, and old Felt Hat.

JOHN MARSH, about 5 Feet 5 Inches high, a well set Fellow, has black Hair, dark Eyes, and is very talkative: Had on, when he went away, a Fearnought Jacket, Cotton under ditto, Crocus Trousers, Osnabrig Shirt, old Shoes, and a Felt Hat. They also took with them, a Castor Hat, about half worn, and a Pair of Buckskin Breeches.

Whoever takes up said Servants, and secures them, so that their Master gets them again, shall receive Three Pounds for each if taken in the Province, and if out of the Province the above Reward of Forty Dollars, or in Proportion for either of them, paid by
JOHN ROBERT HOLLIDAY.

The Maryland Gazette, June 6, 1771; June 13, 1771; June 20, 1770.
See *The Pennsylvania Chronicle,* From Monday, May 13, to Monday, May 20, 1771.

SIX DOLLARS REWARD,

May 14, 1771.

RAN away from the Subscriber on the 25th of *April* last, an indented *Irish* Servant Man, named *Charles Dogood*, about 34 Years of Age, 5 Feet 6 or 7 Inches high, a little marked with the Small-Pox, a down looking Fellow, and rather round shouldered, long Visage, has dark brown Hair tied behind, talks with the *Irish* Accent, and waddles much in his Walk, is sturdy and well legged, by Trade a Watch-maker, and lately lived Servant in *Lancaster*; took with him, Two lightish Knap Coats, One of them tared behind, a blue Jacket, black knit Breeches, with One Pair of old Leather, Three good white Shirts, and Three ditto Neckbands, with Silver Buckles in his Shoes. Supposed to have taken with him, a small Pinchbeck Watch (not his own) with a black Shagreen Case to it, studded on the Back with Gold Pins, in form of a Sprig. He is much addicted to Liquour and low Company, and is thought to have taken a Woman with him.

Whoever takes up and secures the said Runaway, so that his Master may have him again, shall receive the above Reward and reasonable Charges, paid by
SAMUEL JEFFERYS, Watch-maker, in *Philadelphia.*

N. B. He has been used to work at a Ferry, and to the Sea, and may possibly offer himself to Masters of Vessels, who are forbid to take him off.
The *Maryland Gazette*, June 6, 1771; June 13, 1771.

RUN away the 20th of May last, at night, from Mount Royal Forge, near Baltimore-Town, Maryland, an English indented servant man, named EDWARD DAVIS, about 30 years of age, by trade a shoemaker, 5 feet 2 inches high, swarthy complexion, and pitted with the small-pox, has short black hair, cut close on the top of his head, black beard, talks Dutch and Welsh; had on, and took with him, a castor hat, coarse brown cloth coat and breeches, trimmed with mohair buttons, claret coloured cloth jacket, with metal buttons, blue cloth ditto, with mohair buttons, ozenbrigs shirt, milled yarn greyish stockings, old shoes, and blue cloth breeches. Whoever takes up said servant, and secures him, so that his master gets him again, shall receive, if taken in the county, Forty Shillings; *or, of out of the province,* FIVE POUNDS, *and reasonable charges, if brought home.*
JAMES FRANKLIN.
The *Pennsylvania Gazette*, June 6, 1771; June 20, 1771; July 4, 1771; July 25, 1771.

FIVE POUNDS Reward.
RUN away, last night, from Mount Royal Forge, near Baltimore-Town, Maryland, an English convict servant man, named *John Carr*, by trade a brick-layer, born in Cheshire, and speaks in that dialect, he is about 48 years of age, 5 feet 8 or 9 inches high, has short brown hair, which is turning grey, his nose has been broke, and is crooked, lisps a little in his speech, and is bow-legged; had on, when he went away, a felt hat, cocked two ways, old brown cloth coat, with metal buttons of different sorts, ozenbrigs trowsers, new white kersey breeches, which has on the seat two stripes, between which are some letters, it being the end of the piece of cloth, coarse speckled yard stockings, and country shoes, tied with strings. Whoever secures said servant, so that he may be had again, shall have, if taken in the county, Forty Shillings, and if out of the province, the above reward, and reasonable charges, if brought home.
May 3, 1771.   JAMES FRANKLIN.
The *Pennsylvania Gazette*, June 6, 1771; June 20, 1771; July 4, 1771.
See *The Pennsylvania Gazette*, July 25, 1770.

RUN away from the subscriber, living in Kent county, Maryland, on the twenty-sixth ult. an English servant man, named STEPHEN PHIPPS, a

Taylor by trade, about 50 years of age, 5 feet 7 inches high, pale complexion, black hair; had on, when he went away, a light coloured bearskin coat, much worn, spotted flannel jacket, old snuff coloured velvet breeches, light blue yarn stockings, old shoes, with brass buckles, two white shirts, and an old felt hat. Whoever secures the said servant, and brings him to the subscriber, shall receive, if taken in the province, Thirty Shillings; *if out of the province,* Fifty Shillings, *and reasonable charges, paid by*
CHARLES ALLEN.
The Pennsylvania Gazette, June 6, 1771.

RUN away from the subscriber, living near Chester-Town, in Kent county, Maryland, on the 21st of May last, an English convict servant man, named JOHN BARTLETT, *about 43 years of age, by trade a Tinker, took tools with him, about 5 feet 9 inches high, well set; had on, or took with him, a felt hat, white shirt, bearskin vest, lined with white flannel, old leather breeches, black worsted stockings, white metal buckles in his shoes, and a Spanish great coat, called a grego; has lost the thumb of his right hand. Whoever takes up the said servant, and secures him, so that his master may get him again, shall have* FOUR POUNDS *reward, paid by*
OLIVER HASTINGS
The Pennsylvania Gazette, June 6, 1771; June 20, 1771; July 4, 1771.

COMMITTED to *Anne-Arundel* County Jail as a Runaway, a certain JOHN KING, an elderly Man, about 5 Feet 9 Inches high: His Apparel a white Linen Frock, a black flowered Waistcoat, and old Leather Breeches. His Master is desired to take him away and pay Charges, to
JOHN CLAPHAM, Sheriff.
The Maryland Gazette, June 13, 1771.

Calvert County, *June 5, 1771.*
THERE are in my Custody, committed as Runaways, Two Men, *viz.* John Graves, a well made Man, about 5 Feet 10 Inches high, of a ruddy Complexion; had on a Country Cloth Jacket, Osnabrig Shirt, check Trousers, old Shoes, and Felt Hat. *John Barset*, about 5 Feet 7 or 8 Inches high, of a brown Complexion, has several large Warts on the Back of his right Hand; his Cloathing is a Country Cloth Jacket, Osnabrig Shirt, old greasy Leather Breeches, old Pumps and Felt Hat. They are both young, and say they belong to Col. Tayloe, of Virginia. Their Owner is requested to take them away and pay Charges.
ALEXANDER SOMERVELL, Sheriff.
The Maryland Gazette, June 13, 1771.

Philadelphia, June 6, 1771.
FOUR DOLLARS Reward.
RUN away, the 1st instant, from the subscriber, living in George-Town, Kent county, Maryland, a Portuguese servant man, named *Anthony Socea*, about 5 feet 9 inches high, of a dark complexion, and very meagre look, speaks broken English, and wears his hair tied; by trade a shoemaker; had on, when he went off, an old felt hat, bound with broad yellow binding, dark brown cloth jacket, old leather breeches, yarn stockings, leather spatterdashes, with white metal buttons; a person so clothed, and of such appearance, was seen near the Lower Ferry, on Schuylkill, on Monday, the third instant, so that it is likely he may be in or near this city. Whoever takes up and secures said servant, so that I may have him again, shall be paid the above reward of Thirty Shillings, and reasonable charges, by *John Cummings*, at the House of Employment, to whom they will please apply, if the servant should be taken in or about this city, or if more convenient to me, in George-Town aforesaid.
ARCHIBALD WRIGHT.

The Pennsylvania Gazette, June 13, 1770,

TWENTY POUNDS REWARD.
RAN away from the Subscriber's Plantation, near *Elk-Ridge Landing*, the Four following Convict Servants, viz.

JAMES BARBER, about 5 Feet 6 Inches high, of a brown Complexion, short light brown Hair, and about 25 Years of Age: Had on and took with him, a Country Cloth Jacket and Breeches, an old Felt Hat, Two new Osnabrig Shirts, old Shoes, with flat Iron Buckles.

JOHN BATE, [sic] about 23 Years of Age, 5 Feet 5 Inches high, of a fair Complexion, with short straight brown Hair: Had on when he went away, a blue Halfthick Jacket, a Felt Hat, about half worn, a new Osnabrig Shirt, old Crocus Trowsers, no Shoes or Stockings.

JOHN BATES, [sic] about 27 or 28 Years of Age, a stout well looking Fellow, of a fair Complexion, with short brown Hair, about 5 Feet 8 or 9 Inches high: Had on when he went away, a Country Cloth Jacket, much worn, old Leather Breeches, old Felt Hat, and Osnabrig Shirt.

JOHN TOM LISON, about 35 Years of Age, 5 Feet 7 or 8 Inches high, a well set Fellow, with sandy Hair and Beard, a little knock-kneed, and his Ancles sore: Had on when he went away, an old Felt Hat. Country Cloth Jacket, much worn, greasy Buckskin Breeches, Osnabrig Shirt, old gray ribbed Stockings, and old Shoes.

Whoever takes up and secures the aforesaid Servants, or either of them, shall receive, if taken in the Province, Forty Shillings; but if taken out of the Province, Five Pounds for each, paid by

BENJAMIN HOWARD.
N. B. They are all Englishman.
The Maryland Gazette, June 20, 1771; June 27, 1771; July 11, 1771.

RAN away from the Subscriber, living in *Kent* County, *Maryland*, an *English* Convict Servant, named *Thomas Randall*, about 5 Feet 8 Inches high, round shouldered, of a brown Complexion, black Hair, has had a sore Leg, which makes it appear less than the other, and full of Knots: Had on, and took with him, a new Felt Hat, One Osnabrig Shirt, One fine ditto, One black Handkerchief, and One red ditto, a light coloured Coat, let out at the Sides, and Two blue Jackets without Sleeves, Two Pair of light coloured Breeches, and One Pair of Leather ditto, Two Pair of Thread Stockings, Two Pair of blue ditto, and Two Pair of new Shoes. He took with him a new Spade, and may pass for a Banker. It is supposed he has a good deal of Money with him, and went in Company with an old Woman and her Daughter, whose Names are *Marr*. Whoever takes him up, and secures him, shall have a Reward of Forty Shillings, besides what the Law allows.
CHARLES FOREMAN.
The Maryland Gazette, June 20, 1771; July 4, 1771; July 16, 1771.

Elk-Ridge Landing, May 31, 1771.
FIVE POUNDS Reward.
RAN away last Night from the Subscriber, Four Servant Men, lately imported from *Ireland*, viz. *James Routlidge, John Worgar, Roger Mealy*, and *Thomas Bryan*; the First Two are *Englishmen*, the other *Irishmen*. I cannot particularly describe them, but they are likely healthy Men; Three of them had on, when they went away, striped Lincey Jackets, with striped Woollen Caps. Whoever takes them up, and secures them in any Jail, shall have the above Reward, or Twenty-five Shillings each, besides what the Law allows, and reasonable Charges, if brought home.
JAMES FRENCH.
The Maryland Gazette, June 20, 1771; July 4, 1771; July 11, 1771; July 18, 1771; July 25, 1771. See *The Maryland Gazette*, August 8, 1771 and October 31, 1771.

Kent County, *Maryland*, June 23, 1771.
RAN away last Night, Two English Convict Servant Men, *viz.*
WILLIAM JAMES, about Twenty one Years of Age, about Five Feet Nine Inches high, he is a stout well set Fellow, wears his Hair short, fair

Complexion, has had the Small-Pox; he has a large Scar on One of his Knees.

THOMAS DYER, about Twenty-two Years of Age, about Five Feet Six Inches high, fair Complexion, wears his Hair short, has a large Scar on the inside of One of his Legs; they talk much in the West Country Dialect. They had on, and took with them, Four white Shirts, Four Osnabrig ditto, Seven Pair of Cotton and Thread Stockings, Three Pair of Trousers, One striped, One Osnabrig, One brown Roll; Five Pair of Shoes, Three Hats, Three Handkerchiefs, Two Coats, One blue Broad Cloth, One Wilton; Six Jackets, One blue Fearnought, One Wilton; Six Jackets, One blue Fearnought, One Wilton, One blue Cloth, One Damask, Two Linen; Five Pair of Breeches, One Pair Buckskin, and a Gun.

Whoever takes up and secures the said Convicts, if in the County, Three Dollars, and if out of the County, Six Dollars Reward for each of them, exclusive of what the Law allows, and if brought home, reasonable Satisfaction, made by
JOHN CARVILL HYNSON,   RICHARD HYNSON.

N. B. We suspect they will attempt to cross the Bay, and those that have Vessels we beg will take care of them.

The Maryland Gazette, June 27, 1771. See *The Pennsylvania Gazette,* April 4, 1771 and *The Maryland Gazette,* March 28, 1771.

June 15, 1771.

COMMITTED to *Talbot* County Jail, as a Runaway, a Man by the Name of *William Bradshaw,* who says he belongs to a certain *John M'Kenzie,* of *Anne-Arundel* County. His Master is desired to take him away and pay Charges.
JOSEPH BRASSUP, Jailer.

The Maryland Gazette, June 27, 1771.

FIVE POUNDS Reward.

RUN away from the subscriber, living in Baltimore county, 12 miles from Baltimore-Town, an English servant man, named WILLIAM LANGLEY, *about 26 years of age, about 5 feet 7 or 8 inches high, pale complexion, down look, short black hair; had on, or took with him, a new felt hat, grey fearnought jacket, two new ozenbrigs shirts, and trowsers of the same, blue ribbed yarn stockings, half worn pumps, small square steel buckles. Whoever secures the said servant, so as the subscriber may get him again, shall have Forty Shillings, if taken in the county; if 50 miles from home, Three Pounds; if 100 miles, Four Pounds; and if out of the province, the above reward, with reasonable charges, paid by*

May 1, 1771.   ABRAHAM PATTON.
The Pennsylvania Gazette, June 27, 1771; September 5, 1771. See *The Maryland Gazette*, January 10, 1771, July 11, 1771, October 17, 1771, and December 5, 1771.

THREE POUNDS REWARD.

Baltimore, June 28, 1771.

ESCAPED out of my Custody last Night, a certain *Andrew Williams*, about 5 Feet 6 or 7 Inches high, of a fair Complexion, has scarce any Appearance of a Beard, and about 27 or 28 Years of Age: Had on, an old Osnabrig Shirt, and a Pair of old Leather Breeches, he speaks much in the West of *England* Dialect; it is supposed he will steal other Cloaths (as he is a noted Villain) he being committed to my Custody for thieving, he may very probably try to pass himself as a Soldier and Deserter, which he attempted to do here; he has served his Time and likely will produce a Discharge from his first Master, named *George Hail*. Whoever takes up and secures said *Williams* in any Jail, shall have the above Reward, and if brought home the same Reward and reasonable Charges, paid by
JOHN R. HOLLIDAY, Sheriff.

The Maryland Gazette, July 4, 1771. See *The Pennsylvania Chronicle,* From Monday, July 29, to Monday, August 5, 1771.

June 17, 1771.

RAN away last Night from the Subscriber, living on Elk-Ridge, 2 indented Servants, *viz.*

ABRAHAM MILSON, abut 5 Feet 5 or 6 Inches high, well made, of a brown Complexion, brown Hair, commonly tied, gray Eyes, is not inclined to talk much, and has a down look when spoke to: Had on, and took with him, a black and white Country Cloth Jacket, a brown Holland ditto, Two Osnabrig Shirts, and One white ditto, a Pair of Osnabrig Trousers, black Breeches, and a Pair of *Russia* Drab ditto, white Yarn Stockings, old Shoes, and a half worn Hat; his other Apparel unknown.

SUSANNA MILSON, an *Irishwoman*, his Wife, about the same Height, is much freckled, and has sandy coloured Hair: Had on when she went away, a striped Linsey Gown, green Petticoats, bordered with different Sorts of Calico, and One white ditto; her other Cloaths unknown.

Whoever takes up said Servants, and brings them home, shall receive Three Pounds, including what the Law allows, if in the Province, and, if out of the Province Five Pounds, paid by
CHARLES G. RIDGELY.
They may probably have a forged Pass with them.

The Maryland Gazette, July 4, 1771.

TEN POUNDS REWARD.

June 26, 1771.

RAN away last Night from the Subscribers, living within 2 Miles of *Baltimore-Town*, 2 Convict Servant Men, the One is a young Fellow, much pock marked, well set, about 5 Feet 7 or 8 Inches high, and took with him a young bay Mare, with a Boy's Saddle newly mended on the Pummel, and also behind: Had a Fustian Coat and Jacket of a light Colour, with yellow Buttons, Osnabrig Breeches and Trousers, Country Thread Stockings, talks broad, was a Schoolmaster, is a good Scholar, and took with him a Silver Watch. The other is about 44 or 45 Years of Age, by Trade a Blacksmith, has a Scar on his left Wrist, near the Back of his Hand; took with him a Fearnought Pea Jacket, white Shirt and Osnabrig ditto, Crocus Trousers, old Leather Breeches, Worsted Stockings; has black Hair and a Wig with him; he is well set, about 5 Feet 8 or 9 Inches high, and talks broad, they are both *Englishmen*, the first is named *Paul Higton*, the other named *William Roberts*.

Whoever secures the said Servants, so that the Owners may have them again, shall have Fifty Shillings, if in the County; if out of the County, Five Pounds, and, if out of the Province, the above Reward, paid by
JOHN GORSUCH.   JOB GARRETSON.

N. B. They have stole a light coloured Country Cloth Coat and blue Jacket, and Two Holland Shirts. It is supposed they will forged Passes.
All Masters of Vessels are forewarned from carrying them off.

The Maryland Gazette, July 4, 1771.

EIGHT DOLLARS REWARD.

RAN away from the Subscriber, living near *Annapolis*, on Tuesday Night the 18th of *June* last, a Country born Servant Man, named *Luke Bullin*, a lusty well set Fellow, about Six Feet high: Had on, a coarse short Bearskin Coat, Osnabrig Shirt and Trousers, Country made Shoes, and Felt Hat. Whoever secures the said Servant in any Jail, shall have the above Reward, including what the Law allows, paid by
THOMAS RUTLAND.

The Maryland Gazette, July 4, 1771; July 11, 1771; July 25, 1771; August 8, 1771. See *The Maryland Gazette*, December 17, 1772.

FIVE POUNDS REWARD.

Baltimore, June 24, 1771.

RAN away last Night from the Subscriber, a Convict Servant Man, named *William Springate*, a Gardiner by Trade, about 5 Feet 4 Inches high, a dark ruddy Complexion, black Eyes, and wears his own Hair which curls

naturally; he was born in *Wales*, bred in *Bristol*, and speaks in that Dialect, he is much addicted to drinking and thieving, and when drunk is very quarrelsome and abusive, he has the Marks of a severe Whipping given him lately for breaking into a House: Had on and took with him, a Suit of light coloured Wilton, Buckskin Breeches, white Thread Stockings, and a black Silk Handkerchief about his Neck. Whoever brings him home to his Master, shall have Five Pounds Reward, and if delivered into any Jail in this Province, Three Pounds, paid by
DANIEL CHAMIER.

The Maryland Gazette, July 4, 1771; *The Pennsylvania Gazette*, July 4, 1771; July 25, 1771. Minor differences between the papers. See *The Maryland Gazette*, July 18, 1771.

FIVE POUNDS Reward.

RUN away from the subscriber, living in Caecil county, Maryland, on the 29th day of May last, a native Irish servant man, named JOHN MARA, *about 5 feet 8 inches high, about 20 years of age, wears his own light coloured hair, of a ruddy complexion, speaks pretty good English, can write a tolerable good hand, and it is probable will forge a pass; had on, and took with him, a reddish mixed coloured coat, an old light coloured jacket, with metal buttons, a blue ditto, old leather breeches, middling good shoes and buckles, grey yarn stockings, new felt hat, and several shirts, of country made linen; it is likely he may change his clothes and name, as he has been seen to pass by Dunkers Town and Padle Town, near Lancaster, when he had on a red jacket, and called himself* James Daughadey, *and was in company with one* Frances Yetts, *a woman, of a lusty size, pitted with the small-pox, of a freckled dark complexion, has a child, of about 18 months old, a boy, with very fair hair; it is probable they may attempt to pass for man and wife, and may change their names and clothes, in order to get clear; she is an idle vagabond woman, and has inticed him away. Whoever secures said servant in any goal, so that his master may get him again, or brings him home, shall have the above reward, and reasonable charges, paid by* SAMUEL GILPIN.

The Pennsylvania Gazette, July 4, 1771; July 25, 1771; August 22, 1771; September 5, 1771. See *The Pennsylvania Chronicle*; From Monday, May 27, to Monday, June 3, 1771. The ad for September 5 ends with: "N. B. He understands farming, and dressing flax, is a grand rogue, and should he be taken, will make his escape the first opportunity, was at Pittsburg about 18 months ago, and was taken in Philadelphia." This appears to be a printer's error, as that text is found in ads for John Read, which begin in *The Pennsylvania Gazette*, April 4, 1771.

THREE POUNDS REWARD.

ABSCONDED from his bail, on the 12th day of June, 1771, at Pine-Grove Furnace, on the Head of Nanticoke, in the province of Maryland, BOSTON AILE, a well set man, about 5 feet 6 inches high, of a fair complexion, wears his own hair, of a sandy colour, has an impediment in his speech; had on, and took with him, a new light-coloured cloth coat, and breeches of the same, check shirt, ozenbrigs trowsers, old buckskin breeches, and an old blue grey halfthick jacket, with sleeves. Whoever takes up and secures said *Boston Aile*, in any goal, so as his bail may have him again, shall have the above reward, paid by
THOMAS and WILLIAM LIGHTFOOT, and COMPANY.

The Pennsylvania Gazette, July 4, 1771.

RUN away from the subscriber, living in Gloucester county, near Cooper's Creek, N. Jersey, an Irish servant man, who calls himself *William Wilson*, but whose right name is said to be *M'Cullum*, about 30 years of age, near 5 feet and a half high, has been about 7 years in the country; he has very sandy hair tied behind, big under-lip, grey eyes, and has a sour look. Had on, when he went away, a brownish broadcloth coat, a blue grey broadcloth jacket, leather breeches, almost new, pretty good hat, a hempen sheeting shirt, black yarn stockings, and half worn shoes. It is supposed he is now somewhere in Maryland, having been twice advertised and taken; the first time he was confined in Cecil county gaol, and the last in Chester. Whoever takes up and secures said servant in any of his Majesty's gaols, or brings him home, shall have the above reward, paid by
BENJAMIN INSKEEP.   July 2, 1771.

The Pennsylvania Chronicle, From Monday, July 1, to Monday, July 8, 1771; From Monday, July 8, to Monday, July 15, 1771; From Monday, July 15, to Monday, July 22, 1771; From Monday, July 22, to Monday, July 29, 1771; From Monday, July 29, to Monday, August 8, 1771; *The Pennsylvania Gazette*, September 12, 1771. Minor differences between the papers. All but the first of the *Chronicle* ads have "THREE POUNDS REWARD." headlined at the top. See *The Pennsylvania Chronicle,* From Monday, February 4, to Monday, February 11, 1771, also *The Pennsylvania Chronicle,* From Monday, February 25, to Monday, March 4, 1771.

TEN POUNDS Reward.

RAN away, last night, from the subscribers living within two miles of Baltimore-town, two convict servant men; the one is a young fellow much pock marked well set, about 5 feet 7 or 8 inches high; and took with him a young bay Mare, with a boy's saddle newly mended on the pummel, and also behind. Had a fustian coat and jacket of a light colour, with yellow buttons, oznabrigs breeches and trowsers, country thread stockings; talks broad; was a schoolmaster; is a good scholar; and took with him a silver watch. The other is about 44 or 45 years of age, by trade a blacksmith, has a scar on his left wrist, near the back of his hand. Took with him a fearnought pea jacket, a white shirt, an oznabrigs ditto, crocus trowsers, old leather breeches, worsted stockings; has black hair and a wig with him; he is well set, about 5 feet 8 or 9 inches high, and talks broad; they are both Englishmen, the first is named PAUL HIGTON, the other named WILLIAM ROBERTS. Whoever secures the said servants, so that the owners may have them again, shall have FIFTY SHILLINGS, if in the County; if out of the County, FIVE POUNDS; and, if out of the province, the above reward, paid by

June 26, 1771. JOHN GORSUCH. JOB GARRETSON.

N. B. They have stole a light coloured country cloth coat, and blue jacket, and two holland shirts. It is supposed they will forge passes.

All masters of vessels are forewarned from carrying them off.

The Pennsylvania Chronicle, From Monday, July 1, to Monday, July 8, 1771. See *The Maryland Gazette*, July 4, 1771.

FIVE POUNDS REWARD.

May 1, 1771.

RAN away from the Subscriber living in *Baltimore* County, about Twelve Miles from *Baltimore-Town*, an *English* Servant Man, named *William Langley*, about 26 Years old, 5 Feet 7 or 8 Inches high, pale Complexion, down Look, short black Hair: Had on and took with him, a new Felt Hat, gray Fearnought Jacket, Two new Osnabrig Shirts, and Trousers of the same, a Pair of blue ribbed Yarn Stockings, a Pair of Pumps, and a Pair of small square Steel Buckles; he can spin both Wool and Cotton, and can wash Linen well, and as he has served some Time in the Country may endeavour to pass as a Freeman. Whoever takes up said Servant and secures him so as the Subscriber may have him again, shall receive Forty Shillings if taken in this County, Three Pounds in out of the County, and if out of the Province the above Reward, with reasonable Charges, paid by
ABRAHAM PATTON.

The Maryland Gazette, July 11, 1771; July 18, 1771; August 1, 1771. See *The Maryland Gazette*, January 10, 1771, October 17, 1771, December 5, 1770, and *The Pennsylvania Gazette*, June 27, 1771.

Annapolis, June 9, 1771.
COMMITTED to my Custody as Runaways, *Donald Clark*, a Sailor, who says he belongs to the Ship *Thornton*, Capt. *M'Dougall*....
The Maryland Gazette, July 11, 1771. See *The Maryland Gazette*, June 11, 1772.

RUN away on the 4th of June last, at night from the subscriber, living in Baltimore county, Maryland, an English servant man, named WILLIAM HIPIT, a Collier by trade, about 40 years of age, 5 feet 10 or 11 inches high; he has been in the country a long time, and has worked at the coaling business in the Jerseys, and at Mr. Morgan's Iron-works, in Philadelphia county; and, last winter, cutting wood in Merryan Furnace, in York county; had on, and took with him, an old felt hat, a white cotton jacket, an ozenbrigs shirt, old buckskin breeches, a pair of hempen-roll trowsers, pale blue stockings, old shoes, and it is thought he has got a good blanket with him; he is a little round shouldered, and wears his own dark coloured hair. Whoever takes up said servant, and brings him home, or secures him in any goal, so that his master may have him again, receive *Four Dollars* reward, if taken in the county; if out of the county, *Three Pounds*; if out of the province, *Five Pounds*; if taken in the Jerseys, *Six Pounds*, and reasonable charges, paid by me DANIEL REESE, Blacksmith, living in Gunpowder Forest, near Nathan Wheeler's mill, or by WILLIAM LEVELY, in Baltimore-Town.   DANIEL REESE.
The Pennsylvania Gazette, July 11, 1771,

Calvert County, *July* 12, 1771.
COMMITTED to my Custody as Runaways the Two following Men, *viz. William Springate*, a young Man, and says he belongs to *Daniel Chamier*, Esq; of *Baltimore* County. *James Barris*, about 5 Feet 8 Inches high, fair Complexion, appears of be about 30 Years old, hath scarce any Beard, he says he belongs to Capt. *John Pitt*, of *Annapolis*. Their Owners are desired to take them away and pay Charges.
ALEXANDER SOMERVELL, Sheriff.
The Maryland Gazette, July 18, 1771; July 25, 1771. See *The Maryland Gazette*, July 4, 1771.

July 9, 1771.
RAN away on the 16th of *June* last from the Subscriber, living in *Marsh-Creek Settlement*, in *York* County, *Pennsylvania*, an *Irish* Servant Man, named *David Clark*, by Trade a Woolcomber and Tobacco-spinner, about 4

Feet 7 or 8 Inches high, has a large long Nose, and loves Drink: Had on when he went away, a course [sic] blue Jacket with broad white metal Buttons, and since he first went away, he was taken and committed to Prison in *Alexandria*, in *Fairfax* County, *Virginia*, from whence he broke Jail, in Company with a Negro Fellow...calls himself *Will Jones*.... It's probable that the white Man *David Clark*, may claim the said Negro, in order to entitle them to travel unmolested.

Whoever takes up the said white Man, and brings him to the Jailer in *Alexandria*, shall have Forty Shillings *Pennsylvania* Currency Reward, and reasonable Charges, paid by me
ALEXANDRIA RAMSAY.

The Maryland Gazette, July 18, 1771.

SIX POUNDS REWARD.

Baltimore, July 15, 1771,
RAN away last Night from the Subscribers, living in *Baltimore-Town*, Two Servant Men, *viz.*

THOMAS TOWNSEND, and JOHN JOLLY,
(but might change their Names.) *Townsend* is a Cabinetmaker by Trade, a pretty well set Fellow, about 5 Feet 5 Inches high, of a light sandy Complexion, sandy Hair, Pock-marked, and freckeled, a small Scar on the upper Part of his Forehead, talks so as to be known as an *Irishman*: Had on, a lightish coloured tight Bearskin Coat that has been turned, but is little worn since, a Fustian Jacket without Sleeves, an old Pair of Blossom coloured Cloth Breeches, white Shirt, Thread Stockings, Shoes that have been soled, and Pinchbeck Buckles; he might alter his Cloaths, as he took several Things with him belonging to other Persons, particularly a brown Cloth Coat, a red and brown striped Persian Jacket, Buckskin Breeches, white Ticking ditto, Check Shirts, white Shirt ruffled at the Bosom, Osnabrig Trousers, &c. *John Jolly* is a Saddle-Treemaker, about 40 Years of Age, about 5 Feet 9 Inches high, stoops in his walk, has his own light Hair, lightish Complexion, large gray Eyes, and looks awry, and a remarkable large Nose: Took with him, a new red Surtout Coat, a purple broad Cloth Coat with Silver Basket Buttons, a Pair of Leather Breeches, a Pair of white Ticking ditto, and several white Shirts, a Felt Hat, and other Cloaths.—Whoever secures said Servants, so as their Masters may have them again, if taken in the Province shall have Three Pounds, for each, and if out of the Province Five Pounds, paid by
ROBERT MOORE, & AWBRAY RICHARDSON.

The Maryland Gazette, July 18, 1771; July 25, 1771; August 8, 1771.

RAN away from the Subscriber, living in *Chester-Town, Maryland*, Two white Servant Lads, *viz*. The one named JAMES FRANCIS, belonging to *Stephen Bordley*, junr. the other named GEORGE TIPPINS, belonging to *William Bordley*. JAMES FRANCIS, is short thick set, of a fair Complexion, has fair Hair, and down look, can write a tolerable good Hand, and pretends to know something of Navigation: Had on and took with him, a brown Country made Coat, Country Linen Trousers, a Pair of white broad Cloth Breeches that will not fit him, Two Silver Knee Buckles not Fellows, and a Pair of Shoes that were not made for him, and upon Examination will appear too long and narrow for him. GEORGE TIPPINS, is slender made, of a fair Complexion, short light coloured Hair, has been for some Time on board of a Man of War, can neither read or write: Had on and took with him, an old blue lapelled broad Cloth Coat, an old Nankeen Coat patched at the Elbows and under the Arms, and a Pair of white Breeches made of Ticking. It is probable JAMES FRANCIS may forge Passes for them both.—Whoever takes them up and secures them, so that the Subscribers may get them again, shall receive Five Pounds Reward, from
STEPHEN BORDLEY, junr, WILLIAM BORDLEY.

The Maryland Gazette, July 25, 1771; August 8, 1771; August 22, 1771; September 5, 1771; September 19, 1771; October 3, 1771; October 10, 1771; *The Pennsylvania Gazette*, August 1, 1771. Minor differences between the ads. *The Pennsylvania Gazette* has the date July 17, 1771 at the bottom

RUN away from the subscriber, living in Frederick county, Maryland, an Irish servant man, named JOHN BRIAN, by trade a baker, near 30 years of age, about 5 feet 6 or 7 inches high, short black hair, of a fair complexion, has a scar under his chin, and on his breast, that resembles the King's evil; had on, when he went away, a brown beaver coating surtout, a black velvet jacket, a castor hat, half worn thread stockings, a pair of pumps, with steel buckles. He speaks very good English, he having lived near ten years in London. Whoever takes up said servant, and secures him, so that he may be had again, shall receive Three Pounds reward, paid by the subscriber, or by David Cumming, innholder, in the Manor of Moreland, Philadelphia county. ROBERT CUMMING.
N.B. All masters of vessels are forbid to conceal or carry him off, at their peril.

The Pennsylvania Gazette, July 25, 1771; August 8, 1771; August 29, 1771.

FIVE POUNDS REWARD.

July 30, 1771.

RAN away from the Coffee-House in *Annapolis*, an indented Servant Man, named OLIVER STEPHENS, about 23 Years of Age, 5 Feet 8 Inches high, wore his own Hair, light coloured Cloaths, and also carried some light coloured Jennet, which had been cut out, but not made up, away with him; he is very slender, and has a remarkable thin Face, is a Native of *Ireland*, as may be easily gathered from his Conversation, he plays tollerably on a Variety of musical Instruments, viz. The Violin, Clarinet, Guitar, German Flute, &c. Tho' not yet Nine Months in the Country, yet this is his Second Elopement; he has shewn great Ingratitude to mild and even genteel Treatment. 'Tis supposed he is either gone by Water to *Philadelphia*, or lies concealed in this Town. If any Person through Ignorance of the Law has harboured him, by securing him and giving immediate Notice thereof to Mrs. *Howard*, at the Coffee House, he will not only avoid a Prosecution, but be handsomely rewarded. Five Pounds will be paid by the said Mrs. *Howard*, to the Person who apprehends said *Oliver Stephens*, if taken more than 10 Miles from *Annapolis*, or Three Pounds if nearer, and lodged in Jail, so that Mrs. *Howard* may have him.

The Maryland Gazette, August 1, 1771; August 8, 1771; August 22, 1771; September 12, 1771; September 27, 1771; October 3, 1771; October 10, 1771.

FIVE POUNDS REWARD.

April 9, 1771.

RAN away from the subscriber, living in *Roxborough Township, Philadelphia* County, on the 7th Instant, a *Dutch* Servant Lad, named *Philip Lutts*, about 18 Years of Age, about 5 Feet 5 Inches high, and grows fast, of a lean Visage, light brown short Hair, being lately cut, he is a little knock-kneed, flat-footed, speaks good *English*, but is aukward, and of a down bashful Look, and has been in the Province between 4 and 5 Years, and served chief of the Time at the Cooper's and Miller's Business: Had on when he went off, a new blossom coloured Cloth Coat and Vest, a Pair of Leather Breeches, a Felt Hat, and Check Shirt; and took with him, a blue flowered Flannel Vest, a Pair of blue Ever-lasting Breeches, a white Shirt, and had Two Pair of Stockings, with good Shoes. Whoever takes up the said Servant, and will convey him to the Work-House, in *Philadelphia*, or secure him in any Jail, so that I may get him again, shall have the above Reward, paid by   EDWARD MILNER.

N. B. He has since been seen near *Joppa*, in *Baltimore* County, *Maryland*, and it is thought will endeavour to get settled in some of the Mills in that Province.

The Maryland Gazette, August 1, 1771; August 8, 1771; August 15, 1771.

Baltimore, July 26, 1771.
ESCAPED from my custody the 28th ult. a certain ANDREW WILLIAMS (who listed with Lieutenant John Joyner Ellis, Esq; of his Majesty's 18th regiment of foot) having been taken on a precept for debt. He is about 5 feet 6 or 7 inches high, about 27 or 28 years of age, of a fair complexion, has scarce any appearance of a beard, speaks much in the West Country dialect, served his time with Mr. George Hart, and will probably produce a discharge from him; he has since been tried and convicted of a felony, and is a noted villain. He was seen on the road to York-Town, inquiring the way to Philadelphia, and then had on a blue surtout and leather breeches. Whoever secures said Andrew Williams in any of his Majesty's gaols, shall receive Three Pounds reward; and, if brought home, the above reward, and reasonable charges, paid by
JOHN ROBERT HOOLIDAY, Sheriff of Baltimore county.
The Pennsylvania Chronicle, From Monday, July 29, to Monday, August 5, 1771. See *The Maryland Gazette*, July 4, 1771.

Caecil *County*, July 30, 1771.
COMMITTED to my Custody as a Runaway, a Man who calls himself *Charles Connelly*, about 5 Feet 6 Inches high, well made: Has on, a brown Cloth Coat and Breeches, old white jacket, and blue Worsted Stockings, says he came into *Baltimore-Town* with Captain *Richard Hunter*; he has a Pass signed by Mr. *Andrew Buchanan*, but it is supposed to be forged.—His Master (if any) is desired to pay Charges and take them away.
RICHARD THOMAS, Sheriff.
The Maryland Gazette, August 8, 1777; August 15, 1771; August 22, 1771; August 29, 1771; September 5, 1771.

FIVE POUNDS REWARD.
RAN away last Night from the Brigantine *Watters*, lying at Mr. *William Digges's* Landing, *Patowmack* River, the following Servants, *viz.* JOHN GRAYHAM, born in *Ireland*, about Eighteen Years of Age, pitted with the Small-Pox, knock-kneed HUGH BURNS, born in *Ireland*, about Eighteen Years of Age, swarthy Complexion, and a little pitted with the Small-Pox. They wear their own Hair, and dressed in Sailors Dress. Any Person that will deliver the said Servants to Mr. *Alexander Hamilton*, at *Piscataway*, or

to the Master *Christopher Dixon*, on board said Vessel, shall have the above Reward, or Fifty Shillings for either of them.
The Maryland Gazette, August 8, 1771; August 15, 1771; August 22, 1771; August 29, 1771.

COMMITTED to *Charles* County Jail, a white Man, about 25 or 30 Years of Age, pale fair Complexion, about 5 Feet 8 Inches high: He is supposed to be a Servant belonging to some Person in *Frederick* County, *Virginia*; he was taken in Company with another white Man, who made his Escape from the Persons who were bringing him to Jail. Committed also, a Negro Man, the Property of a certain *Henry Scott*, near *Bladensburg*. Their respective Owners are desired to take said Prisoners away, and pay charges.
RICHARD LEE, Sheriff.
The Maryland Gazette, August 8, 1771.

July 25, 1771.
RAN away last Night from the Subscriber's Plantation, about 10 Miles from *Baltimore-Town*, 2 Convict Servants, *viz.* DAVID TOOLE, about 5 Feet 4 or 5 Inches high, a well set Fellow, has black Hair, gray Eyes, fresh ruddy Complexion, he is an *Irishman*, but doth not talk much in that Dialect: Had on and took with him, an old Fearnought Jacket, Osnabrig Shirt, Crocus Trousers, Felt Hat, and half worn Shoes. JOHN ROBERSON, an *English* Convict Boy, about 4 Feet high, and about 14 or 15 Years old, has black Hair, black Eyes, and a good Complexion; he is a very smart talkative Boy, and can read and write pretty well; he has had both of his Legs broke by a Cart, which occasions them to be somewhat crooked. Had on when he went away, an Osnabrig Shirt, Felt Hat, a good blue Coat, brown Holland Jacket, and blue Breeches: They may not be dressed as is described, as they took sundry Cloaths with them, *viz.* A half worn Gold laced Hat, which has a very narrow Brim, a redish Wilton Coat, with Pockets in the Skirts, a Check Shirt, and striped Holland Trousers, an old blue under Jacket, old white Shirt and a new white ditto, 8 Pair of Thread Stockings, and One Pair of worsted ribbed ditto; the Boy has a Pair of Boots.—Whoever takes up and secures the said Servants, so that their Master gets them again, shall have 30 Shillings, if taken about 20 Miles from home, if out of the County, 40 Shillings, and if out of the Province 3 Pounds for each, and reasonable Charges if brought home.
JOHN R. HOLLIDAY.
The Maryland Gazette, August 8, 1771; August 22, 1771; September 5, 1771; September 19, 1771; October 10, 1771; October 31, 1771; November 14, 1771; November 28, 1771; December 5, 1771;

December 12, 1771; December 19, 1771; December 26, 1771; January 9, 1772; January 16, 1772; January 23, 1772; January 30, 1772; February 6, 1772; February 13, 1772; February 20, 1772; February 27, 1772; March 5, 1772; March 12, 1772; March 19, 1772; March 26, 1772; April 9, 1772. *The Pennsylvania Gazette*, August 15, 1771; August 29, 1771; *The Pennsylvania Chronicle,* , From Monday, August 5, to Monday, August 12, 1771; From Monday, August 26, to Monday, September 2, 1771. Minor differences between the papers. The *Chronicle* adds a line at the bottom: "N. B. The boy has a good voice, and is fond of singing." *The Pennsylvania Gazette* shows the boy's name as "Robertson." See *The Maryland Journal, and the Baltimore Advertiser*, From October 9, to Saturday, October 16, 1773 and *Dunlap's Pennsylvania Packet or, the General Advertiser*, August 15, 1774, for "David Tool."

RAN away from the Subscriber, living on *Elk-Ridge*, on Thursday the First of *August*, a Convict Servant Man, named *John Worgar*, about Thirty-five Years of Age, Five Feet Seven or Eight Inches high, has black Hair, and is of a dark Complexion: Had on and took away with him, an old Snuff-coloured Broad-Cloth Coat and Jacket, a Cotton ditto, a Pair of Linen Breeches, Hempen Roll Trousers, Yarn Stocking, and old Shoes. It is supposed he took away with him a small black Horse, about Twelve Hands and a Half high, branded on the near Shoulder and Buttock thus, S; his Shoulders are galled with plowing. He also took away with him a Russia Drab Bedtick, and Five Ells Hempen Rolls.—Whoever takes up the said Servant, and secures him in any Jail, so that the Owner may have him again, shall receive a Reward of Forty Shillings, besides what the Law allows, and reasonable Charges, if brought home, Fifteen Shillings for the Horse, paid by   STEPHEN STEWART.

The Maryland Gazette, August 8, 1771. See *The Maryland Gazette*, June 20, 1771 and *The Maryland Gazette*, October 31, 1771.

SEVEN POUNDS Reward.

RUN away, on the 21st of July last, from the Subscriber, living in Baltimore-town, Maryland, a servant man, named SAMUEL DEALE, about 24 years of age, 5 feet 6 or 7 inches high, slender made, pale complexion, down look, pretends to be a Doctor and a great Horse-farrier, and will pretend to any thing; is handy in a kitchen, and is a low artful insinuating fellow, much addicted to lying; he can write, and probably will forge a pass; he took with him a blue lapelled surtout coat, white flannel waistcoat, two new linen shirts, and two pair of oznabrigs trowsers; his hair is cut off. He ran away last December, and passed some time by the name of William Johnson; it is likely he will change his name.

Whoever takes up said servant, and secures him in any gaol, so as his Master may get him again, shall have Four Pounds reward, and the above reward if brought home (including what the law allows) paid by
MARK ALEXANDER.

> *The Pennsylvania* Gazette, August 8, 1771; August 29, 1771; The *Pennsylvania Chronicle,* From Monday, August 5, to Monday, August 12, 1771; From Monday, August 12, to Monday, August 19, 1771. See *The Maryland Gazette,* January 17, 1771; *The Maryland Gazette,* January 31, 1771 and *The Pennsylvania Gazette,* March 14, 1771.

July 9, 1771.

RUN away, yesterday, from the Subscriber, living near Gunpowder Falls, 9 miles from Baltimore-town, a convict servant woman, named SARAH HILL, about 22 years of age, of a middling size, grey eyes and short yellow hair, she has a boil on one of her arms. Had on when she went away, a black bonnet, a red handkerchief bird's-eyed, a blue calimanco gown almost new, a black quilted petticoat with large diamonds; he has neither shoes nor stockings; she is fresh-coloured, and has one or two large marks near her mouth from the small-pox.

Whoever takes up said woman, and secures her, so that her Master may get her again, shall have FOUR POUNDS reward, and reasonable charges if brought home, paid by
JOHN CHRISTOPHER.

> *The Pennsylvania Chronicle,* From Monday, August 5, to Monday, August 12, 1771; From Monday, August 12, to Monday, August 19, 1771; From Monday, August 26, to Monday, September 2, 1771.

August 8, 1771.

RAN away from the Subscriber, living in *Piscataway,* on Monday last, an indented Servant Man, named THOMAS PHILLIPS, by Trade a Tailor: Had on when he went away, a light coloured Frize Coat with Gold Basket Buttons, a mixt Cloth Waistcoat, Osnabrig Trousers, a Pair of old Shoes and Buckles, white Dowlais Shirt much worn, wears his own Hair, which is long, black, and tied behind, is of a dark Complexion, and of a grim sour Look; he has a Hurt in his Hip, and when he walks limps, and stoops on one Side: He is about Five Feet Nine or Ten Inches high, and was born in England. Whoever brings him to the Subscriber, if taken up in the Province Three Pounds, besides what the Law allows, paid by
WILLIAM DUVALL.

The Maryland Gazette, August 15, 1771. See *The Maryland Gazette*, September 29, 1771 and *The New-York Journal, or, the General Advertiser*, October 17, 1771.

SIX POUNDS REWARD.
Kent County, *Maryland, July* 24, 1771.
RAN away from the Subscriber, last Night, Two *Irish* Servant Men, *viz.* TIMOTHY CONNER about 5 Feet 8 or 9 Inches high, has middling thick Lips, large Nose, short brown Hair, has a Sore on his right Breast, and a large Wart on his left Hip: Had on and took with him Two brown Country Linen Shirts and Two Pair of Trousers of the same, a brown Kersey Vest without Sleeves, an old brown great Coat, half worn Shoes with large Copper Buckles, and Felt Hat; his other Cloaths not known if any. The other named MICHAEL GOULDSBOURY, about 5 Feet 6 or 7 Inches high, long black Hair, a large Mouth, large Teeth, and brown Complexion: Had on and took with him Two new brown Country Linen Shirts, Two Pair of Trousers of the same, a new light coloured Country Cloth Vest lined with white Country Flannel, with Cuffs to the Sleeves, with white Metal Buttons, a Felt Hat, half worn Shoes, to One of which has lately been put a new Patch. They took with them a coarse Sheet and some Provisions. Whoever takes up the said Servants, and brings them Home, shall receive the above Reward; or if secured in any Jail, and Notice given to their Master, so as he may get them again, shall receive Forty Shillings for each.
GEORGE BROWNING.

N. B. All Masters of Vessels and others are forbid to harbour or carry them off at their Peril.
The Maryland Gazette, August 15, 1771; August 22, 1771; August 29, 1771; September 5, 1771. See *The Pennsylvania Gazette*, August 22, 1771 and *The Pennsylvania Gazette*, December 26, 1771.

July 20, 1771.
RAN away on the 19th Inst. from the Subscriber, living on *Elk-Ridge, Maryland*, an *Irish* Servant, named *James Henderson*, about 28 Years of Age, about 5 Feet 5 Inches high, of a brown Complexion, black Hair and Eyes, pitted with the Small-Pox, and has a large Scar on his left Breast: Had on, a Felt Hat, Kersey Coat, spotted Cotton Jacket, brown Linen Shirt, Osnabrig Trousers, and it is supposed that he has a Pair of Shoes; he is a Schoolmaster, and it is likely that he has forged a Pass, being well known. He taught School in *Maryland* and *Pennsylvania*, about Two Years ago, and since was put into *Baltimore* Jail for Debt, and was sold out for his Prison Fees.—Whoever takes up the said Servant, and secures him, so that his

Master may get him again, if 10 Miles from home, shall receive 20s; if 20 Miles, 40s; and if out of the Province, 5 Pounds, paid by me JOHN BROWN, Son of Joshua.
The Maryland Gazette, August 15, 1771; August 22, 1771.

August 1, 1771.
COMMITTED to *Queen-Anne's* County Jail, the following Persons as Runaways: *William Philips* (as he calls himself) an elderly Man, about 5 Feet 8 Inches high, light coloured Hair, and bald on the fore Part of his Head, has Shackles round his Ancles. *Joseph Warle*, about 25 Years of Age, a lusty well made Man, light coloured Hair, lisps much, and has lost his left Thumb, says he run away from *Baltimore* for Debt. *Richard Brown*, about 30 Years of Age, middle sized Man, with short sandy coloured Hair, says he run away with *Philips* from a Man of War, lying at *Hampton Road.* These Persons came to *Kent-Island* in a Yawl, where they were apprehended. Their Owners are desired to take them away and pay Charges, to   JAMES BUTLER, Jailer.
The Maryland Gazette, August 22, 1771.

FIVE POUNDS Reward.
RUN away, the 11th of this instant August, from near Lower Cross Roads, in Baltimore county, an Irish servant man, named *Thomas Preston*, about 24 years of age, about 5 feet 9 inches high, wears short brown hair, is fresh coloured, and middling likely; he wore a brown linsey jacket, a sailor's blue jacket, country linen shirt, tow trowsers, and a pair of old grey silk stockings; he writes a good hand. With him went a young Negroe man, named *Toney*, is pitted with the small pox; wore an old fustian coat, and plays well on the fiddle. Whoever secures the said servant, and Negroe, shall have *Thirty Shillings* reward for each, and if out of the province of Maryland, shall have *Fifty Shillings* for each, paid by me JAMES MOORE.
The Pennsylvania Gazette, August 22, 1771.

TEN DOLLARS Reward.
Escaped *from my custody, on the 23d of May last, a certain* JAMES LATHIM, *an English man, aged about* 30 *years, about* 5 *feet* 7 *inches high, of a fair complexion, and sandy beard, and wears his own long light coloured hair, either plaited or tied with a ribbon, his religion a Papist; had on an English castor hat, a mixed coloured coat, of light blue cloth, a claret coloured lappelled jacket, made of an old coat, buckskin breeches, and carved silver buckles; but it is probable he may change his name, and*

also his dress, as it is supposed he took 50 or 60 pounds money with him; he is a shoemaker by trade, of which business he is a compleat master; he has, for some time past, worked with Mr. John Patrick, at Deer-Creek, in Baltimore county, in the province of Maryland; he took away with him, a small bay trotting Mare, about 12 hands high, 4 years old, neither ear-mark nor brand; also a new bridle and new hog-skin seated saddle, the tuft-nails of the saddle covered with leather, and a new cross barred saddle-cloth. Whoever secures said Lathim in any goal in America, and gives notice thereof, shall have the above reward; or if brought home to me, at my dwelling house in Baltimore-Town, shall receive the above reward of Ten Pounds, besides reasonable charges, paid by
John Robert Holliday, *Sheriff of Baltimore county.*
   The Pennsylvania Gazette, August 22, 1771.

SIX POUNDS REWARD.
RUN away from the subscriber, living in Kent county, Maryland, the 23d of July, at night, two Irish servant men, viz. TIMOTHY CONNER about 5 feet 8 or 9 inches high, has middling thick lips, large nose, short brown hair, has a sore on his right breast, and a large wart on his left hip: had on, and took with him, when he went away, two brown country linen shirts and trowsers of the same, a brown kersey vest, without sleeves, an old brown great coat, half-worn shoes, old broad-rimmed brass buckles, and a felt hat. The other, named MICHAEL GOULDSBOURY, about 5 feet 6 or 7 inches high, long black hair, a large mouth, and large teeth, and of a very brown complexion; had on, and took with him, two new brown country linen shirts, and trowsers of the same, a new jacket of Devonshire kersey, of a lightish brown colour, with cuffs to the sleeves, and lined with white linsey, country made with old metal buttons, a felt hat, and half-worn shoes. Their other clothes not known, if any. Whoever takes up the said servants, and brings their master, shall receive the above reward, and reasonable charges; or if secured in any goal, and notice sent to their master, so as he may get them again, shall receive *Forty Shillings* apiece, paid by
GEORGE BROWNING.
   N. B. All masters of vessels, and others, are forbid to harbour or carry them off, at their peril.
   The Pennsylvania Gazette, August 22, 1771; August 29, 1771; September 12, 1771. See *The Maryland Gazette*, August 15, 1771.

FIVE POUNDS Reward.
RUN away from the Upper Cross Roads, in Baltimore county, the 4th of this instant August, two English convict servant men, viz. *William Smart*, a

low well set fellow, about 22 years of age, speaks very broad, his hair is cut off; he served part of his time with Jeremiah Chance, and often tells about dealing with, or for, gentlemen in Baltimore Town; it is likely he will pass for a Waggoner. *John Brown*, is a low middle sized man, wore black curled hair, has a down look, small grey eyes, by trade a Miller; it is supposed they have the following cloaths, a superfine white jacket, 1 pair of leather breeches, 1 pair of redish broadcloth breeches, several pair of trowsers, sundry shirts, 2 pair of thread stockings, 3 silk handkerchiefs, 1 castor hat, 1 coarse felt hat, and 2 needle worked pocket books, with many papers belonging to Edward M'Cormick. Whoever secures the said servants, shall have Thirty Shillings for each, paid by us,

WILLIAM DITTO,   ABRAHAM JARRETT.

N.B. They cannot write, but may change their names.

The Pennsylvania Gazette, August 22, 1771.

Talbot County, August 12, 1771.

ESCAPED from my custody, the 29th of July, a certain GEORGE KITCHEN, having been taken, on a precept, for debt; he is about 5 feet 8 inches high, about 18 years of age, of a fair but blotted complexion, born in England, and talks in the West country dialect, by trade a Wheelwright, stoops in his walk, and is very apt to get in liquor; had on, when he went away, a brown broadcloth coat and jacket, leather breeches, and a light grisle cut wig. Whoever takes up the said runaway, and secures him in any goal, so that the subscriber may have him again, shall receive *Three Pounds* reward; if brought to him, shall receive *Seven Pounds*, paid by

JOSEPH BRUSCUP, Goaler.

The Pennsylvania Gazette, August 22, 1771; September 5, 1771; November 28, 1771.

SIX POUNDS REWARD.

Kent County, *Maryland.*

MADE their Escape from the Constable of *Eastern Neck* Hundred, a certain *David M'Carty* and Wife who were apprehended for dealing with Servants and Slaves: He was born in *Ireland*, a tall strait Fellow near Six Feet high, about 30 Years of Age, Sandy Complexion, has long Hair tied behind, his Apparel uncertain; he has been a Soldier, and may have several Discharges. His Wife is a likely tight Body, but is a great Villain; she was born in *Virginia*, and they may pretend to be going there to receive some Money due to her by some Friend. They stole a Canoe, and on their Way were examined and said they intended for *St. Mary's* County. Whoever secures the said *M'Carty* and Wife, so that they may be brought to Justice, shall

receive the above Reward, or Four Pounds for securing *M'Carty* only, paid by   RICHARD GRESHAM.
The Maryland Gazette, August 29, 1771.

Elk-Ridge, August 20, 1770.
RAN away last Night from the Subscriber, an *Irish* indented Servant Man, named NILL DUFFEY. He is a short well made Fellow, has a remarkable large Beard, and wears his own dark Hair: Had on a Felt Hat, a dark coloured Cloth Coat lined with yellow, a striped Flannel Waistcoat without Sleeves, a Check Shirt, a Pair of striped Ticken Breeches, one Pair ditto coarse Country Lining, a Pair of dark coloured Yarn Stockings, and an old Pair of Shoes. Whoever secures the said Servant, so that the Subscriber gets him again, shall receive 40 Shillings Reward, including what the Law allows, if 20 Miles from Home; if out of the Province Three Pounds, and reasonable Charges if brought Home, paid by
HENRY HOWARD.
The Maryland Gazette, August 29, 1771; September 5, 1771; September 12, 1771.

Baltimore County, Maryland, 8th Month (Aug.) 20, 1771.
FIVE POUNDS Reward.
RAN away last Night from the Subscriber, an indented Irish Servant Man, named EDWARD WALL, about 21 Years of Age, dark Complexion, dark curled Hair (which he may perhaps cut off) pretty much pitted with the Small-pox, and near 6 Feet high. Had on, when he went away, an Ozenbrigs Shirt, coarse Country Linen Trowsers, a Pair of coarse Shoes, tied with Strings, new soaled, and has a large Foot; A Fly Coat or Jacket of Country made Cloth, with Apple tree Buttons, and a small Felt Hat. Whoever takes up said Servant, and brings him home, or secures him in any Goal, so as his Master may have him again, shall be paid the above Reward, and reasonable Charges, by
WILLIAM COX.
N. B. All masters of vessels are forbid to carry off, or employ said servant.
The Pennsylvania Gazette, August 29, 1771.

Baltimore, July 23, 1771.
FIVE POUNDS Reward.
RUN away last night from Mrs. ENSOR's Quarter, Gunpowder Forest, an English Convict Servant Man, named JOHN CHAFFY, about 5 feet 6 or 7

inches high, well set, but a remarkable coward, wore his own hair, of a yellowish colour, tied behind, has a down look, and took with him an old felt hat, green cotton jacket, two good ozenbrigs shirts, three pair of pompon roll trowsers, two pair of old shoes, with a pair of strong open work brass buckles. He likewise took with him a small BLACK HORSE four years old, well made, carries a high head, with a short switch tail. Whoever takes up and secures the said Man and Horse, so that the owner gets them again, shall have, if 20 miles from home, THIRTY SHILLINGS, if forty miles FORTY SHILLINGS, and if out the province the above reward, and reasonable charges paid, if brought home, or THREE POUNDS for the Man, and FORTY SHILLINGS for the Horse, paid by
NATHAN GRIFFITH.
The Pennsylvania Gazette, August 29, 1771.

THREE POUNDS Reward.
RAN away from the subscriber, living on Ladies Manor, Baltimore County, a convict servant, named WILLIAM RANSON, about 5 feet 8 or 9 inches high, dark complexion, has black hair which he may probably disguise, as he took with him a brown cut wig, wore an old blue surtout, calico jacket, old leather breeches, coarse worsted stockings, old shoes, yellow metal buckles and a fine linen shirt. He took with him a fearnought jacket, oznabrigs shirt, tow linen trousers and an old felt hat, and went off the 12th instant, it is supposed in company with one Thomas Mason, a convict servant belonging to Charles Bond, living in Baltimore County. Whoever secures said William Ranson, so that his master may have him again, shall have the above reward from   JOHN MARSHALL.
Ladies Manor, Baltimore County, August 13, 1771.
The Pennsylvania Chronicle, From Monday, August 26, to Monday, September 2, 1771; From Monday, September 2, to Monday, September 9, 1771; From Monday, September 16, to Monday, September 23, 1771.

RAN away from the Subscriber, living in *Charles* County, on the 10th of *August*, a Convict Servant Woman, named *Catherine Miller*, an Irish Woman, middle Size and well made, very fleshy, has a broad Face, much pitted with the Small-Pox, and has black Hair: Had on when she went away, a striped Holland short Gown, Felt Hat, and a Country Cloth Petticoat.— Whoever takes up the said Servant, and secures her, so that her Master may have her again, shall have Four Dollars if taken in the County, if out of the

County Forty Shillings, and if out of the Province Three Pounds Reward, besides what the Law allows, paid by
JOSEPH EVINS.
The Maryland Gazette, September 5, 1771; October 3, 1771; October 10, 1771.

Maryland, Dorsey's *Forge*
RAN away from the Subscriber, Two Convict Servant Men, *viz.*
WILLIAM HUNT, an *Englishman,* about 19 Years of Age, 5 Feet 7 Inches high, has a good Countenance, speaks well, and says he was brought up a Farmer: Had on when he went away, a Cotton Jacket, an old Felt Hat bound round the Brim with black Binding, an Osnabrig Shirt and old leather Breeches.
JOSEPH DUNN, an *Irishman,* about 40 Years of Age, 5 Feet 6 or 7 Inches high, has short gray Hair, and a blemish in one of his Eyes: Had on when he went away, a short striped Flannel Jacket, an old Hat, tarred over the Crown, an Osnabrig Shirt, and old Buckskin Breeches. These Fellows were both lately put in Irons for running away, but have found means to get them off; they also took with them, a new Match-coat Blanket, Three Yards of strip Holland, and several other Things.—Whoever apprehends said Servants, and brings them home, shall have for each, if taken Twenty Miles from home, Thirty Shillings, if Thirty Miles, Forty Shillings, and if out of the Province, Five Pounds Reward (including what the Law allows) paid by
CALEB DORSEY.
The Maryland Gazette, September 5, 1771.

FIVE POUNDS Reward.
RUN away from the subscriber, living on the Fork of Gunpowder, in Baltimore county, Maryland, the 20th of August, 1771, at night, a convict servant man, named WILLIAM LOWED, about 5 feet 7 or 8 inches high, of a sandy complexion, brown hair and beard, a mole on his chin, and one of his eye-teeth sticks out on the left side; had on, when he went away, a snuff coloured coat, a blue jacket, old black leather breeches, oxenbrigs trowsers, and an old beaver hat, with the crown greased : He took with him a chestnut sorrel HORSE, about 14 hands high, his hoofs turn up very much, with being foundered; also a half-worn hunting saddle, and a new half-curb bridle. As he is a good scholar, it is supposed he has forged a pass. Whoever takes up the said servant, and horse, and secures them, so that the owner may have them again, shall receive, if taken in the county, Forty Shillings *for the man, and* Twenty Shillings *for the horse; and if out of the county,* Three Pounds *for the man, and* Forty Shillings *for the horse, paid by* SKELLTON STANDIFORD.
The Pennsylvania Gazette, September 5, 1771.

FIVE POUNDS Reward.

ABSCONDED from his bail in the beginning of July last, from Deer-Creek, near Rock Run, Baltimore county, a man who went under the name of WILLIAM BARRELL, by trade a taylor, with short brown hair, of a swarthy complexion, somewhat pitted with the small-pox; he is very talkative, much given to drinking, swearing, lying, and inclines to thieving; when walking, goes very upright and fast, with a comical air in his body, and his arms stretched down his sides almost unmovable; he is an Englishman born, and says he served his time in London; he came to this country from either Pennsylvania or the Jerseys, to either of which places he is supposed to have made his elopement; he wore a reddish broadcloth coat, with yellow metal buttons, but probably may have changed his dress and name. Whoever takes up and secures said man in any of his Majesty's gaols in America, by writing a line to the subscriber, miller, upon Deer-Creek, Baltimore county, or to John Rodgers, at the Prince Ferdinand, near the Lower-Ferry, Susquehanna, shall have the above reward, and if brought home all reasonable charges, paid by
JOHN LATHIM.

The Pennsylvania Chronicle, From Monday, September 2, to Monday, September 9, 1771; From Monday, September 16, to Monday, September 23, 1771.

September 10, 1771.

RAN away about the Middle of *July* last from the Subscriber, living in *Prince-George's* County on the *Paint* Branch, a Convict Servant Man, who was imported in the *Tryall,* Captain *M'Dougal,* in *September* 1768, he is a stout *Irish* Man, 5 Feet 10 Inches high, named *Lawrance Thomson,* wears short brown Hair, has grey Eyes, and a down Look: Had on when he went away, a Cotton Waistcoat with Cuffs, Osnabrig Short and Trousers.

Whoever takes up the said Servant, and brings him home, shall have Forty Shillings besides what the Law allows, if taken in the Province, and if out of the Province, Four Pounds and reasonable Charges.
GEORGE WILSON, senr.

The Maryland Gazette, September 12, 1771; October 3, 1771; October 10, 1771. Minor differences between the first ad and the other two.

TWELVE POUNDS REWARD.

September 1, 1771.

RAN away last Night from the Subscriber, living at *Legh* Furnace, *Little-Pipe* Creek, *Frederick* County, the Two following *Irish* Servant Men, *viz.*

ANDREW REDMOND, a well made Man, about 5 Feet 10 or 11 Inches high, about 30 Years of Age, wears his own Hair, and is of a dark

Complexion, by Trade a Turner and Spinning-Wheel maker: He had on when he went away, a light grey Surtout Coat, green Waistcoat, Leather Breeches, Thread Stockings, and Check Shirt: he took with him some Shirts, and a rifled Barrel Gun,

JOHN O'BRIEN, a tight slim made Fellow, about 5 Feet 8 Inches high, about 26 Years of Age, of a fair Complexion, wears his Hair tied, by Trade a Weaver: He had on when he went away, a light brown Coat, red Waistcoat, Leather Breeches, and a Pair of new Shoes nailed in the Heels and Soles, and some Shirts.—Whoever apprehends both or either of the said Servants, and brings them to the Subscriber at Little-Pipe Creek, shall receive Six Pounds reward for each, paid by me

LEGH MASTER.

The Maryland Gazette, September 12, 1771; October 3, 1771. *The New-York Gazette; and the Weekly Mercury*, October 7, 1771; October 14, 1771. Minor differences between the papers.

RUN *away from the subscriber, an indented servant man, named* JANUS NOWER, *by trade a Bricklayer, about 5 feet 7 or 8 inches high, of a swarthy complexion, stoops in his shoulders, turns his toes in when he walks, is much addicted to drink, wears his hair, which is black; had on, when he went away, a light coloured duffil coat, ozenbrigs trowsers, or green shag breeches, and white linen shirt, country made shoes and stockings, and felt hat; but as he has some persons that assist him, he may have changed his dress. Whoever takes up said servant, and brings him back to his master, living near Bushtown, in Baltimore county, Maryland, shall receive* FIVE POUNDS *reward, and reasonable charges; or if secured in any goal, so that his master may have him again, shall receive the above reward of* FIVE POUNDS, *paid by* AQUILA HALL.

The Pennsylvania Gazette, September 26, 1771; October 24. 1771.

FIVE POUNDS REWARD.

Piscataway, September 21, 1771.

RAN away last Night from the Subscriber, an *English* indented Servant Man named *Thomas Philips*, by Trade a Tailor, he is about 5 Feet 8 or 9 Inches high: Had on, when he went away, a light coloured Frize Coat,bound, trimm'd with Gold Basket Buttons, Nankeen Jacket and Breeches, new Dowlas Shirt, Thread Stockings and turned Pumps, wears his own long black Hair tied behind, of a dark Complexion, and a grim sower Look. He ran away about a Month ago, and got to *Baltimore*, to which Place it is probable he may make again. Whoever secures said Servant, so that his Master may get him again, shall have a Reward of

Three Pounds Currency, if above Thirty Miles from home, and if out of the Province the above Reward, and reasonable Charges paid, if brought home, by   WILLIAM DUVALL.

The Maryland Gazette, September 29, 1771; October 3, 1771; October 10, 1771. See *The Maryland Gazette*, August 15, 1771 and *The New-York Journal, or, the General Advertiser*, October 17, 1771.

THIRTY DOLLARS Reward.

RAN away last night from the subscriber, living in Baltimore town, Maryland, an indented servant man named JOHN GREEN; he was born in Ireland, is about 5 feet 9 inches high, and about 24 years of age, he is a likely well-made man, and has a very good countenance, wears his own dark hair, smooth faced, has but little beard, a small scar near his mouth, speaks good English, and writes a good hand; it is said he forged a pass; he says he served several years in the Earl of Drogheda's regiment of Light Dragoons; he arrived here the third day of August, 1769; took with him, when he went away, a blue cloth coat, half worn, with a hole in one skirt eaten by the rats, one check shirt, one white ditto, a black handkerchief, one white diaper lapelled jacket, and one thick-set ditto of an olive colour, a castor hat, about half worn, a pair of new buckskin breeches, a little soiled, and some spots of shoemakers wax on them, a pair of blue worsted stockings, a pair of yarn ditto, a pair of old oznabrigs trowsers, a leather apron, a pair of new turned pumps, and a pair of pinchbeck buckles; also, took with him, a set of shoemaker's tools, he being by trade a shoemaker; he is an exceeding good workman, and, by his own account, worked some time as a journeyman at the trade; he is also an excellent fiddler, and very apt to get in liquor; it is remarkable when talking he is apt to say *eath* instead of *yes*; he may change his clothes, but the above-mentioned scar will make him very remarkable, except he puts a patch on it; inquire for his indenture. Whoever takes up said servant, and secures him in any gaol, so that his master may have him again, shall receive, it taken in the county, *Five Pounds*, if out of the county, *Seven Pounds Ten Shillings*, but if out of the province, the above reward, and reasonable charges, paid by
JOSEPH HAYWARD.   JOHN GREY.
N. B. He goes by the name of JOHN GREY.

The Pennsylvania Chronicle, From Monday, September 23, to Monday, September 30, 1771; From Monday, September 30, to Monday, October 7, 1771. See *The Pennsylvania Chronicle, and Universal* Advertiser, From Monday, May 7, to Monday, May 14, 1770.

COMMITTED to the Custody of the Sheriff of *Frederick* County, as Runaways, *John Cochran, John Moran,* and *Joseph Ridrom,* who says he belongs to John *Brellossic* of *Prince-George's* County. Their Masters are desired to take them away and pay Charges.
ERASMUS DORCIAS, Jailor.
The Maryland Gazette, October 3, 1771.

TWELVE DOLLARS REWARD.
RAN away from the Subscriber, *May* 27, 1771, living in *Manington* Township, *Salem* County, *West New-Jersey,* an *Irish* Servant Man, named RICHARD HANDLEY, about 20 Years of Age, wears his own fair Hair, 5 Feet 4 or 5 Inches high, a likely well-set Fellow, stoops as he walks, speaks in the *Irish* Dialect, and is remarkable for calling working Cattle *Oxens:* Had on, and took with him a Felt Hat, old Homespun Cloth Jacket of a lightish Colour, a fine Shirt, a Tow Cloth ditto, 2 Pair of Trousers, one of Check Linen, a Pair of Buckskin Breeches, and Shoes tied with Strings; he may probably have a forged Pass with him. Whoever takes up the said Servant, and secures him, so that his Master may have him again, shall receive the above Reward, and all reasonable Charges, paid by me,
JOHN ROBERTS.
The Maryland Gazette, October 3, 1771; October 10, 1771; October 24, 1771; November 7, 1771; November 14, 1771; November 21, 1771; November 28, 1771.

THIRTEEN DOLLARS Reward.
RAN away, on the 23d of February last, from the Subscriber's plantation, in Frederick County, Maryland, an Irish servant man named ANDREW DUNLOP, has been some years in the country, since which he has come under indenture; he is about 5 feet 10 inches high, has dark brown hair, tied behind, thin vissage and pale complexion, talks much of his being a soldier in the last war, is subject to drink, and very impertinent: Had on, and took with him, a suit of brown drab cloth, old blue camblet coat and jacket, old castor hat, one narrow ax and mattock, and sundry other things unknown, he having formerly cut wood at the Principio works, near Susquehannah. It is supposed he is now near that place.

Whoever takes up said servant, and delivers him to his master, or to the sheriff of Baltimore County, shall receive the above reward, and reasonable charges paid, by
Baltimore, Oct 3, 1771.   MORDECAI GIST.

N. B. His wife being a free woman, has since left her place of residence, and gone off to him.

The Pennsylvania Chronicle, From Monday, September 30, to Monday, October 7, 1771. See *The Maryland Gazette*, April 30, 1772.

RAN away last June, from the Subscriber, living in *Frederick* County, near the *Great Falls* of Patowmack, an *English* convict Servant Man, named JOSEPH JAMES, about 20 Years old, 5 Feet 9 Inches high, and has worked at the Blacksmiths Trade about Three Years; his Cloaths are unknown; he was taken up in Charles County, but made his Escape. Whoever takes up said Servant, and brings him home, if in Maryland, Four Pounds, if in Virginia, Six Pounds, and reasonable Charges, paid by
NINIAN BEALL, Son of Ninian.
The Maryland Gazette, October 10, 1771; October 24, 1771; November 7, 1771.

FIVE POUNDS REWARD.

RAN away from the Forge near *Elk-Ridge* Landing, on the 9th of *September* last, a Servant Man, by Name JOHN WINTERS, he is about Five Feet Eight Inches high, Pock marked, bald headed, and about Forty-five Years old: Had on a Fearnought Jacket, coarse Linen Shirt, Osnabrig Trousers, and a Felt Hat. He has served Four Years, and pretends that he is a Freeman. Whoever brings him to his Master, living near *Elk-Ridge* Church, *Anne-Arundel* County, or to *William Hammond*, at the Forge, shall receive Three Pounds, if within the Province, and if out, the above Reward, paid by   EPHRAIM HOWARD.

N. B. He has taken with him some old Cloaths, in particular, an old Cloth Coat lined with red Flannel.
The Maryland Gazette, October 10, 1771; October 24, 1771; November 7, 1771.

September 18, 1771.
FIVE POUNDS REWARD.

RAN away from the Subscriber, the 17th Inst. living on *Monockasy*, about 3 Miles from *Frederick-Town*, an indented Servant Man, named THOMAS CONNER, born in *Limmerick*, in *Ireland*, about 5 Feet high, 17 Years of Age, of a dark Complexion, wears his own Hair, which is black and pretty thick, has much of the *Irish* Brogue, and is greatly addicted to lying: Had on, when he went away, Two Linsey Jackets, One with Sleeves, the other without, lined with striped Linsey, a Pair of Tow Linen Trowsers, and a Shirt of ditto, a new Felt Hat, and an old Pair of Shoes tied with Leather Strings Whoever takes up said Servant, and brings him to the Subscriber, shall receive the above Reward, and reasonable Charges, paid by

JACOB WINDRODE.
The Maryland Gazette, October 10, 1771; October 24, 1771; October 31, 1771.

COMMITTED to *Charles* County Jail, a Servant Man, named *William Langley,* who says he belongs to *Abraham Patton,* in *Baltimore* County: Also, a Servant Man, named *William Stephens,* a Shoemaker by Trade, lame in one of his Feet, he says he belongs to *Joseph Duvall,* in *Frederick* County.—Their Masters are desired to take them away, and pay Charges.
RICHARD LEE, junr. Sheriff.
The Maryland Gazette, October 17, 1771; October 24, 1771; October 31, 1771. See *The Maryland Gazette,* January 10, 1771, July 11, 1771, December 5, 1771, and *The Pennsylvania Gazette,* June 27, 1771.

October 6, 1771.
RAN away from the Subscriber, living in *Fredericksburg, Virginia,* an indented Servant Man, by Trade a Tailor, named *John Driver,* sometimes calls himself *Windsor Driver,* was born in the west of *England,* he is about Five Feet Five Inches high, speaks quick and short, and of an effeminate Voice: Had on, when he went away, a brown Frock Coat with gilt Buttons, a light blue Pair of Breeches, a dark Bath Coating Waistcoat, brown Thread Stockings, a Pair of new Shoes, double stitched at the Eyes, a Felt Hat, bound with Tape, brass Buckles not Fellows, a blue Silk Handkerchief spotted white, a Check Shirt, dark brown Hair commonly tied, has a dark Complexion, and a thin Visage. Whoever takes up said Servant, and lodges him in any of his Majesty's Jails, so as his Master shall get him again, shall receive Forty Shillings, and if brought home to his said Master, Four Pounds, besides what the Law allows, paid by me
JAMES NEWTON.
N. B. As he pretends to know a little of the Sea, this is therefore to forewarn all Masters of Vessels, on their Peril, not to carry said Servant out of the Colony.
The Maryland Gazette, October 17, 1771; October 24, 1771; November 7, 1771.

TWENTY DOLLARS REWARD,
Maryland, Piscataway, Sept. 30, 1771.
RAN AWAY from the Subscriber, on the 21st Instant, an English indented Servant Man named THOMAS PHILIPS, by Trade a Taylor, 5 Feet 8 or 9 Inches high. Had on when he went away, a light coloured Frize Coat,

bound, trimm'd with Gold Basket Buttons, unlined, and about half worn, Nankeen Jacket and Breeches, the Button Holes of the Jacket bound with the same, a new Dowlas Shirt, Thread Stockings, turned Pumps, and a Felt Hat, commonly cock'd up behind, wears his own black Hair, tied behind, of a dark Complexion, and a grim sower Look. He ran away some Time ago, and then he got inlisted with Soldiers at Baltimore Town, but was apprehended before they left that Place; if it probable he will endeavour to get to Philadelphia, to the Soldiers there. Whoever apprehends said Servant, and secures him in any Gaol, so that his Master gets him again, shall have the above Reward and reasonable Charges paid if brought home, by
WILLIAM DUVALL.

The New-York Journal, or, the General Advertiser, October 17, 1771; October 31, 1771; November 7, 1771. See *The Maryland Gazette*, August 15, 1771 and *The Maryland Gazette*, September 29, 1771.

RAN away from the Subscriber, on the first Day of *September*, 1771, living in *Prince George's* County, near Mess. *Snowdens* Iron-works, a Convict Servant Man, named WILLIAM SHEPPERD, by Trade a Shoemaker, though he calls himself a Tobaccco-stemmer. [*sic*] He is about 5 Feet 6 Inches high, lame in his right Foot, limps very much, and his left Shoulder is disabled: Had on, when he went away, an Osnabrig Shirt and Trousers, 2 Cotton Waistcoats, one with Sleeves the other without, and an old Castor Hat bound round with black Ferrit. He wears his own brown short Hair, is of a yellow Complexion, and spare in his Body. Whoever takes up the said Servant, or confines him, so that his Master may get him again, shall receive Five Pounds Currency Reward, paid by
JOSEPH DUVALL.
N. B. *All Masters of Vessels are forewarned carrying him off at their Peril.*
The Maryland Gazette, October 24, 1771.

RAN away from the Subscriber, living on *Swan* Creek, in *Kent* County, on Friday the Nineteenth of *October*, a Convict Servant Man named JOHN GILSOM, about 24 Years of Age, 5 Feet 8 Inches high, has a middling long Nose, a thin Face, a smiling Countenance, and is pitted with the Small-Pox: Had on and took with him a black Kersey Jacket, Two Osnabrig Shirts, Osnabrig Trousers, a blue Cloth ditto, and an old Felt Hat; he probably has other Cloaths. Whoever takes up the said Fellow, and secures him in any Jail, so that the Owner may have him again, shall have 20 Shillings Reward if in the County, if out of it 40 Shillings, paid by
ROBERT AYRES.
The Maryland Gazette, October 24, 1771.

RUN away from the subscriber, last July, living in Frederick county, Maryland, near the Great Falls of Potowmack, an Irish indebted servant man, about 5 feet 9 inches high, a well set fellow, very much freckled in his face; he had a large brown surtout coat when he went away, and was taken up, and put in Charlestown goal, but got away; he pretends to be a butcher, and is very likely to have a forged pass. Whoever takes up the said servant, and secures him, shall have THREE POUNDS, or if brought home, ONE SHILLING per mile, and reasonable charges, paid by RINIAN BEALL, Son of RINIAN.

N. B. His proper name is CORMACK LAPPEN, but he has changed his name in a forged pass, which he had when taken at Charlestown, at the head of the Bay.

The Pennsylvania Gazette, October 24, 1771.

RAN away from the Subscriber, living on *Elk-Ridge,* on Sunday the 18th of *August* 1771, a Convict Servant Man, named JOHN WORGAR, about 35 Years of Age, 5 Feet 7 or 8 Inches high, round shouldered, has short black curled Hair, is of a dark Complexion, and talks very much like an *Irishman*: Had on an old Snuff coloured Broad-Cloth Jacket, a Cotton ditto, a Pair of Linen Breeches, Hempen Roll Trousers, Yarn Stockings, old Shoes, Check Shirt, Osnabrig and Irish Linen ditto; he took with him a Russia Drab Bedtick. Whoever takes up said Servant, and secures him in any Jail, so that his Master may get him again, shall receive Three Pounds in taken in the Province, and if out of the Province Five Pounds, and reasonable Charges if brought Home, paid by   STEPHEN STEWARD.

The Maryland Gazette, October 31, 1771; November 7, 1771; November 14, 1771; November 21, 1771. See *The Maryland Gazette,* August 8, 1771 and *The Maryland Gazette,* June 20, 1771.

October 28, 1771.

COMMITTED to *Anne-Arundel* County Jail, as Runaways, the Three following Persons, *viz.*

George Griffin, a lusty young Man, about 22 Years of Age, says he is a free Man, and lived in *Dover* in *Delaware* Government, and followed the Trade of a Sadler.

Negro *Whitehaven*.... Negro *Joe*....

Their Masters are desired to take them away and pay Charges to JOHN CLAPHAM, Sheriff.

The Maryland Gazette, October 31, 1771.

TWENTY-FIVE DOLLARS REWARD.
September 30, 1771.

RAN away last Night from the Subscriber, living about a Mile from *Baltimore-Town*, a Convict Servant Man named ISAAC PINKENEY, about 35 Years of Age, 5 Feet 8 or 9 Inches high, of a fresh Complexion, short brown Hair very thin before and tied behind: Had on when he went away, a middling good Felt Hat, a blue Sailors upper Jacket, a striped under ditto, several Sailor like Jackets, Two Osnabrig Shirts, a Pair of Country Tow Linen Trousers, and under them a Pair of Linen or Ticken Drawers, a Pair of gray ribb'd Stockings, light blue ditto, and a Pair of Country made Shoes almost new. As he has been a Sailor, it is very likely he will go on Board some Vessel; he is very talkative and pert if he gets in Liquor. It is supposed he is in Company with Three more belonging to *Kayton* and *Heeston*. He was on board one of his Majesty's Ships at the latter End of the last War, towards the Northward. Whoever takes up the said Servant, and brings him Home, shall receive, if taken in the County, Ten Dollars, and if out of the Province the above Reward and reasonable Charges, paid by   DAVID GORSUCH.

N. B. All Masters of Vessels are forbid to carry him off at their Peril.

The Maryland Gazette, October 31, 1771, November 14, 1771; November 21, 1771; November 28, 1771. See below.

NINE POUNDS REWARD.

RAN away from the Subscribers, living at Mr. *Lersh's* Mill near *Baltimore-Town*, Three Servant Men, *viz.* JOHN JOHNSON, a smart young Man, about 24 Years of Age, a little marked with the Small-Pox, wears his own flaxen colour'd Hair, was us'd to the Sea all last War: Had on a blue Pea Jacket, a black Coat rent in the Back, good Shoes and Stockings; says he has many Relations in *London*, who follow the Grocery Business, to which he was brought up. THOMAS BERNS, about 24 Years of Age, about 4 Feet 10 Inches high, black Hair and Beard, of a brown Complexion, and has some small impediment in his Speech: Had on when he went away, either a coarse whitish Cloth or a black Coat, a Pair of Buckskin Breeches, a Pair of black Stockings, a Felt Hat, and a Pair of middling good Shoes. SOLOMON LEETCH, about 25 Years of Age, 5 Feet 5 Inches high, of a fair Complexion, down Look, low Speech, has short Hair, and chiefly wears a Cap, or else a brownish Wig; has lost Two Joints of his fore Finger on his right Hand, his Cloaths but mean: Had on when he went away an Iron Collar, which it is supposed he has filed off, as he attempted it once before; he may pretend to many Trades, as he was brought up in *Birmingham*. They have all been in the Country about 4 Months and they probably have

Passes, as *Johnson* can write a very good Hand. It is supposed they are gone in Company with one *Isaac Pinkeney* belonging to *David Gorsuch*.

Whoever takes up the said Servants and secures them, so as their Masters may get them again, shall receive if taken in the Province 50 Shillings, if out of the Province 3 Pounds for each, and reasonable Charges if brought Home, paid by
JOHN HEESTON and JOHN KAYTON.

The Maryland Gazette, October 31, 1771; November 14, 1771; November 21, 1771; November 28, 1771; *The Pennsylvania Gazette*, October 31, 1771. Minor differences between the papers. *The Pennsylvania* Gazette show the name of the second man as "BURNS" and shows Leetch as about "24 or 26 years of age." See above.

RUN away from the subscriber, on the 18th of October, a servant lad, who calls himself JAMES JACKSON, about 19 years of age, says he was born in London, about 5 feet 6 inches high, of a fair complexion, stoops in his shoulders, of a thin visage, straight brown hair, cut off at top; he says he served his time in Baltimore county, Maryland, and it is likely, as he can write a pretty good hand, that he will forge a pass; had on, when he went away, a half worn castor hat, an old ozenbrigs shirt, a striped lincey waistcoat, the stripes go round him, a large blue sailor jacket, lined with white flannel, somewhat tarry, a pair of buckskin breeches, too large for him, a pair of home made blue and white yarn stockings, and half worn shoes, with carved Pinchbeck buckles. Whoever takes up said servant, and brings him home to his said master, living in Woolwich township, Gloucester county, and province of West New Jersey, or secures him in any goal, so as his master may get him again, shall receive THIRTY SHILLINGS reward, and reasonable charges, paid by
BENJAMIN THOMPSON.

The Pennsylvania Gazette, October 31, 1771.

Dorchester county, September 20, 1771.
Run away from the Subscribers, a servant man named CHARLES EAST, he has a notable mark on his left cheek, a large nose and wears his hair, which is black; he passes for a school-master, or stay-maker; had on, when he went away, a mixed coloured Wilton coat, a striped lapelled jacket, a pair of check trowsers, and a new fine hat: He took away with him a BAY STALLION, with a blaze in his forehead. Whoever apprehends the said servant man, and horse, so that the subscribers may get them again, shall have TWENTY DOLLARS reward, besides what the law directs.
ISAAC NICOLLS, RISDON MOORE.

The Pennsylvania Gazette, October 31, 1771. See *The Pennsylvania Gazette*, January 25, 1770 and March 1, 1770.

Annapolis, November 13, 1771.
COMMITTED to *Anne-Arundel* County Jail as a Runaway, a Man who says his Name is *Alexander Harris*, and that he served his Time in *Virginia* near *Alexandria:* He has on a blue Surtout Coat and Worsted Shag Jacket of a Red Colour, Leather Breeches, &c. His Master, if any, is desired to take him away and pay Charges to
JOHN CLAPHAM, Sheriff.
The Maryland Gazette, November 14, 1771.

November 11, 1771.
RAN away last Night from the Subscribers, Three Convict Servant Men, lately imported from *Bristol* in the *Restoration*, Captain *Thomas, viz.* GEORGE M'CARTY, about 30 Years old, 5 Feet 8 Inches high, fresh Complexion: Had on a Snuff-coloured Cloth Coat, brown Holland Waistcoat, striped Cotton Trousers, old Buckskin Breeches. He has been in the Country before and talks of having a Wife at *Duck-Creek*; it is probable he may endeavour to pass for a Sailor. JOHN HINTON, a Gardener by Trade, about 5 Feet 7 Inches high, fair Complexion: Had on a light-coloured Thick-set or Fustian Waistcoat, old Buckskin Breeches, and Silver plated Buckles in his Shoes; has light-coloured Hair, and is about 25 Years old. WILLIAM RUDGE, by Trade a Whitesmith, pale Complexion, about 27 Years old, 5 Feet 6 or 7 Inches high: Had on an old blue Coat with yellow Metal Buttons, Flannel Waistcoat, and old Buckskin Breeches. They have been in the Country about 3 Weeks, were born in the West of *England*, and speak much in that Dialect.

Whoever takes up said Servants and secures them in any Jail, or either of them, shall have Four Dollars Reward for each, besides what the Law allows, and if brought home to *Ebenezer Mackie* at *Baltimore*, or *James French* at *Elk Ridge Landing*, reasonable Charges will be allowed by
EBENEZER MACKIE,   JAMES FRENCH.
The Maryland Gazette, November 14, 1771; November 28, 1771; December 5, 1771; December 12, 1771; December 19, 1771; December 26, 1771.

RUN away, on the 17th of September last, from the subscriber, living in Frederick county, Maryland, about 3 miles from Frederick-Town, an Irish servant lad, named THOMAS CORNER, 17 years old, about 5 feet high, black thick hair, dark complexion, hath much of the brogue; had on, when he went away, a new felt hat, two light coloured lincey jackets, one with

sleeves, and the other without, both lined with striped ditto, a tow linen shirt, and trowsers, old shoes, tied with strings, and is much given to lying and stealing. Whoever takes up the said servant, and brings him to his master, shall have FIVE POUNDS reward, and all reasonable charges, paid by   JACOB WINDRODE.
  The Pennsylvania Gazette, November 14, 1771.

Baltimore County, *Nov.* 12, 1771.
FIVE POUNDS REWARD.

RAN away from the Subscriber, living in *Garrison Forrest*, an indented Servant Man, named ROGER FIELDS, by Trade a Baker, about 35 Years old, about 6 Feet high, has the Palsy in his Head, and dark Hair and black Eyes: Had on and took with him, a light coloured Cloth Coat, blue Jacket, Buckskin Breeches, gray Yarn Hose, good Shoes, Osnabrig Shirt and Trousers, and a good Hat.

  Whoever will take up and secure the said Servant in any Jail, so that his Master may get him again, shall receive, if taken Twenty Miles from home, Thirty Shillings, if Thirty Miles Forty Shillings, if Forty Miles Three Pounds, and if out of the Province the above Reward, and reasonable Charges if brought home.   CHARLES WALKER.
  The Maryland Gazette, November 21, 1771; November 28, 1771.

Port-Tobacco, Nov. 12, 1771.
TWENTY DOLLARS REWARD.

RAN away from Subscriber, on Sunday Evening last, an *English* Convict Servant Man, named WILLIAM DAY, who has been brought up to the Farming Business; he is middle aged, very swarthy, wears short black curled Hair, has a quick artful Way of talking, and is of middle Size: Had on and took with him, an old blue Surtout Coat, an old blue Jacket, an old Pair of Leather Breeches, a new Dowlas Shirt, a checked Linen ditto, an old Pair black Stockings, an old Pair light coloured ditto, a Pair coarse Shoes, almost new, with Strings in them, and an old Hat.

  Whoever will take up said Servant, and contrive him [sic] to my House, about 4 Miles below *Port-Tobacco*, shall have the above Reward; and if he is secured in a Jail, so that I can hear of him, shall have Eight Dollars Reward   GERARD B. CAUSIN.
N. B. I suspect that he has an Inclination to make for Carolina.
  The Maryland Gazette, November 21, 1771; November 28, 1771; December 5, 1771; December 12, 1771; December 19, 1771; December 26, 1771; January 9, 1772.

RUN away from the subscriber, living in Baltimore county, near-Elk Ridge Landing, the 15th of September last, a convict servant man, named JOHN HILYEAR, about 30 years of age, 5 feet 6 or 7 inches high, wears his own short brown hair, is of a fair complexion; he is hard of hearing; had on a castor hat, red silk handkerchief, holland shirt, brown jacket and breeches, grey stockings, and country shoes. Whoever takes up said servant, and secures him in any goal, so that his master may have him again, shall have THREE POUNDS reward; but if brought home FIVE POUNDS, and reasonable charges, paid by
EDWARD NORWOOD.

LIKEWISE,

RUN away from said Norwood, the 26th of October last, another convict servant, named JOHN BOTTIN, a Brick layer by trade, about 5 feet 8 inches high, wears his own short brown hair, some of which grey, about 25 years old, a little pock-marked, has a sore on his left knee; had on, when he went away, a castor hat, holland shirt, brown duffil coat, flannel jacket, white buckskin breeches, English worsted stockings, and shoes. Whoever takes up said BOTTIN, and secures him, so that his master may get him again, shall be entitled to the like reward as is offered above for HILYEAR, paid by   EDWARD NORWOOD.

The Pennsylvania Gazette, November 21, 1771; January 2, 1772. See *The Maryland Gazette*, November 28, 1771.

November 1[6], 1771.

RAN away from the Subscriber, living in *Baltimore* County, near *Elk-Ridge Landing*, some time in *July*, an *Irish* Convict Servant Man, named *William Perry*, about 20 Years of Age, much Pock-marked, about 5 Feet 7 Inches high, a Tailor by Trade, and pretends to understand something of Horses: Had on, an took with him, when he went away, a brown Broad Cloth Coat, striped Linsey Jacket, Dowlas Shirt, Osnabrig Trousers, old Shoes and Steel Buckles, and a new Castor Hat. Whoever secures the said Servant, so that his Master gets him again, shall have Five Pounds Reward, including what the Law allows, and reasonable Charges, if brought home, paid by
EDWARD NORWOOD.

The Maryland Gazette, November 28, 1771.

November 18, 1771.

RAN away from the Subscriber, living in *Baltimore* County, near *Elk-Ridge* Landing, on the 15th of *September* last, Two Convict Servant Men, *viz.*

JOHN HILYEAR, about 30 Years of Age, 5 Feet 6 or 7 Inches high, wears his own short brown Hair, is of a fair Complexion, and hard of hearing: Had on, a Castor Hat, red Silk Handkerchief, Holland Shirt, brown

Jacket and Breeches, gray Stockings, and Country Shoes.—JOHN BOTTIN, a Bricklayer by Trade, about 5 Feet 8 Inches high, wears his own short brown Hair, some of which is gray, about 25 Years of Age, a little Pock-mark'd, has a Sore on his left Knee: Had on when he went away, a Castor Hat, Holland Shirt, brown Duffil Coat, Flannel Jacket, white Buckskin Breeches, English Shoes, and Worsted Stockings.—Whoever takes up said Servants, and them in any Jail, [sic] so that their Master may have them again, shall have Three Pounds Reward for each, if brought Home Five Pounds, and reasonable Charges, paid by
EDWARD NORWOOD.

N. B. BOTTIN is supposed to be carried away by Thomas Corbin, Joiner, who lately came from Philadelphia; there shall be, if taken, the same Reward for this Corbin, as is for either of them.

The Maryland Gazette, November 28, 1771; December 5, 1771; December 12, 1771; December 19, 1771; December 26, 1771; January 9, 1772. See *The Pennsylvania Gazette*, November 21, 1771.

November 28, 1771.

RAN away last Night from the Subscriber, an indented Servant Man, named WILLIAM LEE, a short thick Fellow, of a swarthy Complexion, has a remarkable thick Neck, and talks very broad: Had on and took with him, a light coloured Jacket, and a blue under ditto pretty much worn, a Felt Hat bound round with black Worsted Binding, old Stocking Breeches, light coloured Stockings, and Country made Shoes.—Whoever takes up the said Servant and brings him to his Master, living in *London-Town*, shall receive Forty Shillings Reward, if taken in the County, and if out of the County, Three Pounds and reasonable Charges, paid by
EDWARD AMIES.

The Maryland Gazette, November 28, 1771; December 5, 1771; December 19, 1771; December 26, 1771.

EIGHT DOLLARS REWARD.

RAN away from the Subscriber, in *Baltimore* County, an *English* Servant Man, named WILLIAM LANGLEY, about 25 Years old, 5 Feet 7 or 8 Inches high, has long black Hair, pale Complexion, down Look, and thin Beard, can spin both Wool and Cotton; he was in Custody in *Charles* County Jail, from whence he was released and brought to *Lower-Marlborough*, and there made his Escape the Third of *November*: Had on when he went away, a Castor Hat, red and white striped Lincey Jacket, brown Holland Jacket, without Sleeves, Osnabrig Shirt and Trousers, brown and white mixed Yarn Stockings, old Pumps, Brass Buckles, not Fellows.—

Whoever secures said Servant in any Jail, or brings him to *Fielder Bowie's* Store, at *Nottingham*, shall receive the above Reward, paid by
ABRAHAM PATTON.

The Maryland Gazette, December 5, 1771; December 12, 1771; December 19, 1771; December 26, 1771; January 9, 1772; January 16, 1772; January 23, 1772; January 30, 1772. See *The Maryland Gazette*, January 10, 1771, July 11, 1771, October 17, 1771, and *The Pennsylvania Gazette*, June 27, 1771.

Annapolis, December 4, 1771.
COMMITTED to *Anne-Arundel* County Jail as a Runaway, *William Wood*, says he belongs to *Humphry Godman*, on *Elk-Ridge*. His Master is desired to take him away and pay Charges.
JOHN CLAPHAM, Sheriff.

The Maryland Gazette, December 5, 1771. See *The Maryland Gazette*, October 22, 1772, and October 21, 1773.

WAS committed to Carlisle Goal, the following runaway servants, viz.

ROBERT PATRICK, about 17 years of age, red haired, and says he belongs to Henry Bitting, living near the Great Swamp, in Bucks county.

JOHN GLASS, a Dutch lad, about 22 years of age, says he belongs to David Crawford, near Sam's Creek, in Frederick county, Maryland.

PATRICK SULLIVAN, and JOHN HAMERSLEY, advertised by David and John Brown, both of the Forks of the Great Falls, in Baltimore county, Maryland.

Their masters (if any they have) are desired to come and pay their cost, and take them away, in six weeks from this date, otherwise they will be sold for the same, by
December 12, 1771.   ROBERT SEMPLE, Goaler.

Also, a certain JOHN BAGNELL, who was advertised in the Chronicle, by Patrick Ford, Taylor, of Philadelphia. Said Ford is desired to come, and lay in his charge, otherwise he will be released from his confinement, in ten days from the date hereof.

The Pennsylvania Gazette, December 12, 1771; December 19, 1771.

Dec. 18, 1771.
RAN away from the Subscriber on Sunday Night last, living in *Bladensburg*, a Servant Man, 5 Feet 3 Inches high, aged 25 Years: Had on, when he went away a brown Cloth Jacket, blue Breeches; he is a pert spoken Man, has a round fair Face, black Eyes, an *Englishman*, and a Shoemaker by Trade.— Whoever shall take him up, and bring him to his

Master, shall receive Forty Shillings Reward, over and above what the Law allows, from
JOHN FRANCIS

N. B. He has a Scar under his left Knee about the Size of Half a Dollar, his Name is *William Daniel Angess.*

The Maryland Gazette, December 26, 1771; January 9, 1772. See *The Maryland Gazette,* January 9, 1772 and *The Pennsylvania Gazette,* May 7, 1772.

Lancaster December 13, 1771.

COMMITTED to my custody, the 11th of this instant, a certain servant man, named TIMOTHY CONNER, who says he belongs to a certain George Brown, in Kent county, Maryland, in Ryle's Neck, near George Town. His said master is desired to come, pay charges, and take him away, in three weeks from the date hereof, otherwise he will be sold for his charges, by me GEORGE EBERLY, Goaler.

The Pennsylvania Gazette, December 26, 1771. See *The Maryland Gazette,* August 15, 1771 and *The Pennsylvania Gazette,* August 22, 1771.

RUN away on the second day of December, from the subscriber, living in Baltimore-Town, Maryland, an apprentice lad, named ARCHIBALD DOUGHERTY, between 13 and 14 years of age, by trade a potter, about 4 feet 9 or 10 inches high, fair complexion, light hair, stoops in his walk, is round shouldered; had on, when he went away, a half worn wool hat, without loops, a cloth coloured double breasted jacket, with sleeves, and an under jacket of the same, pretty much worn, brown sheeting shirt, blue serge trowsers, and new shoes. Whoever takes up said apprentice, and brings him to his said master, shall have Two Shillings and Six pence reward, paid by JOHN BROWN.

The Pennsylvania Gazette, December 26, 1771.

1772

CECIL COUNTY, MARYLAND Dec. 28, 1771.

RUN AWAY from the Subscriber, last night, an Irish Servant man, named MORGAN MURPHY, about five feet ten inches high, well made, of a ruddy complexion, has black hair that curls a little, is about forty-five years of age, and will probably pretend to be a gardener. Had on when he went away, a grey wilton coat, with white metal buttons, a light coloured cloth

him again shall have SIX DOLLARS, if taken in Maryland, and TEN DOLLARS, if taken out of it, with all reasonable charges, paid by
GEORGE MILLIGAN.

The Pennsylvania Packet; and the General Advertiser, January 6, 1772; January 20, 1772.

December 18, 1771.
RAN away from the Subscriber on Sunday Night last, living in *Bladensburg*, a Servant Man, named WILLIAM DANIEL ANGESS, a Shoemaker by Trade, an *Englishman*, about Five Feet Three Inches high, aged Twenty-five Years, light brown Hair, round Face, with black Eyes, and a very fair Skin, has a Scar under his left Knee the Size of an Half Dollar: Had on when he went away, a brown Cloth Jacket, and blue Breeches, but may have changed his Cloaths, and have forged himself a Pass; is a pert bold spoken Man, and likely to behave with a great deal of Assurance if examined.

Whoever shall take him up, and bring him to his Master, shall receive Five Pounds Reward and reasonable Charges, from
JOHN FRANCIS.

The Maryland Gazette, January 9, 1772; January 16, 1772; January 23, 1772; January 30, 1772; February 6, 1772; February 13, 1772; February 20, 1772; February 27, 1772; March 12, 1772. See *The Maryland Gazette*, December 26, 1771 and *The Pennsylvania Gazette*, May 7, 1772.

Annapolis, Jan. 15, 1772.
RAN away from the Subscriber Yesterday, a Servant Man, named *James Royston*, he is about Five Feet Three Inches high, fair Complexion, and light Hair, a Turner by Trade, his Clothes are not well known to me, therefore can't describe them: He went off with one *Walter Osborn*, who is a Turner by Trade also, of middling Stature, and marked with the Small-Pox, and is a *Scotchman*. *Royston* had been working under *Osborn* for some Time past, they both went down *South River* in a Canoe, and it's probable they are gone up or down the Bay in some Vessel.

Whoever takes up *James Royston*, and secures him in any Jail, so that he may be had again, shall if taken in this County, receive Twenty Shillings Reward, if in any other County, Forty Shillings, and if out of the Province, Three Pounds, and reasonable Charges if brought home, paid by
WILLIAM REYNOLDS.

The Maryland Gazette, January 16, 1772.

TWENTY DOLLARS REWARD.

Poor house, *Charles* County, *Dec.* 22, 1771.

RAN away on Sunday the 15th of *Dec.* a Scotch convicted Servant Man, named *James Hunter*, a Joiner and Carpenter by Trade, of a middle Age, and swarthy Complexion, he has short black Hair, about Five Feet Eight or Nine Inches high: Had on, and took with him, a Felt Hat, a blue plain Jacket, lined with white Plaid, an under Ditto of knit Silk and Worsted of a clouded Colour, with Silver washed Buttons, an Osnabrig Shirt, Leather Breeches, and Nankeen ditto, dark Worsted ribbed Stockings, Two Pair turned Pumps, with Iron Buckles.

Whoever will apprehend the said Servant, and contrive him [sic] to us at the Poor-house, about Three Miles from *Port-Tobacco*, in *Maryland*, shall have the above Reward, and if secured in any Jail so that we may get him, shall receive Eight Dollars Reward, paid by
WILLIAM CRAIGHI[L]L, & SPENCE MONROE.

The Maryland Gazette, January 16, 1772.

January 22d, 1772.

ON Sunday the 12th of this instant, came to the Subscriber in Queen Ann's county, Maryland, a stranger, under the pretence of a gentleman, and called himself WALTER DELANY, *jun.* and hired a black Horse to ride about 12 miles, with saddle, bridle, whip and loose coat, which he has carried off. This person is about thirty or forty years of age, five feet nine or ten inches high: He had on a red close bodied coat, light broadcloth waistcoat, leather breeches, a half worn castor hat, long black hair tied behind, and grey about the temples. The Horse is about seven years old, fourteen hands two or three inches high; has one white hind foot, hanging main, [sic] a long cut tail and a snip on his nose. Whoever takes up the said Horse, so as his master may get him again, shall have Forty Shillings reward; if they secure the Man, Three Pounds, paid by
THOMAS ELLIOTT HUTCHINGS.

N. B. He plays on the German flute; and he may perhaps go by another name.

The Pennsylvania Packet; and the General Advertiser, January 27, 1772; February 3, 1772; February 10, 1772.

THIRTY DOLLARS REWARD.

January 22, 1772.

RAN away from the Subscribers, living in *Fredericksburg, Virginia*, on Friday the 15th of *November* last, the Two following Convict Servants, both *Yorkshiremen*, (which may easily be discovered by their Dialect) *viz. Thomas Henry Enman*, alias *Eaman*, a Schoolmaster, has lost one of his

Eyes, which has a Mark all round it, had pretty long light Hair when he went away, but may probably cut it off: Had on, a light coloured Cloth Coat, red Jacket, with a striped lapelled one under it, and a Pair of black everlasting Breeches. *William Moor*, a Farmer, about Five Feet Nine or Ten Inches high, well set, full faced, with black curled Hair: Had on when he went away, a light coloured *Newmarket* Coat, blue Cloth Jacket, and Buckskin Breeches, a blue Bonnet [*sic*] bound round with blue Ribbon, which ties in a Rose Knot behind.

Whoever takes up and secures the said Servants, so as we get them again, shall have the above Reward, and reasonable Charges if brought home, paid by   HESLOP & BLAIR.

N. B. We suspect they are gone towards *Philadelphia*.

The Maryland Gazette, January 30, 1772; February 6, 1772; February 13, 1772; February 20, 1772; February 27, 1772.

FORTY SHILLINGS REWARD.

RUN AWAY from Mr. Richard Dallam's on Swan Creek, in Baltimore county, on Monday the 13th ult. a servant man belonging to the Subscriber, imported the last season from Dublin, middle aged, of low stature, well set, calls himself NEAL M'LACHLAND, a native of Ireland, and speaks much in that country dialect. Had on when he went away, a dark olive coloured cloth coat, with a brown cloth jacket, sheepskin breeches, ribbed stockings, and good shoes; he has also carried several other clothes with him. He wears his own hair, which appears very grey, and say, he lived several years in Philadelphia, with Mr. David Franks and Mr. John Reynolds, for the latter of which he drove a carriage, and professes that as his business. Whoever takes up the said servant, and secures him in any goal, so that his master may have him again, shall receive the above reward; and if brought home, reasonable charges by
AMOS GARRETT.

The Pennsylvania Packet; and the General Advertiser, February 3, 1772; February 10, 1772; February 17, 1772.

RUN away from the subscriber, living near the Head of Elk, in Caecil county, Maryland, on the 14th day of this instant February, a native Irish servant lad, named JOHN STANTON, about 17 years of age, about 5 feet 8 or 9 inches high, brown hair, and often wears it tied behind, talks with the brogue, is likely well looking lad when well, but has now the ague every third day; had on, or took with him, one large jacket of country made cloth, of a whitish colour, and 2 under jackets of striped lincey, one of them mixed with cotton, 2 or 3 pair of woollen stockings, two shirts, one of tow,

and the other of flax, a half worn felt hat, a pair of half worn shoes, which have been half soaled. Whoever takes up and secures said servant, so as his master may have him again, shall receive THIRTY SHILLINGS reward, and all reasonable charges, paid by BENJAMIN BRAVARD.
The Pennsylvania Gazette, February 20, 1772.

FIVE POUNDS Reward.

RUN away, on the 18th of January, 1772, from his special bail, in Caecil county, Maryland, a certain WILLIAM BROWN, about 27 years of age, a Weaver by trade, about 5 feet 8 or 9 inches high; had on, when he went away, a dark coloured coat, a mixed surtout ditto, and blue stockings; a down look, a fair complexion, very much inclined to gambling, and it is thought that he went towards Virginia, being followed as far as Skippack Town, Cumberland county, in Pennsylvania, by his bail, and found he had then changed his name from Brown to Johnson, and is rogue enough to change his clothes. Whoever apprehends the said William Brown, and secures him in any of his Majesty's goals, so as the subscriber may have proper notice of him, shall receive the above reward, and reasonable charges, paid by JOHN GUFFEY, *living near Charles-Town, Caecil county, Maryland.*
The Pennsylvania Gazette, February 27, 1772; April 4, 1772.

SIXTY POUNDS REWARD.

February 25, 1772.

RAN away from the Subscriber, living on *Little Pipe Creek,* in *Frederick* County, *Maryland,* the Five following Servant Men, viz.

EDWARD RYLOT, about 5 Feet 6 or 7 Inches high, pale yellow Countenance, straight black Hair and black Eyes, had One of his Ancles put out of Place, very bad sore Shins, and is about 27 Years of Age.

JOHN POLLARD, about 5 Feet 6 or 7 Inches high, middling clear Skin, down Look, gray Eyes, straight black Hair, a large Scar on his Breast which came by a Scald, about 25 Years old, and is well set.

JOHN BISSEY, about 5 Feet 6 or 7 Inches high, bold saucy Look, gray Eyes, straight black Hair, much pitted with the Small-Pox, and is about 22 Years of Age.

WILLIAM NORRIS, about 5 Feet 4 or 5 Inches high, a well set Fellow, fresh Countenance, Pot-belly'd, has a flat Nose and straight brown Hair.

HENRY WITMORE, about 5 Feet 4 or 5 Inches high, a slim Fellow, frown Skin, fresh Colour, black Eyes, and curled black Hair.

All the above Servants have on under Jackets of white Linsey, Breeches of white Kersey, white Yarn Stockings, Country made Shoes the bottoms of which are well nailed, and old Felt Hats; Three of them had on blue Fearnought Jackets, and Two had on white Kersey Jackets; they all had on coarse Country made Shirts. They took with them a new Felt Hat, Country Cloth great Coat, new gray Bearskin close body'd Coat, old white Cotton ditto, and an old Linen jacket. They took also 5 Horses, *viz* 4 Waggon Horses, and One black riding Horse and 15 Hands high, 3 Years old, has a Scar on his near Side with some white Hairs; the 4 are shod all round; One is a black Stallion, has some Saddle Spots, about 15 Hands high, and 11 Years old; One large bright bay, about 15 Hands and a Half high, 10 Years old, they both pace; One dark bay, about 14 Hands high, 9 Years old, branded **B. O.** on the near Buttock; One bright bay, 13 Hands and a half high, 7 Years old, they both trot.

Whoever takes up the said Servants and Horses shall be entitled to the above Reward under the following Conditions, *viz*. For each and every Horse 40 Shillings, and for each and every Man Four Pounds if taken within a Mile from Home, if taken within 100 Miles from Home 40 Pounds, and if taken within 200 Miles from Home 60 Pounds, as in Proportion for each Man and Horse. The above Reward to be paid if brought Home to the Subscriber, but if secured in any Jail, so that the Owner gets them again, Two Thirds of the above Reward shall be paid as above proportioned, by
EDWARD STEVENSON.

The Maryland Gazette, March 5, 1772; March 12, 1772; March 19, 1772; *The Pennsylvania Gazette,* March 12, 1772. Minor differences between the papers. See *Dunlap's Pennsylvania Packet or, the General Advertiser*, January 9, 1775, Bissey and Witmore are assumed to be Byset and Witmon. See *The Maryland Journal, and the Baltimore Advertiser*, August 2, 1775.

Cecil county, Maryland March 9th 1772.
THREE POUNDS REWARD.
THERE was stolen from the Subscriber, living at the head of Elk, by a certain THOMAS RING, a BLACK HORSE, about 15 hands high, has a long manE and tail, a small star in his forehead, is a natural pacer, and has a swelled nose from his eyes to his mouth. Said fellow is about 35 years of age, five feet, eight inches high, of a dark complexion, has short curled hair, and had on a light coloured surtout. Whoever secures the above mentioned thief and horse, shall have the above reward; or for the horse Thirty Shillings, and reasonable charges, by applying to
THOMAS BIDDLE.

The Pennsylvania Packet; and the General Advertiser, March 16, 1772; March 23, 1772; March 30, 1772.

BALTIMORE, *March 7th*, 1772.
THREE POUNDS REWARD.

RUN AWAY from the Subscriber, a Scotch servant woman, named ANN M'DONALL, about 40 years of age, has red hair, marked with the smallpox, and speaks in the Scotch dialect. Had on when she went away, a broad strip'd gown, strip'd lincey petticoat, an apron of the same of the gown, leather shoes with low heels, blue stockings, one tweelled [sic] linen shift, and one ditto country linen, with some other things not known: She had a child with her, about three years old, who also speaks in the Scotch dialect. Whoever takes up and secures said servant, so that her master may have her again, shall receive the above reward and reasonable charges paid by JAMES HOLLADAY. Or, JOHN JONES, in PHILADELPHIA.

The Pennsylvania Packet; and the General Advertiser, March 30, 1772; April 6, 1772; April 13, 1772. See *The Pennsylvania Chronicle, and Universal Advertiser*, From Monday, May 25, to Monday, June 1, 1772.

March 31, 1772.

RAN away from the Subscriber, living on *Great Senica*, in *Frederick* County, *Maryland*, on Friday the 27th Instant, a Convict Servant Man named THOMAS READY, about 5 Feet 3 or 4 inches high, of a fair Complexion, light Hair, about 25 Years of Age, the fore Finger of his left Hand is strait, occasioned by a Cut: Had on when he went away a German-Serge Coat of a mixed light Colour, a Waistcoat near the same, white Cotton Breeches with black Spots, much worn on the Knees and patch'd, One Pair of mixed Worsted Hose, One Pair of Country ditto, and a Halfworn Felt Hat; is a talkative Fellow and fond of Liquor He took with him a small HORSE, about 14 Hands high, a Star on his Forehead, about 10 Years old, paces, trots and gallops, branded on the near Buttock **CR**, and has a short Tail; a new English Saddle and strip'd Saddle-Cloth bound with green. Whoever takes up the said servant and Horse, and secures them as the Owner may have them again, shall receive Five Pounds Reward, or Fifty Shillings for either, and reasonable Charges of brought Home, paid by JOHN FORREST DAVIS.

N. B. He took a Cadder Blanket with him.

The Maryland Gazette, April 9, 1772; April 16, 1772.

FIVE POUNDS REWARD

April 13, 1772.

RAN away from the Subscriber, living in *Prince-George's* County, near *Bladensburg*, on the 31st Day of *March* last, The Two following Servants, viz.

THOMAS ELTON, a Convict Servant Man, about Five Feet Four Inches high, wears his own short black Hair, is of a swarthy Complexion, pretty much marked with the Small-Pox, and is a well made Fellow: Had on when he went away, an old blue Waistcoat, white Broadcloth Breeches, an Osnabrig Shirt, black Yarn Stockings, and a Pair of old Shoes nailed in the Soles, one of his great Toes is so sore that he cannot get his Foot into his Shoe; 'tis probable he may change his Dress.

WILLIAM HUGHS, a well made Country born young Fellow, about Nineteen Years of Age, Five Feet Nine Inches high, of a swarthy Complexion, wears his own short black Hair, is Beetle-browed, has black Eyes, and an ugly down Look: His Cloaths are unknown: He was whipped and pillory'd at Court about Three Weeks ago, for Stealing a Gun.

Whoever takes up said Servants, and brings them Home, or secures them so that their Master may get them again, shall receive the above Reward, or Fifty Shillings for either of them, paid by
CHARLES DUVALL.

N. B. It is presumed they will not go together, as they are unacquainted with each other.

The Maryland Gazette, April 16, 1772; April 23, 1772; April 30, 1772; May 7, 1772; May 14, 1772; May 21, 1772.

Chester-Town, Kent County, April 8, 1772.
BROKE Jail on Tuesday Night the 7th Instant, Three Prisoners committed for Debt, the one named *Joseph Corman,* middle aged, about Five Feet Nine or Ten Inches high, has a pert impudent Look, limps in his Walk, and stammers a little in his Speech, by Trade a Sawyer: Had on when he broke Jail, a Pair of Nankeen Breeches, Nankeen Coat, a striped Silk and Cotton Jacket, a lightish coloured Surtout of Bath Coating, almost new, a Pair of white worsted ribbed Stockings, old Shoes, Check Shirt, a brown Cut Wig, and a coarse Felt Hat, near Half worn; but it is probable he may change his Cloaths; it's thought he would make towards *George-Town,* and from thence to the *Jerseys:* Another named *Richard Skees,* a Country born, [sic] about Twenty-five Years of Age, Five Feet Nine or Ten Inches high, slim made, dark thin Visage, talks pert and bold: Had on when he broke Jail, a light coloured Sagothy or Shalloon Coat, much worn, an old blue Jacket patched with white, a Pair of light blue Worsted Stockings, a Pair of Pumps, a Pair of narrow rimmed Silver Buckles, has a very old flapped Hat, an old Pair of Leather Breeches, has long strait black Hair tied behind: The other named *James Floyed,* middle aged, down Look: Had on when he broke Jail, an old brown short Coat, a Calico Jacket, a Pair of green Cloth Breeches, a Pair of Osnabrig Trousers over the Breeches, his Beard is very red, and wears short brown Hair, by Trade a Flax Breaker.

Whoever takes up the abovementioned Persons, or either of them, and secures them in any Jail, so that they may be delivered to the Subscriber, shall have Three Pistoles Reward for *Corman* and *Skees* each, if taken out of the Province, and Fifty Shillings each, if taken within the Province, and Thirty Shillings for *Floyed*, paid by
THOMAS SMYTH, Sheriff.

The Maryland Gazette, April 16, 1772; April 23, 1772; April 30, 1772; May 14, 1772.

TEN POUNDS REWARD.

April 9, 1772.

BROKE out of the Cecil county goal, on Tuesday the 7th instant, ALEXANDER MORE and WILLIAM ARNETT, who were committed to my custody as criminals.—Moore is about 23 years of age, five feet eight or nine inches high. Had on when he went away, a greyish coat and jacket, leather breeches blue worsted stockings, and plain silver shoe buckles. Arnett is about twemty-five years of age, five feet ten inches high: Had on when he went away, a brown half-coat, leather breeches, and white stockings. Whoever secures and delivers them to the subscriber, shall have the above reward, or Five Pounds for each.
RICHARD THOMAS, Sheriff.

The Pennsylvania Packet; and the General Advertiser, April 20, 1772; April 27, 1772; May 11, 1772. See *The Maryland Gazette*, April 23, 1772.

TEN POUNDS REWARD.

April 9, 1772.

BROKE out of the *Caecil* County Jail on Tuesday the 7th Inst. *Alexander Moore*, and *William Arnett*, who were committed to my Custody as Criminals.—*Moore* is about 23 Years of Age, 5 Feet 8 or 9 Inches high: Had on, a grayish Coat and Jacket, Leather Breeches, blue Worsted Stockings, and plain Silver Buckles in his Shoes.—*Arnett* is about 25 Years of Age, 5 Feet 10 Inches high: Had on, a brown Half Coat, Leather Breeches, and white Stockings.—Whoever secures them, and delivers them to the Subscriber, shall have the above Reward, or Five Pounds for each.
RICHARD THOMAS, Sheriff.

The Maryland Gazette, April 23, 1772; April 30, 1772; May 7, 1772; May 14, 1772; May 28, 1772; June 4, 1772; June 11, 1772; June 18, 1772; June 25, 1772; July 2, 1772; July 9, 1772; July 16, 1772. See *The Pennsylvania Packet; and the General Advertiser*, April 20, 1772.

St. Mary's County, *March* 12, 1772.
COMMITTED to my Custody as a Runaway, *Reuben Fraugher*: Has on, a blue Jacket, Country Cloth Breeches, white Yarn Hose, and a Pair of old Shoes, is about 5 Feet 4 or 5 Inches high. His Master (if any) is desired to take him away, and pay Charges.
JENIFER TAYLOR, Sheriff.
The Maryland Gazette, April 16, 1772; April 23, 1772; April 30, 1772.

THIRTY DOLLARS REWARD.
Virginia, Fredericksburg, April 8, 1772.
RAN away on Monday Night the 6th Inst. from my Plantation, in *Culpepper*, near *Frederick Zimmerman's* Ordinary, an *English* Convict Servant Man, named JOHN BOCKER, about 33 Years old, 5 Feet 6 Inches high, narrow Visage, ruddy Countenance, a little pitted with the Small-Pox, dark Hair not tied, born in *Yorkshire*, speaks broad, fond of Liquor, and talkative; he has been near Two Years in the Country, a good Ditcher and Farmer: His Clothes consisted of a Frize Frock almost new, not lined, with flat Metal Buttons, cut in the Fashion with a Button and Strap to the Hip, his Breeches the same Cloth, but more wore, if any Jacket, an old black one, new Felt Hat, Yarn Stockings, Country Shoes tied with Strings, the Heels and Soles thick nailed.—Went off at the same Time with the above, another *English* Convict Servant Man, belonging to Mr. *William Allan*, adjoining to my Plantation, named THOMAS DRYBROW, a tall stout Fellow, full swarthy Face, which appears as if swelled or bloated, wears his own thick curled sandy coloured Hair: Had on and took with him, Two Osnabrig Shirts, a Pair of old brown Trousers, old Leather Breeches, coarse Kersey Fly Coat, and Metal Buttons, the Body lined with Plaid, an old blue Jacket without Sleeves, good Shoes, old Felt Hat, and Country white Yarn Hose, much wore; it is probable they may change Clothes with each other. The above Reward shall be paid to any Person who will deliver the said Servants to Mr. *Edward Stevens*, Merchant, at *Culpepper* Court-House, the Overseer of my Plantation, or to myself in *Fredericksburg*, or Fifteen Dollars if secured in any Jail, so we get them again, or in Proportion for either of them. JAMES DUNCANNSON.
The Maryland Gazette, April 23, 1770; April 30, 1772; May 7, 1772.

Prince-George's County, *February* 16, 1772.
COMMITTED to my Custody as a Runaway, a certain *Joseph Abair*, who says he is one of the *French* Neutrals, and a free Man. His Master (if he has one) is desired to take him away and pay Charges.

JOSEPH FORSTER, Sheriff.
The Maryland Gazette, April 16, 1772; April 23, 1772.

THIRTY SHILLINGS REWARD.

RAN away, on Monday the 13th of this instant, from the subscriber, living on Carroll's Manor, in the Fork of Gunpowder, a convict servant man, named JAMES SPARROW, about 5 feet 10 inches high, 33 years old, of a dark complexion, has short black hair, and has lost his right eye: Had on, an old felt hat, a cotton jacket, a great coat, of a lightish colour, with horn buttons, an old shirt, country made shoes, with strings in them, and a pair of stockings. Whoever takes up said servant, and secures him, so that his master may have him again, shall have *Twenty Shillings*, besides what the law allows; and if out of the county, the above reward of *Thirty Shillings*, besides what the law allows, and reasonable charges, paid by
April 13, 1772.   EDWARD BOSMAN.
The Pennsylvania Chronicle, From Monday, April 20, to Monday, April 27, 1772.

FIVE POUNDS REWARD.

RUN AWAY from the subscriber, living in Baltimore county, Miladas manor, Deer Creek Hundred, an English servant man, named RICHARD HINDMAN, about five feet eight inches high, thirty years of age, of a sandy complexion, with a pearl on one of his eyes, and has a down look. Had on when he went away, a white coloured surtout coat, a blue broadcloth coat lined with green, a scarlet lapelled jacket, buff coloured worsted breeches, good shoes and stockings, and plated buckles. He also took with him a Bay Mare, about 13 hands high, with saddle and bridle, and has a small strake of white over her nose. Whoever secures the said servant in any of his Majesty's goals, so that his master may receive him again, shall have the above reward and reasonable charges paid by
ALEXANDER ELLISON.
N. B. It is supposed he will change his name and apparel, and dispose of the mare.
The Pennsylvania Packet; and the General Advertiser, April 27, 1772; May 4, 1772; May 11, 1772.

FIFTEEN DOLLARS REWARD.
Baltimore, April 22, 1772.
RAN away about Fourteen Months ago, from the Subscriber's Plantation, in *Frederick* County, an *Irish* Servant Man named ANDREW DUNLOP, has

been some Years in the Country, since which he has come under Indenture; he is about 5 Feet 10 Inches high, has dark brown Hair tied behind, thin Visage and pale Complexion, talks much of his being a Soldier in the last War, is subject to drink and very impertinent: Had on, and took with him a Suit of brown Drab Cloth, old blue Camlet Coat and Jacket, old Castor Hat, Two Pair of Shoes, and sundry other Things unknown.

Whoever brings said Servant to his Master, living in *Baltimore-Town*, delivers him in Custody of the Sheriff of said County, shall receive the above Reward by
    MORDECAI GIST.

N. B. His Wife being a free Woman, has since gone off to him, and they have lately been heard of in *Pennsylvania*.

The Maryland Gazette, April 30, 1772; May 7, 1772; May 28, 1772; June 4, 1772. The second ad lacks the place and date at the top. See *The Pennsylvania Chronicle,* From Monday, September 30, to Monday, October 7, 1771.

FIVE POUNDS REWARD.

Head of Severn, April 27, 1772.

RAN away, on Sunday the 26th Instant, from the Subscribers, the Two following Convict Servants, *viz*. JOSEPH ADLEY, of a middle Size, a well made Fellow, wears his own Hair of a reddish Colour, red Beard, is about Thirty Years of Age: Had on and took with him a Snuff coloured Coat, white Shirt and white Linen Waistcoat, Buckskin Breeches, white ribbed Cotton Stockings, Two new turned Pumps, white Metal Buckles, and a half worn *Carolina* Hat. The other named JOSEPH WARD, a small pert impudent Fellow, his Hair is short and brown, and common keeps it tied, his Beard is very thin, he has lost the First Joint of his left Thumb: His Cloathing is a half worn blue Fearnought Waistcoat, a Pair of old Crocus Trousers, a Pair of old blue Stockings, a Pair of turned Pumps; it is probable he will change his Dress, as there are Cloaths missing; he is very fond of Liquor, and when attacked is very saucy. They had Plenty of Cash with them. Whoever takes up the above Servants and secures them in any Jail in the County shall have Thirty Shillings for each, if out of the County Forty Shillings, if out of the Province Fifty Shillings for each, and reasonable Charges if brought Home, paid by
 ABRAHAM WOODWARD, GILBERT YEALDHALL.

The Maryland Gazette, April 30, 1772.

FIVE POUNDS Reward.
RUN away from the subscriber, living at the head of Choptank River Branch, Queen Ann's county, Maryland, the 16th of this instant, a servant man, named JOHN TUTLE, about nineteen years of age, born in England, by trade a sweep chimney, but has not followed it these three or four years; he is a short fellow, about five feet three inches high, of a fair complexion, thin visage, has had the small-pox, but dont show it much, has light hair which reaches his shoulders, and when he laughs or opens his mouth, shews he has lost an under jaw tooth near his eye tooth; had on when he went away, a coarse homespun shirt, moss coloured jacket, breeches made of linsey woolsey, sheeps black stockings, and old shoes, with strings in them, all very ragged; he had also a coarse homespun linen cap on. Whoever takes up and secures said servant in any goal, so that his Master may see him to say, How do you John Tutle again? [sic] shall have the above reward, paid by THOMAS STECTHAM.

The Pennsylvania Gazette, April 30, 1772 See *The Pennsylvania Gazette*, March 29, 1775.

Gloucester County, New-Jersey, April 18th, 1772.
YESTERDAY was committed into my custody, two certain persons, one named JOHN MORPHEY, the other NICHOLAS HAMILTON, suspected to be runaways. They had with them two horses, and are supposed to belong to some person in Maryland or Virginia. Their masters, if any they have, are desired to come within three weeks from the date hereof, and pay charges and take them out, otherwise they will be sold for their charges. Any person to whom the horses belong, on proving their property and paying harges, [sic] shall have them again by applying to
RICHARD JOHNSON, Goaler.

The Pennsylvania Packet; and the General Advertiser, May 4, 1772; May 11, 1772.

TEN POUNDS Reward.
RUN away from the subscriber, living in Bladensburgh, on Sunday night last, a convict servant man, named *William Daniel Angess*, a Shoemaker by trade, an Englishman, about 5 feet high, aged 25 years, light brown hair, round face, dark hazel eyes, a very fair skin, and has a scar under the left knee, about the size of a round half dollar; is a pert spoken, square made man, and likely to behave with a great deal of assurance, if examined. Had on, when he went away, a brown jacket, made of coarse rough cloth, with turned up sleeves, and an under ditto, something lighter, with white metal buttons, and pale metal buckles; and had both pumps and shoes, with

yellow metal buckles; but may have changed his dress, and forged himself a pass, a practice he has used. Whoever shall take the above servant, and bring him to his matter, shall have the above reward; or if any body will give intelligence of him, so that he may be had again, shall receive Three Pounds, from
December 18, 1771. JOHN FRANCIS.

The Pennsylvania Gazette, May 7, 1772. See *The Maryland Gazette*, December 26, 1771 and *The Maryland Gazette*, January 9, 1772.

FOUR DOLLARS Reward.
RUN AWAY from the subscriber, living in Kent county, near the province Bridge, an apprentice lad, named JOSHUA REW, aged 17, about 5 feet 6 inches high; had on, and took with him, a lightish brown coat, of coating, an unfulled kersey jacket, with sleeves, a blue cloth jacket, without sleeves, old buckskin breeches, an oxenbrigs shirt, mixed blue yarn stockings, and a new felt hat. Whoever takes up and secures said servant, so that his master may have him again, shall have the above reward, and reasonable charges, paid by JOHN LEWIS.

N. B. He was born in Bucks county, but I suppose is gone to some part of Queen Anne. He is a well set fellow, but a remarkable sloven.

The Pennsylvania Gazette, May 7, 1772.

May 1, 1772.
RUN AWAY *from the subscriber, living in Baltimore county, between the 22d and 23d of February last, an English servant man, named BENJAMIN PENNY, about 5 feet 5 inches high, and about 35 years of age, he is a Plummer by trade, wears his own hair, has a scar on his face; it is probable he may forge a pass, and change his name. Whoever takes up the said servant man, and brings him to his said master, at Deep Creek Furnace, in Worchester county,* or CORBIN LEE, *Esq; at Nottingham Forge, in Baltimore county, Maryland, shall have a reward of FIFTY SHILLINGS, if taken in this province, and FOUR POUNDS reward, if taken out of the province, and all reasonable charges, paid by* JAMES SMITH.

The Pennsylvania Gazette, May 7, 1772.

Frederick County, *April* 30, 1772.
COMMITTED to my Custody as a Runaway, JOHN DOYL, about 5 Feet 5 Inches high, with black Hair and a long Beard; Has on, a Fearnought Coat, brown Jacket, a short Leather Apron, and Breeches of many Colours. He

says he came into *Philadelphia* with Capt. *Miller*. His Master is desired to take him away and pay Charges.
JAMES HACKMAN, Sheriff.
The Maryland Gazette, May 14, 1772; May 21, 1771; May 28, 1771.

TWENTY-FIVE POUNDS REWARD.
RAN away from the Subscriber, living near Mr. *James Brooke's* Mill, in *Frederick* County, about 20 Miles from *George-Town*, on 4th Instant, *May*, a Convict Servant Man, named WILLIAM WARD, about 22 Years of Age, 5 Feet 6 or 8 Inches high, well set, round Visage, short brown Hair tied behind: Had on and took with him, a blue Drugget or German Serge Coat, trimmed with yellow Metal Buttons, a light coloured Duroy Waistcoat, a Pair of Buckskin Breeches almost new, one Pair of Thread, and Two Pair of dark coloured Yarn Stockings, a Pair of old Shoes, one of them patched on the Side, odd Buckles, one brass and the other Steel, a Pair of Osnabrig Trousers, white Shirt, Two Handkerchiefs, one Linen and the other black Silk, a new coarse Felt Hat, and an Eight Dollar Bill; also a sorrel Horse, about 14 Hands and an Inch high, branded on the near Buttock and Shoulder PD, paces, trots and gallops with good Spirit, his hind Legs are white about half way, and has a large Blaze in his Face. Whoever delivers the said Servant and Horse to the Subscriber, or secures them so as he may get them again, shall receive the above Reward, or Twenty Pounds for the Servant only, and Five Pounds for the Horse, paid by
SAMUEL RIGGS.
The Maryland Gazette, May 14, 1772; *The Pennsylvania Gazette*, May 21, 1772; July 23, 1772. Minor differences between the papers.

Prince George's County, *May* 2, 1772.
COMMITTED to my Custody as Runaways, *Robert Campbell*, who says he had agreed to work his Passage to *Scotland* in a new Ship, Capt. *Miller*, in *Patowmack*, but that he belongs to the 14th Regiment of Foot, commanded by Col. *Dalrymple* at *Boston*. Negro *Prince*....Their Masters are desired to pay Charges and take them from
RALPH FORSTER, Sheriff.
If *Campbell* is not taken out in Two Months, he will be sold for his Fees.
The Maryland Gazette, May 14, 1772; May 21, 1772.

RAN away from the Ship *Molly, William Maynard* Commander, now lying at *Benedict*, Two indented Servant Men; the one named ROBERT CUMMINS, by Trade a Barber and Peruke maker, is about 5 Feet 8 Inches high, wears his own Hair of a light Colour tied behind: Had on when he went away, a dark brown Coat and Buckskin Breeches, and a Hat covered with Oilskin. The other named RICHARD JONES, by Trade a House Carpenter and Joiner, about the same Height as the former, wears his own dark Hair, and is pitted with the Small-Pox: Had on a light coloured Coat and dirty Buckskin Breeches. Whoever takes up the above Servants, and secures them in any Jail within this Province, shall receive Three Pounds Reward, or Thirty Shillings for either, besides what the Law allows; and if taken out of the Province Five Pounds for both, or in Proportion.
WILLIAM MAYNARD.

The Maryland Gazette, May 21, 1772; May 28, 1772; June 4, 1772; June 11, 1772; June 18, 1772; June 25, 1772; July 2, 1772; July 9, 1772; July 16, 1772; July 23, 1772; August 13, 1772; August 20, 1772; September 3, 1772.

THREE, FIVE, or SEVEN POUNDS Reward.

RUN away from the subscriber, near the Lower Cross-roads, Baltimore county, Maryland, the second day of May instant, a Convict Irish Servant Man, named WILLIAM DELANY, about 45 years old, about five feet eight or nine inches high, red hair, dark hollow eyes, has lost the most of his teeth, round shouldered, freckled hands, a round black mark between the thumb and fore finger of his right hand, thus O, bow legged, his ancles something swelled, large scars on his legs, and often sore, one large one on the outside of one of his legs, appears to be an old cut; had on when he went away, a plain brownish coat, and vest of the same, a tow and linen shirt, sheep-skin breeches, blush stockings, old shoes, a wool hat, bound with ferret; he has some money with him, and loves to drink. Any person taking up said servant in Maryland, and confining him in any goal, and giving notice thereof to his Master, so that he may have him again, shall have the above reward of THREE POUNDS, and all reasonable charges; if taken in Pennsylvania, the reward of FIVE POUNDS, on giving notice, and securing, as above; and if in New Jersey or New York Provinces, the reward of SEVEN POUNDS, on the above terms, paid by
May 21.   DAVID BARCLAY.

The Pennsylvania Gazette, May 21, 1772.

EIGHT DOLLARS Reward.

RAN away from the subscriber, on the 27th of April, a Convict Servant Man, named JAMES BROWN, about 5 feet 6 or 7 inches high, and appears to be about 35 or 36 years of age, is of a darkish complexion, has strait brown hair, thin visage, very much addicted to strong liquor, and chews tobacco to a great excess; had on and took with him, a felt hat, a greyish coloured cloth jacket, with sleeves, an under ditto of flowered flannel, white flannel breeches, ozenbrigs shirt, old shoes, with pinchbeck buckles; it is supposed he will change his name and clothes. Whoever takes up said servant, and secures him in any goal in this province, shall have FORTY SHILLINGS reward, with reasonable charges, if brought home; if out of the province, THREE POUNDS, with reasonable charges, paid by WILLIAM GRAHAM, in Market-street, Philadelphia, or by me RICHARD GRAHAM, junior, living in Baltimore county, Maryland.

N. B. It is supposed he will write a pass, as he is a very ready clerk.

Baltimore County, May 16, 1772

The Pennsylvania Gazette, May 21, 1772.

May 27, 1772.

COMMITTED to *Anne-Arundel* County Jail, William *Gullokey*, a Lad about 18 Years of Age, says he came into *Patapsco* in Capt. *Miller* [sic] from *Ireland*, and belongs to *James Duke*, living in *Frederick*, who is desired to take him away and pay Charges to

JOHN CLAPHAM, Sheriff.

The Maryland Gazette, May 28, 1772.

Baltimore, May 14, 1772.

RAN away, from the subscriber, a Scotch servant woman, named ANN M'DANIEL, about 40 years of age, speaks much in the Scotch dialect, has red hair, and is pock-marked: Had on, when she went away, a check gown, with broad striped, stripe linsey petticoat, and a blue linsey bed gown, with some other clothes, not known what sort.—She is a good spinner, of wool or flax, and it is thought will go about either begging or spinning. She took with her a child about three years of age, speaks much in the same dialect. Whoever takes up said woman, and secures her, so that her master may have her again, shall receive the reward of TWENTY SHILLINGS, and reasonable charges, if brought home, paid by

JAMES HOLLIDAY, Shoemaker.

N. B. As she is an old offender, it is hoped that any honest person knowing her will take her up.

The Pennsylvania Chronicle, and Universal Advertiser, From Monday, May 25, to Monday, June 1, 1772; From Monday, June 1, to Monday, June 8, 1772; From Monday, June 8, to Monday, June 15, 1772. See *The Pennsylvania Packet; and the General Advertiser,* March 30, 1772.

RAN away from the Subscriber the 20th of *May*, from the Ferry opposite *Alexandria, Maryland*, an *Irish* Servant Man named JOHN MATTHEWS, about 5 Feet high, of a fair Complexion and black Hair: Had on when he went away an old brown Coat, blue Pea Jacket, Drilling Breeches, gray Stockings, old Shoes, and a half worn Felt Hat. Whoever takes him up and secures him in any Jail, so that his Master may get him again, shall receive Three Pounds Reward, paid by
JOHN CLIFFORD.
The Maryland Gazette, June 4, 1772; June 11, 1772; June 18, 1772; June 25, 1772.

Fredericksburg, May 26, 1772.
RAN away on the 20th Instant, a Servant Woman named MARY CLARK, born in *Scotland*, talks very broad, is well set, has brown Hair, a fresh Complection, is subject to Fits, and is about 23 Years of Age: Had on when she went away a brown Linen Petticoat, a blue Country Cloth ditto, and a dark County Cloth Bed-gown filled in with black Yarn. She is gone off with a Servant Woman belonging to *Lewis Jones*, named MARGARET JOE, her Shipmate of the same Age and Country, pale Complection, and brown Hair; she has robbed her Mistress of sundry wearing Apparel: Had on when she went away a Check Bonnet and blue Calimanco Shoes. As they are gone together, it is probable they will change their Cloaths and endeavour to get on Board some Vessel, therefore I forwarn all Masters of Vessels from concealing them. I will give 40 Shillings for the Two, or 20 Shillings for each, besides what the Law allows, for securing them in any Jail, so that I may get them again. JOHN BAGGOTT.
The Maryland Gazette, June 4, 1772; June 18, 1772; June 25, 1772.

June 10, 1772.
RAN away last Night from the Subscriber, living near *Snowden's* Iron Works, in *Anne-Arundel* County, a Convict Servant Man, named JOHN TINK, a well set Fellow, about 22 Years of Age, of a pale Complexion, short brown curled Hair: Had on and took away with him, Two Osnabrig Shirts, Two Pair of Osnabrig Trousers, a strip'd Holland Jacket, Two Pair

of Shoes, a Castor Hat, and also an Indenture in a Pocket-Book, and some other Papers of *Marmaduke Pindelbury's*; it is very probable he will pass by that Name.—Whoever takes up the said Servant, and secures him in any Jail, so that his Master may get him again, shall receive Six Dollars, (besides what the Law allows) paid by
HENRY GRIFFITH, junr.
The Maryland Gazette, June 11, 1772; June 18, 1772; June 25, 1772.

Annapolis, June 11, 1772.
RAN away from the Subscriber, living near *Annapolis*, an indented Servant Man, named DONALD CLARK, a *Scotchman*, has been used to the Sea: Had on such Cloaths as Sailors generally wear, and has remarkable crooked Legs, occasioned by their being broke.—Whoever takes up and secures said Servant, so that his Master gets him again, shall have Forty Shillings Reward, besides what the Law allows, paid by
THOMAS WALKER.
The Maryland Gazette, June 11, 1772; June 18, 1772; June 25, 1772.
See *The Maryland Gazette*, July 11, 1771

TEN POUNDS REWARD.
June 9, 1772.
RAN away on the 18th of *May* last from the Subscriber, on *Elk-Ridge*, in *Anne-Arundel* County, *Maryland*, a Servant Man, named JOHN HAGGET, Five Feet Eight or Ten Inches high, about Twenty-four Years of Age, ruddy Complexion, a little pitted with the Small-Pox, black Hair: Had on and took with him, a new Castor Hat, a white Linen Shirt, an Osnabrig ditto, a white Country Cloth Jacket half worn, One ditto, the Fore-Parts brown Velvet, the Hind-parts light coloured Cloth, a Pair of brown German Serge Breeches, a Pair of strip'd Holland Trousers, a Pair of blue Worsted Stockings, a Pair of Thread ditto, a Pair of turned Pumps, a Pair of large white Metal Buckles, and a Country Linen Bag; it's supposed he is gone down the Bay in a Shallop. Whoever secures the said Servant, so that I get him again, shall receive if taken within Forty Miles of home Five Pounds, if upwards of Forty Miles, the above Reward, and reasonable Charges paid if brought home. JAMES HOWARD.
The Maryland Gazette, June 11, 1772.

RUN away, on the 17th of May, 1772, from the subscriber, at the Head of Chester river, in Kent county, Maryland, an English servant man, named TIMOTHY SMALLY, about 35 years of age, 4 feet 10 inches high, fair

hair, pitted with the small pox; had on, and took with him, a light blue saggathy coat, a green lappelled vest, tied with yellow ferritting, half worn sheepskin breeches, a pair of coarse yarn milled hose, half worn shoes, with buckles, a large half worn beaver hat, commonly wore it cocked up, one ozenbrigs shirt; he is fond of company, and delights much in singing, and, is examined, will appear much confused. Whoever takes up said servant, and secures him in any goal, so that the owner may have him again, shall have a reward of THIRTY SHILLINGS, and reasonable charges, paid by THOMAS JUREY.
The Pennsylvania Gazette, June 11, 1772; July 29, 1772.

Chester Town, May 21, 1772.
THREE POUNDS Reward.
RUN away from his bail, in Chester-Town, Kent county, Maryland, JOHN BARNHOLD, *a Butcher by trade, he is about 5 feet 6 or 7 inches high, thin, lively complexion, and has lost his fore finger from his left hand, born in Germany, but brought up in or near Philadelphia, where it is supposed he is gone. Whoever apprehends the said fellow, and secures him in any of his Majesty's goals, shall have the above reward; but if brought to his bail, shall have FIVE POUNDS.*
WILLIAM GEDDES.
The Pennsylvania Gazette, June 11, 1772.

June 17, 1772.
RAN away from the Subscriber, on the 15th Instant, an indented Servant Man named JOHN BRAND, a short thick Fellow, about 5 Feet high, short black Hair, very much pitted with the Small-Pox, and his right Eye very red: Had on, an Osnabrig Shirt and Trousers, Country made Shoes, an old Felt Hat, and Cotton Jacket; is supposed to have taken with him a brown Cloth Jacket with Mohair Buttons; and professes to be a Seinemaker and Groom. Whoever takes up the above Servant, and secures him, so as his Master may have him, shall receive a Reward of One Pistole, and all reasonable Charges, paid by
STEPHEN STEWARD.
The Maryland Gazette, June 18, 1772; June 25, 1772; July 2, 1772; July 9, 1772; July 16, 1772; July 23, 1772; July 30, 1772.

Charles County, *Maryland, June* 16, 1772.
COMMITTED to my Custody, as a Runaway, a white Man, by the Name of *John Buck*, but since his Commitment says his true Name is *John Caton*,

and that he belongs to *Peter Rufner*, in *Frederick* or *Augusta* County in *Virginia*. His Dress is a blue Coat, Calico lapelled Jacket, white Shirt, with a Broach in it, and Osnabrig Trousers. He is pitted with the Small-Pox, has light Hair, and says he is about Twenty Years of Age. His Master is desired to pay Charges, and take him from
GEORGE LEE, Sheriff.
The Maryland Gazette, June 25, 1772; July 2, 1772; July 9, 1772.

June 22, 1772.
RAN away from the Subscriber, living on *Elk-Ridge*, in *Anne-Arundel* County, and Province of *Maryland*, an *Irish* Convict Servant named *Lawrence Robertson*; appears to be about 16 or 17 Years of Age, slim made, about 5 Feet 8 Inches high, swarthy Complexion, thin Visage, dark brown Hair, his Apparel but mean. Whoever secures the said Servant, and brings him Home, shall have a Reward of 20 Shillings if taken within 20 Miles, 30 Shillings if 30 Miles, and if a greater Distance 50 Shillings, besides what the Law allows.
JOHN DORSEY.
The Maryland Gazette, June 25, 1772; July 2, 1772; July 9, 1772; July 16, 1772; July 23, 1772; July 30, 1772.

Baltimore county, Maryland, June 26, 1772.
RUN away the 20th instant, an English convict servant man, named THOMAS LOVELY, about 6 feet high, and well made, red complexion, red haired, wears it tied behind, also red bearded; had on, when he went away, a half worn felt hat, a country made cloth jacket, of a lightish colour, with sleeves and cuffs to it, the lining all wore out of it, linen shirt and trowsers, the trowsers mended before with new linen, half worn pumps, with pewter buckles; he stole a bridle, and it is expected he will steal a horse, and is intending for Frederick road. Said fellow was in the army in England and is a good drummer, and can play on several instruments of music. Whoever takes up said servant, and secures him in any of his Majesty's goals, so as his master may get him again, shall have FORTY SHILLINGS reward, and if out of the province THREE POUNDS, and reasonable charges, if brought home, paid by ANDREW MEEK, living within 3 miles of the Lower Ferry, on Susquehanna.
The Pennsylvania Gazette, July 2, 1772; July 16, 1772; July 29, 1772.

EIGHT DOLLARS REWARD.
RUN AWAY on the 15th of June, from the Subscriber, living at my Lady's manor, near St. John's Chapel, Fork Gunpowder, Maryland, an indented

servant man, named GEORGE BURN, between 20 and 30 years of age, 5 feet 6 inches high, of a fair complexion, has a scar across his nose, and his head shaved. Had on and took with him, two dark coloured wigs, one curl'd and the other cut; a felt hat half worn; a country cloth coat, of a light colour, lined with homespun white flannel, with white metal buttons; a short blue jacket; old buckskin breeches; a holland shirt and two country linen ditto; country trowsers, much worn; country shoes and pinchbeck buckles. Whoever takes up said servant, if ten miles from home Fifteen Shillings; if twenty miles Thirty; if out of the county Forty, and if out of the Province the above reward, and reasonable charges if brought home, paid by
THOMAS GALLOWAY.

The Pennsylvania Packet; and the General Advertiser, July 6, 1772; July 20, 1772.

Annapolis, July 7, 1772.
RAN away from the Subscriber, on the 5th Instant, an indented Servant Man named JOHN BROOKS, upwards of 30 Years of Age, of a dark Complexion, black Hair and black Beard, a long Chin, and is a Barber by Trade: Had on when he went away a Drugget Coat and Felt Hat, the rest of his Cloaths unknown. Whoever secures the said Servant in any Jail, that his Master may get him again, shall receive a Reward of three Pounds and reasonable Charges, paid by
JAMES REID.

The Maryland Gazette, July 9, 1772.

Prince-George's County, *June* 30, 1772.
BROKE JAIL,
On the Night of Wednesday the 10th *Instant, and the following Prisoners escaped, viz.*
JAMES SMITH, a stout Fellow, about 40 Years of Age, a Butcher by Trade, and has but One Hand, used formerly to row in the Ferry-Boat over *Severn* from *Annapolis*.

ROBERT CAMPBELL, about 25 or 30 Years of Age, 5 Feet 5 or 6 Inches high, has a Scald Head, and wears sometimes a marine Cap of the *Royal George* Man of War, and plays a little on the Fife.

JOHN EARLS, a tall raw-boned Fellow, of a very swarthy Complexion, 25 Years old or thereabouts—Their Dress is uncertain. I will five 10 Dollars Reward for *Smith*, and 20 Shillings Current Money for *Campbell* and *Earls*, if secured in any Jail, so that I may get them again, and reasonable Charges if brought home to
RALPH FORSTER,

Sheriff of *Prince-George's* County.

Committed as Runaways, *Alexander Downey* and *Henry Bayley*, Sailors, and they say free Men, are willing to enter on Board any Ship whose Commander they can agree with, for which Purpose they were travelling from *Virginia*, not knowing it was necessary to have a Pass. They are clean looking Men, and have much the Appearance of Seamen.
R. F.
The Maryland Gazette, July 9, 1772.

THREE POUNDS REWARD.

Frederick County, *June* 18, 1772.

RAN away from the Subscriber, the 16th Instant, an *Irish* Servant Man named PATRICK CANNON, between 40 and 45 Years of Age, about 6 Feet high, gray Hair, and a remarkable crooked Finger on his right Hand: Had on a Claret colour'd Jacket, a strip'd flannel Waistcoat, a blue cotton Jacket, white Plush Breeches, Two Osnabrig Shirts, One Check ditto, Two Hats, Three Pair of Stockings, Crocus Trousers, and some other Cloathing. It is suspected he has a Pass, and it is probable he will change his Cloathing. He pretends to speak bad *English*. Whoever takes up the said Servant, and secures him so as his Master may get him again, shall receive the above Reward, and reasonable Charges if brought Home, paid by
CHARLES PERRY.
The Maryland Gazette, July 9, 1772; July 16, 1772; July 30, 1772.

Kent County, Maryland, July 8, 1772.

RUN away on the 20th of last month, from the subscriber, an indented servant man, named WILLIAM VICKERS, born in Talbot county, Maryland, about 40 years of age, 5 feet 9 or 10 inches high, thin visage, has lost one of his eyes; he is very apt to get drunk, whenever he can get strong liquor; he has been some years a Soldier, in the Royal Americans : Had on, when he went away, a coarse brown jacket, with sleeves, ozenbrigs shirt and trowsers, a felt hat, about half worn, but as he had some money with him it is thought he has changed his clothes, and his name. Whoever takes up and secures said servant, so that the subscriber may get him again, shall have the above reward, and if brought home, reasonable charges, paid by
ISAAC PERKINS.
The Pennsylvania Gazette, July 16, 1772; July 29, 1772; September 2, 1772; September 16, 1772; September 23, 1772; October, 28, 1772.

RUN AWAY *June* 12, 1772, *from the subscriber, living in George-Town, Kent county, Maryland, an apprentice lad, named* DANIEL JACKSON, *about* 16 *years of age, dark complexion, and dark brown hair, about* 5 *feet* 4 *or* 5 *inches high, slim built, had a down look; had on, when he went away, a dark brown cloth jacket, made sailor fashion, and a pair of kersey trowsers, of the same colour. Whoever apprehends and secures the said apprentice lad, shall have a reward of* FOUR DOLLARS, *and all reasonable charges, paid by* THOMAS BIVENS.

The Pennsylvania Gazette, July 16, 1772; July 29, 1772.

TEN POUNDS REWARD.

July 20, 1772.

RAN away last Night from the Subscribers, near the Head of *Rock-Creek*, *Frederick* County, *Maryland*, Two Irish Convict Servant Men, *viz*.

PATRICK DUFFEE, about 35 Years of Age, 5 Feet 7 or 8 Inches high, a thick set Fellow, red Complexion, short black Hair, and has a Blemish in one of his Eyes: Had on an old *Russia* Drab Coat and Breeches, Osnabrig Shirt, Felt Hat, and Country made Shoes and Stockings. He has been in the Country about Eight Months.

THOMAS MARTIN, 25 Years of Age (about the same Heighth of *Patrick Duffee*, though not so lusty), dark Complexion, black Eyes, short black Hair, and is marked with the Small-Pox: Had on and took with him Two Osnabrig Shirts, Country Linen Trousers, old blue worsted Stockings, half worn Shoes, dark coloured Pea Jacket, striped Flannel ditto, and a new Felt Hat. He has been in the Country about Six Weeks.

Whoever takes up the said Servants, and secures them, so that their Masters may get them again, shall receive the above Reward, or Five Pounds for either of them, and reasonable Charges if brought Home, paid by JOHN BAKER, BASIL BROOKE.

The Maryland Gazette, July 23, 1772.

RAN away from the Subscriber near the City of *Annapolis*, on the 26th Day of this Inst. *July*, a Convict Servant Man, named GEORGE BATHUM, about 5 Feet 5 Inches high, born in the West of *England*, a thick set Fellow, of a ruddy Complexion, and short black Hair: Had on, when he went away, a Felt Hat about half worn, an Osnabrig Shirt and Crocus Trousers; he is very much addicted to Liquor, and when drunk is very impudent. Whoever takes up and secures the said Servant, so that he may be had again, if taken up out of the County shall have 3 Pounds Currency, if 20 Miles from Home 40 Shillings, if 10 Miles 30 Shillings, and if within 10 Miles 20 Shillings, and all reasonable Charges if brought Home, paid by

SAMUEL HOWARD.
The Maryland Gazette, July 30, 1772.

FORTY DOLLARS REWARD.
RAN away from the Subscriber, living on *Morgan's Run*, near *Little Pipe Creek* in *Baltimore* County, *Maryland*, an *Irish* Convict Servant Man, named JAMES RILEY, about 30 Years of Age, a stout well set Fellow, about 5 Feet 9 or 10 Inches high, round shouldered, short sandy coloured Hair trimmed on the Top of his Head, red Beard, gray Eyes, down Look, slow in Speech, and has lost the little Finger of his left Hand: Had on and took with him, a light mixed coloured Broad Cloth Coat with yellow Buttons, which has been turned and the Pockets moved from the Side to the Folds, Leather Breeches patched in the Crotch, a Holland Shirt and Jacket, a Pair of Thread Stockings, a Pair of white Worsted ditto, black in the Grain Shoes with plain Silver Buckles, Felt Hat trimmed round the Edge, black Barcelona Stock with a plain Copper Buckle. Whoever takes up the said Servant, shall have, if taken 50 Miles from Home 3 Pounds, if 100 Miles 5 Pounds, if 150 Pounds 7 Pounds ten Shillings, if 200 Miles 10 Pounds, and if 300 Miles the above Reward (including what the Law allows) if brought Home, paid by   RICHARD OWINGS, Son of Samuel.
  The Maryland Gazette, August 6, 1772; August 20, 1772; September 3, 1772; October 1, 1772; October 8, 1772; October 15, 1772. See *The Maryland Gazette*, June 30, 1774 for Riley.

Patuxent Iron-Works, *August* 3, 1772.
RAN away from the Subscribers last Night, Six *English* Servant Men, just imported in the Ship *Friendship*, Captain *James Nesbitt*.—*Thomas Bevers*, a likely well made Fellow, about Six Feet high: Had on, and took with him, a blue Coat and Jacket, white Linen Shirt, Russia Drab Breeches, Thread Stockings, a Pair of Shoes with Silver Buckles, and a Felt Hat, about Twenty-five Years of Age.—*John Oliver*, a lusty well made Fellow, about Six Feet high: Had on, and took with him, a brown Coat and Breeches, Thread Stockings, Irish Linen Shirt, a Pair of Shoes with plated Buckles, Felt Hat, about Twenty-six Years of Age, and is very talkative.—*James Cookman*, a lusty Fellow, about Five Feet Ten Inches high: Had on, and took with him, a striped Gingham Jacket, white Linen Shirt, Buckskin Breeches, blue Worsted Stockings, a Pair of Shoes, and Felt Hat. *John Barrowcliff*, a well made Fellow, about Five Feet Nine Inches high: Had on, and took with him, a blue Pea Jacket, Osnabrig Shirt, Cloth Breeches, Thread Stockings, a Pair of Shoes, and Felt Hat.—*Francis Stoakes*, a lusty Fellow, about Five Feet Eleven Inches high: Had on, and took with him, a

light coloured Broad Cloth Coat, Buckskin Breeches, Worsted Stockings, a Pair of Shoes, and Castor Hat.—*Jeremiah Pollingbrook*, a middle Size Fellow, about Five Feet Eight Inches high: Had on and took with him, a dark coloured Coat and Jacket, white Linen Shirt, Fustian Breeches, Worsted Stockings, and Felt Hat.

Whoever take [sic] up the above Servants, and delivers them to the Subscribers, shall receive if Ten Miles from Home, Twenty Shillings; if Twenty Miles, Thirty Shillings; if Thirty Miles, Fifty Shillings; and if out of the Province, Five Pounds for each, and reasonable Charges if brought home, paid by
THOMAS SNOWDEN, & RICHARD CRABB.

N. B. It is supposed the above Servants have some Cash, and sundry Cloaths unknown.

The Maryland Gazette, August 6, 1772. See *The Maryland Gazette*, July 21, 1774, for Cookman.

RAN away from the Subscriber, living about 10 Miles from *Bladensburg*, a Convict Servant Man named THOMAS BAILEY, about 27 Years of Age, 5 Feet 8 Inches high, fair Complexion, light coloured short Hair, speaks pretty broad, and has a Scar on one of his Arms: Had on and took with him when he went away, a Holland Shirt pretty fine, an Osnabrig ditto, a striped Lincey Jacket, a brown Cloth ditto, both without Sleeves, an old brown Cloth Coat much torn, a Linen Frock much daubed with Tar, a Pair of old black Cloth Breeches torn at the Knees, 2 or 3 Pair of old Yarn Stockings, a small felt Hat, a Pair of new Shoes, old ditto with Hobnails in the Heels, a Pair of Brass Shoe-Buckles, and a Pair of plated ditto. Whoever secures the said Servant, so that his Master gets him again, if taken up in Prince-George's County, shall have 20 Shillings, if out of the County 40 Shillings, and if 50 Miles from Home 50 Shillings, and if out of the Province Three Pounds, paid by   CHRISTOPHER HYTCH.

The Maryland Gazette, August 6, 1772; August 20, 1772; September 3, 1772.

THREE POUNDS Reward.
WHEREAS a certain John Tittle, of Baltimore Town, Maryland, was intrusted with a Parcel of Tin Ware to sell, together with a Mare to carry them, and the said Tittle having disposed of all the Tin Ware and Mare, at Charlestown, in the Province of Maryland, and not returning, agreeable to Expectation, the Subscriber therefore offers the above Reward to any Person who will secure him in any of his Majesty's Goals: He is between 30 and 40 Years of Age, about 5 Feet 9 or 10 Inches high, stout made, but

not lusty, wears his own short dark Hair, and one of his little Fingers crooked: He has chang'd his Dress to a blue and white striped Holland Banyan and Jacket: He was seen at Wilmington, with a Pair of Saddle Bags almost full; was likewise seen to go through Pennsylvania and the Jerseys, and assumes the Name of Folks, and says he is Brother to Mr. Folks the noted Performer in Horsemanship. Whoever secures him, so that he may be brought to Justice, shall have the above Reward, with reasonable Charges, from William Bowen, Tinman, at Baltimore Town, or Thomas Russell, Blacksmith, at Princetown, in the Jerseys.

The New-York Gazette; and the Weekly Mercury, August 10, 1772; August 17, 1772; August 24, 1773.

Caecil county, Maryland, August 1, 1772.
WHEREAS *MATTHEW SEDGWICK* has absconded from his special bail, in an action brought in the Provincial Court of this province, we, the subscribers, who are his bondsmen, do engage the reward of TEN POUNDS to any person who may take up and secure said *Sedgwick*, so that he may be rendered up in discharge of his bail. Said *Sedgwick* is about 45 years of age, and about 5 feet 10 inches high; had on, when he went away, a blue coat, of country cloth, and jacket of the same, without sleeves, pretty fine, half-worn striped linen trousers, new 800 linen shirt, no stockings, half-worn shoes, with brass buckles, and a coarse half-worn hat. He went away the 13th day of July, and is supposed to be gone towards Philadelphia.
ANDREW BARROT, ARTHUR ALEXANDER.

The Pennsylvania Gazette, August 12, 1772.

Head of Elk, August 2, 1772.
EIGHT DOLLARS REWARD.
RUN away from the subscriber, the 27th of July last, an indented servant man, named WILLIAM ABBOT, about 22 years of age, 5 feet 5 inches high, or thereabouts, his hair of a light brown, his complexion rather tawny, he was born in Middlesex, and pretends to have been some time in the smuggling trade; is very fond of strong liquor, his disposition savage, and is very abusive in his language; had on, when he went away, a new felt hat, country shirt and trowsers, a good homespun cloth jacket, of an ash colour, in the back of which are some dark stripes, old shoes, and large brass buckles. Whoever takes up and secures said servant, so that his master may have him again, shall receive *Three Pounds* reward, and reasonable charges, if brought home, from   HENRY HOLLINGSWORTH.

All masters of vessels, and others, are forbid to carry him off, or to harbour him, at their peril.

The Pennsylvania Gazette, August 12, 1772. See *The Pennsylvania Packet; and the General Advertiser*, August 17, 1772, and *The Pennsylvania* Gazette, July 7, 1773.

Patuxent Furnace, *August* 11, 1772.
WENT away a few Days since from the Subscriber, an English Convict Servant Man, named *Jeremiah Boythroid*, about 25 Years of Age, 5 Feet 7 or Inches high, has a ruddy Complexion, and short sandy Hair: Had on, and took with him, when he went away, several white Linen Shirts, a brown Cloth Coat and Waistcoat, Linen Breeches, Felt Hat, blue worsted Stockings, and tolerable good Shoes, with plated Buckles.—Whoever takes up said Servant, shall be paid on delivering him at the *Patuxent* Furnace, if taken within 20 Miles from home, 30 Shillings; if 30 Miles, 40 Shillings; and if 50 Miles, 5 Pounds; (including what the Law allows) paid by me
RICHARD CRABB.

N. B. He had Money with him, and it's not improbable but he may get other Apparel.

The Maryland Gazette, August 13, 1772.

EIGHT DOLLARS REWARD.

RAN away from the Subscriber, living on *Elk-Ridge*, on Sunday the 9th of this Inst. the Two following Servant Men, *viz.* JOHN MEAVIS, a Convict, by Trade a Weaver, about Six Feet high, black Hair tied behind, pale Complexion, and a remarkable down look, bow legged, and limps in his Walk: Had on, a brown Country Cloth Jacket, with mettle Buttons, and one at each Hip, Osnabrig Shirt, and Country Linen Trousers, half worn, old Shoes, and Block Tin Buckles.—DAVID BRUCE, a *Scotch* indented Servant Man, by Trade a Weaver, about Five Feet Two or Three Inches high, black Hair tied behind: Had on, an Osnabrig Shirt, and Country Linen Trousers, old fulled Country Cloth Jacket, with plain Metal Buttons.— Whoever takes up the said Servants, and brings them home, shall receive the above Reward, and reasonable Charges, paid by
JOHN GAITHER, senr.

The Maryland Gazette, August 13, 1772.

THREE POUNDS REWARD.
Fredericksburg, June 16, 1772.

RAN away from the Subscriber, on Tuesday the 9th Inst. a Convict Servant Man, named *William Jenkins*, by Trade a Cabinetmaker, he is about Forty-five Years of Age, about Five Feet One or Two Inches high, is of a fair Complexion, wears his own Hair, which is short and gray: He carried with him, an old dark gray Kersey Coat, Osnabrig Shirt and Trousers; as he has been on board several of his Majesties Ships, he will very likely endeavour to get on board some Vessel as a Sailor. Whoever takes up the said Servant, and conveys him to me, shall have the above Reward.
THOMAS MILLER.

The Maryland Gazette, August 13, 1772; September 3, 1772; October 1, 1772.

Fredericksburg, August 4, 1772.
RAN away from the Subscriber, the 11th of *July* last, a Convict Servant Man, named *James Buchannan*, by Trade a Tailor, he is a thick well set Fellow, about Five Feet Five Inches high, sandy Hair, and his Face much freckled: He had on, when he went away, a light coloured mixt Broadcloth Coat lappeled, a Waistcoat nearly the same Colour, with welted Pockets, a new furred Hat; the Rest of his wearing Apparel I cannot describe, he having different Changes.—Whoever takes up the said Convict, and secures him in any of his Majesty's Jails in *Maryland*, so that I may have him again, shall receive Forty Shillings Reward, or if brought to me in *Fredericksburg*, shall have Three Pounds, paid on Delivery, by me
WILLIAM PAUL.

N. B. I am credibly informed he was carried from here, by one *William Williams*, a Waterman, to *Great Wiccomico*.

The Maryland Gazette, August 13, 1772; August 27, 1772; September 10, 1772; September 24, 1772.

Octarara Hundred, Cecil county, Maryland, Aug. 10, 1772.
WHEREAS a certain JOHN NEILSON, labourer, came, on the 5th of this instant, to the house of DENNIS M'FADING, with a pretended token from his son (who was at some distance at the time) and received and carried off the following CLOTHES, viz. one Wilton coat, of a light mixture, lined all through with durant, and has a spot of tar on the right elbow; one red, yellow and white damascus waistcoat; one pair of linen breeches; one pair of thread stockings; one fine shirt, with broad turn up wristbands; and a beaver hat.—He is about 5 feet 4 inches high, and has dark-coloured hair. Whoever takes up and secures said NEILSON, so that he may be brought to justice, shall have FORTY SHILLINGS reward, and reasonable charges, paid by

PATRICK M'FADING.
The Pennsylvania Chronicle, From Saturday, August 8, to Saturday, August 15, 1772; From Saturday, August 15, to Saturday, August 22, 1772; From Saturday, August 22, to Saturday, August 29, 1772.

EIGHT DOLLARS REWARD.
RUN AWAY from the Subscriber, living at the Head of Elk, on the 27th of July last, an indented servant man, named WILLIAM ABBOT, about 22 years of age, five feet five inches high, has light brown hair, of a brown or tawny complexion, and was born in Middlesex; he pretends to have been some time in the smuggling trade, is very fond of strong liquor, has a savage disposition, and is very abusive in his language. Had on when he went away, a new felt hat, country linen shirt and trowsers, a good homespun cloth jacket of an ash colour, in the back of which are some dark stripes, old shoes with large brass buckles. Whoever takes up and secures said servant, so that his master may have him again, shall receive the above reward, and reasonable charges, if brought home, paid by
HENRY HOLLINGSWORTH.
N. B. All masters of vessels, and others, are forbid to harbour or carry him off, at their peril.
The Pennsylvania Packet; and the General Advertiser, August 17, 1772; August 24, 1772. See *The Pennsylvania Gazette*, August 12, 1772, and *The Pennsylvania* Gazette, July 7, 1773.

NEW GERMANTOWN,
BALTIMORE COUNTY, *July* 22, 1772.
TEN DOLLARS REWARD.
RUN AWAY last Saturday morning from the Subscriber, an Irish indented servant lad, named DANIEL RAFTEN, about sixteen years old, five feet four or five inches high, fresh complexion, black hair tied behind, strong built, in particular very thick and unportionable legs, much addicted to sore shins, and speaks very much in the Irish dialect. Had on and took with him, a blue cloth coat with yellow metal buttons, a red coating jacket, a black cloth ditto, two white ditto, five or six white linen shirts, a pair of leather and a pair of drilling breeches, several pair of cotton, thread and worsted stockings, one of two pair of linen trowsers, and a half wore beaver hat. Whoever takes up and secures said servant in any of his Majesty's goals in this province, shall receive Six Dollars reward; but if out of the province, the above reward, including what the law allows, paid by
DANIEL BOWER.

N. B. Said lad has a good voice and sings well.
The Pennsylvania Packet; and the General Advertiser, August 17, 1772, August 24, 1772; September 14, 1772; September 21, 1772.

RAN away from *Westmoreland* County, in *Virginia*, on Monday the Third Day of *August*, 1772, one *Benjamin Brooks*, a Fuller and Weaver by Trade; and also, One *Daniel James*, a Fuller and Dyer by Trade, and has Stolen from me the Subscriber, living in *Westmoreland* County, One Iron gray Horse, and Thirteen Hands Two Inches high, branded on the near Buttock with the Figure of **8**, Five Years old last Spring, and has a good Breast, thin Body, his Mane hangs on both Sides, he gallops, trots, and paces. The said *Benjamin Brooks* is about Twenty-Six Years of Age, wears his own dark brown Hair, gray Eyes, of a ruddy Complexion; the said *Brooks* carried off with him, a blue new Market Coat, which he borrowed of Mr. *David W[is]d[r]ope*; he also took a *Virginia* Cloth Coat of a mixed Colour from *William Jewell*, and they had a roan Horse, which they led, well loaded with Cloth and Cloaths, they took with them from the fulling Mill, in the said County of *Westmoreland*, belonging to Mess. *Turberville* and *Lee*: The said *Brooks* and *James* are *Englishmen*, and came here from *Philadelphia*.

Whoever will take the said Horse and deliver him to me, shall receive a Reward of Four Pounds.   STEPHEN SELF.

N. B. All Persons are hereby forewarned from purchasing the said Horse from him: The said *Brooks* and *James* were seen cross [sic] at *Tyler's* Ferry over to *Maryland*.

The Maryland Gazette, August 20, 1772.

TEN DOLLARS REWARD,
Philadelphia, August 12, 1772.

RAN away from the Subscriber, on Tuesday Morning the 11th Instant, an *English* Servant Lad, named JOHN SPRAGUE, about 20 Years of Age, 5 Feet 6 Inches high, has dark curled Hair, large Eyebrows, a down Look, a pretty good Complexion, good Teeth, a Dent on one Side of his Mouth, a peaked Nose, a large Scar on his right Leg where it was broke, and is pretty thick: Had on, when he went away, a Check Shirt and Trousers, and a light Fustian Jacket: he took with him One or Two Check Shirts: He also had a large Pair of oval Silver Shoe and Knee Buckles. It is supposed he will try to get off by Water; but it was thought he was seen going down *Parscion* Road the same Day. Whoever will take up and secure said Servant in any Jail, so that his Master may have him again, shall receive the above Reward and reasonable Charges, paid by
ROBERT BASS.

The Maryland Gazette, August 27, 1772; September 10, 1772; October 8, 1772.

Prince George's County, *August* 19, 1772.
Committed to my Custody as Runaways,

RICHARD PENDERGEST, a good looking Fellow, about 21 Years of Age, 5 Feet 5 Inches high, dark Hair, which he wears short and curled: Has on a blue Slop Jacket, Check Shirt (and has Three white ones with him in a Wallet) Osnabrig Trousers, a good Castor Hat, is (by his Dialect) an *Irishman*, and says he came from on Board the *Gibraltar* Man of War, at *Charles-Town, South Carolina.*

WILLIAM OSBORNE, an *Englishman*, about 21 Years of Age, 5 feet 7 or 8 Inches high, wears his Hair, which is light coloured, very short and curled a little: Has on an old Fustian or Jeans Coat and Breeches, white Shirt and Muslin Neckcloth, a Pair of brown Thread Hose marked WB, half worn Shoes nailed on the Heels, and a Felt Hat almost new. Says he came into *Rappahannock* about 6 Weeks ago, in the *Thornton*, Capt *Kidd*, and that he, with 3 others, ran away from the Person that purchased them on their Way Home from the Ship.

These Two Men were committed the same Day from distant Parts of the Country, and though they do no acknowledge an Acquaintance, may probably be Two of the Six advertized in the *Virginia* Gazette, as run away from the *Thornton*, Capt. *Kidd.*
RALPH FORSTER, Sheriff.

The Maryland Gazette, August 27, 1772; September 3, 1772; September 17, 1772. See *The Maryland Gazette*, December 3, 1772.

RAN away on the 22d of *July*, from *Norfolk*, with a 30 Hogshead Flat, Sloop rigged, *James Nickolson*, and carried with him a Negro Man belonging to the Flat, and about 40 Barrels of Tar, which the said *Nickolson* was to have delivered at Norfolk: He is a middle sized Man, about 45 Years old, black Hair and Beard, sharp Chin, has lost several of his Teeth, walks slow, and stoops in the Shoulders. The Negro is....named *Boston*...the Flat has lately been raised upon about Ten Inches with a thick Piece of Timber on her Gunwales, has Staples drove in her Bends instead of Chain Plates for her Shrouds, her Mast fixed through Two Cross Pieces of Timber from her main Beams to her Forecastle, she has a Mainsail and Jib, a Pump fixed with a Trough to carry the Water off, her Sealing broke and gone in several Places, she has been employed in carrying of Tar, her raised Work and other Parts of her have been paid [sic] with brown Paint but is very dull now; I have heard that such a Flat and Hands were seen going up the Bay

near the Mouth of *Peanketank* River; the said *Nickolson* has been used up the Bay and on the Eastern Shore of *Maryland*. If any Person can get the Flat and Negro, and any Tar that may be left, and bring them to me at *Suffolk-Town* on *Nansemond* River, shall receive Ten Pounds Reward; and if they can take the said *Nickolson*, and bring him to me, then they shall receive 12 Pounds 10 Shillings, paid by me,
JOSIAH RIDDICK.
The Maryland Gazette, August 27, 1772; September 10, 1772.

TEN POUNDS REWARD.
RAN away the 23d of *August* from the Subscriber, living in *Prince-George's* County, near *Bladensburg*, the Two following Convict Servant Men, *viz.*

JOHN RICHARDSON, born in the County of *England*, understands reaping, mowing and ditching, about 35 or 40 Years of Age, a thin, spare, swarthy Fellow, about 6 Feet high, one of his Knees stands a little in: He had on and carried away with him an old Castor Hat, a white Wig, a Dowlas Shirt, an Osnabrig ditto, a Pair of Osnabrig Trousers, a Pair of old blue Cloth Breeches, an old Linen Jacket lined with Flannel, Three Pair of old Worsted Stockings, a Pair of old Shoes with Holes cut in the Tops of them for Corns on his Feet, and a Bundle with some Things unknown.

JAMES MARSHMAN, 30 or 35 Years of Age, about 5 Feet 8 or 9 Inches high, a very down looking Fellow, pitted with the Small-Pox: Had on when he went away an old Castor Hat, short Hair, an old brown Cloth Coat, a Dowlas Shirt, an Osnabrig ditto, a Pair of Crocus Trousers, and a Pair of old Shoes with Nails in the Bottoms of them.—It is thought they will make for the Water.—Whoever takes up and secures the said Servants, so that they may be had again, shall receive Forty Shillings Reward for each if 20 Miles from Home, or the above Reward if out of the Province, paid by
BENJAMIN BERRY, jun.
The Maryland Gazette, September 3, 1772. See below.

COMMITTED to *Anne-Arundel* County Jail, as Runaways, the Two following Persons, *viz.*

JAMES MARSHAM, about 5 Feet 6 or 7 Inches high, born in the West of *England*, and speaks in that Dialect: Had on when committed, an old brown Cloth Coat, coarse Trousers and Shirt, no Shoes, Stockings or Hat, says he belongs to *Zachariah Berry* in *Prince George's* County, and that he has been in the Country about Six Weeks.

JOHN WILLIAMSON, a Companion of the above *James Marsham*, but will not own his Master: His Cloathing is an old Hat, white Wig, a

Linen short Coat and Jacket of the same with Lining and Back of reddish coloured Woollen Cloth, coarse Trousers, &c. Their Masters are desired to take them away and pay Charges to
JOHN CLAPHAM, Sheriff.
N. B. Said *Williamson* says he was bred to the Sea.
The Maryland Gazette, September 3, 1772. See above.

Prince-George's County, *September* 8, 1772.
COMMITTED to my Custody as a Runaway, *William Colloquher*, alias *Williamson*, says he belongs to *William Duke*, in *Frederick* County. His Master is desired to pay Charges and take him, from
RALPH FORSTER, Sheriff.
The Maryland Gazette, September 10, 1772.

RAN away from the Subscriber, living near *Annapolis*, on Sunday the 13th of *September*, an indented Servant Man, named *William Lee*, about Five Feet high, has straight yellow Hair: Had on, when he went away, a Cotton Jacket, Osnabrig Shirt and Trousers, Felt Hat, and Country made Shoes. Whoever takes up the said Servant, and secures him in any Jail, so that the Owner may get him again, shall receive a Reward of Six Dollars, and reasonable Charges if brought home, paid by
THOMAS RUTLAND.
N. B. The above Servant has got a Copy of his Indentures, and it is probable he may forge a Discharge.
The Maryland Gazette, September 17, 1772.

FIFTEEN PISTOLES REWARD.
Maryland, Queen-Anne's County, *Sept.* 11, 1772.
RAN away from the Subscriber's Plantation, in *Murther Kiln* Hundred, in *Kent* County, on *Delaware*, on Wednesday, the 2d Day of *September* Instant, Two Men (by Profession Ditchers) who were under Articles to the Subscriber: One named *James Dickson*, alias *Edward Rogers*, for whom I stand Bail, and took out of *Queen-Anne's* County Jail, in the province of *Maryland*; he is about Five Feet Six Inches high, supposed to be between 32 and 35 Years of Age, smooth faced, a well made squat Fellow, very talkative, boasts much of Knowledge in his Business, and reports himself to be the Heir to a considerable Estate in *England*. The other, named *John Cole*, about Five Feet Seven Inches high, a well made fellow, and Hump backed. Their wearing Apparel cannot be well described, as they took with them Changes of Cloaths. It is supposed they will make for the *Jerseys*.

Whoever will take up, and secure the said Two Fellows in any Jail within the Province of *Maryland*, shall have for *Dickso*n, Ten Pistoles, and for *Cole*, Five Pistoles Reward, paid by
JAMES HUTCHINGS, junr.

    The Maryland Gazette, September 17, 1772. See *The Pennsylvania Gazette*, September 23, 1772 and *The Pennsylvania Packet; and the General Advertiser*, September 28, 1772.

FIFTEEN PISTOLES REWARD.

RUN AWAY *from the subscriber's plantation, in Murtherkiln Hundred, in Kent county, on Delaware, on Wednesday, the 2d of this instant, September, Two Men, by profession ditchers, (who are under articles to the subscriber) the one named* JAMES DICKSON, *alias* EDWARD ROGERS, *and for whom I stand bail, and took out of Queen-Anne's county goal, in the province of Maryland; he is about 5 feet 6 inches high, supposed to be between 32 and 35 years of age, smooth faced, a well made squat fellow, is very talkative, boasts much of knowledge in his business, and reports himself to be the heir of a very considerable estate in England. The other, named* JOHN COLE, *about 5 feet 7 inches high, a well made fellow, and bump backed. Their wearing apparel cannot be well described, as they took with them a change of clothes. It is supposed they will make for the Jerseys. Whoever will take up the said two fellows, and secure them in any goal, within the province of Maryland, shall have, for* Dickson, *TEN PISTOLES, and for* Cole, *FIVE PISTOLES reward, paid by*
JAMES HUTCHINGS, junior.

    The Pennsylvania Gazette, September 23, 1772. See *The Maryland Gazette*, September 17, 1772 and *The Pennsylvania Packet; and the General Advertiser*, September 28, 1772.

FORTY SHILLINGS Reward.

RUN away from the subscriber, living in Baltimore county, on the 14th day of August, 1772, a servant man, named THOMAS CROSS, 25 years of age, 5 feet 7 or 8 inches high, well set, down look, thick lips, hollow eyed, short black hair, and speaks hoarse; had on a tow linen shirt and trowsers, and a half-worn castor hat. Whoever takes up said servant, and secures him, so that his master may have him again, shall have Thirty Shillings, if 20 miles from home, and the above reward, and reasonable charges, if out of the county, and brought home, paid by JOSIAH HITCHCOCK, near the Upper Cross-roads.

    The Pennsylvania Gazette, September 23, 1772.

Chester-Town, August 18, 1772.
RUN away from the subscribers, living in Chester-Town, on the 16th instant, two servant men, viz. WILLIAM FAGAN, born in Ireland, about 5 feet 8 or 9 inches high, of fair complexion, dark brown hair, tied behind, full smooth face, has a mole on his upper lip, and is a Taylor by trade; had on, and took with him, a blue broadcloth coat, with yellow buttons, a scarlet lapelled jacket, with buttons of the same, brown holland breeches, broad chequered trowsers, and sundry other cloaths. ROBERT CAMPBELL, born in the north of Ireland, about 5 feet 10 inches high, of a dark complexion, short black hair, has a tolerable education, and will probably forge a pass; he is also a Taylor by trade; had on a raven grey coat, short jacket, ticken breeches, and new shoes, with silver buckles, marked I. S. Whoever apprehends the said servants, so that their masters may have them again, shall receive SIX POUNDS reward, if taken within this province, if out of the province, TEN POUNDS, and all reasonable charges, paid by EDWARD SCANIAN, and CHARLES ALLEN.
The Pennsylvania Gazette, September 23, 1772; October 21, 1772; October 28, 1772.

September 23, 1772.
RAN away from the Subscriber, on Monday last, an indented Servant Man named JOSEPH WELCH. He is about 24 Years of Age, small in Stature, wears his own black Hair, is sparing in Speech and hard of Hearing, He has many Scars in his Body, which he says proceeded from Boils. He has on, when he went away, an Osnabrig Jacket, and Breeches or Trousers, Dowlas Shirt, Country made Shoes and Worsted Stockings, and a small Beaver Hat, but may have taken other Cloaths with him: He is much addicted to drinking, and apt to be intoxicated with a small Quantity. Whoever will apprehend the said Runaway, and deliver him to me at *Annapolis*, shall have 20 Shillings Reward if taken in the County, and if taken out of the County 40 Shillings and reasonable Charges.
It is suspected he is lurking at some little Distance from *Annapolis*. He was seen by Mr. *Brice Worthington* in Company with Two other Men. He went off on Foot, but probably will steal a Horse, and his Course it is imagined will be towards Frederick.
WALTER DULANY.
The Maryland Gazette, September 24, 1772; October 1, 1772.

COMMITTED to *Anne-Arundel* County Jail, as Runaways, the Two following Persons, *viz. Bartholomew Burn*, who pretends to be a *Frenchman*, but can give no Account of himself, though he speaks good

English: His Cloathing is, an old Suit of black Cloaths, very bad Shoes and Stockings, old Hat and Wig.—Negro *Jack*....Their Owners are desired to take then away and pay Charges to
JOHN CLAPHAM, Sheriff.

 N. B. The above Negro was taken up in a Poplar Canoe, Twenty-eight Feet long, Two and a Half wide, Gunwale round, she has Places for Six Oars, and is branded at each End, inside and out C S: There was in her, a Pair of Oyster Rakes, and an Ash Paddle, with an Iron Ring round it. The Owner may have her again, proving his Property and paying Charges, by applying to the Subscriber in Annapolis.
JOHN STEELE.
 The Maryland Gazette, September 24, 1772; October 1, 1772.

FIFTEEN PISTOLES REWARD.

 MARYLAND, *Queen Anne's county, Sept* 11, 1772.
RUN AWAY from the Subscriber's plantation, in Murtherkiln Hundred, in Kent county, on Delaware, on Wednesday, the 2d of September inst. (who are under articles to the Subscriber) two men, by profession ditchers; the one named JAMES DICKSON *alias* EDWARD ROGERS, and for whom I stand bail, and took out of Queen-Anne's county goal, in the province of Maryland: he is about five feet six inches high, supposed to be between thirty-two and thirty-five years of age, smooth faced, a well made square fellow: He is very talkative, boasts much of knowledge in his business, and reports himself to be the heir of a very considerable estate in England. The other, named JOHN COLE, about five feet seven inches high, a well made fellow, and hump backed. Their wearing apparel cannot be well described, as they took with them change of clothes. It is supposed they will make for the Jerseys.—Whoever will take up and secure the said two fellows in any goal within the province of Maryland, shall have for Dickson, Ten Pistoles, and for Cole, Five Pistoles reward, paid by
JAMES HUTCHINGS, Jun.
 The Pennsylvania Packet; and the General Advertiser, September 28, 1772; October 5, 1772.

FORTY SHILLINGS REWARD.

RUN AWAY from the Subscriber, living in Baltimore county, on the 27th ult. an English convict servant named EDWARD JACKS, five feet six inches high, has a down look, wears his own hair, and is a settled fellow. Had on and took with him, a lightish coloured jockey coat, with metal buttons, a pair of buckskin breeches, a coarse shirt, white stockings, shoes

with brass buckles, a castor hat, the brim and hole sticht together with white thread, and took with him a short gown, which it is supposed he will make an under jacket of: He is a good waggoner, and as he took a bridle with him, it is supposed he will steal a horse: He can neither read nor write. Whoever takes up said servant, and secures him, so that his master may get him again, shall have the above reward; but if out of the county, Three Pounds, paid by
ABRAHAM BRITTEN.

The Pennsylvania Packet; and the General Advertiser, September 28, 1772; October 5, 1772.

COMMITTED to *Frederick* County Jail, the following Persons, viz. SARAH HALL, from *Virginia*, who says that she belongs to *Ralph Loftis*. JAMES GENTS, an *Irishman*, who says he belongs to *Thomas Wilson*, of *Annapolis*. JOHN ROBERTSON, an *Englishman*, who says he is a free Man, and a Sailor, has lost his middle Finger, and is about 40 Years of Age. Negro GILBERT....The Owners of each, are desired to come and pay Fees according to Custom.
JAMES HACKMAN, Sheriff.

The Maryland Gazette, October 1, 1772; October 8, 1772.

Baltimore, September 22, 1772.
FIVE POUNDS Reward.
RAN away, last night, from the subscriber, living in Baltimore, an English convict servant man, named Thomas Lacey, but may change his name to Payne, about 23 or 24 years of age, 5 feet 6 or 7 inches high, brown complexion, round shouldered, stoops in his walk, has a large dent in his head, and a large mark in the instep of his right foot, occasioned by the small pox; he can talk Dutch, had on and took with him a brown coarse cloth short coat, two oznabrigs shirts, one pair ditto trowsers, and a pair of check trowsers, good double soled shoes, yarn stockings spotted blue and white, yellow buckles, a felt hat bound with black ferrit, white lining and loops, a red silk handkerchief with white spots round his neck. He is left handed, and pretends to be a cobler by trade. Stole, with him, a bay horse, about 14 hands high, small ears, bob tail, and trimmed mane, a natural trotter and shod all round; he is hurt on his rump by the crupper buckle; some saddle sports and hurt on his neck, with the collar; an old saddle without housing; a snaffle bridle; a short Dutch gun, square barrel, two sights, and a small piece broke off the stock. Whoever takes up said servant, and brings him, together with the horse, saddle, bridle and gun, to the

subscriber, shall, if taken in this county, receive Forty Shillings, if out of the country Three Pounds, and if out of the province the above reward; or for the servant alone, Five Pounds, and reasonable charges paid, by
PHILIP LIDIG.

The Pennsylvania Chronicle, From Saturday, September 26, to Saturday, October 3, 1772; From Saturday, October 3, to Saturday, October 10, 1772; From Saturday, October 17, to Saturday, October 24, 1772; *The Pennsylvania Gazette,* October 7, 1772. Minor differences between the papers.

Charles-Town, Caecil County, Sept. 30, 1772.
COMMITTED to my Custody as Runaways, Two Men, named *John Murien* and *Richard Ewel,* who says they belonged to a Ship from *Bristol,* commanded by Capt. *Brown,* and that they left her in *Norfolk.* Their Masters (if any) are desired to take them away and pay Charges, to
JOHN HAMILTON, junr. Sheriff.

The Maryland Gazette, October 15, 1772.

September 29, 1772.
RAN away from the Subscriber, living near the Head of *South* River, an indented Servant Man named JAMES GRIBBINE, by Trade a Weaver, about 20 Years of Age, 5 Feet 4 or 5 Inches high, wears his own black Hair, is of a pale Complexion, pitted a little with the Small-Pox, and has large dark gray Eyes: Had on, when he went away, a Felt Hat much worn, Osnabrig Shirt and Trousers patched at the Knees, a Devonshire Kersey Jacket with metal Buttons, an under Jacket of a brown Colour, with the back Part of another Colour, lined with Linen; black Shoes and odd Buckles: he probably may endeavour to pass for a Cripple. Whoever takes up the said Runaway, and secures him, so that his Master may get him again, shall be entitled to a Reward of 40 Shillings if out of the County, if Ten Miles from Home 20 Shillings, if 20 Miles 30 Shillings, excluding what the Law allows, and reasonable Charges if brought Home to
THOMAS TOFFT.

The Maryland Gazette, October 15, 1772. See *The Maryland Gazette,* October 22, 1772.

TEN POUNDS REWARD.

October 4, 1772.
RAN away from the Subscriber, living on *Elk-Ridge, Anne-Arundel* County, *Maryland,* a Servant Man, named *Francis Sellers,* he is about 21 or

22 years old, about 5 Feet 8 or 10 Inches high, brown Hair: Had on and took with him when he went away, an old Castor Hat, a brown *Bath-coating* Sourtoat [*sic*] Coat, a brown Broad Cloth close bodied ditto, a sky blue coloured Jacket without Sleeves, a pair of Nankeen Breeches, a Pair of Cotton Stockings, a Pair of blue Worsted ditto, Two Pair of Shoes, a Bird-eyed Silk Handkerchief, Two Osnabrig Shirts, and had Ten Shillings Cash.—Whoever takes up said Servant and secures him, so that I may get him again, shall have if taken 10 Miles from home 3 Pounds, if 20 Miles 6 Pounds, if farther the above Reward. He can write, and will no doubt forge a Pass. JAMES HOWARD.

N. B. The above Servant came in the Country about 6 or 7 Years ago, indented for 5 Years, he served the first Part of his time on *Elk-Ridge*, with *Nicholas Greenbury Ridgely*, the remaining Part with *Joshua Griffith*, at *Elk-Ridge Landing*; after being free he worked for some Time with *George Gale*, a Stone Mason, then hired to *Samuel Poole*, some Time past he and some others robbed a Store-house, on which Account he indented himself to *Samuel Poole*, who consigned him to me.

The Maryland Gazette, October 15, 1772; October 29, 1772; November 12, 1772; November 19, 1772; November 26, 1772; December 3, 1772; December 10, 1772; *The Pennsylvania Chronicle,* From Saturday, October 10, to Saturday, October 17, 1772; From Saturday, October 17, to Saturday, October 24, 1772; From Saturday, October 24, to Saturday, October 31, 1772. Minor differences between the papers. *The Chronicle* does not have the date at the top. See *The Maryland Gazette*, April 8, 1773 for "Sellars."

Stafford County, *Virginia, October* 6, 1772.
FIVE POUNDS REWARD.
FOR apprehending a Convict Servant, named SAMUEL GASFORD, imported in the *Kidd*, Capt. *Thornton*, into *Rappahannock*, last Year, and ran away from the Rev. Mr. *Boucher's*, in *Prince-George'* County, yesterday. His Person is rather likely, being about 5 Feet 6 or 8 Inches in Stature, 23 Years of Age, with light coloured brown Hair; which, however, being artful, he will probably cut off. He had with him a blue Coat and Waistcoat, with a red Cape to the Coat: and also a brown Holland Suit, and a Wilton Cloth Waistcoat and Breeches, and a Leathern Pair of ditto. He sings, and plays tolerably well on the German Flute, which he is fond of. He carried off with him my Portmanteau, with Sundries of my wearing Apparel; and a small bay Horse, trimmed according to the *Virginia* Custom, with his Mane and Fore-top cut close, and a Bob-tail. branded **IM**. He enquired the Road to *Baltimore*, and so is probably gone thitherwards; and from thence may proceed on into some of the Northern Colonies, having, it

is supposed, been in *America* before. Whoever will apprehend, and convey him to Dr. *Richard Brooke* in *Prince-George's* County, *Maryland*, or to me in *Virginia*, shall be entitled to the above Reward, over and above what the Law allows.   CLEMENT BROOKE.

The Maryland Gazette, October 15, 1772. See *The Maryland Gazette*, October 22, 1772.

SIX DOLLARS REWARD.

September 29, 1772.

RAN away from the Subscriber, living near the Head of *South* River, an *Irish* indented Servant Man, named JAMES GRIBIN, by Trade a Weaver, about 20 Years of Age, 5 Feet 3 or 4 Inches high, wears his own black Hair, is of a pale Complexion, pitted a little with the Small-Pox, and has large dark gray Eyes: Had on, when he went away, a Felt Hat much worn, Osnabrig Shirt and Trousers patched on the Knees, a light coloured *English* Cloth upper Jacket with metal Buttons, an under ditto of a Snuff Colour, the back Part of another Sort, much daubed with Tar, black Shoes and odd Buckles: he probably may endeavour to pass for a Cripple. Whoever takes up the said Runaway, and secures him, so that his Master may get him again, shall receive, if taken Ten Miles from Home 20 Shillings, if 20 Miles 30 Shillings, and if out of the County the above Reward.
THOMAS TOFT.

N. B. He is fond of Liquor and very talkative, and pretends to know something of many Trades, particularly Seine knitting. He very likely may change his Name.

The Maryland Gazette, October 22, 1772; November 5, 1772. See *The Maryland Gazette*, October 15, 1772.

COMMITTED to *Anne-Arundel* County Jail as a Runaway, *William Wood*, says he belongs to *Humphry Godman*, on *Elk-Ridge*. His Master is desired to take him away and pay Charges.
JOHN CLAPHAM, Sheriff.

The Maryland Gazette, October 22, 1772. See *The Maryland Gazette*, December 5, 1771, and October 21, 1773.

FORTY DOLLARS REWARD.

October 13, 1772.

RAN away from the Rev. Mr. *Boucher's*, in *Prince-George's* County, *Maryland*, on Sunday the 4th of *October*, a Convict Servant Man belonging to the Rev. Mr. *Brooke*, in *Stafford* County, *Virginia*, his Name is *Samuel*

Gasford, he is an *Englishman*, about 23 Years of Age, came into *Virginia* a few Months ago, in the Ship *Thornton*, Captain *Copland*; It has been discovered since he ran away, that this is not the first Time of his having been convicted to *America*, and that he is well acquainted with the Country Northward; he is middle sized, or rather below it, wears his own Hair, which however it is not improbable he may cut off, the better to disguise himself; he rode off a small bay blooded Horse, trimed with a ridge Mane, his Foretop cut off, with the Tail bobbed short, and has a small and remarkable white Spot upon one of his Ears, it is thought, but not certainly known, to be branded with the Letters **IM** in one Piece: The Servant took with him a Portmantua containing some wearing Apparel belonging to his Master: He has with him of his own, a blue Coat with a red Cape, and Waistcoat of the same, together with a Suit of brown Holland, and a Wilton Waistcoat and Breeches, and a Pair of Leather ones; he plays tolerable well on the German Flute, which he is fond of doing. Twenty Dollars will be paid to any Person who will deliver him and the Horse to his Master in *Virginia*, or Dr. *Brooke* in *Maryland*, provided he be taken in *Virginia* or *Maryland*; Thirty if taken in *Pensylvania*, or Forty if taken in any other Colony.

The Maryland Gazette, October 22, 1772; November 5, 1772; November 12, 1772; November 19, 1772; November 26, 1772; December 3, 1772. See *The Maryland Gazette*, October 15, 1772.

October 17, 1772.
RAN away from the Subscriber, living on *Kent-Island*, the 11th Inst. a Convict Servant Man, named *Edward Davey*, about 20 Years of age, a well set Fellow, about 5 Feet high, dark coloured Hair: Had on, old blue and white Jacket, a Pair of old Tow Trousers, and Two Tow Shirts, One of them had no Button-holes, but in the Wristband, old Felt Hat tarred, a Pair of old Shoes; he had on an Iron Collar when he went off. Whoever takes up the said Servant, and secures him in any Jail, so that his Master may get him again, shall have Fifty Shillings Reward, including what the Law allows, paid by   ROBERT WEEDEN.

The Maryland Gazette, October 22, 1772; October 29, 1772; November 5, 1772.

FOUR DOLLARS REWARD.
RAN away from the Subscriber, living in *Annapolis*, on the 10th Day of *October*, 1772, a Convict Woman, named *Catharine Pardon*, of a middling Size, has dark Hair, a fresh Colour, and is pitted with the Small-Pox: Had on, when she went off, it is supposed, a purple and white Bedgown, a pink

stuff Petticoat, and a black Bonnet; but as she took many Things with her, it is likely she may disguise herself, and change her Name. She is subject to all manner of Vice, and is supposed to have gone towards *Baltimore.* She appears to be with Child, and is an artful deceiving Hussey. Any Person giving Intelligence of her, so that her Master may get her again, shall be paid the above Reward, by
CONSTANTINE BULL.

The Maryland Gazette, October 22, 1772; October 29, 1772; November 5, 1772.

BALTIMORE COUNTY, *Maryland, Oct.* 26, 1772.
TEN POUNDS REWARD.
RAN AWAY from the Subscriber, two convict servant men, viz. THOMAS WHEATLEY, about five feet eight or nine inches high, strait limbed, small featured, sandy hair and beard, with double teeth, and about 27 years of age: Had on a brown coat, white drab breeches, and pumps. The other named DANIEL UNTHANK, near the same height, about 20 years of age, has a fair smooth face, light brown hair, no beard, or very little. He took from me a great coat, of fine cloth, dove colour, basket buttons, small wooden buttons to the cape, moth-eaten in the back under the cape, and one pair of double soaled shoes. Both of them had fine shirts and felt hats. As they have some money, it is likely they will change their clothes. Whoever takes up and secures said servants in any goal, so that their master may have them again, shall have the above reward, paid by
AQUILA PRICE.

The Pennsylvania Packet; and the General Advertiser, November 9, 1772; November 16, 1772; November 23, 1772; *The Pennsylvania Gazette,* November 25, 1772. Minor differences between the papers. See *The Maryland Gazette,* November 12, 1772.

TEN POUNDS REWARD,
Baltimore County, *October* 26, 1772.
RAN away from the Subscriber, Two Convict Servant Men, *viz.* THOMAS WHEATLEY, about 5 Feet 8 or 9 Inches high, 27 Years of Age, is straight limb'd, small featured, has sandy Hair, and double Teeth: Had on a brown Coat, white Drab Breeches and a Pair of Pumps. DANIEL UNTHANK, near the same Heighth, about 20 Years old, has a fair smooth Face, light Hair, and little or no Beard: He took with him a Great Coat of fine Cloth, with light coloured basket Buttons, and small wooden ditto on the Cape; it is Moth eaten on the Back below the Cape. They both had white Shirts, felt Hats, and a Pair of double soaled Shoes, but they have some Money and

will likely change their Cloaths. I would fetch them from any Part of the Continent, and any Person that will secure or bring them home shall have the above Reward.   AQUILA PRICE.

The Maryland Gazette, November 12, 1772; November 19, 1772; November 26, 1772; December 3, 1772; December 10, 1772; December 24, 1772. See *The Pennsylvania Packet; and the General Advertiser*, November 9, 1772.

Baltimore, October 25, 1772.
TEN POUNDS REWARD.

RUN away from the subscriber, on Monday the 25th of this instant October, an Irish servant man, named Robert Lewis, 5 feet 6 or 7 inches high, well made, and of a brown complexion, has black hair, and sometimes puts a false tail to it, has a smooth and soft flattering speech and can speak the French language, by trade a saddler and harness maker, came over this fall in the Maremaid, and consigned to Mr. Thompson in Baltimore: Had on when he went away, a new coarse felt hat, has a white shirt and stock, a light broadcloth coat, red cloth jacket, brown cloth breeches, blue worsted stockings, a pair of shoes and plated buckles: but it is probable may change his dress and name.

Whoever takes up said servant man and brings him to the subscriber living in Gay-street, Baltimore, shall receive, if within ten miles, thirty shillings, if out of the county five pounds, and if out of the province the above reward, paid by   JOHN GORDON,

N. B. He hath been in the army, and it is probable will pretend that he is a free man.

The Pennsylvania Chronicle, From Saturday, November 7, to Saturday, November 14, 1772; From Saturday, November 14, to Saturday, November 21, 1772; From Saturday, November 21, to Saturday, November 28, 1772; From Saturday, November 28, to Saturday, December 5, 1772.

Charles County, *November* 11, 1772.

RAN away last Night, an indented Servant, a *Frenchman*, by Trade a Weaver, named *Nicholas Be[ss]on*, about 30 Years of Age, 5 Feet 7 Inches high, well set, brown Hair, combs it back: Had on and took with him, when he went away, a blue Broadcloth Coat, light Cloth Waistcoat, black knit Breeches, Three fine Shirts, and several Things to sell, such as Sleeve Buttons, Razors and Scissars; and took with him, a sorrel Horse, about 14 Hands high, a blaze Face, and Four white Feet.

Whoever secures the said Servant and Horse, so as the Owner may get them again, shall receive 3 Pounds Reward, paid by
WALTER CLEMENTS.
The Maryland Gazette, November 19, 1772.

FIVE POUNDS Reward.

RAN AWAY from the subscriber, living in Caecil county, North Sasquehanna Hundred, Maryland, the 15th of November inst. an indented servant man, named WILLIAM HAMILTON, alias WILLIAM HAMLON, came from Ireland in the ship Pennsylvania Farmer, Capt. Robert Johnston, in June 1771; he is about 26 years of age, five feet eight or nine inches high, slim made, pale hair, thin beard, apt to swear, has large lumps on his great toes, and walks somewhat splaw-footed: Had on, when he went away, an old grey surtout coat, and a close bodied claret coloured drab cloth coat, without lining, a spotted flannel jacket, with horn buttons and long skirts, a pair of old fustian breeches, a pair of old black stockings, newly footed, new shoes and iron buckles, a felt hat, and wears a silver breast buckle. Whoever takes up the said servant, and secures him in any of his Majesty's goals, giving intelligence to me, so that I may get him again, shall have the above reward, and all reasonable charges, paid by
CHARLES PORTER.
The Pennsylvania Gazette, November 25, 1772; December 9, 1772; December 16, 1772.

Dumfries, Virginia, November 17, 1772.
RUN away from Baltimore, in Maryland, about the 6th instant, a convict servant man, named THOMAS BOWLING, he is a likely well made fellow, about 5 feet 10 or 11 inches high, short dark brown hair, a little inclining to curl, about 25 years of age, and Irishman born, and retains the brogue peculiar to most of his country, is very talkative, especially when in drink, which he is much subject to, he has been about 12 months in the country, and been employed in tobacco craft, therefore it is imagined he will endeavour to get off in some vessel, or cross the country to Philadelphia; he went round from hence in the Molly and Betsey, Captain Jackson, and took with him three or four shirts, of different sorts, a coat and waistcoat, of mixed brown broadcloth, one blue fearnought, and one green frize jacket, both with sleeves, horn buttons, and without lining, blue cloth breeches, tarred ozenbrigs trowsers, and sundry other clothes; he has a discharge from the vessel, signed by Iris Hair, clerk to Mr. M'Gachen, of Baltimore. Any person who will secure said servant in goal, so that I get him again, shall

have FIVE POUNDS reward, and if delivered to me in Dumfries, shall be paid TEN POUNDS, Virginia currency, by
RIGINALD GRAHAM.
The Pennsylvania Gazette, November 25, 1772; December 23, 1772.

November 25, 1772.
RAN away from the Subscriber, living near *Queen-Anne*, in *Anne-Arundel* County, on Tuesday the 17th Instant, a Convict Servant Man named MATTHEW FIELD; he is about 30 Years of Age, about 5 Feet 3 or 4 Inches high, has brown hair and a Cast in his left Eye; his Apparel is unknown unless it is a red Cloth Jacket. He took with him a large bay Horse about 14 and a Half Hands high, paces, trots and gallops; he has a small Star on his Forehead and some gray Hairs in his Tail. Whoever secures the above Fellow and Horse, so as the Owner may get them again, shall receive, if taken in the County, Three Pounds, if out of the County Four Pounds, if out of the Province Five Pounds, and if brought Home reasonable Charges, paid by
THOMAS ELLIOTT.
N. B. It is supposed he is gone off with *John Iiams*, jun. a Waiting Man, as they both went off the same Evening.
The Maryland Gazette, November 26, 1772; December 3, 1772; December 10, 1772.

November 10, 1772.
RAN away from the Subscriber, an Apprentice Boy; named WILLIAM DODSON, Country born: Had on, when he went away, a blue Jacket, long striped Trousers, new Shoes, yellow Metal Buckles, and Yarn Stockings; he also took with him, belonging to his Master, a Nankeen Coat, ditto Waistcoat double breasted, a white Flannel Jacket, a white Shirt, ditto Match Cloth, black Stockings, and a Linen Handkerchief marked WR in one Corner of it; he has a likely Face, having never had the Small-Pox, his Hair was cut off about 10 Days, he sprained his Wrist about 6 Weeks ago, and wears on it a Piece of red Flannel bound up with blue Ribband. Whoever takes up and secures the said Apprentice, so that the Subscriber may get him again, shall have 40 Shillings Reward.
WILLIAM RICKETS,   Carver and Guilder in *Annapolis*.
The Maryland Gazette, November 26, 1772.

November 19, 1772.
RAN away from the Subscriber, living in *Annapolis*, on Friday the 13th Instant, an Indented Servant Man named *John Powell*, born in *Ireland*,

which may be plainly discovered by his Tongue; he is by Trade a Turner, and pretends to the Cabinet Making Business; is about 5 Feet 10 Inches high, blind of one Eye, and halts much in his Walk, occasioned by this Thigh-Bone being out of its Place: He had on and took with him a good Bearskin Surtout Coat with Metal Buttons, one Swanskin and one Flannel striped Jacket, new Check Shirt, Woollen Stockings, good Shoes with Brass Buckles, a gray Wig and half worn Castor Hat. He has been formerly a Soldier, say he is now a Pensioner, is very much given to Liquor, at which Time he is very talkative and abusive. Whoever brings him to me or confines him in any Jail shall receive a Reward of Thirty Shillings, including what the Law allows, and if brought Home reasonable Charges, paid by   FRANCIS HEPBURN.

The Maryland Gazette, November 26, 1772; December 3, 1772; December 10, 1772; December 17, 1772; December 24, 1772; December 31, 1772; January 7, 1773; January 21, 1773.

Prince George's County, *November* 28, 1772.

COMMITTED to my Custody as a Runaway, RICHARD PENDERGEST, a good looking Fellow, about 21 Years of Age, 5 Feet 5 Inches high, dark Hair, which he wears short and curled: Has on a blue Slop Jacket, Check Shirt (and had Three white ones with him in a Wallet), Osnabrig Trousers, a good Castor Hat, is (by his Dialect) an *Irishman,* and says he came from on Board the *Gibraltar* Man of War, at *Charles-Town, South Carolina.*

The said *Pendergest* is a very good Thresher and Ditcher (as he says), and is now to be sold by the Subscriber for his Prison Fees.
RALPH FORSTER, Sheriff.

The Maryland Gazette, December 3, 1772; December 10, 1772; December 24, 1772; December 31, 1772. See *The Maryland Gazette,* August 27, 1772.

Baltimore County, *November* 23, 1772.

RAN away Yesterday from the Subscriber, living in the Fork of *Gunpowder,* a Convict Servant, named BARTHOLOMEW MARTIN, about 25 Years of Age, 5 Feet high, has short brownish Hair, and is much pitted with the Small Pox; he is a well looking Fellow: Had on and took with him, when he went away, a blue Jacket, Two Cotton Jackets without Sleeves, a Pair of old Cotton Breeches pretty much worn, with a Fearnought Flap, a coarse Country Linen Shirt, a Pair of white Yarn Stockings, Two Pair of Shoes, one with Straps the other with Strings, and a new Felt Hat. Whoever takes up and secures the said Servant, so that his Master may have

him again, shall receive, if taken in the County, Four Pounds, and if out of the County Five Pounds Reward, paid by
WILLIAM ALLEN.

N. B. It is supposed he is in Company with WILLIAM DAWSON, a free Man, who has a Pass, and it is likely *Martin* may obtain it for himself, and change his Name to answer it. The same reward shall be given for apprehending him as for *Martin*. Masters of Vessels, and others, are desired not to harbour or carry off said Runaway, as the will answer the contrary at their peril.   W. A.

The Maryland Gazette, December 3, 1772; December 10, 1772; December 17, 1772.

TWENTY POUNDS Reward.

RUN away from the subscribers, on Elk-Ridge, in Anne Arundel county, Maryland, November 9, 1772, two convict servant men, viz. JAMES FIELD, by trade a Taylor, is about 22 years of age, 5 feet 8 or 9 inches high, is of a fair complexion, and has short light coloured hair. WILLIAM HAWK, of a swarthy complexion, has black eyes, short black hair, and is about 5 feet 7 or 8 inches high: Had on, and took with them, a light coloured red German serge coat, a dark bearskin frock, with white metal buttons, a pair of blue sergedenim [*sic*] breeches, a pair of snuff coloured broadcloth ditto, with gold basket buttons, an old castor hat, a new furred ditto, two fine white shirts, and sundry other things unknown. It is supposed they have also taken with them two horses, one of them a dark bay, about 14 hands high, six years old, well gaited, and is branded on the near shoulder E.I. The other is a bright sorrel, with a blaze face, about 13 1/2 hands high, six years old, and is branded on the near shoulder O. Whoever apprehends and secures said servants, so that the subscribers may get them again, shall have EIGHT POUNDS for each, and FORTY SHILLINGS for each of the horses. WILLIAM SELMAN, JOHN SHIPLEY.

The Pennsylvania Gazette, December 9, 1772; December 16, 1772; December 23, 1772.

TWENTY DOLLARS REWARD.

RAN away, on the 20th of *August* last, from the Subscriber, living near *Patapsco* Ferry, in *Anne-Arundel* County, in the Province of *Maryland*, a Convict Servant Man named JOSEPH LAMB, about 5 Feet 10 Inches high, swarthy Complexion, down Look, short brown Hair, a large Mole under his left Eye: Had on, an Osnabrig Shirt and Trousers, old Beaver Hat, and Negro Shoes with Brass Buckles. It is likely he may change his Cloaths and Name, as he sometimes calls himself *Joseph Hannon*; he also stole an

Indenture from a certain *James Moalson*, and it is likely he may pass by that Name. Whoever secures the said Servant, so that his Master may get him again, shall receive, if 10 Miles from Home, Ten Dollars including what the Law allows, and if out of the Province the above Reward and reasonable Charges if brought Home.
THOMA HAMMOND.
The Maryland Gazette, December 10, 1772; December 17, 1772; December 24, 1772; December 31, 1772; January 7, 1773; January 21, 1773.

December 5, 1772.
COMMITTED to my Custody as a Runaway, a Man who calls himself *John Holmes*, who says he belongs to *William Conn*, near *Bladensburg*. His Master is desired to pay Charges and take him from
RALPH FORSTER, Sheriff.
The Maryland Gazette, December 10, 1772; December 17, 1772; December 24, 1772.

TEN POUNDS REWARD.
RAN away from the Subscriber, living in *Anne-Arundel* County, near *Elk-Ridge* Church, on Sunday the 8th Day of *November*, 1772, a Convict Servant Man, named *Edward Elliott*, about Thirty Years of Age, Five Feet Eight or Nine Inches high, short light Hair, fair Complexion, and one of his Shoulder Blades appears much larger than the other, he is much given to Drink, and when taxed with any Thing has a remarkable wild Look: Had on and took with him, a new coarse Castor Hat, a blue and white figured Stuff Coat, lined with white Shalloon, the Cuffs large and turned up with blue Satin, a long Bearskin Jacket lined with white Flanel, with small turned up Cuffs, Two white Shirts, One Osnabrig ditto, One Pair Russia Drab Breeches, One Pair dark Bearskin ditto, lined with white Flanel, one Pair of turned Pumps, One Pair of Shoes, One Pair ribbed Thread Stockings, One Pair Yarn ditto, Two Silk Handkerchiefs, 1 black the other dark flowered; he may have other Cloaths unknown.

Whoever takes up the said Servant shall be entitled to the above Reward, and reasonable Charges if brought Home, paid by
CHARLES WORTHINGTON.
N. B. He has been since seen to go through *Frederick-Town* towards the New Country, and is supposed to have a Pass.
The Maryland Gazette, December 17, 1772; December 24, 1772; December 31, 1772.

RAN away from the Subscriber, living near *Annapolis*, on Sunday the 6th Day of *December*, 1772, a Country born Servant Man, named LUKE BULLIN, a lusty well set Fellow, about Six Feet high: Had on and took with him a blue Broad Cloth Coat, dark coloured Bearskin Jacket, Two Pair of Osnabrig Trousers, a coarse Irish Linen Shirt, Country made Shoes, with a plain Pair of Copper Shoebuckles, blueish Yarn Stockings and Felt Hat. He was brought Home from Mr. *Joseph Ogle's*, on *Monockasy*, some Time in *June* last, and it is supposed he will go the same Way again. He is a great Lover of Liquor, and when drunk will both swear and lie. Whoever secures the said Servant in any Jail, or will bring him to the Subscriber, shall receive Six Dollars Reward, paid by
THOMAS RUTLAND.

The Maryland Gazette, December 17, 1772. See *The Maryland Gazette*, July 4, 1771.

December 11, 1772.

WENT away last Night from the *Patuxent* Iron-Works, the Two following Servant Men, just imported in the *Isabella*, Captain *Spencer, viz. William Foard*, an *American*, born in *New-England*, about 22 Years of Age, 5 Feet 6 or 7 Inches high, has a dark Complexion, and wears his own short brown Hair: Had on and took with him, a coarse white Linen Shirt, old dirty Trousers, an Olive coloured Thickset Coat, with yellow Metal Buttons, a red and white striped Linsey Jacket, gray Worsted Stockings, black Leather Shoes with Metal Buckles, and a Felt Hat. *William Hunt*, an *Englishman*, about 23 Years of Age, 6 Feet high, has a fair Complexion, wears his own short brown Hair, and answers very boldly when spoke to: Had on and took with him, a new Osnabrig Shirt, dirty Leather Breeches, a light coloured Frize close-bodied Coat, a blue Surtout ditto with a Velvet Cape, a Variety of Worsted Stockings and Silk Handkerchiefs, a Pair of black Leather Shoes with plated Buckles, and an old Felt Hat bound round the Edge with some Kind of black Binding. Whoever takes up said Servants, shall be paid on delivering them at *Patuxent* Iron Works aforesaid, if taken 10 Miles from Home, Twenty-Five Shillings; if 20 Miles, Thirty Shillings for each, including what the Law allows, and so in proportion for a greater Distance, by   SAMUEL & JOHN SNOWDEN.

The Maryland Gazette, December 17, 1772; December 24, 1772; December 31, 1772; January 7, 1773; January 21, 1773; February 18, 1773.

RUN away, on Sunday, the 13th of December, 1772, from the subscriber, living in Cambridge town, in Maryland, an Irish servant man, named

THOMAS SHERIDAN, about 5 feet 8 or 9 inches high, between 19 and 20 years of age, of a redish complexion, with large eye-brows, has long sandy coloured hair, combed up before, and wears it tied behind in a large club, talks loud, and is very apt to swear by his maker; had on, and took with him, when he went away, a snuff-coloured old surtout coat, an old cloth-coloured ditto, without sleeves, a brown cloth jacket, with black horn buttons, old white breeches, grey ribbed worsted stockings, half-worn shoes, with large plated buckles, wears his hat cocked up behind, two old white shirts, and commonly wears a stock and stock-buckle. Whoever takes up the said servant, and secures him, so that his master may get him again, shall have SIX DOLLARS reward, and reasonable charges, paid by
JOHN MANNING.
All masters of vessels are forbid to carry him off.
The Pennsylvania Gazette, December 23, 1772; December 30, 1772; January 20, 1773; February 3, 1773; February 17, 1773.

RUN away from the subscriber, near George Steuart's tavern, at the Lower Cross Roads, in Baltimore County, the 10th of December 1772, an English convict servant woman, named MARY PARKER, about 23 years of age, pretty lusty and fat, marked with the small-pox, of a fresh complexion, dark sandy coloured hair, has a blemish on her right eye, so that it looks whitish; had on, and took with her, a chints gown, a brown worsted gown, a red ditto, a red plain worsted petticoat, a redish pennella ditto, a light coloured cloth cloak, a black silk bonnet, a black Barcelona silk handkerchief, a red flowered ditto, also a linen handkerchief, with St. Paul's church, and the various cries of London, stamped on it, a man's hat, red worsted stockings, red calimancoe shoes, a pair of women calf-skin ditto, a black hood, and several other kinds of head clothes, some lincey jackets and petticoats, a wrought-pocket-book, and silver ring, which it is probable she will wear on her finger, two silver table spoons, one of which is marked W.T. also a bay mare, about 14 hands high, with a white streak in her face, very small towards her nose, and paces pretty fast; an old side-saddle, covered with buckskin. Whoever takes up and secures said servant woman, if within this county, shall have THREE POUNDS reward, and reasonable charges; and if out of the county FIVE POUNDS; and for taking up and securing the mare only, FIFTY SHILLINGS reward, paid by WILLIAM THOMPSON.
The Pennsylvania Gazette, December 23, 1772; February 17, 1773.

Baltimore, December 28, 1772.
RUN *AWAY from his bail, on Friday, the 25th instant, a certain JAMES M'MAHON, a labouring man, about 5 feet 7 inches high, much pitted with*

the small-pox, very talkative in company; had on, when he went away, a rough hat, brown coloured coat, green waistcoat, flesh coloured cotton velvet breeches, white stockings, a pair of speckled ditto, and a pair of half boots. Whoever takes up the said James M'Mahon, and brings him to any of the subscribers, living in Baltimore town, Maryland, shall receive FIVE POUNDS reward, and all reasonable charges, paid by
JAMES MARSHALL, JOHN TAYLOR, HENRY WEAVER, and WILLIAM LAVELY.
The Pennsylvania Gazette, January 6, 1773; February 3, 1773.

RUN AWAY from the subscriber, living at Deer-creek, in Baltimore county, in the province of Maryland, on the 28th of July last, an English convict servant MAN, named JOHN SHELDON, about 30 years of age, is about 6 feet high, fair skin, light hair, and a Nailer by trade. Whoever takes up said servant man, and brings him to his master, or secures him in the nearest goal, so that his master gets him again, shall have FORTY SHILLINGS reward, paid by   JOHN FORWOOD.
The Pennsylvania Gazette, January 6, 1773.

TEN POUNDS Reward.
RUN AWAY *from the subscriber, living in Great Pipe-Creek, Frederick county, Maryland, a Dutch servant man, named* JOHN KINSINER, *by trade a taylor, about 5 feet 6 inches high, black complexion, straight black hair, he is a noted thief; had on, when he went away, an old red jacket, and a white one over it, old stuff breeches, blue stockings, new pumps, aged 35 years. Whoever secures said servant, in any of his Majesty's goals, shall have FIVE POUNDS reward, and if brought home, the above reward, and reasonable charges, paid by*
MICHAEL M'GUIRE.   Dec. 21, 1772.
N. B. His father lives in Sixth street, the corner of Race street, in the city of Philadelphia.
The Pennsylvania Gazette, January 6, 1773; January 20, 1773; February 3, 1773.

December 4, 1772.
RUN *away, last night, from the subscriber, living near Charles-Town, Caecil county, a servant man, named* THOMAS SALTER, *country born, about 6 feet high, about 42 years of age, has a scar on his eyelid; had on, when he went away, an old hat, an ash coloured boy's great coat, the button holes bound with white cloth, with white metal buttons, a blue cloth*

jacket, a striped linsey ditto, with blue stocking sleeves, an ash coloured great coat, without buttons, old brown woollen trowsers, and old striped ditto, new shoes, and blue grey stockings. Took with him a black MARE, her mane trimmed, and her tail short and bushy, has a white spot on one of her eyes, paces and hand gallops, is about six years old, and 15 hands high; he also took a saddle, with blue housings, having two yellow flowers on the corners, and a pair of black leather saddle bags. Whoever secures the said Runaway and Mare, so that the subscriber may have them again, shall have FIVE POUNDS reward, or THREE POUNDS for the Mare only, and FORTY SHILLINGS for the runaway, and reasonable charges, paid by BENJAMIN MEVE.

N. B. The said runaway wears black curled hair, has a strong rough voice, and is addicted to drinking and card playing. It is supposed he is gone towards Bethlehem, and may travel from thence towards Staten Island or New-York.

The Pennsylvania Gazette, January 6, 1773; January 20, 1773.

SIXTEEN POUNDS REWARD.

RAN away from the subscribers living on Elk-Ridge, Ann-Arundle county, Maryland, two servant men, one of them an Englishman named JOHN HACKIT, about 24 years old, 5 feet 8 inches high, dark hair, ruddy complexion, had on a new felt hat, oznabrigs shirt, a white jacket and breeches made of country cloth, a pair of white yarn stockings, and a pair of coarse nailed shoes   The other an Irishman, named NATHANIEL MACMIN, about 29 years old, 5 feet 11 inches high, light short hair, has a cast in his eyes and is near sighted; had on and took with him a felt hat about half worn, two check shirts, a blue pea jacket, a spotted flannel ditto, blue cloth breeches, two pair of brown ribbed stockings, a brown great coat, two pair of shoes, a pair of pumps, and a pair of large pewter buckles. Whoever will take up said servants and bring them home shall receive, if taken twenty miles from home, Four Pounds, if thirty miles, Six Pounds, if forty miles Ten Pounds, and further the above reward, or half for either of them.   JAMES BARNES, JAMES HOWARD.
Dec. 19, 1772.

The Pennsylvania Chronicle, From Saturday, January 2, to Saturday, January 9, 1773; From Saturday, January 9, to Saturday, January 16, 1773.

THIRTY POUNDS REWARD.

RUN AWAY on the 5th instant, from the subscriber, living near Baltimore-town, two servant men, SAMUEL COWAN, a joiner, who indented himself by that name in England, but since his arrival here, says his name is BOLLORD, was born in this country, and learned his trade in Philadelphia, where, he says, he has ten brothers; he is about 25 years of age, about 5 feet 10 inches high, is very straight and well made, has black eyes, is of a fresh complexion, has a lively countenance, and wears black hair tied behind: Had on when he went away, a blue nap coat, lined with white shalloon, a coarse fulled country cloth jacket and breeches, part white and part dark grey, old check shirt, leather breeches, coarse white yarn stockings, and a pair of shoes with strings, and nailed.—PATRICK QUINN, an Irishman, about forty years of age, about five feet ten inches high, has black hair, a large black beard, of a dark complexion, a thin visage, has a high thin nose, and stoops in his walk; he had on, when he went away, a coarse country cloth fulled jacket and breeches, with buttons of the same cloth, black and white stockings, oznabrigs shirts, and a pair of shoes with strings, and nailed.—Whosoever secures said servants in any gaol, so that their master gets them again, shall receive Five Pounds, and if 40 miles from home, Seven Pounds Ten Shillings; if 100 miles, Ten Pounds; if 200 miles, Fifteen Pounds; if 300 miles, Twenty Pounds; if 400 miles, Twenty-five Pounds; and if 500 miles, the above reward, or in proportion for either, and Six Shillings per day, with reasonable charges for the time of any person who brings them home, or 4s. a day, with reasonable charges for either, paid by SAMUEL OWINGS, jun.   Baltimore County, January 11, 1773.

The Pennsylvania Chronicle, From Saturday, January 9, to Saturday, January 16, 1773; From Monday, February 1, to Monday, February 8, 1773; *The New-York Gazette; and the Weekly Mercury*, February 15, 1773; March 1, 1773. Minor differences between the papers. The *Gazette* does not show the date they ran away, nor does it have the date and location at the bottom. Also it shows the seven pounds reward if they are taken 50 miles from home, not 40. See *The Pennsylvania Packet; and the General Advertiser*, June 21, 1773, and September 20, 1773.

January 1, 1773.
RAN away from the Subscriber, near the Head of *South* River, *Anne-Arundel* County, an indented Servant named *Edward Willard*, about Five Feet Two Inches high, of a dark Complection, has dark Eyes and dark coloured Hair: Had on when he went away a light coloured Jacket with slash Sleeves and Metal Buttons, lined throughout with white Flannel, blue Breeches pretty much worn, Country made Shoes and Stockings, a Felt Hat and Osnabrig Shirt. Whoever takes up said Servant and secures him so that the Subscriber gets him again, shall have a Reward of Twenty Shillings if taken Ten Miles from Home, Thirty Shillings if Twenty Miles, if Forty

Miles Fifty Shillings, if out of the Province Five Pounds, including what the Law allows, and reasonable Charges if brought Home, paid by
OTHO FRENCH.
The Maryland Gazette, January 21, 1773.

Patuxent Iron-Works, *January* 12, 1773.
RAN away last Night from the *Patuxent* Iron-Works, a Servant Man named *Robert Wharton*, born in *England*, by Trade a Blacksmith; he is a very lusty well made Fellow, 6 Feet high, about 30 Years of Age, much pitted with the Small-Pox, dark brown Hair and very thin on the Top of his Head: Had on and took with him a Hat bound round the Brim with Binding, Two Osnabrig and One Check Shirt, a dark coloured Cloth Coat and lappelled Jacket, a dark short Bearskin Coat, blue Halfthick Breeches, white Yarn Stockings and black Leather Shoes. Whoever takes up said Servant, on delivering him at said Works, if Ten Miles from Home shall have Twenty-five Shillings, if Twenty Miles Forty Shillings, and a greater Distance Three Pounds, and if out of the Province Five Pounds, including what the Law allows, paid by
SAMUEL & JOHN SNOWDEN.
The Maryland Gazette, January 21, 1773; January 28, 1773; February 4, 1773; February 11, 1773.

Baltimore, Jan. 13, 1773.
FIFTEEN POUNDS REWARD.
RUN AWAY from the Neabsco Iron works, Two Servant men, belonging to the Hon. John Taylor, Esq; viz.
JOSEPH LOVEDAY, an English Convict, about 23 years old, five feet eight inches high, and of a ruddy complexion, sandy coloured hair, red beard and smooth faced, squeaking voice and a halt in his walk, owing to having one of his knees dislocated, and therefore cannot bend it but trails his leg after him. He run away about the first of November last, and had on when he went away, a blue Fearnought, and a cotton jacket, oznabrig shirt and trowsers, the trowers [*sic*] he had dyed brown with tan bark; his other clothes are such as servants commonly have, but imagine he will endeavour to change them as soon as he can. The other is named JAMES M'LANE, a Scotch indented Servant, of great volubility of language; but may easily be known to be a Highlandman by his tongue, he is a short well made fellow, wears his own hair, which is a little of the sandy colour, dresses and ties it behind in the soldier's fashion, and talks largely of his feats in the last war, and has more assurance than a great many of his countrymen has, an instance of which he gave, in undertaking the management of a schooner

which I made him master of, tho' now believe he knew little or nothing about, and has ungratefully left the Schooner in Northumberland about the 14th of December last, sold his bedclothes and sundry other things, and run off. He had a variety of clothes with him of his own, particularly a leaden coloured coat which he daily wore.

Whoever apprehends the two servants and secures them, so that their master may have them again, shall receive for Joseph Loveday, FIVE POUNDS, and for James M'Lane TEN POUNDS, paid by
THOMAS LAWSON.

N. B. If the above mentioned servants are taken up towards Philadelphia, the person or persons concerned, are desired to apply to John Colvert in Baltimore.

The Pennsylvania Packet; and the General Advertiser, February 8, 1773; February 15, 1773; February 22, 1773; March 1, 1773; March 8, 1773.

COMMITTED to my Custody as a Runaway, a certain *James Clarke*, who says he belongs to *James Martin*, on *Kent-Island*; he had a Collar round his Neck, and his left hand is much [   ]ed; he crossed the Bay in a Yawl with two other Persons. His Master his requested to take him away and pay Charges.
WILLIAM NOKE.   Sheriff of Anne-Arundel County.
The Maryland Gazette, February 18, 1773; March 11, 1773.

N. B. The Subscriber had some Time Past assigned to him, the Indentures of a certain *William Noble*, who indented himself to a certain Dr. *John M'Donald*, for the space of Three Years, and Three Months; and as it appears he never served his Time: There are to acquaint the Publick, that if any Person will apprehend the said *William Noble*, and bring him to the Subscriber, shall have good Compensation for their Trouble, and all reasonable Expence, paid by
RICHARD YEATES.

The Maryland Gazette, February 18, 1773; March 11, 1773.

February 6, 1773.
RUN AWAY, from the subscriber, living in Strates Hundred, Dorchester County, Maryland, an Irish servant man, named WILLIAM CARROLL, *about 5 feet 2 or 3 inches high, has very thick short coarse hair, a little marked with the small-pox, a large nose, and a pretty good countenance; had on, and took with him, a blue kersey jacket, lined with coarse white*

flannel, *and has large white metal buttons, an old green coat, the lining partly tore out, country flannel breeches, and a pair of drilling ditto, nits and lice stockings, shoes one half soaled, one pewter and one metal buckle, and a coarse hat, with yellow binding; he is a Shoemaker by trade, and has been about 8 months in the country. Whoever takes up said servant, and secures him in any goal, so as his master may have him again, shall have FIVE POUNDS reward, paid by*
JOB SLACUM.
The Pennsylvania Gazette, February 24, 1773.

RUN AWAY, *the 28th of February last, from the subscriber, an English servant man, named JOHN WHITE, about 5 feet 4 inches high, brownish coloured hair, of a yellowish complexion, had a scar on one of his cheeks, an ill-looking fellow; had on, when he went away, a brown coat and jacket, blue red and white drawers, worsted stockings, and coarse shoes, with strings, an old felt hat, a good home made shirt, with flowered wristbands; the clothes described do chiefly belong to some of the rest of the family; I think he will wear them, and sell his own to get money, for he is a grand rogue; he was a servant in Maryland, and run from thence, and by his thieving and running away has been kept a servant these ten years, and scarcely worth his victuals at the best, for when he is affronted he will pretend to be sick or lame, and will not do any thing for several days; he carried his arm in a sling for 3 or 4 weeks before he went away, and said it was dead, that he had no use of it, but was seen to use it, when he thought no body observed him; I think he will try to pass for an object of charity, and go a begging. Whoever secures said servant, and brings him home, shall have one Shilling and Six pence reward, and no charges, paid by*
CURTIS LEWIS.
The Pennsylvania Gazette, March 10, 1773.

February 27, 1773.
EIGHT DOLLARS Reward.
RAN away, on Wednesday last from the subscriber living at Petapsco Lower Ferry, in Baltimore County, near Baltimore-Town, in the province of Maryland, an English convict servant man, named WILLIAM HILL, about five feet six inches high, of a swarthy complexion, down look, has short brown hair, and a large scar on his forehead. He had on, when he went away, an old blue coat with a black velvet collar, button holes on the skirts, and broad white metal buttons on the breast, old broken trowsers, old felt hat, the rim of which is cut off, except a little before, an old check shirt with patches on the shoulders of it, a pair of Negro shoes nailed in the heels and

soles, and brass buckles.—It is likely he may change his name and clothes, as he is a great rogue. Whoever secures the said servant, so that his master may have him again, shall receive, if 10 miles from home, Two Dollars; if 20 miles, Twenty Shillings; if 30 miles, Thirty Shillings; and, if out of the Province, the above reward, and reasonable charges paid, if brought home, by   JAMES LONG.

The Pennsylvania Chronicle, and Universal Advertiser, From Monday, March 15, to Monday, March 22, 1773; From Monday, March 22, to Monday, March 29, 1773; From Monday, March 29, to Monday, April 5, 1773.

Baltimore, March 10.
TWENTY DOLLARS REWARD.
RUN AWAY from the subscriber, in Newfoundland, Baltimore county, on Sunday night the 7th inst. (March) Two indented servant men, viz. WILLIAM COLLINS, about five feet five or six inches high; had on and took with him, a small brim'd hat, bound with black binding, and very likely may take it off; wore a brown surtout, and snuff coloured bodied coat, striped linen jacket, and breeches of the same kind of cloth, white linen shirt, worsted stockings, old shoes and buckles, black curled hair cut on the crown and turned up before, and much mixed with grey hairs, one of his eyes he commonly keeps shut, about thirty years old, and is a weaver by trade: He has a wife which he probably may have took with him; she is short and much pock-marked.

TOBIAS BURK, about five feet eight or nine inches high, had on and took with him, a half worn coarse hat, a lightish long surtout coat, ditto bodied coat, black jacket with sleeves, light mixed breeches, yarn stockings very much darned in the heels, a pair of old country shoes, and a white linen shirt; he is about nineteen or twenty years old, much pock marked, has sandy hair; he served his time over the Bay, and has lived at New-Castle. Whoever takes up said fellows and secures them in any gaol, shall have EIGHT DOLLARS if in the county, and if out TWELVE DOLLARS; and if out of the province the above reward, and reasonable charges, paid by PHILIP HALL.

N. B. All masters of vessels are forbid to harbour him [*sic*] at their peril.

The Pennsylvania Packet; and the General Advertiser, March 22, 1773; April 12, 1773.

York Town, Goal, March 1, 1773.
WAS committed to my custody, the 15*th day of February last past, a certain* Thomas Ward, *who says he served his time with Mr. William Burten, about*

4 *miles from Baltimore-Town, near Annapolis road; had on, when committed, an old felt hat, a blue cloth coat, with brass buttons, a blue cloth jacket, without sleeves, with metal buttons, a pair of linen drawers, white knit hose, flaxen linen shirt, he is about 5 feet 7 or 8 inches high, hath a sandy beard, thin visage, well made otherwise, a bushy brown head of hair, and about 20 years old, an Irishman. And, on the 23d day of February last past, there was also committed, a certain* Conrad Founder, *who says he is a servant to Jacob Dautistel, a butcher, in Philadelphia; he is a lad of about 18 years of age, and about 5 feet high, thin visage, long dark brown hair; had on, when committed, a dark-blue napped short jacket, with sleeves, with metal buttons thereon, a pair of buckskin breeches, light blue worsted hose, a blue cloth cap; talks pretty good English. Their masters (if any) are desired to come, pay charges, and take them away, from*
MICHAEL GRAYBIL, Goaler.
The Pennsylvania Gazette, March 24, 1773; April 7, 1773.

Annapolis, April 5, 1773.
BROKE Jail, in the Night of the 4th Instant, *Timothy Ragan*, committed for Horse-stealing; the said *Ragan* is about 20 Years of Age, about Six Feet high, of a fair Complexion; Had on when he made his Escape a blue Coat and Waistcoat of the same, Country made Leather Breeches, Yarn Stockings and Country made Shoes. *Francis Sellars*, committed on Suspicion of Felony: Had on when he made his Escape a brown Cloth Coat, Leather Breeches, Yarn Stockings, Country made Shoes, all very much worn. The said *Sellars* is about 5 Feet 9 or 10 Inches high, of a dark Complexion, with black straight Hair. Whoever apprehends and secures the said *Ragan* and *Sellars*, so that they may be had again, shall receive Five Pounds Reward, or Fifty Shillings for either of them.
WILLIAM NOKE, Sheriff of Anne-Arundel County:
The Maryland Gazette, April 8, 1773; April 15, 1773; April 29, 1773.
See *The Maryland Gazette*, October 15, 1772 for "Sellers."

TEN POUNDS REWARD.
RAN AWAY from the subscribers, living in Baltimore County, Maryland, about twelve miles from Baltimore Town, on the road leading to Frederick Town, on Sunday night the 28th of February last, the two following English convict servant men, viz. JOHN MORGAN, about five feet six inches high, and about twenty years of age, down look, round shouldered, a small face, blue eyes, short brown hair, and a middling fair complexion, can speak Welch, is a great lover of strong liquor, and well built; had on when he went away, an old felt hat, an old black handkerchief, an old oznabrig shirt, a

good white kersey outside jacket, and an under ditto, white Kersey breeches patched between the thighs, old grey yarn stockings, double soaled shoes nailed, and a patch on one of the toes. ROBERT JONES, about thirty years of age, but appears to be more, can speak Welch, and is about five feet seven or eight inches high, well set, pale complexion, grey eyes, and short brown hair; had on and took with him an old hat bound with black, an old cotton jacket, old country cloth coat, and striped waistcoat, all much patched and darned, two oznabrig shirts, white plush breeches lined with shammy, had a leather apron, a pair of hose with grey legs and white feet, white yarn ditto with half feet, shoes with the straps pieced, plated square buckles, but very likely may change them for cash; he has a scar on the left side of his under jaw, which he says came from the kick of a horse; he has an old worked pocket-book with him: He served part of his time with Mr. Chew, on Herring Bay, in St. Mary's County, and part with Mr. William Barney, in Baltimore, and is acquainted with most of the lower counties in Maryland. Whoever takes up and secures said servants, so that their masters may get them again, shall have TWELVE DOLLARS, or SIX DOLLARS for either; and if one hundred miles from home, the above reward, or FIVE POUNDS for either, and reasonable charges (if brought Home) paid by
JOHN OWINGS, son of Richard
JOSHIA OWINGS, Junior
N. B. Said JONES is a thief, a liar, and very deceitful.
The Pennsylvania Packet; and the General Advertiser, April 12, 1773; April 19, 1773; May 3. 1773.

RAN away from a waggon on its way from Baltimore-Town to Frederick, near Hood's mill, a convict servant man, imported in Capt Thomas [sic] from Bristol the other day, named Stephen Woolridge He is about twenty-three years of age, five feet eight inches high, born in Cornwall, a brisk looking well made fellow, brown complexion, blue eyes, wears his own dark hair, and is or pretends to be a farmer, but has rather the appearance of a sailor: Had on a small bound hat, coarse cotton jacket, old trousers, old shoes and odd buckles. Whoever secures him in any jail, or delivers him to Mr. Lux at Baltimore, Jacques and Johnson in Annapolis, or James Johnson at Fort Frederick furnace, shall have forty shillings if taken in the province, and three pounds in taken out of the province.

There is another convict servant who was imported in the same ship, the property of Mr. Russell, in company with him.
The Maryland Gazette, April 15, 1773.

Kent County, Maryland, April 9, 1773.
RUN AWAY from the subscriber, living near the Province Bridge, Duck Creek, on the seventh of this instant, an apprentice lad named JOSHUA RUE, about nineteen years old, and about five feet eight or nine inches high; had on when he went away, a brown cloth over jacket without lining, and a blue under ditto with white lining and pewter buttons, a wool hat, a pair of old leather breeches, a pair of black and white yarn stockings, and a pair of half worn shoes. The cause of said boy's running away was for stealing a horse from one of the neighbours and riding about 30 or 40 miles. Whoever takes up said Joshua Rue, and confines him in any gaol, or brings him to his master, shall have THREE DOLLARS reward, and reasonable charges, paid by   JOHN LEWIS.
The Pennsylvania Packet; and the General Advertiser, April 19, 1773; May 3, 1773.

RAN away from the subscriber, living near the head of Patapsco river, in Baltimore County, on the 9th of march last, an English convict servant man named Joseph Manyfold, a lusty well set fellow, about five feet eight or nine inches high, wears his own short dark hair which curls a little, his right ear is split, and has a scar on his throat which I believe to be cut by himself. Had on, an osnabrig shirt, an old felt hat, and strong shoes with iron plates to the heels; the other part of his dress is country made white kersey. Whoever secures the said servant so that his master may get him again, shall receive, if ten miles from home thirty shillings, if thirty miles fifty shillings, and if out of the province five pounds including what the law allows, and reasonable charges if brought home, paid by
SAMUEL NORWOOD.
The Maryland Gazette, April 22, 1773; April 29, 1773; May 6, 1773.

Queen Anne's County, Maryland, April 19, 1773.
RUN away from the Subscriber, the 11th of this Instant, a Convict Servant Man, who calls himself JOHN INMAN, but perhaps may change his Name; is about 5 Feet 3 Inches high, fresh coloured, and very talkative; had on, when he went off, a white Cloth Jacket, with yellow Metal Buttons, Nankeen Breeches, white Linen Shirt, blue grew Worsted Stockings, tolerable good Shoes, with large plated Buckles; he took with him an old blue great Coat, very much worn. Whoever takes up said Servant, and secures him in any of his Majesty's Goals, shall receive THREE POUNDS Reward, paid by
MICHAEL BATEMAN.
The Pennsylvania Gazette, April 28, 1773; May 12, 1773.

April 26, 1773.

A CERTAIN Richard Flemming, a native of Ireland, and by trade a weaver, about five feet nine or ten inches high, well set, long dark curled hair, brown complexion, speaks tolerable good English, but has a small scar on his nose, down look, and has remarkable small eyes; he has a flesh mark on his right wrist nearly the colour of claret, and has very bad sore legs, but the right leg the worst; wears a lightish cloth coat about half wore, a wilton jacket that has been turned, and lined with fine Shaloon, leather Breeches, mixed blue and white stockings, over which he wears brown knit leggings, old shoes, and wears a grayish surtout coat about half wore, and a small country made hat with white lining; came and lived with the subscriber in Baltimore county, from December until the twenty-ninth of March last, as a weaver, and then pretended business at Charles-Town, in Caecil county, borrowed to ride there a saddle, bridle, and a bay horse, about fifteen hands high, paces well and trots, used to the draught, has a snip and small star in his face, branded on the near buttock **G C** but not very plain, on the upper part of his neck, under where the collar has wore is some white hairs, and his tail has also white hairs in it, and what is most remarkable has no under bridle teeth; but the said Richard Flemming, not returning to the time proposed, caused suspicion in the subscriber who pursued him, but found he has altered his rout, and instead of going to Charles-Town, took through York county, and it's expected has either gone to the back settlements, or turned off towards Virginia or Carolina. Whoever apprehends said Flemming, and secures him in any jail, that the said horse may be got again, or damaged recovered for him, shall receive five pounds reward, or three pounds for securing the said horse that the subscriber may obtain him again.
GEORGE CHAUNCEY.

The Maryland Gazette, April 29, 1773.

April 27, 1773.

RAN away from the subscriber on the 11th inst. an Irish convict servant man, named William Weldon, about five feet five inches high, sandy coloured short hair, and his beard when grown entirely red, with a remarkable mould [*sic*] on his right cheek, surrounded with red hair which he will not have shaved off; a joiner by trade, speaks much with the brogue, and is very fond of liquor: had on and took with him, a check and an osnabrig shirt, country made shoes, old felt hat, halfthick jacket, and a pair of dark coloured broad cloth breeches.

Whoever takes up the above servant, and secures him, so that his master may have him again, shall receive five pounds reward, and all reasonable charges paid by   STEPHEN STEWARD.

The Maryland Gazette, May 6, 1773; May 27, 1773.

May 2, 1773.

RAN away from the subscriber, a servant man named James Roper, about twenty-one years of age, by trade a tailor, is about five feet eight or nine Inches high, dark complexion, much pitted with the small-pox, wears his own hair, which is black: had on when he went away, a dark bearskin frock bound round, white russia drab breeches, white thread stockings, and good shoes; he also took with him, a light coloured fustain [*sic*] frock with a red cape, and sundry waistcoats. Whoever takes up the said servant, and brings him to his master, living in Annapolis, shall receive, if taken ten miles from him, forty shillings; if twenty miles, three pounds, and if fifty miles or upwards, five pounds; including what the law allows, paid by
THOMAS CALLAHAN.
The Maryland Gazette, May 6, 1773.

TEN POUNDS REWARD.
Mount Clare, Baltimore county, April 27, 1773.

RAN away from the subscriber, a convict servant man, named John Adam Smith, a well set fellow, five feet six or seven inches high, about 30 years of age, fair complexion short light curled hair, gray eyes, and light eyebrows, by trade a Gardener; has with him, it is supposed, a treatise on raising the pine apple, which he pretends is of his own writing, talks much of his Trade, and loves liquor: Had on when he went away, a red striped linen waistcoat, white shirt, buckskin breeches, fine yarn stockings, and black leather shoes, but may have other cloaths, and perhaps may have a pass. Whoever secures him and gives the subscriber notice, shall have if taken in Baltimore or Anne-Arundel counties five pounds, and if in any other county the above reward, paid by
CHARLES CARROLL.
The Maryland Gazette, May 6, 1773; May 13, 1773.

RAN away, from the subscriber, living in Blandensburg, an Irish servant man, named BRYAN FITZPATRICK, a well set fellow, about 5 feet 3 inches high, light complexion, light brown hair, cut short, yellow buckles in the diamond fashion; he is a shoemaker by trade, and is a proud saucy fellow. Had on when he went away, a claret coloured surtout coat, a light blue coat, waistcoat and breeches, brown worsted stockings, pumps half worn, with a French cock'd hat, tarred on the top of the crown, and is supposed to have a forged pass. Whoever takes up the said servant and secures him, or gives intelligence so as his master may get him again, shall receive, if taken out of the province, THREE POUNDS, Maryland

currency, or otherwise, if taken in the province of Maryland, FORTY SHILLINGS.
Maryland, May 4, 1773.   JOHN FRANCIS.
The Pennsylvania Chronicle, From Monday, May 3, to Monday, May 10, 1773; From Monday, May 10, to Monday, May 17, 1773; From Monday, May 17, to Monday, May 24, 1773. See *The Maryland Gazette,* May 13, 1773.

Baltimore, April 27, 1773.
RAN away, last Friday night, from the subscriber, a servant woman named MARY WILKINS, lately imported in the snow Restoration, Captain James Thomas, from Bristol; she is a lusty well-looking young woman, remarkably fresh coloured, and speaks quick and bold; she carried off many clothes of her own, besides robbing her master of several things of value. At the same time, ran away, from the above-mentioned vessel, two sailors, who are supposed to have assisted her in robbing her master, and are gone off with her.—One an Irishman, named NATHANIEL MADDIN, about 5 feet 8 inches high, of a ruddy complexion, has black hair, and a cast in one of his eyes.—He wore a blue upper jacket, and a red and white striped waistcoat. The other an Englishman, named GEORGE ROBINSON, about 5 feet 7 inches high, of a ruddy complexion, has black curled hair, and dressed in seamen's clothes.—Whoever takes up the said servant woman, and secures her, so that her master may have her again, shall receive FIVE POUNDS reward, and the like sum for each of the said men, if taken up and convicted of the robbery, to be paid by
JAMES CHAMBERS.

N.B. All masters of vessels, and others, are forbid to harbour, conceal or carry off the said persons, or either of them, at their peril; and the same reward will be given to any person who informs against and such master or masters, upon conviction.
The Pennsylvania Chronicle, From Monday, May 3, to Monday, May 10, 1773; *The New-York Journal, or, the General Advertiser,* May 13, 1773.

May 1, 1773.
THREE POUNDS REWARD.
RUN AWAY from the subscriber, in Charles Town, Caecil County, Maryland, a servant man named THOMAS WILKIN, near forty years of age, about five feet ten or eleven inches high, thin visage, of a dark complexion, wears his own hair, his head a little bald; he is a blacksmith by trade, came into Maryland a convict, and served his time near Sassafras; has now a wife and two children; he lately lost his eldest son at the Crooked

Billet wharf at Philadelphia, when attempting to run away, but was retaken; he is often very talkative and much in his own favour; being pretty artful he may probably (as he cannot write) prevail on some person to counterfeit a discharge on the back of his part of the indentures, in which he bound himself to RICHARD THOMAS, late Sheriff of Caecil County, for 4 years from September 1770; had on when he went away, a short blue bath coat, a purple and white serge jacket, old light blue velvet breeches, and a new felt hat. Whoever takes up and secures the said servant man, so that he his master may have him again, shall have the above reward, and all reasonable charges, paid by   JAMES PRITCHARD.
N. B. The subscriber is bail for him in a considerable sum of money, exclusive of what he indented for.

The Pennsylvania Packet; and the General Advertiser, May 10, 1773; May 17, 1773; May 31, 1773.

Newcastle Gaol, April 28, 1773.
EIGHTEEN DOLLARS REWARD,
BROKE out of the gaol of this county on Sunday night last, the following persons, to wit. PATRICK M'DANIEL....MATTHEW SIMPSON, about five feet six inches high, short dark brown hair, full faced, fresh complexion, a well made fellow and a notorious rogue; had on an old ragged greyish coat, new felt hat, and hat an iron collar on his neck when he broke goal; he served his time (as he said) in or near Lancaster, afterwards became servant to ROBERT JOHNSON, tinker, in Penns Neck, West New-Jersey, who sold him to ADAM LITTLE, in Kent County, Maryland. Also a negro man named POMPEY....Whoever apprehends and secures the above named prisoners, and lodges them in any of his Majesty's gaols so that the subscriber may have them again, shall have the above reward, or SIX DOLLARS for each, and reasonable charges, paid by
ROBERT MACK, Gaoler.
N. B. Was committed to my custody, a certain ALEXANDER HASLET, who says he belongs to PATRICK GAMBLE, of Chester County; his said master is desired to come and pay charges and take him away.

The Pennsylvania Packet; and the General Advertiser, May 10, 1773; May 24, 1773; June 7, 1773.

RUN AWAY *from the subscriber, living in Queen-Anne's county, Maryland, near Minor's tavern, a Dutch servant man, named* JOHN PETERSON, *a shoemaker by trade, had on, when he went away, an old blue broadcloth coat, a pale blue jacket, white Russia drilling breeches, white yarn stockings, and new pumps; he is remarkably small sized, and talks very bad English, scarcely to be understood. Whoever takes up the*

said servant, and brings him home, shall have FIVE POUNDS, *and all reasonable charges paid, or* THREE POUNDS, *if secured in any of his Majesty's goals, so that his master may get him again, paid by*
JOSEPH NABB.   April 14, 1773.
The Pennsylvania Gazette, May 12, 1773.

THREE POUNDS REWARD.

May 4, 1773.
RAN away from the subscriber, living in Bladensburg, an Irish servant man, indented for four years, about twenty-two years of age, named Bryan Fitzpatrick, a shoemaker by trade: had on, when he went away, a claret coloured surtout coat, a light blue coat, waistcoat and breeches, brown worsted stockings, pumps half worn, with a French cocked hat tarred on the top of the crown, and is supposed to have a forged pass.

Whoever brings the said servant to his master, or gives intelligence, so that he may be got again, shall receive if taken out of the province, three pounds Maryland currency, or otherwise if taken in the province of Maryland, forty shillings.
JOHN FRANCIS.

N. B. He took with him, a pair of yellow buckles cut in diamond fashion, a case of razors marked G. W. a dark flaxen hair curl, he is a proud saucy fellow.

The Maryland Gazette, May 13, 1773; May 20, 1773; June 3, 1773.
See *The Pennsylvania Chronicle*, From Monday, May 3, to Monday, May 10, 1773.

May 4, 1773.
COMMITTED to the jail of Charles county the 30th of April last, as a runaway, Daniel Duoneilly, an Irishman, who says he is a servant to Henry Howard of Meclinburg county, in Virginia, has an impediment in his speech, thin visage, wears his own dark hair: has on, an old bearskin coat, a red striped linsey woolsey jacket, both trimmed with black horn buttons, leather breeches, osnabrig shirt, shoes, yarn stockings, and hat. The owner of said servant is desired to take him away and pay charges, to
WILLIAM HANSON, deputy sheriff.

The Maryland Gazette, May 13, 1773; May 20, 1773; June 3, 1773.

ADVERTISEMENT.
Bush-Creek, Frederick County, Maryland, Oct. 11.
RUN away from the subscriber, a convict servant maid, named Sarah Wilson, but has changed her name to Lady Susanna Carolina Matilda,

which made the public believe she was his Majesty's sister, she has a blemish in her right eye, black roll'd hair, stoops in the shoulders, makes a common practice of writing and marking her cloaths with a crown and a B. Whoever secures the said servant women, or takes her home, shall receive five pistoles besides all costs and charges.
WILLIAM DEVALL.

I entitle Michael Dalton to search the city of Philadelphia, and from thence to Charlestown, for the said woman.
(*A true copy*)   William Devall.

Boston Post Boy, May 17, 1773; *Connecticut Journal*, May 21, 1773; *Essex Gazette*, From Tuesday, May 18, to Tuesday, May 25, 1773; *The Providence Gazette; And Country Journal*, May 29, 1773; *The Newport Mercury*, May 31, 1773.

Wilson had been a servant to one of the Queen's maids of honour. She was arrested and transported in 1771 after the disappearance of some of the Queen's jewels. She had been sold in Maryland but escaped. After conning her way through polite society along the eastern seaboard, she was caught in Charleston and brought back to the man who had bought her.

May 10, 1773.
SEVENTY DOLLARS Reward.
RAN AWAY, from Annapolis, the two following indented servants, viz. WILLIAM TANKARD, a native of Ireland, about twenty years of age, about five feet six or seven inches high, of a ruddy complexion, has light hair and very little beard. He took with him, a blue duffil coat with a red collar, a red duffil waistcoat, leather breeches, boots turned down, with plated spurs. He also took with him, a livery suit of cloaths, the coat being a superfine blue cloth, waistcoat and breeches superfine white cloth, the buttons plain white metal, the sleeves and cape of the coat of white cloth, and a silver laced hat, but he may have taken off the trimmings. He may also have other cloaths.

BERNARD BARRY, also a native of Ireland, about twenty-eight years of age, five feet ten inches high, of a ruddy complexion, black beard, and large eye brows. He is a stout man, and in the right side of his upper jaw has a remarkable tooth sticking out so that in speaking he shews it. He took with him, a new sky blue coat with plain white metal buttons, red waistcoat, black cotton velvet breeches lined with shammy. His hair is short in curl, but he took with him a light-coloured wig with one curl, and he may cut off his hair; he is a bricklayer, stone mason, and plaisterer. They took with them a sorrel gelding, about fourteen hands high, or upwards, with a white face, his mane remarkably thick; also a bright bay gelding known by the name of Chatham, about fifteen hands high, nine years old, is a blooded horse, has lost three of his upper teeth by an accident; likewise took with them, two saddles, made by Witkers of London, one of them has four raised silver plated nails, has been cut in the seat, and sewed; the other a portmanteau saddle, the stirrips of both double barr'd; two bridles, one of them plated with silver, the other a steel one; also, a large whip with a silver cap, with the letters D D in a cypher. They have also, a brace of silver mounted screw barrel pistols.

The subscriber, D. DULANY, will pay to any person who will apprehend and secure William Tankard, the sum of TWENTY DOLLARS, and also TWENTY DOLLARS more for the sorrel horse, saddles, bridles, and pistols, on delivery to him.

The subscriber, UPTON SCOTT, will pay any person for the bay horse, the sum of FOURTEEN DOLLARS, on delivery to him; and the subscriber, JAMES MAWE, will pay to any person who shall apprehend and secure BARNARD BARRY, in any of his Majesty's goals, the sum of SIXTEEN DOLLARS, and reasonable charges if brought home.

It is supposed they were seen pass [sic] by the Rising Sun, on the Old York Road.

D. DULANY, UPTON SCOTT, JAMES MAWE.

N. B. All masters of vessels are forbid to carry them off at their peril.

The Pennsylvania Packet; and the General Advertiser, May 17, 1773; May 24, 1773; June 7, 1773; June 14, 1773. *The New-York Gazette; and the Weekly Mercury,* May 24, 1773. Minor differences between the papers. The *Gazette* does not have the date at the top. See *Rivington's New-York Gazetteer*, June 3, 1773.

TWENTY DOLLARS Reward.

RUN AWAY, on the 10th Day of November last, from the Subscriber, living in Baltimore County, near Nathan Wheeler's Mill, on the Great-Road leading from York to Baltimore Town, an English Servant Man, named NOAH BROWN, by Trade a Blacksmith, about 45 Years of Age, 5 Feet 10 Inches high, he is stoop shouldered, and wears his own black Hair, has a down Look, and is pitted with the Small-pox: Had on, when he went away, a Felt Hat, a blue Kersey Jacket, good Buckskin Breeches, white Stockings and old Shoes; he has lived some Time in Barbados, and followed the Barber's Business. Whoever takes up said Servant, and brings him Home, shall have the above Reward, and all reasonable Charges, paid by
April 20, 1773.   DANIEL REES.

The Pennsylvania Gazette, May 19, 1773; June 2, 1773.

York-Town, May 11, 1773.

WAS committed into my custody, on the 5th day of April last, a certain RICHARD PENDERGRASS, as he calls himself, says that he is a servant to Francis Casteel, of Frederick county, Maryland. Also, on the 23d day of April last, was committed to my custody, a certain THOMAS MAYFIELD, who says he is a servant to Bernard Sweeny. Their masters, therefore, are desired to come and take them away, in four weeks from the date hereof, or else they will be sold out for their fees, by MICHAEL GRAYBIL, Goaler.

The Pennsylvania Gazette, May 19, 1773.

TWENTY POUNDS REWARD,

BROKE out of Caecil County Gaol, on Saturday night the 15th of May, the following persons, *viz.*

WILLIAM DAVIDSON, committed for felony; a tall thin fellow, about thirty years of age; had on a light coloured coat, a brown jacket, an old hat, and wore his own hair tied behind.

PATRICK M'DONALD, committed as a runaway, lately broke out of Newcastle county Gaol; about twenty-two years of age, had on a brown jacket with a linen frock almost worn out, and a half worn pair of buckskin or sheepskin breeches, black hair and smooth face, and looks as if he had been pretty long confined in gaol.

HUGH BROWN, about forty-seven or forty-eight years of age, had on a brown jacket, blue duffil trowsers, old hat and shoes.

SARAH DAVIDSON, about twenty-five years of age, yellow complexion, long black hair, and a lincey petticoat. Whoever takes up the above described persons, and delivers them to me, shall have the above reward, or FIVE POUNDS for each.

JOHN HAMILTON, Sheriff.

The Pennsylvania Packet; and the General Advertiser, May 24, 1773; June 28, 1773; *The Pennsylvania Gazette*, June 9, 1773. The *Gazette* ad has the date May 16, 1773 at the bottom.

TWENTY DOLLARS Reward.

RUN away from the subscriber's plantation, near Colonel Cresap's, in Maryland, on the 6th of April last, a servant man, named WILLIAM COADY, aged 27 years, 5 feet 5 inches high, thick set, tender eyed, a down look when spoke to, round shouldered, and the one much higher than the other; he pretends to be a butcher by trade, but knows nothing of it, speaks much on the Irish dialect, is very fond of drink and smoking; it is supposed he will make for Philadelphia or Baltimore. Whoever will secure him in any goal, so that I get him again, shall receive Ten Dollars reward, and if brought home to me, near Winchester, shall receive Twenty Dollars reward, paid by me   ANGUS M'DONALD. *May* 26.

The Pennsylvania Gazette, May 26, 1773; June 9, 1773; June 23, 1773; August 25, 1773. See *The Pennsylvania Gazette*, June 30, 1773.

TWELVE POUNDS REWARD.

May 17, 1773.

RAN away last night from the subscribers, living on Elk Ridge, in Anne-Arundel county, Maryland, two convict Servant men, viz. Anthony Jackson, born in the west of England, speaks a little in that dialect, about twenty-five years of age, five feet eight or nine inches high, a red faced well-looking fellow, stoops in the shoulders, has short brown hair, and thin dark beard, has a down look when spoken to: had on, and took with him, when he went away, two osnabrig shirts, a pair of coarse country linen trousers, two pair of country made old shoes, a felt hat, white cotton and kersey jacket much worn, and an iron collar.—John Jones, an Irishman, about eighteen years of age, five feet three or four inches high, short dark hair, black eyes, fair complexion, and fresh coloured: Had on, and took with him, a light coloured forest cloth coat, with a piece of linsey about two inches broad down the back, a jacket of the same, old felt hat, a pair of greasy leather breeches, coarse yarn stockings, one pair of thread ditto, osnabrig shirt, and an iron collar.

Whoever takes up the said servants, and secures them in any jail, so that their masters may get them again, shall receive if taken ten miles from home, forty shillings; if twenty miles, four pounds; if forty miles, eight pounds; and if out of the province, the above reward; or half for either one of them (including what the law allows) and reasonable charges if brought home to

JOHN HOOD, junr.   JOSEPH HOBBS, junr.

N. B. It is probable they may cut off their hair and get their collars taken off. All masters of vessels are forwarned carrying them off at their peril.

The Maryland Gazette, May 27, 1773; June 3, 1773; June 17, 1773; June 24, 1773. Only the first ad has the date at the top. See *The Maryland Gazette*, September 13, 1770, *The Pennsylvania Gazette*, September 20, 1770, and *The Pennsylvania Chronicle,* From Monday, June 14, to Monday, June 21, 1773, for Jackson.

Baltimore, May 22, 1773.

RAN away on Wednesday the 5th inst. an apprentice lad, named Arthur Shane, between fifteen and sixteen years old, is country born: had on, when he went away, an old check shirt, new osnabrig trousers, his own light

brown hair, little eyes sunk in his head; by report is gone off in a boat to Virginia. Whoever will bring or send him home to the subscriber in Baltimore-town, shall have five shillings for their trouble.
ROBERT MOORE.
The Maryland Gazette, May 27, 1773.

May 20, 1773.
SIXTEEN DOLLARS REWARD.
STOLEN from the subscriber, in Baltimore, on the 19th of this instant, a BAY HORSE, about 14 hands high, trots fast and very lively, no particular brand, a switch tail, crooked snip down his face, a white hind and fore foot on the contrary side, a hanging mane on the right side, has two small white spots, about the bigness of an English shilling, just behind his ears, which are exactly under the bridle, has a scar on his right side, occasioned by the saddle, lately shod before, and is in very good order.

The Horse was stolen by an Irish servant lad, belonging to Mr. Jacob Myers, named DENNIS NEAL, between 17 and 18 years of age, about 5 feet high, has a smooth full face, pleasant countenance, and is fresh-coloured; has black eyes and hair, his hair tied behind, and was lately cut before; he can write a tolerable good hand; and has been in the country about two years, and is acquainted with gentlemen from all parts of the country, having attended in a tavern in Baltimore-Town. Had on, when he went away, a drab-coloured cloth coat, with either a red or a blue jacket, oznabrigs trowsers, good shoes with metal buckles, and an old felt hat, but probably may change his dress. Whoever secures said Horse, so that he may be had again, shall have Eight Dollars reward, and Eight more for the thief, if convicted.   WILLIAM AISQUITH.
The Pennsylvania Chronicle, From Monday, May 24, to Monday, May 31, 1773; From Monday, May 31, to Monday, June 7, 1773.

May 10, 1773.
Thirty Six DOLLARS Reward.
RAN AWAY, from Annapolis, the two following indented servants, viz. WILLIAM TANKARD, a native of Ireland, about twenty years of age, about five feet six or seven inches high, of a ruddy complexion, has light hair and very little beard. He took with him, a blue duffil coat with a red collar, a red duffil waistcoat, leather breeches, boots turned down, with plated spurs. He also took with him, a livery suit of cloaths, the coat being a superfine blue cloth, waistcoat and breeches superfine white cloth, the buttons plain white metal, the sleeves and cape of the coat of white cloth, and a silver laced hat, but he may have taken off the trimmings. He may also have other cloaths.

BERNARD BARRY, also a native of Ireland, about twenty-eight years of age, five feet ten inches high, of a ruddy complexion, black beard, and large eye brows.

He is a stout man, and in the right side of his upper jaw has a remarkable tooth sticking out so that in speaking he shews it. He took with him, a new sky blue coat with plain white metal buttons, red waistcoat, black cotton velvet breeches lined with shammy. His hair is short in curl, but he took with him a light-coloured wig with one curl, and he may cut off his hair; he is a bricklayer, stone mason, and plaisterer. They have also, a brace of silver mounted screw barrel pistols.

The subscriber, D. DULANY, will pay to any person who will apprehend and secure William Tankard, the sum of TWENTY DOLLARS; And the subscriber, JAMES MAWE, will pay to any person who shall apprehend and secure BARNARD BARRY, in any of his Majesty's goals, the sum of SIXTEEN DOLLARS, and reasonable charges if brought home.
D. DULANY,   JAMES MAWE.

N. B. All masters of vessels are forbid to carry them off at their peril.
Rivington's New-York Gazetteer, June 3, 1773. See *The Pennsylvania Packet; and the General Advertiser*, May 17, 1773.

RAN away the 30th of May last from the subscriber, living in the Long Green, in the Forks of Gunpowder, Baltimore County, Maryland, an Irish servant man, named JOHN FARIS, 19 or 20 years old, 5 feet 10 or 11 inches high, freckled and pock marked, has dark brown hair, sometimes tied behind. He is much addicted to strong drink, and when intoxicated he is very talkative and *brags* much of his strength, activity and courage. He also has a propensity to singing, and frequently displays his sing-song abilities. He had on and took with him, when he went away, a bearskin coat, a spotted swanskin jacket, a pair of Russia drab breeches, one holland shirt, oznabrigs ditto, a pair of pumps and silver plated buckles. It is suspected that he hath stolen several other articles of cloathing, and that he will charge his dress as much as possible.—Whoever takes up the said servant, and secures him, so that his master may have him again, shall receive, if taken in the county of Baltimore, TWENTY SHILLINGS; if out of the county THREE POUNDS, and if out of the province FIVE POUNDS reward, paid by   PETER HUNTER, Tanner and Currier.

N. B. All masters of vessels and others are forbid harbouring, concealing or carrying off said servant.
June 9, 1773.

The Pennsylvania Chronicle, From Monday, June 7, to Monday, June 14, 1773; From Monday, June 14, to Monday, June 21, 1773; From

Monday, June 21, to Monday, June 28, 1773; From Monday, June 28, to Monday, July 5, 1773.

June 12, 1773.
TEN POUNDS Reward.

RAN away, the 17th of last month, from the subscriber, living on Elk Ridge, in Anne-Arundel county, Maryland, a convict servant man, named ANTHONY JACKSON, born in the West of England, and speaks a little in that dialect, about 25 years of age, 5 feet 8 or 9 inches high, a red- fac'd well-looking fellow, stoops in the shoulders, has short brown hair, thin dark beard, and has a down look when spoken to; had on, and took with him, when he went away, two oznabrigs shirts, a pair of country coarse linen trousers, two pair of country made old shoes, a felt hat, white cotton and kersey jacket, much worn, and an iron collar.—I am informed by a servant, who ran away with the above, that he has stolen a brown cloth jacket, without sleeves, two pair of yarns stockings, one pair of shoes, a pair of oznabrigs trousers, a linen handkerchief, a pair of boots, and a matchcoat blanket, and 17/6 in money—I am also informed, that he has a pass, signed Jonathan Plowman, dated May, 1773, and will endeavour to pass by the name of Thomas Ryan, and has got his collar off. Whoever takes up the said servant, and secures him in any gaol, so that his master may get him again, shall receive, if taken 20 miles from home, FORTY SHILLINGS, if 40 miles, FOUR POUNDS, and if out of the province the above reward, including what the law allows, and reasonable charges, if brought home to JOHN HOOD, jun.

The Pennsylvania Chronicle, From Monday, June 14, to Monday, June 21, 1773. See *The Maryland Gazette,* September 13, 1770, *The Pennsylvania Gazette,* September 20, 1770, and *The Maryland Gazette,* May 27, 1773.

Deer Creek, in Baltimore County, June 3, 1773.
THREE POUNDS REWARD.

RAN AWAY, last night, from the subscriber, an Irish convict servant man, named OWEN COYL, a smooth faced fellow, about twenty years of age, and about five feet seven or eight inches high; had on when he went away, a new felt hat cut in the fashion, a sailors grey jacket, a striped linsey under ditto with sleeves, a check shirt, old ticken breeches, good shoes, and ribbed stockings with no feet to them: He was imported in the schooner Polly and Sally, Capt. Slacum, to Newcastle, about three weeks ago. Whoever secures said servant in any gaol, so that his master may have him again, shall receive the above reward (including what the law allows) and reasonable charges if brought home, paid by

WILLIAM WEBB.

N. B. He is a very great rogue, and says he has broke seven gaols in Ireland.

The Pennsylvania Packet; and the General Advertiser, June 14, 1773; June 21, 1773; July 5, 1773; *The Pennsylvania Gazette*, June 16, 1773; June 30, 1773. After three weeks ago, The *Gazette* has the line "He pretends to be a horse-rider or jockey."

Chester-town, Maryland, June 2, 1773.

FIVE POUNDS Reward.

RUN away from the subscriber, the 31st of May, at night, two English servant men, both joiners, one named *Robert Duffey*, upwards of 40 years of age, thin shrivelled or wrinkled face, about 5 feet 8 inches high, is very apt to get drunk; had on, when he went away, a new felt hat, old fearnought jacket, without buttons, new ozenbrigs shirt and trowsers, old yarn stockings, and black-grained shoes, almost new. The other, named *Thomas Harvey*, about 28 years of age, 5 feet 6 inches high, with dark hair, which is generally cued; had on, and took with him, a brown cloth coat and waistcoat, an old striped silk ditto, old drilling breeches, old thread stockings, shoes, two Russia shirts, almost new, felt hat; he is very talkative and fond of drink. Whoever secures said servants, so as they may be had again, shall have what the law allows, if taken within this province, and if out of it Five Pounds, including what the law allows, and if brought home, all reasonable charges, paid by

WILLIAM BOWERS.

The Pennsylvania Gazette, June 16, 1773; June 30, 1773.

THIRTY POUNDS REWARD.

RUN AWAY, *the* 5th *of January last, from the subscriber, living near Baltimore-town, two servant men, viz.* SAMUEL COWAN, *a joiner, who indented himself by that name in England, but since his arrival here, says his name is* BOLLORD; *was born in Pennsylvania, and learned his trade in Philadelphia, where he has several brothers and sisters, a brother in Reading, and several in different parts of that province, and the Jerseys; he is well acquainted in almost every part of this continent; he is about* 25 *years of age, about* 5 *feet* 10 *inches high, is remarkable straight and well made, has black eyes, is of a fresh complexion and lively countenance, and wears black hair tied behind: Had on, when he went away, a blue napped coat, lined with white shaloon, and coarse fulled country cloth jacket and breeches, part white and part dark grey, old check shirt, leather breeches, coarse white yarn stockings, and a pair of shoes with strings in them and*

nailed. PATRICK QUINN *(Yeoman) an Irishman, about 40 years of age, about 5 feet 5 inches high, slow of speech, has black hair, a large black beard, of a dark complexion, a thin visage, has a high thin nose, and stoops in his walk: Had on when he went away, a coarse fulled country cloth jacket and breeches, with buttons of the same cloth, ozenbrigs shirt, black and white stockings, and a pair of shoes with strings and nailed. They may have cut off their hair, changed their clothes, and altered their names. They are great rogues, and very artful, and will, if possible, make their escape when apprehended. Whoever secures said servants in any gaol, so that their master gets them again, shall receive Ten Pounds; and if 50 miles from home, Fifteen Pounds; if 100 miles, Twenty Pounds; if 200 miles, Twenty-five Pounds; and if 300 miles, the above reward, or in proportion for either of them, paid by*
June 10, 1773.   SAMUEL OWINGS, *junior.*

The Pennsylvania Gazette, June 16, 1773; June 30, 1773; August 18, 1773; *The Pennsylvania Packet; and the General Advertiser,* June 21, 1773; July 5, 1773; August 9, 1773; August 30, 1773. Minor differences between the papers. See *The Pennsylvania Chronicle,* From Saturday, January 9, to Saturday, January 16, 1773 and *The Pennsylvania Packet; and the General Advertiser,* September 20, 1773.

FIFTEEN POUNDS REWARD.

May 20, 1773.

RAN away from the subscriber's plantation, in Frederick county, on the head of Bennett's creek, on the 17th inst. at night, a convict servant man, named William Flint, about 22 years of age, born in the west of England, a spare slim fellow, about 5 feet 8 inches high, of a swarthy complexion, short black hair, and has lost one of his fore teeth: he had on, and took with him, a white cotton jacket, brown cloth ditto much worn, a pair of leather breeches black and dirty, two white shirts, two pair of stockings and shoes, and a new felt hat; it's possible he may have changed his name and apparel, as he has a sum of money with him.

Whoever takes up the said servant, and brings him either to John Plummer, overseer on the above-said plantation, or the subscriber living in Anne-Arundel county, near Elk Ridge church, shall have the above reward for their trouble, besides what the law allows, paid by
HENRY RIDGELY.

The Maryland Gazette, June 17, 1773; July 1, 1773; July 15, 1773; July 22, 1773; August 5, 1773; August 19, 1773; September 2, 1773; September 16, 1773; September 30, 1773; October 14, 1773; October 28, 1773; November 11, 1773; November 18, 1773; November 25, 1773; December 2, 1773; December 9, 1773; December 16, 1773;

December 23, 1773; December 30, 1773; January 6, 1774; January 13, 1774; January 27, 1774; February 3, 1774; February 10, 1774; February 17, 1774; March 10, 1774; March 17, 1774; March 24, 1774; March 31, 1774; April 3, 1774; April 14, 1774; April 21, 1774; April 28, 1774; May 5, 1774; May 12, 1774; May 19, 1774; May 26, 1774; June 2, 1774; June 9, 1774; July 7, 1774.

TWELVE DOLLARS Reward.

RAN away, from the subscriber, living in Baltimore County, Maryland, within 18 miles of Baltimore-Town, an Irish servant man, named JOHN CARROL, about 21 years of age, 5 feet 9 or 10 inches high, slim made, fair complexion, has little or no beard, short straight black hair, which has lately been cut round the bottom, black eye-brows and blue eyes; is a lively quick-spoken person, and a vile rogue for riding horses; had on, when he went away, a country full'd grey cloth coat, a pair of country cloth white breeches, old oznabrigs shirt, old felt hat, and shoes and stockings. It is probable he will get other clothes, change his name, and endeavour to pass as a free man, as he has done before. Whoever takes up the said servant, and brings him home, if in the county, *Forty Shillings*, and if out of the province, the above reward, including what the law allows.

May 13, 1773.   SAMUEL WORTHINGTON.

N. B. All masters of vessels are forbid to carry him off at their peril.

The Pennsylvania Chronicle, From Monday, June 21, to Monday, June 28, 1773; From Monday, June 21, to Monday, June 28, 1773; From Monday, July 5, to Monday, July 12, 1773.

Baltimore County, June 21, 1773.
FIVE POUNDS REWARD.

RAN AWAY, last Saturday night, from the subscriber, living on Garrison Ridge, nine miles from Baltimore Town, an English convict servant man named WILLIAM TALBEY, a shoemaker by trade, about five feet seven or eight inches high, about thirty-five years of age, has yellow short curled hair, is pitted with the small-pox, and talks in the West Country dialect; had on and took with him when he went away, a black broadcloth coat, a brown fustian ditto, and a red broadcloth jacket with sleeves; a white holland, a striped holland, and two oznabrigs shirts; two hats, a beaver and a felt; black Barcelona handkerchief, a pair of new oznabrigs trowsers, a pair of white cotton stockings, black grain turn pumps, and white metal buckles. It is supposed he has a pass. Whoever takes up the said servant, and secures him in any goal, so that his master may get him again, shall have, if taken in

the county, THREE POUNDS reward, and if out of the county, the above reward, and reasonable charges if brought home, paid by
MICHAEL KRANER.
The Pennsylvania Packet; and the General Advertiser, June 28, 1773; July 5, 1773.

Baltimore County, June 21, 1773.
RAN AWAY, last night, from the subscriber, living about ten miles from Baltimore, an indented servant man named WILLIAM JEFFRIES, an Englishman, twenty-five years of age, five feet ten inches high, of a dark complexion, is very much pock-marked, and has black hair curled; he has taught school in the neighbourhood for seven months past: Had on and took with him when he went away, two check shirts, a white flannel jacket bound round with black worsted, two pair of osnabrigs trowsers, worsted stockings, and old shoes; he has been used to the sea, and has a sailor's hat with him. Whoever takes up the said servant, and brings him to the subscriber, shall have, if ten miles from home, TWENTY SHILLINGS; if twenty miles, FORTY SHILLINGS; and if out of the province, THREE POUNDS reward, and reasonable charges if brought home, paid by
JOHN COCKEY.
The Pennsylvania Packet; and the General Advertiser, June 28, 1773; July 5, 1773.

JUNE 29, 1773.
NOW in the goal of the county of Philadelphia, several runaway servants, viz. JAMES COLEMAN, belonging to Robert Barr, in Milford hundred, Caecil county, Maryland. THOMAS MORGAN, belonging to Benjamin M'Vaven, Caecil county, Maryland. HUGH M'MAHAN, belonging to William Beakes, Caecil county, Maryland. WILLIAM EDWARDS, on suspicion of being a runaway servant. JOHN GOOD, belonging to John Guttrey, Caecil county, Maryland. Their masters are desired to come, pay the charges, and take them away, or they will be sold in three weeks from this date, to pay their fees.
The Pennsylvania Gazette, June 30, 1773; July 7, 1773.

Lancaster Goal, June 14, 1773.
THIS day was committed to my custody, on suspicion of being a runaway servant, a certain John M'Laughlin, as he calls himself, and says that he worked last with Robert Robin, or Robert Robe, within 2 miles or Carlisle; he is about 5 feet 9 inches high, and about 21 years of age, and of a freckled complexion; had on, when committed, a flannel jacket, spotted with black, old long trowsers, old hat, and has straight short light hair. Also was committed to my custody, in the 19th instant, a certain WILLIAM

ROBINSON, alias COADY, aged 27 years, and answers all the descriptions of the person, advertised in the Pennsylvania Gazette, that ran away on the 6th of April last, from Angus M'Donald, near Col. Cresap's, in Maryland. The masters of the said servants, if any they have, are desired to come and pay their charges, and take them away, in four weeks from the date hereof, otherwise they will be sold out for their fees, by me GEORGE EBERLY, Goaler.

The Pennsylvania Gazette, June 30, 1773. See *The Pennsylvania Gazette*, May 26, 1773, for Coady.

RUN away on Sunday last, from the subscriber, living in Baltimore county, Maryland, about 15 miles from Johnson's Ferry, an Irish servant man, named PATRICK NEVIN, but may change his name, 25 years of age about 5 feet 4 inches high, wears his own black hair, of a swarthy complexion, blue eyes; had on and with him, when he went away, an old pair of trowsers, old homespun shirt, a short linsey-woolsey jacket, of a dark colour, a swanskin spotted ditto, a brown homespun cloth jacket, with sleeves, a new silk handkerchief, and a half worn felt hat: He has his indenture with him. Whoever takes up said servant, and secures him, so as his master may get him again, shall have FORTY SHILLINGS reward, and reasonable charges, paid by
JOHN VANCLEAVE.
N. B. All masters of vessels are forbid to carry him off at their peril.
June 23, 1773.

The Pennsylvania Gazette, June 30, 1773; July 21, 1773.

Baltimore, June 10, 1773.
RAN AWAY, last night, from the subscriber, an Irish servant lad, named MEREDITH THOMAS, about five feet six inches high, and twenty years of age, or thereabouts; he is much pitted with the small pox: Had on when he went away, a blue nap'd coat and jacket, light coloured plush breeches, dark check shirt, woollen stockings, old shoes and hat: 'Tis unknown what other things he may have taken with him. He came in the brigantine Boscawen, Capt. Marshall, from Londonderry, to this place, and it is supposed that he is on his way to Philadelphia, in company with a run-away fellow from Fell's-point, about his own size, who was taken up with this servant at Bush Town, where they were handcuffed together, and made their escape with their irons on. 'Tis probable he may change part of his cloathing. Whoever takes up the said servant, and brings him home, or secures him in any gaol, so that his master may get him again, shall have the above reward, and all reasonable charges, paid by
CHARLES YOUNG.

N. B. Said servant has a forged pass, and, as he can write, he may forge one for his comrade. All masters of vessels, and others are forbid to harbour, conceal or carry him off.

The Pennsylvania Packet; and the General Advertiser, June 28, 1773; July 5, 1773; August 16, 1773; August 30, 1773; *The Pennsylvania Gazette*, June 30, 1773; July 14, 1773; July 28, 1773; August 18, 1773. See *The Maryland Journal, and the Baltimore Advertiser*, From Friday, August 20, to Saturday, August 28, 1773.

Maryland, June 21, 1773.
TWENTY DOLLARS Reward. RUN away from the subscriber, living in Anne-Arundel county, near Elk-Ridge Church, a convict servant man, named JOHN COLLIER, born in England, about 5 feet and an half high, well made, of a brown complexion, has a hoarseness in his speech, he wears his own short dark hair, took with him a new castor hat, a dark coloured bearskin outside jacket, made long, with cuffs, and lined with white flannel, one white linen under ditto, one white shirt, one ozenbrigs ditto, white Russia drab breeches, white worsted stockings, and a pair of pumps; he has with him a pass, formerly belonging to one John Fleming, by which name he now goes; it is signed by Henry Ridgely, of Anne-Arundel county, and Thomas Price, of Frederick county, Maryland, by Richard M'Collister, of York county, William Henry, of Lancaster county, and William Clingan, of Chester county, Esquires, Pennsylvania. Whoever takes up the said servant, and secures him, so that the subscriber gets him again, shall have the above reward, paid by
CHARLES WORTHINGTON.

N. B. The above servant has had one of his legs broke, near the ancle, which stands somewhat out; it is thought to be the left.

The Pennsylvania Gazette, July 7, 1773; July 21, 1773.

FIFTEEN POUNDS Reward.
RUN away, last night, from the subscriber living in Baltimore county, about 12 miles from Baltimore town, in Maryland, three English convict servant men, viz. JAMES HICKMAN, about 22 years of age, about 5 feet 7 or 8 inches high, straight and well made, with short dark brown hair, round face, dark eyes, a little cross, fresh complexion, and some freckles. He speaks in the west country dialect. THOMAS AGER, about 25 years of age, about 5 feet 4 or 5 inches high, straight and well made, dark brown hair, tied, long face, bluish eyes, long chin, pale complexion, pert and proud; he is a good scholar, and no doubt has changed his name, and forged passes: He ran away some time ago, and can give some account of Virginia, and the lower parts of Maryland. WILLIAM ABBOTT, about 25 years of age, about 5

feet 2 or 3 inches high, well set, round shouldered, with short brown hair, full face, white eyes, very weak; served part of his time with Henry Hollingsworth, at the Head of Elk, ran away, and made into the back lands, was put into Bedford goal, can give an account of Shamokin, on Sasquehanna, Shearman's and Path Vallies, and other parts of the back country. They took with them, felt hats, several coarse shirts, and trowsers, one old hunting shirt, died yellow, two coarse brown cloth jackets, one white kersey ditto with sleeves, one red cloth ditto, bound at the pocket holes; one ditto, country fulled and lapelled, with metal buttons, and without sleeves; two pair of strong country made shoes well nailed, one pair of ditto without nails, and several other things. Whoever takes up said servants and secures them, so as their masters may get them again, shall have *Seven Pounds Ten Shillings*; if 50 miles from home, *Ten Pounds*; if 100 miles the above reward, or in proportion for each, including what the law allows, and reasonable charges, if brought home, paid by
ALEXANDER WELLS, CHARLES HOWARD, THOMAS OWINGS.
June 21, 1773.

    The Pennsylvania Gazette, July 7, 1773; July 21, 1773; The *Pennsylvania Chronicle,* From Monday, July 5, to Monday, July 12, 1773. Minor differences between the papers. See *The Maryland Journal, and the Baltimore Advertiser*, From Thursday, February 24, to Thursday, February March 3, 1774, for Hickman. See *The Pennsylvania Gazette*, August 12, 1772 and *The Pennsylvania Packet; and the General Advertiser*, August 17, 1772, for Abbott/Abbot.

                                                           Prince George's county, June 23, 1773.
COMMITTED to my custody as a runaway, a person who calls himself Francis John Salmon, a well made man, about 23 years old, 5 feet 4 or 5 inches high, gray eyes, dark brown hair, which he wears short, and it curls naturally; says he is a free man, that he kept school some time in Essex county in the Jerseys, and also that he lived some time with Mr. James Boyd, merchant, at Cohansie bridge in Cumberland county in the Jerseys, from whom he shews a letter of recommendation to Mr. John White, merchant in Philadelphia; he shews also a letter signed James Shields and John White, recommending him generally to the merchants in Maryland, but as the bodies of those letters appear to be wrote in the same hand, it is supposed they are forged. His master, if he has one, is desired to pay charges and take him from
RALPH FORSTER, sheriff.

    The Maryland Gazette, July 8, 1773; July 15, 1773; July 22, 1773.

Maryland, June 30, 1773.
RUN away, last Sunday night, from the subscriber, two convict servant men, viz. *Henry Frazer,* appears to be about 26 years of age, about 5 feet 8 or 9 inches high, has lightish hair, full cheeks, and is a fleshy fellow; had on, when he went away, a striped shirt, ozenbrigs trowsers, English shoes, worsted stockings, oldish hat, and a sailor's jacket.—*Robert Armstrong,* about 21 years of age, 5 feet 8 or 9 inches high, and of a lightish complexion; had on, when he went away, a claret-coloured broadcloth coat and jacket, a new hat, cut in the fashion, check shirt, ozenbrigs trowsers, English shoes, plated buckles, and worsted stockings; he said that his father and mother keeps tavern in some part of England, and that he used to tend the bar of the tavern; he appeared to be well brought up. They both came in the ship Thornton, Captain John Kidd, from London. Whoever takes up the said servants, and brings them to WILLIAM PANCOAST, on Hawling's river, in Frederick county, or to their master, living about 4 or 5 miles from the Great Falls of Patowmack river, shall have FIFTEEN POUNDS reward; if confined in any goal in this province, so that they may be got again, TEN POUNDS, and reasonable charges; if taken in New York, TWENTY POUNDS, paid by ADIN PANCOAST.

N. B. it is likely they have parted, and that *Robert Armstrong* has got ruffled shirts, and took with him about Sixty Pounds in gold and silver, a silver watch, a woman's necklace, worth Fifty or Sixty Guineas, which have all been seen with him since he ran off; and he has changed his name, and passes by the name of *Captain Frazer.* All masters of vessels and others are forbid to harbour, conceal, or carry them off, at their peril.
The Pennsylvania Gazette, July 14, 1773; August 18, 1773.

Queen-Anne's County, Maryland, July 3, 1773.
TWENTY DOLLARS REWARD.
BROKE Jail, on the 2d Instant, JAMES NUNAR, *who was committed on Suspicion of Horse stealing, he is a middle- aged Man, Country born, about 5 Feet* 10 *Inches high, and has long brown Hair; had on a Snuff coloured Coat and Vest, Check Trowsers, and Shoes. Whoever delivers him to the Subscriber, shall receive, if taken in the County, Ten Dollars, and if out of the County the above Reward, from*
CHARLES GOLDSBOROUGH, *Sheriff.*
The Pennsylvania Gazette, July 14, 1773; August 11, 1773.

Anne-Arundel county, July 14, 1773.
COMMITTED to my custody as runaways, the four following persons, viz. John Hambleton, and James Adams, both Irishmen, and says they belong to

a ship from Glasgow, commanded by Captain William Mackie, and they left her in Patowmack.—Bartholomew Leary, an elderly Irishman, who says he belongs to James Offord, near the falls of Patowmack.—John Obriant, an Irishman, and says he belongs to Mr. Samuel Dorsey, Ironmaster, on Elk-Ridge. Their masters are requested to take them away and pay charges.
WILLIAM NOKE, Sheriff.
The Maryland Gazette, July 15, 1773.

Gunpowder mill, July 5, 1773
RAN away last night from my mill, on the great falls of Gunpowder, in Baltimore county, Maryland, two Irish indented servant men, viz. William Stackabout, about 50 years of age, and about 5 feet 10 inches high: had on, and took with him, an old blue coat, black jacket and breeches, two pair of osnabrig trousers, one check shirt, one osnabrig ditto, an old brown cut wig, a new felt hat, a pair of yarn stockings, and one pair of old patched shoes. Cornelius Shane, about 23 or 24 years old, and about 5 feet 6 Inches high: had on, and took with him, a suit of brown coarse cloth, one check shirt, one osnabrig ditto, one pair of osnabrig trousers, one pair of blue yarn stockings, one pair of old shoes, with yellow metal buckles, a brown dress wig, one old castor hat, one cooper's broad-axe, with the helve drooping; and an old drawing knife; they are both coopers by trade. Whoever takes up the said servants, so as the subscriber may have them again, shall receive, if taken 10 miles from home, three pounds; if 20 miles, four pounds; and if out of the province, six pounds,; and if only one, the above reward in proportion, with reasonable charges, if brought home, paid by
BENJAMIN ROGERS.
N. B. Stackabout is a thin faced man; the other is a round faced man, pitted with the small pox a little; they both talk much in the Irish dialect.
The Maryland Gazette, July 15, 1773; July 22, 1773; July 29, 1773; August 5, 1773.

July 5, 1773.
RAN away from the subscriber, living in Westmoreland county, Virginia, two white men servants, viz. William Walker, alias Smith, a convict who came in 1771, in the Scarsdale, Capt. Reid, by trade a gardener; he is a slim made man, five feet nine or ten inches high, brown complexion, blue eyes, blackish hair, has a remarkable swing in his walk, a coarse voice and a cough; he has with him, kersey and cotton jackets and breeches, white, check, and osnabrig shirts; he likes to drink, and has been severely whipped before a magistrate: this is the third time he has run away; as he had sailors cloaths with him he will attempt to pass for a sailor. Thomas Puttrell, an indented servant, (who came in last April, in the Liberty, Capt. Raison) a

trunchy well made man, fair complexion, brown hair, which curls in his neck, a round face, hazle eyes, speaks quick, a butcher by trade, understands gardening and farming; he has been fourteen months on board a man of war; he has a butcher's steel and knife, and wears quils in his hat: he has with him, a brown cloth coat, second mourning jacket, black breeches, white, check, and osnabrig shirts, and some money; he will attempt to pass for a sailor; and I hear they intend to Baltimore and Philadelphia. Whoever apprehends the aforesaid servants, and secures them in a jail, so that I get them, shall receive a reward of five pounds Virginia currency for each of them.
RICHARD LEE.

The Maryland Gazette, July 22, 1773; July 29, 1773; August 12, 1773; August 19, 1773; August 26, 1773; October 14, 1773.

SIX POUNDS Reward.

RUN AWAY, last night, from Bush-town, in Baltimore county, Maryland, two convict servant men, one named WILLIAM PITT, about 47 years of age, pitted with the small-pox, about six feet high; had on, and took with him, a brown half worn surtout coat, two white shirts, an ozenbrigs frock, with buttons on the shoulder, a pair of trowsers, yarn stockings, small old felt hat, half boots, with iron plates round the heels, and a pair of old shoes, with nails in the heels, a pair of greasy leather breeches; he wears his own short grey curled hair, and speaks on the West country dialect; he says he is a Tallow-chandler and Horse-jockey. The other named EDWARD WILLIAMS, a Cooper by trade, about 40 years of age, is a down-looking stout fellow, of a dark complexion, the fore part of his head shaved, and the back part short brown hair, and speaks much on the West country dialect; had on a new felt hat, a white shirt, a white fustian frock, lined with white flannel, a brown cloth jacket, dirty coarse trowsers, yarn stockings, and half worn shoes. Whoever takes up the above servants, and secures them in any goal, or brings them to the subscribers, shall receive, if 10 miles and under 40 miles from home, FORTY SHILLINGS, besides what the law allows, and if a greater distance, the above reward, paid by WILLIAM YOUNG, junior, RICHARD RUFF.

N. B. They have not been above four weeks in the country.
July 12, 1773.

The Pennsylvania Gazette, July 28, 1773; August 18, 1773; August 25, 1773. See *The Pennsylvania Packet; and the General Advertiser*, August 2, 1773.

RUN away, on the 19th *of July*, 1773, *from the subscriber, living near Elk Ridge Church, in Anne-Arundel county, Maryland, a convict servant man, named* JAMES HICKINS, *about 5 feet 8 inches high, has black hair, and a very dark skin, his left eye is very remarkable, being contracted, occasioned by a wound he received; has on, and took with him, an ozenbrigs shirt and trowsers, a pair of blue and a pair of white breeches, a country cloth jacket, a blue German serge ditto, without sleeves, the right-hand pocket of it smells of mercurial ointment, and is greasy, a pair of old shoes, with common metal buckles, a good felt hat, and a yellow flowered silk handkerchief; it is probable he has forged a pass, and altered his name, as he has been in the country upwards of six years. Whoever takes up and brings home the said servant, shall receive, if within ten miles from home,* FORTY SHILLINGS; *if more,* THREE POUNDS; *and if out of the province or fifty miles off,* SIX POUNDS; *and half those sums, if only secured in gaol, paid by*
EPHRAIM HOWARD.

The Pennsylvania Gazette, July 28, 1773; August 18, 1773; January 12, 1774.

July 21, 1773.
WENT away, last night, from Thomas Snowden's plantation, the six following servant men, viz. William Lowe, an Englishman, about 20 years of age, about 5 feet 8 or 9 inches high, by trade a blacksmith, of a swarthy complexion, and has lost one of his fore teeth; had on, an osnabrig shirt, dirty brown holland trousers, old castor hat, old shoes, and plated buckles. Richard Ellingsworth, born in Yorkshire, about 25 years of age, 5 feet 8 or 9 inches high, of a dark complexion, and pretty well set; had on, an osnabrig shirt, crocus trousers, old flowered lapelled waistcoat, old felt hat, and good shoes. Richard Thompson, born in the north of England, about 27 years of age, about 5 feet 5 or 6 inches high, of a swarthy complexion, and is much pitted with the small-pox, had on, an osnabrig shirt, crocus trousers, old felt hat, and good shoes with copper buckles. Thomas Hogg, born in Yorkshire, about 25 years of age, about 5 feet 6 or 7 inches high, and of a swarthy complexion; had on, an osnabrig shirt, black breeches and stockings, an half worn castor hat, and old shoes with copper buckles. Thomas Sutton, a north countryman, about 25 years of age, about 5 feet 8 or 9 inches high, and of a fair complexion; had on, an osnabrig shirt, canvas trousers, old castor hat, and good shoes with plated buckles. John Driver, an Englishman, born in Norfolk, about 23 years of age, about 5 feet 5 or 6 inches high, and of a dark complexion; had on, an osnabrig short, crocus trousers, old castor hat, old shoes and copper buckles. Whoever takes up the said servants, shall receive, on securing them in any jail, so that their masters get them again, if taken 20 miles from home, 30 shillings for each,

and so in proportion for a greater distance, and, if brought home, reasonable travelling charges, paid by
HENRY and THOMAS SNOWDEN.
The Maryland Gazette, July 29, 1773; August 5, 1773. See *The Maryland Journal, and the Baltimore Advertiser*, From Saturday, August 28, to Saturday, September 4, 1773, for Hogg.

New-Castle Gaol, July 26, 1773.
WAS committed to my care, the 22d inst. two convict servant men, viz. EDWARD WILLIAMS, who says he belongs to Mr. YOUNG, Merchant, in Bush-Town, Maryland: The other said his name is WILLIAM PITT, and belongs to a gentleman near to the above Mr. Young's. Their masters are desired to come, pay charges, and take them away in three weeks from the date hereof, otherwise they will be sold for the same, by
ROBERT MACK, Gaoler.
The Pennsylvania Packet; and the General Advertiser, August 2, 1773; August 9, 1773; August 23, 1773. See *The Pennsylvania Gazette*, July 28, 1773.

THREE POUNDS Reward.
RUN away, last night, from the subscriber, living on Deer Creek, Upper Hundred, Baltimore county, a convict servant man, named PATRICK M'CLUSKY, about 25 years of age, 5 feet 6 inches high, of a dark complexion, has black hair, and a scar over his right eye; had on, when he went away, a double breasted flannel jacket, with black spots, the back part of which is white, tow shirt and trowsers, and an old wool hat; he took with him a sickle, and may endeavour to get work. Whoever takes up said servant, and secures him in any of his Majesty's goals, or brings him home to his master, shall receive, if 20 miles from home, THIRTY SHILLINGS, if 30 miles, FORTY SHILLINGS, and if out of the province, the above reward, and reasonable charges, if brought home, by
June 28, 1773. JAMES GORDON.
The Pennsylvania Gazette, August 4, 1773.

August 2, 1773.
FIVE POUNDS REWARD.
RAN AWAY from the subscriber, living in Baltimore County, near Joppa, an Irish servant man, name THOMAS CORMICK, lately from Waterford, about five feet eight or nine inches high, appears to be twenty-five or twenty-six years of age, smooth full face, thick lips, little out-mouth, full eyed, stoop shouldered, black hair, well built, with thick ancles and feet,

and swears in common discourse: Had on when he went away, an old dirty shirt, old waistcoat without sleeves, the fore parts of a grey colour and the hind parts of a light; and old trowsers, but perhaps he may change his dress: His hair has been lately cut off. Whoever takes up said servant and secures him, so that his master may have him again, shall receive the above reward, and all reasonable charges, paid by
JOHN WILSON.

The Pennsylvania Packet; and the General Advertiser, August 9, 1773; August 16, 1773; August 30, 1773.

Baltimore, July 23, 1773.
COMMITTED to my custody at different times, the following persons, viz. Henry Kenally or Connelly, who says he is a servant to John Owings. Nancy Jones, a servant to Richard Greaves. George M'Cason, a deserter from his majesty's 16th regiment of foot. John Scarran or Skyrme, who says he is a servant to Robert Henwood of Annapolis, and produces an indenture dated Nov. 1772, to serve one year. John Glowen, who says he is a servant to Richard Lawrence. Patrick M'Glaskey, a servant to James Gordon. Daniel Earls, alias Poor, an Irishman, five feet seven or eight inches high, about thirty-five years of age, short fair hair: had on, a white Irish frize jacket, osnabrig shirt and trousers, a labourer, and appears to be one of those advertised by Dr. Ephraim Howard, of Elk-Ridge. John Buttler, a Yorkshireman, about five feet eleven inches high, says he deserted from his majesty's 23d regiment or Welch fusileers, has short curled hair, Russia sheeting trousers, but appears to have changed his apparel, and says he came from Philadelphia, but it is believe he belongs to some person on Elk-Ridge. Letters have been wrote to those persons to whom it is said the servants belong, requesting them to take them, paying charges, but to no effect; have therefore taken this method, hoping due attention will be paid thereto; if not the servants will be sold to pay fees as the law directs, by
JOHN ROBERT HOLLIDAY, sheriff.

The Maryland Gazette, August 12, 1773; August 26, 1773; September 2, 1773.

RAN away from the subscriber, living in Charles county, a servant lad, called Hooper Bennett, about 19 years of age, slender make, about 5 feet 3 inches high, light coloured hair, which he generally wears in a slovingly manner, pale sallow complexion, appears to have had the fever and ague, speaks quick, and calls himself a barber and hair-dresser: had on, when he went away, a brown short skirted coat, red waistcoat, and olive coloured velvet breeches, although it is supposed he may have changed his dress: he was seen, about five weeks ago, at Lyon's-creek, in Calvert county, and I do imagine he is now either in that or the county of St. Mary's. Whoever brings said servant to the subscriber, shall have a reward of forty shillings, paid by   RICHARD LEE.

The Maryland Gazette, August 12, 1773; August 26, 1773; September 2, 1773; September 9, 1773. See *The Maryland Gazette*, October 14, 1772.

THREE POUNDS REWARD.

RAN AWAY the 6th of July last, from the subscriber, living in Charles-Town, Cecil County, Maryland, an indented servant man named THOMAS DOUGHERTY, by trade a shoemaker, and can shave and dress hair very well; he was born in the north of Ireland, is about five feet ten inches high, a black looking fellow, stoops in the shoulders, black hair, very dark beard, and has a very remarkable hair mole on the side of his face; had on, a brown coat, striped jacket, old buckskin breeches, old shoes and old felt hat. Whoever takes up the said servant, and secures him in any gaol, so that his master may get him again, shall receive THIRTY SHILLINGS, and if brought home the above reward, and all reasonable charges, paid by CHARLES HAMILTON.

The Pennsylvania Packet; and the General Advertiser, August 16, 1773; August 30, 1773.

RAN-AWAY from the subscriber, living on Kent-Island, Queen Ann's County, Maryland, on the 9th of July (ult.) an English servant man, named THOMAS NORRINGTON, a spare made fellow, five feet 9 or 10 inches high, pale complexion, sandy beard, brown hair, about 30 years of age; had on when he went away, an oznabrigs shirt, coarse county linen trowsers, old dark country kersey jacket, old felt hat; and an iron collar about his neck. Whoever takes up and secures said fellow, so as his master may have him again, shall have, if taken in the county, THIRTY SHILLNGS, if out of the county, FORTY SHILLINGS, and if out of the province THREE POUNDS reward, paid by   WILLIAM STEPHENS.

The Pennsylvania Packet; and the General Advertiser, August 16, 1773; August 30, 1773; September 20, 1773.

SIXTEEN DOLLARS Reward.

RUN away from the subscriber, living in the Forks of Gunpowder, Baltimore county, and English convict servant man, named EDWARD HUMPHREYS, he pretends to be a Shoemaker, about 5 feet 11 inches high,

well built, dark complexion, and dark brown hair; had on, and took with him, an osnabrig shirt and trowsers, old check shirt, old shoes, and old felt hat; it is likely he may change his name and dress, and forge a pass. Whoever takes up the said servant, so that his master may get him again, shall have, if in the county, SIX DOLLARS, if out of the county, TEN DOLLARS, and, if out of the province, the above reward, paid by
July 30, 1773.   JAMES BAKER.
The Pennsylvania Gazette, August 18, 1773. See *The Maryland Gazette*, August 19, 1773.

guAust [sic] 18, 1773.
RAN away from the subscriber, near Elk-Ridge church, the 8th inst. an English convict servant, named Edmund Nunn, about 5 feet 8 inches high, 21 years of age, well made, fair complexion, gray eyes, wears his hair, one of his teeth stands further forward than the others: had on when he went away, an osnabrig shirt, roll trousers, felt hat, and coarse new shoes: he pretends to know the duties of a sailor, may have changed his name, and forged or otherwise fraudulently obtained a pass.—Whoever takes up and secures said servant, so that he may be had again, shall have if 30 miles from home, three pounds, if out of the province five pounds, (including what the law allows) and reasonable charges if brought home.
THOMAS SAPPINGTON.
The Maryland Gazette, August 19, 1773; September 2, 1773; September 16, 1773; October 21, 1773; October 28, 1773; November 4, 1773; November 11, 1773; November 18, 1773; November 25, 1773; December 2, 1773; December 9, 1773; December 16, 1773; December 23, 1773; December 30, 1773; January 6, 1774; January 13, 1774. The ads from October 21 on have the correct spelling for August.

TAKEN up and committed to Somerset county jail, a certain John Danks, who says he belongs to John Roberts, in Baltimore county His master is desired to pay charges, and take him out.
GEORGE DASHIELL, sheriff.
The Maryland Gazette, August 19, 1773.

SIXTEEN DOLLARS REWARD.
July 30, 1773.
RAN away from the subscriber, living in the fork of Gunpowder, in Baltimore county, a servant man, named Edward Humphreys, about 5 feet 11 inches high, about 40 years of age; he pretends to be a shoemaker, of a

brown complexion, well built, and short brown hair, a very mild sober look: had on when he went away, osnabrig shirt and trousers, felt hat, and old shoes. Whoever takes up the said servant, so that his master gets him again, shall receive if taken in the county, six dollars; if out of the county, ten dollars; and if out of the province, the above reward, paid by
JAMES BAKER.

The Maryland Gazette, August 19, 1773. See *The Pennsylvania Gazette*, August 18, 1773.

August 16, 1773.

RAN away yesterday morning from the subscriber living on Seneca, Frederick county, near the Widow Dowden's tavern, a convict servant man, named John Gardner, about 24 years of age, and about 5 feet 8 or 9 inches high, dark complexion, gray eyes, is very talkative, and has a very bad scald head: Had on and took with him, old felt hat, osnabrig shirt much patched, old striped linsey jacket, white drab breeches, cotton stockings, and good shoes: he pretends to act the slight of hand, so I imagine he will pass for a show-man, and probably may forge a pass. Whoever takes up the said servant, and secures him, so that his master gets him again, shall receive twenty shillings reward, besides what the law allows, and reasonable charges if brought home, paid by
GREENBURY GRIFFITH.

The Maryland Gazette, August 26, 1773; September 2, 1773; September 9, 1773. See below.

August 16, 1773.

RAN away, yesterday morning, from the subscriber, living on *Seneca*, in *Frederick County*, near the widow *Dowden's* tavern, a convict servant named JOHN GARDENER, 5 feet 8 or 9 inches high, of a dark complexion, very talkative, has gray eyes, and a bad scald head. He had on, and took with him, an old felt hat, an oznabrig shirt, much patched, an old striped linsey jacket, white drill breeches, thread stockings, and good shoes. He pretends to act the slight of hand, and I imagine he will endeavour to pass for a show-man. Whoever will secure him, so I may get him again, shall have TWENTY SHILLINGS reward, beside what the law allows, and reasonable charges if brought home, paid by
GREENBERRY GRIFFITH.

N. B. It is imagined he will change his clothes; he has got a forged pass, and probably may go by the name of *John Jennings*.

The Maryland Journal, and the Baltimore Advertiser, From Friday, August 20, to Saturday, August 28, 1773; *The Maryland Journal, and the Baltimore Advertiser*, From Saturday, August 28, to Saturday,

September 4, 1773; From Saturday, September 4, to Thursday, September 9, 1773. See above.

RAN away, on Sunday last, from the Subscriber, living about a Mile from *Hanover-Town*, in *Manheim Township, York County*, Province of *Pennsylvania*, a Servant Woman, named MARY ROWE, about 21 or 22 Years of Age, about 5 Feet 2 or 3 Inches high, of a brown Complexion; one of her middle Fingers is shorter than the rest; she speaks good *English* and *Dutch*. Had on, when she went away, a Linsey Petticoat, with blue and white Stripes, one short half Silk red under Jacket, one fine Cap, and a Straw Hat.—Whoever takes up said Servant, and secures her in any Gaol, so that her Master may get her again, shall have, if taken in the County, FORTY SHILLINGS, if out of the County, THREE POUNDS, and if out of the Province, FIVE POUNDS, and reasonable Charges paid, by
SEPT. 7, 1773.   SOLOMON MILLER.

The Maryland Journal, and the Baltimore Advertiser, From Saturday, September 4, to Thursday, September 9, 1773; From Thursday, September 9, to Saturday, September 18, 1773; From Saturday, September 18, to Saturday, September 25, 1773.

BALTIMORE, *August* 25, 1773.
SIX DOLLARS Reward.

RAN away, on the 9th of June last, from the subscriber, an *Irish* servant lad, named MEREDITH THOMAS, about 5 feet 6 inches high, and 20 years of age, or thereabouts; he is much pitted with the small-pox: had on, when he went away, a blue nap'd coat and jacket, light-coloured plush breeches, dark check shirt, woollen stockings, old shoes and hat. 'Tis unknown what other things he may have taken with him. He came in the brigantine Boscawen, Capt. Marshall, from Londonderry, to this place, and it is supposed that he is on his way to *Philadelphia*, in company with a runaway fellow from *Fell's-Point*, about his own size, who was taken up with this servant at *Bush-Town*, where they were hand-cuffed together, and made their escape with their irons on. It is probable he may change part of his cloathing. Whoever takes up the said servant, and brings him home, or secures him in any gaol, so that his master may get him again, shall have the above reward, and all reasonable charges, paid by
CHARLES YOUNG.

N. B. Said servant has a forged pass, and, as he can write, he may forge one for his comrade. All masters of vessels, and others are forbid to harbour, conceal or carry him off.

The Maryland Journal, and the Baltimore Advertiser, From Friday, August 20, to Saturday, August 28, 1773; From Saturday, August 28, to Saturday, September 4, 1773. See *The Pennsylvania Packet; and the General Advertiser*, June 28, 1773.

Baltimore, August 15, 1773.
THE following persons were lately committed to my custody as runaways John Gambol, a German, appears to be insane, when in his senses which he is a times, his jargon is not to be understood. Thomas Morris, a seafaring man, who says he belonged to the Sims, Capt. Boucher, lying in the eastern branch of Patowmack, he had money concealed about him, and much spare apparel, and is supposed to have robbed some vessel. Richard Slade, says he is a servant to Mr. Levin Lawrence, of Elk-Ridge. Their masters (if any they have) are desired to fetch them away and pay charges, or they will be sold agreeable to law, by
JOHN ROBERT HOLLIDAY, Sheriff of Baltimore county.
The Maryland Gazette, August 26, 1773.

Baltimore, August 19, 1773.
RAN away from the subscriber, living in Gay-street, near Mr. George M'Candless's Tavern, at the sign of George III, an apprentice Boy, named WILLIAM JOHNSON, about 4 feet 8 or 9 inches high, of a brown complexion, has dark short brown hair, an uncommon wide mouth, and pitted with the small-pox; had on, when he went away, a red plush jacket without sleeves, an oznabrigs shirt and trousers, and coarse felt hat. It is supposed he was taken away by a certain Barnett Johnson (father of the said apprentice) by trade a cooper, near 5 feet 10 inches high, about 32 or 33 years of age, of a dark complexion, well made, and wears his own dark brown hair; he has his wife and children with him. Whoever takes up the said apprentice, shall receive THIRTY SHILLINGS reward, and reasonable charges, if brought home, paid by
ANTHONY MAY.
The Maryland Journal, and the Baltimore Advertiser, From Friday, August 20, to Saturday, August 28, 1773; From Saturday, August 28, to Saturday, September 4, 1773; From Saturday, September 4, to Thursday, September 9, 1773.

BALTIMORE, *August* 5, 1773.
RAN away from the subscriber, near the *Blue Rocks*, on the road leading from *Baltimore-Town* to *York-Town*, on *Sunday* the 25th of last month, an indented *Irish* servant man named JEREMIAH LEARY, between 19 and 20 years of age, about 5 feet 5 inches high, talks much on the brogue, is of a

swarthy complexion, with black bushy hair tied behind; had on when he went away, a narrow brim'd hat bound with the same, a brown coat with two capes, the coat bound with lighter edging, a white cotton waistcoat without sleeves, the back parts of linen, two pair of breeches, the one pair black, the other snuff-coloured, blue gray stockings ribbed, good shoes, yellow metal buckles, and two shirts, one check and the other white. Whoever secures him in any gaol, if taken in the county, shall have TWENTY SHILLINGS, if out thereof, THIRTY SHILLINGS, besides what the law allows, and reasonable charges if brought home.
JOHN ALLMERRY.

The Maryland Journal, and the Baltimore Advertiser, From Friday, August 20, to Saturday, August 28, 1773; From Saturday, August 28, to Saturday, September 4, 1773; From Saturday, September 4, to Thursday, September 9, 1773; From Saturday, September 18, to Saturday, September 25, 1773; From Saturday, October 9, to Saturday, October 16, 1773.

BALTIMORE, *August* 23, 1773.
RAN away, last night, from the subscriber's plantation, near Mr. *Samuel Worthington's*, where *Nicholas Britton* now lives, in *Baltimore County*, three convict servant men, lately brought into this country, viz. HENRY BOSWELL, an *East-India Indian*, about 6 feet high, a remarkable well made fellow, with high cheek bones, short black hair, brown eyes, with a cast in them, shorter arms than common, short thick fingers, and a place almost between his shoulders where he has been scalded; he came from the west of *England*, and talks that dialect; he has been a soldier in *America* last war; had on, when he went away, oznabrigs shirt and trousers; he is very artful and pretends to a great many things. TIMOTHY BOSWELL, a half brother to *Henry*, but no part *Indian*; he is of a dark complexion, very high cheek bones, dark eyes, with a cast in them, short dark hair, and has had a scald over one of his ankles; had on, when he went away, an oznabrigs shirt and trousers, and an old black waistcoat; he is a West country-man, and talks in that dialect. EVAN CONWAN, an old *Welshman*, about 5 feet 6 inches high, of a fair complexion, and has lively black eyes; he is gray with age, and rather deaf; had on, and took with him, when he went away, two flannel shirts, two oznabrigs ditto, a pair of oznabrigs trousers, a pair of old blue plush breeches, and a striped flannel waistcoat. They stole an old claret-coloured broadcloth coat, which has three twist buttons on the breast, two large, and one small.—Whoever takes up the aforesaid fellows, and brings them to me in *Baltimore-Town*, or to my said quarter, if ten miles from home, shall be entitled to the reward of THIRTY SHILLINGS, for

each; if twenty miles, FIFTY SHILLINGS; if out of the county, THREE POUNDS; and if out of the province FIVE POUNDS.
BENJAMIN NICHOLSON.

The Maryland Journal, and the Baltimore Advertiser, From Friday, August 20, to Saturday, August 28, 1773; From Saturday, August 28, to Saturday, September 4, 1773; From Saturday, September 4, to Thursday, September 9, 1773; From Saturday, September 18, to Saturday, September 25, 1773. See *The Pennsylvania Chronicle,* From Monday, September 27, to Monday, October 4, 1773, *The Maryland Journal, and Baltimore Advertiser*, August 24, 1774, and *Dunlap's Pennsylvania Packet or, the General Advertiser*, August 29, 1774, for Henry Boswell.

Three Pounds Reward.

RAN away from the subscriber, on *Caterton-Creek*, about 10 miles from *Frederick-Town*, a convict servant girl named REBECCA CONE, about 28 or 30 years old, a tall woman, with black hair, has a lump on the side of her neck, as long as an egg, and two of her fingers are bent into her hand; she has a mulatto child, and says it is with Mr. *Benjamin Philpot* in *Prince George's* county. Whoever returns her to me shall have the above reward.
JACOB MILLER.

The Maryland Journal, and the Baltimore Advertiser, From Friday, August 20, to Saturday, August 28, 1773.

AUGUST 26, 1773.

RAN away from the subscriber, in *Baltimore County*, about twelve miles from *Baltimore-Town*, on *Sunday* night last, an indented *English* servant man named JOHN HOLLINGSWORTH, who was taken out of *Baltimore* gaol on the 18th instant, and indented for one year. He is about 30 or 35 years old, 5 feet ten inches high, a strong well made fellow, of a dark complexion, with black curled hair, and has a large scar on his upper lip, a small part of which extends to the lower lip. He had on, and took with him, a new felt hat bound round the brim, a new cloth coat of a reddish colour, a gingham jacket with red stripes, a holland shirt, a half worn blue broadcloth coat and jacket, striped holland trousers, one pair of oznabrigs ditto, two pair of worsted stockings, a black silk handkerchief, and old shoes; he may have other clothes as he has not been searched. He says he served his first time in *Queen Anne's* county, near *Tuckahoe*, and that he has a brother living in *Philadelphia*. Whoever secures the said servant, if in *Baltimore County*, shall have FORTY SHILLINGS reward, and if out thereof, THREE POUNDS, and reasonable charges if brought home, including what the law allows.   THOMAS COCKEY.

The Maryland Journal, and the Baltimore Advertiser, From Friday, August 20, to Saturday, August 28, 1773; From Saturday, August 28, to Saturday, September 4, 1773; From Saturday, September 4, to Thursday, September 9, 1773; From Thursday, September 9, to Saturday, September 18, 1773; From Saturday, September 18, to Saturday, September 25, 1773.

TEN POUNDS Reward.

RAN away, on the 6th of July last, from the subscriber, living in Bond's Forest, within eight miles of Joppa, in Baltimore County, an Irish Servant Man, named OWEN M'CARTY, about 45 years old, 5 feet 8 inches high, of a swarthy complexion, has long black hair, which is growing a little grey, and has a remarkable scar under the right eye.—He had on, and took with him, when he went away, a short brown coat, made of country manufactured cloth, lined with red flannel, with metal buttons, oznabrigs trowsers patched on both knees, a white shirt, an old pair of shoes, and an old felt hat.—He was a soldier in some part of America about the time of Braddock's defeat, and can give a good description of the country. Whoever takes up the said Servant, and brings him to Alexander Cowan, or John Clayton, Merchants in Joppa, or to the subscriber, if he is taken in the County, shall receive FIVE POUNDS, and if out of the County, the above-mentioned TEN POUNDS, as a reward and consideration for his trouble and expence.   BARNARD REILY.

The Maryland Journal, and the Baltimore Advertiser, From Friday, August 20, to Saturday, August 28, 1773; From Saturday, August 28, to Saturday, September 4, 1773; From Saturday, September 4, to Thursday, September 9, 1773; From Saturday, September 18, to Saturday, September 25, 1773.

Queen Anne's County, Maryland.
ESCAPED from Jail, on Monday, the 26th of July last, THOMAS CHADDOCK, born in Kent County, Maryland, by Trade a Tanner and Shoemaker, a middle-aged Man, about 6 Feet high, swarthy Complexion, with short black hair, and very fond of Liquor. FORTY SHILLINGS will be given for delivering him to the Subscriber, or securing him in any Jail, if taken in the Province, and if out of the Province,
THREE POUNDS, by CHARLES GOLDSBOROUGH, Sheriff.

The Pennsylvania Gazette, September 1, 1773.

August 11, 1773.
TWELVE DOLLARS Reward.
RUN away, last night, from the subscribers, living in Baltimore county, Nod-forest, near Dear-creek, [*sic*] three English convict servant men, viz. *John Dawson*, about 5 feet 5 inches high, a coarse sour looking fellow, marked with the smallpox, blind of an eye, and about 36 years of age. *George Armstrong*, about 30 years of age, about 5 feet 5 inches high, well set, and of a dark complexion. The other, named *John Bagnall*, about 21 years of age, and about 5 feet 9 or 10 inches high, a likely young fellow, with brown hair. Took with them three fine hats, one of which is bound with velvet, four fine shirts, and some coarse ones, a red surtout coat, for or five jackets, one silk, without sleeves, and a brown broad-cloth jacket, without sleeves, a striped cotton and worsted ditto, the stripes go across, a country cloth lead-coloured ditto, with sleeves, &c. also a light-coloured wig, three pair of breeches, two of leather, half worn, and one pair of thickset, very dirty, several pair of stockings, three pair of new shoes, and a pair of pumps, two pair of silver buckles, and several other pair of buckles, several silk handkerchiefs, and one Half Johannes, and some other money. Whoever takes up said servants, and secures them, so that their masters may get them again, shall have the above reward, or *Four Dollars* for either, and reasonable charges, if brought home, paid by HUGH BRYARLY, WILLIAM JAMES, and WILLIAM HILL.

N. B. All persons are hereby forewarned to put them over the river at their peril, and masters of vessels are forewarned to carry them off, &c.

The Pennsylvania Gazette, September 1, 1773.

July 5, 1773.
RAN away from the subscriber, living in Westmoreland county, Virginia, two white men servants, viz. William Walker, alias Smith, a convict, who came in 1771, in the Scarsdale, Capt Reid, by trade a gardener; he is a slim made man, five feet nine or ten inches high, brown complexion, blue eyes, blackish hair, has a remarkable swing in his walk, a coarse voice and a cough; he had with him, kersey and cotton jackets and breeches, white, check, and osnabrig shirts; he likes drink, and has been severely whipped before a magistrate: this is the third time he has run away; as he had sailors cloaths with him he will attempt to pass for a sailor. Thomas Puttrell, an indented servant, (who came in last April, in the Liberty, Capt. Raison) a trunchy well made man, fair complexion, brown hair, which curls in his neck, a round face, hazle eyes, speaks quick, a butcher by trade, understands gardening and farming; he has been fourteen months on board a man of war; he has a butcher's steel and knife, and wears quils in his hat: he had with him, a brown cloth coat, second mourning jacket, black breeches, white, check, and osnabrig shirts, and some money; he will

attempt to pass for a sailor; and I hear they intend to Baltimore and Philadelphia. Whoever apprehend [sic] the aforesaid servants, and secures them in a jail, so that I get them, shall receive a reward of five pounds Virginia currency for each of them.
RICHARD LEE.
The Maryland Gazette, September 2, 1773; September 23, 1773; September 30, 1773.

BALTIMORE, August 31, 1773.
RAN away, last night, from the subscriber, living in Baltimore-Town, an English convict servant man, named FRANCIS PRATT, by trade a barber, has been transported, as a Convict into this country formerly, by another name, therefore 'tis likely he will change his name; had on, when he went away, a light-coloured broadcloth coat and jacket, Russia drab breeches, white shirt and neckcloth, or red silk handkerchief, long-quartered shoes, with square steel buckles, a Carolina hat, with hooks and eyes; he is about 5 feet 5 inches high, 28 years of age, fair complexion, very full eyed, and his hair curls in the neck, stoops in his walk, and limps with his left leg. Whoever takes up said servant, and brings him to his master, or secures him in any gaol, so that he may be had again, shall have, if taken within 10 miles of this place, Forty Shillings, if 20 miles, Three Pounds, if 50 miles Five Pounds, and if out of the province, Ten Pounds, and reasonable charges paid, if brought home, by
JOHN CLEMENT.
The Maryland Journal, and the Baltimore Advertiser, From Friday, August 20, to Saturday, August 28, 1773; From Saturday, August 28, to Saturday, September 4, 1773; From Saturday, September 4, to Thursday, September 9, 1773; From Thursday, September 9, to Saturday, September 18, 1773; From Saturday, September 18, to Saturday, September 25, 1773; October 9, to Saturday, October 16, 1773; From Saturday, October 16, to Saturday, October 23, 1773; From Saturday, October 23, to Saturday, October 30, 1773. *The Pennsylvania Chronicle,* From Monday, September 6, to Monday, September 13, 1773; From Monday, September 13, to Monday, September 20, 1773. Minor differences between the papers.

AUGUST 30, 1773.
RAN away, last night, from *Patuxent* Iron-Works, the two following servant men, *viz.* NICHOLAS HOWELL, a *Welshman*, about 25 years of age, 5 feet 3 or 4 inches high, with a fair complexion, and very regular features. He had on, and took with him, one white shirt, two oznabrig shirts, old white drilling breeches, oznabrig trousers, a cotton jacket, a new felt

hat, a pair of country made shoes, copper buckles, and an old blue surtout coat, worn through at the elbows.— THOMAS HOGG, a *Yorkshireman*, about 25 years of age, 5 feet seven or eight inches high, of a swarthy complexion, and has on an oznabrig shirt, old black breeches, an old felt hat, and old shoes.—Whoever secures them in any goal, so that they may be had again, shall receive, if taken ten miles from home, TWENTY SHILLINGS, if twenty miles, THIRTY SHILLINGS, and if at a greater distance, FORTY SHILLINGS, for each, besides what the law allows, and all reasonable travelling charges, if brought home, paid by
SAMUEL, JOHN, and THOMAS SNOWDEN.

> *The Maryland Journal, and the Baltimore Advertiser*, From Saturday, August 28, to Saturday, September 4, 1773; From Saturday, September 4, to Thursday, September 9, 1773; From Thursday, September 9, to Saturday, September 18, 1773; From Saturday, September 18, to Saturday, September 25, 1773. See *The Maryland Gazette*, July 29, 1773, for Hogg.

FORTY DOLLARS Reward.

RAN away, from the Subscriber, living in *Maryland*, within 18 Miles of *Baltimore-Town*, one Convict Servant Man, named GEORGE BULMORE, who came from *Yorkshire*, in the North of *England*, and speaks in that Dialect; is about 29 Years of Age, 5 Feet 8 or 9 Inches high, very round shouldered, is of a dark Complexion, thin Visage, short black Hair, and blue Eyes—His Apparel was a Cotton Jacket, hempen Roll Shirt and Trousers, old Leather Breeches, a pair of grey Yarn Stockings, old Hat and Shoes, though perhaps he may get other Clothes, also a Pass, and change his Name. Whoever takes up the said Servant, and secures him in any Gaol, so that his Master gets him again, shall have, if taken up 10 Miles from Home, THIRTY SHILLINGS; If 20 Miles FORTY SHILLINGS; if 50 Miles, THREE POUNDS; if a Hundred Miles, FIVE POUNDS; if 300 Miles, TEN POUNDS; and, if 500 Miles, the above Reward, including what the Laws allows, and reasonable Charges paid, if brought Home, by
AUGUST 11.   SAMUEL WORTHINGTON.

N. B. All Masters of Vessels and others are forbid carrying the above Servant off, at their Peril.

> *The Maryland Journal, and the Baltimore Advertiser*, From Saturday, August 28, to Saturday, September 4, 1773; From Saturday, September 4, to Thursday, September 9, 1773; From Thursday, September 9, to Saturday, September 18, 1773; From Saturday, September 18, to Saturday, September 25, 1773. *The Pennsylvania Chronicle,* From Monday, September 20, to Monday, September 27,

1773; From Monday, September 27, to Monday, October 4, 1773. The *Chronicle* does not have the line beginning with "N. B."

RAN away, from the Subscribers, on the night of the 30th of *August* last, two indented Servants, one named HECTOR WALLIS, an *Irishman*: he is about 6 Feet high, slender made, and of a brown Complexion; had on, when he went off, a long brown coat, and a white Linen Shirt.—The other named Samuel — , an *Englishman*, and 5 Feet 8 or 9 Inches high, has light curled Hair, and fair Complexion; he took with him, two Suits of Clothes, one exceeding good light brown Cloth, several white Linen Shirts, ruffled at the Bosom, a brown Surtout Coat, and two Castor Hats, one very good. Whoever secures said Servants in any Gaol, so that their Masters may get them again, who live in *Bladensburg, Prince George's County*, shall have, if taken in said County, or *Baltimore County*, FORTY SHILLINGS for each, and if in any other County in Proportion.
WAIT STILL SINGELLTON CHURCH.
BENJAMIN BEALL.
 The Maryland Journal, and the Baltimore Advertiser, From Saturday, August 28, to Saturday, September 4, 1773; From Saturday, September 4, to Thursday, September 9, 1773; From Saturday, September 18, to Saturday, September 25, 1773.

August 25, 1773.
FIVE POUNDS Reward.
RUN away from the subscriber, on Bush-creek, about ten miles from Fredericktown, a convict servant man, named JOSEPH WIFFEN, *about 5 feet 10 inches high, is a bold looking fellow, of a swarthy complexion, and has a remarkable sore on one of his legs, near the ancle bone; had on, and took with him, two ozenbrigs shirts, one pair of country spun trowsers, no shoes. He stole, when he went away, a black MARE, about 14 hands and 3 inches high, and an old Saddle. Whoever secure said servant and mare, so that their master may have them again, shall have the above reward, or FIFTY SHILLINGS for each, and reasonable charges, if brought home, paid by* JOHN MACKELFRESH.
 The Pennsylvania Gazette, September 8, 1773.

Wester-Ogle, Baltimore County, August 31, 1773.
TWENTY DOLLARS Reward.
RUN AWAY, from the subscriber, a servant man, named SAMUEL DANGERFIELD, *by trade a Whitesmith, but has, during the two years he has been in the country, been mostly kept to the Blacksmith's business,*

which he now understands pretty well. *He is an Englishman, which may be discovered by his dialect, is about 5 feet 7 inches high, and very well set; has short fair hair, which curls, wants some of his fore teeth, and is about 30 years of age. He has taken with him a new lead-coloured knapped frize jacket, a fine shirt, and a pair of check trowsers. He has also broke upon his master's store, and taken Ten Pounds Ten or Twelve Shillings cash, part of which is a Doubloon, and 3 or 4 Two-dollar bills; one of the bills hath a defect in the middle, supplied with a piece of a newspaper. He, at the same time, took a fine hat, at about 45s. price, 2 or 3 black Barcelona handkerchiefs, 3 or 4 pair of white worsted stockings, 12 yards of calicoe, and perhaps other things not yet missed. He is an artful cunning fellow, and will undoubtedly forge a pass, he writes a tolerable good hand. Whoever brings him to be shall have, if taken in the county, Four Dollars, if 50 miles from home, Eight Dollars, and if 100 miles, the above reward, with reasonable charges.*   WILLIAM LYON.

   N. B. He is supposed to have taken with him a brown thickset coat, and has taken a pocket pistol.

   The Pennsylvania Gazette, September 15, 1773; The Maryland Journal, and the Baltimore Advertiser, From Saturday, October 9, to Saturday, October 16, 1773. Minor differences between the papers.

Chester-Town, Kent County, Maryland, July 10, 1773.
SIX PISTOLES REWARD.
BROKE *goal, on Wednesday night, the 7th instant, a certain* John Anderson, *committed in execution for debt; he is an Irishman, by trade a Ditcher, a bold pert fellow, about 5 feet 10 inches high, very thick and well made, has remarkably large wrists, short curled hair, of a light colour, is a little bald on the fore part of his head, round face, fresh complexion, talks hoarse, is apt to get drunk, and quarrelsome; he has a large bundle of clothes with him, among which are, a claret cloth coat, striped ticken trowsers, good shoes, and a pretty good castor hat: He broke goal on the 7th of June last, and was taken a few days after, and brought back. It is thought he stole a large grey horse, as he has been missing since the night* Anderson *broke goal. Whoever takes up and secures said* Anderson *in any gaol, shall receive the above reward and reasonable charges, if brought back, and safe delivered to him, paid by*
THOMAS SMYTH, Sheriff.
The Pennsylvania Gazette, September 15, 1773.

September 9, 1773.
RAN away, from the Subscriber, in *Nod Forest, Baltimore County,* a Convict Servant Man, named JOHN REED, by Trade a Taylor, is about 5 Feet 7 or 8 Inches high, of a red Complexion, has a red Beard, is about 33

Years of Age; had on, and took with him, a flesh-coloured Coat, a Flannel Jacket, with black Horn Buttons, a Pair of Snuff-coloured Breeches, with Metal Buttons, one white Shirt, one Oznabrigs Ditto, two Pair of Tow Trousers, old reddish Wig, old Felt Hat, and a Silk Handkerchief; he is much freckled, and the Side of his Head is scarrified.—Whoever takes up the said Servant, and secures him in any Gaol, so that his Master may get him again, shall have THIRTY SHILLINGS Reward, besides what the Law allows, paid by   JAMES SCOTT.

The Maryland Journal, and the Baltimore Advertiser, From Thursday, September 9, to Saturday, September 18, 1773; From Saturday, September 18, to Saturday, September 25, 1773.

TWENTY DOLLARS REWARD.

STOLEN, on the night of the 10th of August last, out of the pasture of the subscriber, at Christiana Bridge, a bright BAY HORSE, fourteen hands high, with a long hanging black mane and switch tail, six years old, (but appears to be older) has two colt's teeth in his under jaw, commonly called [fir]asts, paces, trots and hand-gallops, and when riding is apt to throw up his nose; had but one shoe, and that on his near fore foot. He is supposed to be stolen by a certain STEPHEN RATCLIFF, a miller by trade, a pale innocent looking man, about 5 feet 6 or 7 inches high, with black eyes, wears his own hair, of a brownish colour; had on a light-coloured half-worn coat, striped Damascus waistcoat, and blue velvet breeches; he also stole, a half-worn saddle, with brass staple buttons before and behind, the stirrup irons jointed in the sides with two rims above, and a narrow leather girth.—Whoever takes up said horse and thief, so that the owner may have his horse and saddle, and the thief be brought to conviction, shall receive the above reward; and for the horse and saddle only, THREE POUNDS, and reasonable charges.   THOMAS SCULLY,

N. B. If is supposed he is gone towards *New-Virginia*, or *Redstone* settlement, as he has a brother and several relations on the *Monongahela*.

The Maryland Journal, and the Baltimore Advertiser, From Thursday, September 9, to Saturday, September 18, 1773.

EIGHT DOLLARS Reward.

RAN away from the subscriber, living on Lady's Manor, in Baltimore County, an English convict servant man, named JOHN POWEL, came into Baltimore in the Elizabeth, Capt. Thomas Spencer, a copperplate printer by trade, is a stout likely fellow, of a brown complexion, whitish eyes, is about 5 feet 8 inches high, and has short black hair: Had on, a brown cloth jacket, without sleeves, striped plush breeches, check shirt, old blue worsted stockings, silk handkerchief and small castor hat; he has been in the country before, and says he assisted some gentleman as an usher in a school above Philadelphia; it is likely he will forge a pass. Whoever takes up, and brings home the said servant (if ten miles from home) shall have FOUR DOLLARS reward, and if out of the county, the above reward, paid by JAMES GUTHRIE.

The Pennsylvania Chronicle, From Monday, September 13, to Monday, September 20, 1773; From Monday, September 20, to Monday, September 27, 1773. See *The Pennsylvania Chronicle,* From Monday, October 18, to Monday, October 25, 1773.

TWO PISTOLES Reward.

RUN away from the subscriber, living in Chester-town, Maryland, Kent county, an Irish servant man, named *Michael Levey,* alias *Davie,* about 5 feet 6 inches high, pockmarked, black hair, his right leg stands more out than his left, runs fast, a labourer by occupation, he is a great liar and very artful; had of his own, when he went away, a blue great coat, ticking body coat, flowered waistcoat, one striped silk ditto, two pair of ticking breeches, good shoes and stockings, old patched shirt; stole, and took with him, one good Irish linen shirt, one ozenbrigs ditto; he loves liquor, and is apt to sing and swear, when drinking. Whoever takes up said servant, and secures him, so as his master may get him again, shall receive the above reward, paid by EDWARD COSTOLOW. *Sept.* 10, 1773.

The Pennsylvania Gazette, September 22, 1773.

EIGHT POUNDS Reward.

RAN away, from the Antietam Forge, in Frederick county, Maryland, on Sunday the 11th instant, two servant men, viz. DENNIS SULLIVAN, about 5 feet 9 or 10 inches high, or a dark complexion, and has short hair; he was born in Ireland. Had on, an oznabrigs shirt and trousers, a dark brown frize coat with a claret-coloured velvet cape, an half worn felt hat, a pair of good shoes, and yellow metal buckles.—JOHN COPPINGER, about 5 feet 8 or 9 inches high, about 20 years old, and of a sandy complexion; was born in Ireland, from whence he came when about 8 or 9 years old. Had on, and took with him, an oznabrigs shirt, three pair of trousers, a short grey frize jacket, a pair of half worn shoes, and a felt hat; he has been used to work in a forge. Any person who will secure them, so that their masters can have them again, shall be paid the above reward, or FOUR POUNDS for each, if taken above 15 miles from home, with reasonable charges.
DANIEL and SAMUEL HUGHES,
   N. B. All masters of vessels are forbid to take them away.

July 9, 1773.
The Pennsylvania Chronicle, From Monday, September 20, to Monday, September 27, 1773; From Monday, September 27, to Monday, October 4, 1773; From Monday, October 4, to Monday, October 11, 1773; From Monday, October 11, to Monday, October 18, 1773. See *Dunlap's Pennsylvania Packet or, the General Advertiser,* February 21, 1774, for Coppinger.

August 23, 1773.
TAKEN UP and committed to the gaol of the county of Sussex, in West New-Jersey, on suspicion of being a run away, a certain fellow who passes by the name of SAMUEL COWAN, but latterly says his name is BOLLARD, and confesses himself to be the same person advertised in the Pennsylvania Packet, No. 89, by one SAMUEL OWINGS, Jun. near Baltimore. His master is desired to pay the charges, &c. and take him away, in four weeks from the date hereof, otherwise he will be sold out for the same.   JOHN MARTIN, Gaoler.
The Pennsylvania Packet; and the General Advertiser, September 20, 1773; September 27, 1773. See *The Pennsylvania Chronicle,* From Saturday, January 9, to Saturday, January 16, 1773, and *The Pennsylvania Packet; and the General Advertiser,* June 21, 1773.

Annapolis, Sept. 19, 1773.
RAN away from the subscriber, last night about eight o'clock, an indented servant man, named Thomas Hoskins, lately imported in the Lovely Kitty, Capt. Collwell Howard, is a bricklayer by trade, a stout well set man, about 28 years of age, pitted with the small-pox, wears his own hair, and is about 5 feet 8 or 9 inches high: took with him a Jacket and breeches of light coloured bearskin, with osnabrig lining; he also took a new felt hat, a red striped under jacket, dark blue yarn stockings, and copper buckles; he has a discharge from the army in the name of John Holloway, and without doubt will go by that name; he says he has a brother in Philadelphia, and 'tis supposed he will make that way 'tis thought he has a forged pass. Whoever takes up the said servant and delivers him to the subscriber, or secures him in any jail so that he may get him again, shall receive five pounds reward, besides what the law allows.
WILLIAM BUCKLAND.
The Maryland Gazette, September 23, 1773; September 30, 1773; October 7, 1773; October 14, 1773; October 21, 1773; November 11, 1773; November 18, 1773; November 25, 1773; December 2, 1773; December 9, 1773; December 16, 1773.

Newcastle Gaol, on Delaware, Sept, 13, 1773.
WAS committed to my care, the following servants and slaves, to wit, JOHN CLEMENTS, says he belongs to John Barkush, near Bush Town, Maryland. A negro man named DICK...PETER alias PERO, GEORGE, a new negro lad....JAMES CONWAY, an Irishman, says he belongs to David Crafford, near Fishing Creek on Susquehanna. On suspicion the two following: JAMES INSELLOW, as he calls himself, a well set fellow, 5 feet 7 or eight inches high, sandy hair, red beard, full faced, large eyes, and is fond of drink. JAMES MOONEYS, as he calls himself, is about 5 feet 7 inches high, much freckled in the face, had on when committed, a light coloured wilton coat, old trowsers, good shoes, and had a new-fashioned cane with some silver mounting on it: They look very suspicious, and are supposed to have changed their names. The masters of the above servants are once more desired to come, pay charges, and take them away in three weeks, otherwise they will be sold out for their fees, by
ROBERT MACK, Gaoler.

The Pennsylvania Packet; and the General Advertiser, September 20, 1773; October 4, 1773; October 18, 1773. See *The Pennsylvania Packet; and the General Advertiser*, September 23, 1773.

New Castle Goal, August 26, 1773.
WAS committed into my custody, a certain JOHN CLEMONS, who says he belongs to a certain JAMES BARKER, in Queen Ann's county, Maryland; also a negro man named DICK, who says he belongs to a certain JOHN ADDAMS, near Snow Hill; likewise, a negro man who says his name is PETER, and belongs to JACOB LOWRY, near Lancaster. Their masters are desired to come, pay charges, and take them away, in three weeks from the date hereof, otherwise they will be sold for the same, by
ROBERT MACK, Goaler.

The Pennsylvania Packet; and the General Advertiser, September 23, 1773. See *The Pennsylvania Packet; and the General Advertiser*, September 20, 1773, for "Clements," Dick, and Peter.

BALTIMORE-TOWN, *Sept.* 24, 1773.
RAN away from the subscriber, the 18th instant, an *English* convict servant named WILLIAM SCROWFIELD, about 5 feet 3 or 4 inches high, of a fresh complexion, has black eyes, short black hair, and is very likely; he can dress hair and shave pretty well, is an exceeding good waiter and hostler, but very much addicted to liquor. He has been lately whipped, and the stripes, it is thought, still appear on his back. He had on, and took with him, oznabrig shirts, leather breeches, thread stockings, a green broadcloth

lapelled coat, which has been turned, and has yellow buttons; also a coarse light-coloured short working-waistcoat, made without cuffs to the sleeves. It is thought he is now lurking about the *Point,* or *Old-Town.* Whoever takes up the said servant in town, or *Fell's-Point,* shall have Twenty Shillings reward; if ten miles from home, Thirty Shillings; if twenty miles, Forty Shillings; and if out of the county, Three Pounds; and be paid reasonable charges. BENJAMIN NICHOLSON.

The Maryland Journal, and the Baltimore Advertiser, From Saturday, September 18, to Saturday, September 25, 1773. See *The Maryland Journal, and the Baltimore Advertiser,* From Saturday, May 28, to Saturday, June 4, 1774, and *The Maryland Journal, and Baltimore Advertiser,* November 30, 1774.

RAN away from the subscriber, in Baltimore, on Wednesday the 22d inst. (Sept.) an Irish servant man named William Magrath, about 23 years of age, 5 feet 7 or eight inches high, speaks good Dutch, is well set, and had on a felt hat, a red upper Jacket, a striped waistcoat, and a pair of red and blue striped trousers. Whoever secures him so that I may get him again shall have, if 5 miles from home, Fifteen Shillings, and if 30 miles, Four Dollars, besides reasonable charges. JOHN KEYSER.

The Maryland Journal, and the Baltimore Advertiser, From Saturday, September 18, to Saturday, September 25, 1773.

September 21, 1773.
SEVEN POUNDS TEN SHILLINGS REWARD.

RAN away, from the subscriber, living near Soldier's Delight, Baltimore County, Maryland, an indented servant man, named DANIEL M'GUIER, alias GILMER, born in the north of Ireland, and speaks in that dialect, by trade a weaver, about 25 years of age, about 5 feet 10 inches high, has long black hair, tied behind, grey eyes, pitted with the small-pox, thin face, long visage, has a small crook in the end of his nose, straight made, has a lively walk, is much addicted to liquor, and quarrelsome; has been in the army some time, where he has been severely whipped, and has a scar across the small of his back, occasioned by the cut of a sword, and another on the small of one of his legs. He had on, and took with him, a felt hat, a holland shirt, an oznabrig one much mended, a black silk cravat, one stock, a Russia drab jacket double breasted, with buttons of the same, without sleeves, a pair of striped holland trousers much worn, an old pair of shoes much mended, and square white metal buttons. It is probable he may change his name and clothes.—Whoever secures him, so that I may get him again, shall have fifty shillings reward, if fifty miles from home, five pounds, and if a hundred miles, the above reward, and reasonable charges if brought home.   ALEXANDER WELLS.

The Maryland Journal, and the Baltimore Advertiser, From Saturday, September 18, to Saturday, September 25, 1773; October 9, to Saturday, October 16, 1773.

BROKE out of *Frederick County* gaol, on the 16th inst. *(September)* at night, a certain NICHOLAS FITZGARREL, an *Irishman*, under sentence of death, of a fair complexion, about 5 feet 4 inches high, with light curled hair; he had on a nankeen jacket without sleeves, one white linen ditto, a pair of oznabrig trousers, a pair of pumps, old buckles, but no hat. Whoever delivers him to me shall have TEN POUNDS Reward.
LAWRENCE O'NEAL, Sheriff.

The Maryland Journal, and the Baltimore Advertiser, From Saturday, September 18, to Saturday, September 25, 1773.

FORTY SHILLINGS Reward.

RAN away from the Subscriber, living in *Baltimore County*, near the mouth of *Deer Creek*, an *Irish* servant man, named THOMAS TUFF, or DUFF, born in *Dublin*, about 5 feet 6 inches high, has black hair, is round shouldered, a lusty well set fellow, and pretends to understand the brewing business. Had on and took with him, a light-coloured country cloth coat, made plain, one side pocket, no lining, one white linen, and one sagathy jacket, felt hat, old leather breeches, brown worsted stockings, English-made shoes, one old fine shirt, and one coarse county linen ditto.—
Whoever takes up said servant, and secures him in any gaol, so that his master may have him again, shall have the above reward, and if brought home, reasonable charges, paid by
JOSEPH HUSBAND.   15th 9th *mo.* 1773.

The Maryland Journal, and the Baltimore Advertiser, From Saturday, September 18, to Saturday, September 25, 1773; From Saturday, October 16, to Saturday, October 23, 1773; *The Pennsylvania Gazette*, September 29, 1773; *The Pennsylvania Chronicle,* From Monday, September 27, to Monday, October 4, 1773. Minor differences between the papers.

September 18, 1773.

RAN away from the Subscriber, living in Charles county, a servant boy called Hooper Bennett, about 19 years of age, slender make, about 5 feet 3 inches high, light coloured hair, which he generally wears in a slovenly manner, pale sallow complexion, speaks quick, and is by trade a barber and hair-dresser: had on when he went away a brown short-skirted coat, red waistcoat, and olive coloured velvet breeches, and it is supposed he may have now changed his dress. He has the appearance of a country born boy, and therefore will not be readily taken for a runaway. He has been gone above four months, and was seen last July at Leonard's-creek in Calvert County, and it is supposed he is now either in that or St. Mary's county. Whoever brings said servant to the subscriber, or secures him in a jail, so that the owner may have him again, shall receive forty shillings, paid by RICHARD LEE.

The Maryland Gazette, September 30, 1773; October 7, 1773; October 14, 1773. See *The Maryland Gazette*, August 12, 1773.

Chester-town, Kent county, Sept. 25.
RAN away from the subscriber, on Saturday the 5th of June last, a convict servant man named James Lewis, by country an Englishman, aged about 45 years, talks hoarse, much in the west country dialect: he is about 5 feet 8 inches high, round shouldered, stoops in his walk, has a down look, and is of a swarthy dark complexion, and has short dark hair. Had on and took with him two osnabrig shirts, two pair of osnabrig trousers, a mixed coloured fearnought over jacket, a black and white country cloth under jacket, a new felt hat, a pair of black worsted knit breeches, and a pair of country made shoes almost new. He has been near five years in the country, and understands farming and driving an ox team pretty well. He went in company with Mary Philips the wife of John Philips, and pretend to be man and wife. Mary Philips had with her a male child about 7 months old, she is middle sized, round shouldered, has light coloured hair, thin sharp visage, pale complexion, and fair skin; it is thought they are gone over the Bay to the back settlements. Whoever takes up and secures the aforesaid servant man in any jail, so that the subscriber may get him again, shall have 5 pounds reward and if brought home reasonable charges besides the above reward, paid by   THOMAS SMYTH.

The Maryland Gazette, September 30, 1773; October 14, 1773; October 21, 1773; October 28, 1773.

Baltimore-Town, September 25, 1773.
RAN away from the subscriber's plantation, where NICHOLAS BRITTON now lives, in Baltimore county, about 16 Miles from Baltimore Town, on the 22d day of August last, three convict servant men, viz. HENRY BOSWELL, TIMOTHY BOSWELL, and EVAN CONWAN; and on or about the 1st of September, Henry Boswell and Evan Conwan were taken up on an island in Susquehanna river, about 10 miles from York-Town, and

put into York Gaol; the other fellow, Timothy Boswell, made his escape, by concealing himself in the grass on the said island. They were making towards Philadelphia—Timothy Boswell, who is now absent, is a West-Country-man, about 5 feet 6 or 7 inches high, is of a very dark complexion, has short black hair, dark eyes, has a very down look, and when he raises his head to speak, squints and looks with his head awry—He had a scald just over one of his ankles, and has small feet; had on, and took with him, osnabrig shirts and trousers, an old claret colour'd broadcloth coat, with mohair buttons on the breast, and is supposed to have carried off other things unknown. Whoever takes up, and secures the said servant, so that his master gets him again, shall have FIVE POUNDS reward, and all reasonable charges, paid by
BENJAMIN NICHOLSON.

The Pennsylvania Chronicle, From Monday, September 27, to Monday, October 4, 1773. See *The Maryland Journal, and the Baltimore Advertiser,* From Friday, August 20, to Saturday, August 28, 1773, *The Maryland Journal, and Baltimore Advertiser,* August 24, 1774, and *Dunlap's Pennsylvania Packet or, the General Advertiser,* August 29, 1774, for Henry Boswell.

SIXTEEN DOLLARS REWARD.

RAN AWAY from the subscriber, living near Soldiers Delight, in Baltimore county, an English servant man, named THOMAS HANDLEN, about five ten or eleven inches high, about 23 or 24 years of age, a pleasant countenance, round shouldered, down look, straight black hair, had on and took with him, a good felt hat, good oznabrigs shirts, a pair of homespun roll trowsers, and had an iron collar round his neck; it is very likely he will change his name, and get a pass. Whoever takes up said servant, and brings him home, if twenty miles distance shall have FOUR DOLLARS, including what the law allows; if sixty miles TEN DOLLARS, and if a hundred miles the above reward, and reasonable charges, paid by
JOHN OWINGS, son of RICHARD.

The Pennsylvania Packet; and the General Advertiser, October 4, 1773; October 18, 1773; *Dunlap's Pennsylvania Packet or, the General Advertiser,* November 1, 1773.

Maryland, September 18, 1773.
RUN away from the subscriber, living in George-Town, an indented servant man, named HUGH ROGERS, about 5 feet 6 or 7 inches high, fair complexion, light brown strait hair, well set; had on when he went away, a dark brown frize jacket, with sleeves, more than half worn, has a tolerable

good brown sheeting shirt, old ozenbrigs trowsers, with a pair of blue breeches under them, a pair of single channel pumps, a striped silk handkerchief, and a half worn fine hat; he is about 21 years of age, by trade a carpenter and joiner, and can work at the whip-saw; is fond of liquor, and very talkative and quarrelsome when drunk, but put peaceable and of few words when sober; he came from Dublin to Alexandria about 12 months ago, and is supposed to be carried off by a person who hath lived in George-Town four or five months, and called himself John Donaboo, a waterman; the said Donaboo had two passes, one signed by Mr. Buchanan, of Baltimore, where he called himself John Quima; the other by Mr. William Deaken, in George Town, wherein he called himself Donaboo; it is supposed he will give one of those passes to Rogers, and change his name agreeable thereto. Whoever takes up and secures said Rogers, so as his master may get him again, if within 5 miles, shall have Five Shillings; if 15 miles Ten Shillings; if 30 miles Three Dollars, and so on, a Dollar for every ten miles, until 100 miles, and if a greater distance Five Pounds, besides what the law allows, and reasonable charges, paid by THOMAS RIGDEN.
N. B. All masters of vessels are forbid to carry him off.

The Pennsylvania Gazette, September 29, 1773; October 20, 1773; November 17, 1773.

Eight Dollars Reward.

RAN away, from the subscriber, in *Bladensburg,* on the 10th of *October,* an indented *Irish* servant man, named BARNARD FITZPATRICK, 29 years old, of middle stature, well set, of a dark complexion, black hair, has a remarkable scar on one side of his chin, larger than a shilling; had on and took with him, two white shirts, a striped and sprigged calico jacket, a cloth coloured cloth ditto, a felt or wool hat bound with black ferreting, leather breeches, and a pair of black stuff ditto, thread stockings, and a pair of blue ribbed ditto; he says he understands gardening and driving a team, he writes a good plain hand and may forge a pass. Whoever shall take up and bring home said servant, shall receive, if taken within 20 miles, Thirty Shillings, if above 20 miles from home, Three Pounds reward, by
JAMES HUNT.
N. B. He had oznabrigs trousers over his breeches.

The Maryland Journal, and the Baltimore Advertiser, From Saturday, October 9, to Saturday, October 16, 1773; From Saturday, October 16, to Saturday, October 23, 1773; From Saturday, October 23, to Saturday, October 30, 1773. From Saturday, October 30, to Saturday, November 6, 1773; From Saturday, November 6, to Saturday, November 13, 1773. See *The Maryland Gazette,* November 4, 1773.

237

Funk's-Town, Frederick County, Oct. 10, 1773.
FIVE POUNDS Reward.

RAN away, from the subscriber, on *Saturday* the 10th instant, an indented servant man, by name RICHARD PENDERGAST, he is a short thick fellow, about five feet high, and about twenty-five years of age, wears his own hair which is black and inclines to curl, he looks sickly and is lame in one of his arms; had on when he went away, a new short coat and jacket of coarse blue cloth, made sailor fashion, with clear metal buttons, and lined with white plad, a pair of middling old black everlasting breeches, a pair of very good shoes and stockings, and brass buckles, a middling good hat cocked in the fashion, and a new black silk handkerchief about his neck, he looks smiling, is talkative and very much like a sailor, Whoever takes up said servant and secures him in any gaol, so that I may have him again, shall have the above reward, paid by
WILLIAM LEE.

The Maryland Journal, and the Baltimore Advertiser, From Saturday, October 9, to Saturday, October 16, 1773 From Saturday, October 16, to Saturday, October 23, 1773; From Saturday, October 23, to Saturday, October 30, 1773; From Saturday, October 30, to Saturday, November 6, 1773; From Saturday, November 6, to Saturday, November 13, 1773; From Saturday, November 13, to Saturday, November 20, 1773; From Saturday, November 20, to Saturday, November 27, 1773; From Saturday, November 27, to Thursday, December 9, 1773. See *Dunlap's Pennsylvania Packet or, the General Advertiser*, May 9, 1774.

October 12, 1773.

RAN away, last night, from *Tulip Hill*, three servant men, viz. JOHN WHITE, a gardener, born in *Scotland*, a lusty fellow, about 38 years of age; had on and took with, a white country cloth frock and breeches, white shirts, yarn stockings, shoes and trousers; it is likely he will appear in a blue cloth coat, with white metal buttons. ROBERT BRYANT, an *Irish man*, and speaks much in the brogue; had on and took with him, a fine white cloth coat and breeches not much worn, a frock of the same cloth of the gardener's, white shirts, yarn stockings, leather breeches, a gold laced hat with small brim, shoes and boots; 'tis supposed they have stolen many other things. JOHN PARSONS, a shoemaker, about 23 years of age, 5 feet 8 inches high, fair complexion, good features, has light curled hair, and speaks much in the west country dialect; had on when he went away, a short spotted jacket with leather buttons, good oznabrig trousers, shoes and buckles; he took with him an oznabrig shirt, and other things, which cannot be ascertained.

Whoever takes up the said servants, and secures them in any gaol, so that their masters may get them again, shall receive FOUR POUNDS for PARSONS, and TWENTY SHILLINGS each for the other two,
SAMUEL GALLOWAY,   STEPHEN STEWARD.

The Maryland Journal, and the Baltimore Advertiser, From Saturday, October 9, to Saturday, October 16, 1773; From Saturday, October 16, to Saturday, October 23, 1773; From Saturday, October 23, to Saturday, October 30, 1773. See *The Maryland Gazette*, June 21, 1770.

September 28, 1773.
RAN away, from the subscriber, about 9 miles from *Baltimore-Town*, and 2 miles from *Northampton* Furnace, in *Baltimore* County, a convict servant man, named DAVID TOOLE, an *Irishman*, about 5 feet 2 or 3 inches high, a well made fellow, has black hair, gray eyes, and a good skin, one of his thighs has been broken which causes him to walk somewhat lame; he had on when he went away, an oznabrigs shirt and trousers, an old kersey waistcoat, a felt hat, and good strong shoes, which have nails in the soles and heels, 'tis likely he will steal clothes, as he is an arrant thief, and a great drunkard. Whoever apprehends and secures the said servant, so that his master may get him again, shall receive, if taken 20 miles from home, THIRTY SHILLINGS; if 40 miles FORTY SHILLINGS; and if out of province FIVE POUNDS, including what the law allows, and reasonable charges, if brought home, by
JOHN ROBERT HOLLIDAY.

The Maryland Journal, and the Baltimore Advertiser, From October 9, to Saturday, October 16, 1773; From October 16, to Saturday, October 23, 1773. See *The Maryland Gazette*, August 8, 1771, and *Dunlap's Pennsylvania Packet or, the General Advertiser*, August 15, 1774, for "David Tool."

Twenty Pounds Reward
WENT off by stealth, from the *Burnt-House-Woods*, the upper end of *Baltimore County*, two persons, named THOMAS GLYNN, and ELIZABETH GLYNN, who are supposed to have been confederates in robbing *Anthony Haines*, of TWO HUNDRED POUNDS, in gold, silver, and paper money.—The man is of middle size, and of a fair complexion, has snandy [*sic*] brown hair, and a down look; had on, a blue coat, with white lining, a black waistcoat, and green breeches.—The woman, of middle stature, dark complexion, lightish hair, her apparel uncertain, though 'tis thought she can dress well—She has two young female children.—'Tis imagined they will attempt to go by water from *Baltimore Town*, but probably may not go together.—Whoever takes up and secures said *Thomas*

and *Elizabeth Glynn*, so that they are brought to justice, shall have, though none of the money should be recovered, *Five Pounds*, but if half should be recovered, *Ten Pounds*, and it all, or within twenty pounds thereof, the above reward, paid by ANTHONY HAINES, or
Oct, 20, 1773. ANDREW HOOKE.
>*The Maryland Journal, and the Baltimore Advertiser*, From Saturday, October 16, to Saturday, October 23, 1773; From Saturday, October 23, to Saturday, October 30, 1773; From Saturday, October 30, to Saturday, November 6, 1773; From Saturday, November 6, to Saturday, November 13, 1773.

COMMITTED to my custody as a runaway, a person who calls himself William Wood, says he belongs to Humphry Godman, of Frederick county. His master is desired pay charges and take him from
RALPH FORSTER, sheriff of Prince-George's County.
>*The Maryland Gazette*, October 21, 1773. See *The Maryland Gazette*, December 5, 1771; October 22, 1772.

>*City of Burlington, New-Jersey, October* 22, 1773.

AS a certain JOHN POWELL, who has been several times advertised in the Pennsylvania Chronicle by JAMES GUTHRIE, of Lady's Manor, in Baltimore County, Maryland, as a convict servant, is taken up, and now confined in the gaol of said city, the said JAMES GUTHRIE is desired to come or send, and produce a legal claim in three weeks from the date hereof, or he will be sold for his fees, &c.
DANIEL ELLIS, *Sheriff.*
>*The Pennsylvania Chronicle,* From Monday, October 18, to Monday, October 25, 1773; From Monday, November 1, to Monday, November 8, 1773. See *The Pennsylvania Chronicle,* From Monday, September 13, to Monday, September 20, 1773.

>*Three Pounds Reward.*

RAN away from the subscriber, living about 14 miles from *Baltimore-Town, Maryland*, the first day of *July* last, an *Irish* servant man, named THOMAS DOYLE, 21 years of age, about 5 feet 8 or 9 inches high, pock-marked, a well-set fellow, has light brown hair, and lisps in his speech; had on, when he went away, a white country cloth jacket, a red under one, white kersey breeches, a new oznabrigs shirt, marked on the bosom with coloured thread T; has been since taken and put in *York* gaol, and made his escape from *Conrad Miller*, on his return home, the first of *August*, and has since been seen between *York* and *Lancaster*, near *Susquehannah-ferry*, and there passed for a free man: It is supposed he has gone towards *Frederick-Town*. Whoever takes up said servant, and secures him in any of his Majesty's gaols, shall receive the above reward, and if brought home, reasonable charges paid, by   THOMAS TODD.

 The Maryland Journal, and the Baltimore Advertiser, From Saturday, October 16, to Saturday, October 23, 1773; From Saturday, October 23, to Saturday, October 30, 1773; From Saturday, October 30, to Saturday, November 6, 1773; From Saturday, November 6, to Saturday, November 13, 1773. *The Pennsylvania Chronicle*, From Monday, October 25, to Monday, November 1, 1773; From Monday, November 1, to Monday, November 8, 1773; From Monday, November 15, to Monday, November 22, 1773; From Monday, November 22, to Monday, November 29, 1773; From Monday, November 29, to Monday, December 6, 1773. Minor differences between the papers. See *Dunlap's Pennsylvania Packet or, the General Advertiser*, October 24, 1774.

THREE POUNDS REWARD.

October 10, 1773.

RAN away from the subscriber, living near Annapolis, an Irish indented servant lad, named James Garland, about 18 years old, 5 feet 6 inches high, pretty well made, has short brown hair, fresh complexion, but now pale, having had fevers for some time, and is pock marked: had on, a felt hat, fearnought jacket, and osnabrig shirt and trousers.

 Whoever takes up and secured [*sic*] the said servant, so that his master gets him again, shall receive, if taken 10 miles from home, forty shillings currency; and if out of the province, the above reward, paid by
BRICE T. B. WORTHINGTON.

 The Maryland Gazette, November 4, 1773; November 18, 1773; November 25, 1773; December 2, 1773; December 16, 1773; December 23, 1773; December 30, 1773.

THREE POUNDS REWARD.

RAN away, on Sunday the 10th inst. (October) from the subscriber in Bladensburgh, an indented Irish servant man, imported last July from London, named Barnard Fitzpatrick, of middle stature, well set, dark complexion, black hair, has a remarkable scar on one side of his chin larger than a shilling: had on and took with him, two white shirts, a striped callico jacket, a cloth coloured half worn cloth ditto, leather breeches, a felt hat bound with black ferreting, thread stockings, a pair of blue ribb'd ditto, and

it is probable he has forged a pass; he says he has a friend on board a man of war lying off Annapolis. Whoever shall take up and bring home said fellow, shall receive, if taken not more than 20 miles from home, thirty shillings, if above 20 miles, the above reward of three pounds, paid by JAMES HUNT.
All masters of vessels are forbid to employ or carry him off.
> *The Maryland Gazette*, November 4, 1773; November 11, 1773. See *The Maryland Journal, and the Baltimore Advertiser*, From Saturday, October 9, to Saturday, October 16, 1773.

RAN away from the subscriber, living on Elk-Ridge, on the 30th of this Instant, a convict servant man named JOHN ROBERTS, about five feet five inches high, very well made, gray eyes, short yellow hair, and is remarkably fond of liquor, has been about five years and a half in the county, has tended stable, as hostler, he had on and took with him, a short fustian coat, nankeen jacket, calico ditto, dove coloured drugget breeches, thread and worsted stockings, good shoes, plated buckles, castor hat, white shirts, and many other cloths unknown. It is likely he will change his name, and get a pass forged, as he can neither read nor write.—Whoever takes up said servant, and delivers him to the subscriber, near Mr. *Hammond's* shall receive THREE POUNDS, current money, including what the law allows, by   JOSHUA DORSEY, jun.
> *The Maryland Journal, and the Baltimore Advertiser*, From Saturday, October 30, to Saturday, November 6, 1773; From Saturday, November 6, to Saturday, November 13, 1773.

Baltimore, Nov. 11, 1773.
TWENTY SHILLINGS REWARD.
RAN away, from the Brig Betsey, John Patton, Master, a certain RICHARD BLACK, by Trade a Painter and Glazier, about 5 feet 7 inches high, of a yellow Complexion, and is a Native of Ireland.—He has taken several Things from on board said Vessel. Whoever takes up said runaway, and secures him, so that he may be had again, shall have the above Reward, and reasonable Charges paid, by
JOHN CORNTHWAIT, or   JOHN PATTON.
> *The Maryland Journal, and the Baltimore Advertiser*, From Saturday, November 6, to Saturday, November 13, 1773; From Saturday, November 13, to Saturday, November 20, 1773.

Baltimore, Nov.16, 1773.
Five Pounds Reward.

RAN away from the subscriber, living on Fell's Point, an indented English servant man, named JAMES DICKINSON, about 24 years of age, 5 feet 9 or 10 inches high, of a fair complexion, with light coloured curled hair; a little pitted with the small-pox; is a stout well made man, and came into this country in the ship Prince of Wales, Capt. Morrison, on the 15th of October last; had on when he went away, a coarse hat cut in the fashion, a check shirt, and a reddish coloured silk handkerchief round his neck; an orange colour napped coat and jacket, light cloth breeches, with a large hole in the left knee thereof, blue and white cotton stockings, and good shoes, with copper buckles. He is a little crooked knee'd. Whoever secures him so that his master may get him again, shall have the above reward and reasonable charges in brought home, paid by   WILLIAM HAYES.

The Maryland Journal, and the Baltimore Advertiser, From Saturday, November 13, to Saturday, November 20, 1773; From Saturday, November 20, to Saturday, November 27, 1773; From Saturday, November 27, to Thursday, December 9, 1773; From Thursday, December 9, to Saturday, December 18, 1773; From Saturday, December 18, to Thursday, December 30, 1773.

Philadelphia, Nov. 28, 1773.

WENT away, about three weeks ago, from his master, living in Baltimore, an English Servant Man, who goes by the name of WILLIAM FREEMAN, by trade a Cabinet-maker; he is very remarkable, having a crooked back, is of a low stature, has an old-fashioned face, very bad teeth, and a mole on his right cheek; had on, when he went away, a black coat and waistcoat, and stocking or leather breeches, but has been seen since in different sorts of clothes; he stole several things, viz. shirts, stockings, silk handkerchiefs, set stock and knee buckles, and a pair of gold ear-rings, with various other articles, which it is supposed he will offer for sale. He likewise stole, at the same time, a small DARK BAY MARE, with a switch tail, and an almost new saddle and bridle. It is reported he is gone to New-York, where, or at some other place on his way to that city, he has changed the Mare, saddle and bridle, for dressed deer-skins. He pretends to know the art of legerdemain. Whoever takes up the said servant, so that his master gets him again, shall receive, if taken in the city or suburbs, *Twenty Shillings*; if in any other parts of the county, *Forty Shillings*; and if out of the county, THREE POUNDS; to be paid by his master, by applying at Mr. THOMPSON's, in Front-street.

The Pennsylvania Chronicle, From Monday, November 15, to Monday, November 22, 1773; From Monday, November 22, to

Monday, November 29, 1773; From Monday, November 29, to Monday, December 6, 1773; From Monday, December 6, to Monday, December 13, 1773; From Monday, December 13, to Monday, December 20, 1773.

FIFTEEN POUNDS REWARD.

RUN-AWAY from the subscriber, living in Baltimore county, near Garrison Church, two convict servant men, and a negro, viz. WILLIAM JOHNS, a short well made fellow, about 5 feet 5 inches high, has short dark brown hair, tied behind, and blue eyes; took with him a snuff coloured coat and breeches, with yellow buttons, a double-breasted grey beaver coating vest, a white, country made ditto, a pair of coarse yarn stockings, a pair of coarse new shoes, yellow buckles, and a felt hat, He is a stone mason by trade.—WILLIAM MATHEWS, a slim fellow, of a thin visage, about five feet eight inches high, wears a brown wig; has taken with him, a green wilton coat, much faded, made frock fashion, a black jacket, white, country made breeches, two pair of trowsers, two pair of stockings, one of which is brown thread, the other is coarse yarn; a piar [*sic*] of strong nailed shoes, new felt hat, one oznabrigs shirt, and one holland ditto. BERKSHIRE, a large Negro fellow, about five feet nine inches high, has several large scars on each cheek, and sundry others on his forehead, is a little knock-kneed; he took with him, three shirts, one holland, one white sheeting, and one country linen, two country cloth jackets, one dyed, and the other white, a pair of red plush breeches, lined with buckskin, a pair of coarse yarn stockings, and two pair of shoes, one of which is nailed. They also took with them, a light brown jacket, with sleeves, and lined with white flannel, a blue cloth jacket, with white hind parts, a white shirt, and an old felt hat.—Whoever takes up, and secures said servants, so that their master may get them again, shall have, if fifty miles from home, *Three Pounds* for each, and if out of the province, *Five Pounds* for each, or the above reward for the three, if brought home, paid by
CHARLES CARNAN.

N. B. All masters of vessels are forbid to harbour or carry off said servants at their peril, it is supposed they will make for New-York.

The New-York Gazette; and the Weekly Mercury, November 22, 1773.

RAN away, from the Subscriber, living in Dorset County, Maryland, in September 1772, two Servant Men, belonging to the Estate of .William Dunlap, late of said County, deceased, viz. ROBERT VALLIANT, by Trade a Blacksmith, born in Maryland, about 35 Years of Age, a well-set Fellow, about 5 Feet 6 Inches high, dark Complexion; had his Hair cut off

when he went away; his Dress unknown.—.WILLIAM HILL, a Convict, a Native of England, speaks the West-Country Dialect, is a Blacksmith by Trade, a well-set Fellow, 4 Feet 9 Inches high, has black Hair; it is supposed Hill is now in Baltimore County, and Valliant has been seen in Baltimore-Town not long ago. Whoever takes up said Servants, and brings them Home, shall receive for Valliant, FIVE POUNDS, and for Hill, FIFTY SHILLINGS, and reasonable Charges paid by
CHARLES EGLESTON. .

The Maryland Journal, and the Baltimore Advertiser, From Saturday, November 20, to Saturday, November 27, 1773; From Saturday, November 27, to Thursday, December 9, 1773; From Thursday, December 9, to Saturday, December 18, 1773.

November 1, 1773.
TEN POUNDS Reward.

RUN away this morning, from the Subscriber, living in Tawnytown, Frederick county, Maryland, an Irish servant MAN named HUGH M'KAIN, by trade a taylor, about 5 feet 4 inches high, small and slender, of a middle age; the fore-part of his head almost bald, black hair, pale visage, a great snuffer, much given to liquor, and has a mark or scar under his left nostril: Had on and took with him, a half-worn beaver hat, a light coloured half-worn Wilton coat, the hind parts and the left fore-part of a new green duroy jacket, one white shirt, one check ditto, a pair of brown half-worn breeches; a green pair, a ribbed pair, and a plain pair of grey stockings, old shoes with buckles; he is known almost all over Maryland, Virginia, Pennsylvania and the Jerseys. Whoever takes up said Servant, and secures him in any of his Majesty's goals, so that his master may get him again, or brings him home, shall have the above reward, and reasonable charges paid by me,
CONROD BONER.

The Pennsylvania Gazette, December 1, 1773; *The New-York Gazette; and the Weekly Mercury*, December 13, 1773; December 20, 1773; December 27, 1773; January 17, 1774. Minor Differences. The *Mercury* spelled the place McKain left as "Taronytown." See *The Maryland Journal, and the Baltimore Advertiser*, From Saturday, November 27, to Thursday, December 9, 1773.

November 29, 1773.
TEN POUNDS Reward.
RUN away from the subscriber, living at *Great Pipe-Creek, Frederick* county, *Maryland*, a *Dutch* servant man, named *John Balser Kinsiner*, by trade a taylor, about 5 feet 6 inches high, dark frized hair, sandy beard, black eyes, sunk in his head, and very small; had on, when he went away, an old fulled lincey jacket, white flax linen ditto, old check shirt, tow

trowsers, new worsted stockings, and a new silk handkerchief; his father lives in *Philadelphia*, and his wife's father in Germantown, he has many other friends in different parts of that province: He was whipped at *Lancaster*, at October Court, 1772, at *Trenton* last *August*, and is well acquainted with the whipping-post in *Philadelphia*. Whoever secures said servant, so that his master gets him again, shall have, if taken 50 miles from home, FIFTY SHILLINGS, if 100, FIVE POUNDS, if 200, the above reward, and reasonable charges, if brought home, paid by
MICHAEL M'GUIRE, junior.

It is likely he may change his name, clothes and trade, as he can work at the weaving business.

The Pennsylvania Gazette, December 8, 1773; December 22, 1773; January 5, 1774.

Prince-George's county, Nov. 21. 1773.
COMMITTED to my custody as a runaway a certain Jacob Tharp, as he says a Jerseyman born, and has been a soldier in Amherst's regiment, is about 39 years old, 5 feet 9 or 10 inches high, pretty well made, and appears to have had a small cut over his left eye: has on a red lappelled outside jacket with leather buttons, a striped lincey under jacket, a check shirt and a white one under it, osnabrig trousers, worsted hose and a pair of pretty good shoes. His master, if he has one, is desired to pay charges and take him from   RALPH FORSTER.

The Maryland Gazette, December 9, 1773; December 16, 1773; December 23, 1773; December 30, 1773.

Fifteen Pounds Reward.
RAN away from the subscribers, last night, three servant men, viz. JOHN FOGATY, a stout made fellow, a bricklayer by trade, about five feet nine or ten inches high, with short red hair and white eyebrows, pitted with the small-pox, and much freckled; had on, and took with him, one of grey-coloured coat, grey yarn stockings, and leather breeches, with oznabrigs shirt and trousers.

RICHARD SADLER, a plaisterer by trade, about thirty-eight years of age, a stout well made man, about five feet nine or ten inches high, fresh coloured, his beard large and black, wears his own short black hair; had on and took with him, one old black coat, one short light coloured bearskin coat and breeches half worn, dark grey yarn stockings, new country made shoes, and brass buckles. The above two are Irishmen.

CHARLES SAWYER, about four feet four or five inches high, [sic] a bricklayer by trade, is a well set fellow, with short black hair, and large dark eyebrows, is a bold daring fellow, speaks quick, and is remarkably thin visaged; had on and took away with him, one grey coloured bearskin coat, old grey waistcoat and breeches, new yarn stockings, and felt hat. It is supposed they have other things, and forged passes.

    Whoever takes up and secures the said servants, shall have the above reward, or in proportion for either of them, and, if brought home, reasonable charges, paid by
WILLIAM BUCKLAND,   THOMAS PRICE.

    The Maryland Journal, and the Baltimore Advertiser, From Saturday, November 27, to Thursday, December 9, 1773; From Thursday, December 9, to Saturday, December 18, 1773; From Saturday, December 18, to Thursday, December 30, 1773. See *The Maryland Gazette*, April 7, 1774, and *The Pennsylvania Gazette*, April 20, 1774, for Sadler, and *The Pennsylvania Gazette*, April 20, 1774 for Sawyer, and "Fogarthy."

                                                                             Frederick-Town, November 24, 1773.
WHEREAS ROGER AGAN, was committed to the gaol of this County in August last, on suspicion of being a runaway, which, however, he denies; this, therefore, is to desire his master, if he has any, to take him away, paying charges.—He is about 5 feet 4 inches high, 21 years of age, has dark brown hair, and a small scar over his left eye.
LAWRENCE O'NEAL.

    The Maryland Journal, and the Baltimore Advertiser, From Saturday, November 27, to Thursday, December 9, 1773.

                         Eight Dollars Reward.
RAN away, on the 27th of last September, from the subscriber, living in Baltimore County, near Benjamin Rogers, Esqr's mill, a Dutch convict servant woman named Rosannah Unrick, about 30 years of age, 5 feet 9 or 10 inches high; had on and took with her, an old felt hat, a blue flowered Barcelona handkerchief, two check linen ditto, one check apron, one old speckled flannel bed gown, and linen for another, cut out, but not made up, and a linsey petticoat, which were all too short for her, one old quilt, which has been turned and lengthened, two pair of mens stockings, one pair of womens shoes, which are too short for her, one pair of old men's shoes, and likewise 10 yards of home-made linen. She is a leather-dresser by trade. Whoever takes up said woman, and secures her, so that her master gets her again, shall have the above reward, and reasonable charges paid, if brought home, including what the law allows, paid by
DANIEL REES.
N. B. She has a scald head, has her hair cut off, and was under cure for the venereal disorder when she went away.

The Maryland Journal, and the Baltimore Advertiser, From Saturday, November 27, to Thursday, December 9, 1773; From Thursday, December 9, to Saturday, December 18, 1773; From Saturday, December 18, to Thursday, December 30, 1773; From Saturday, January 8, to Thursday, January 20, 1774.

RAN away from the subscriber's plantation, near Poplar Spring Chapel, in Anne Arundel county, an Irish convict servant lad, named LAWRENCE CONNELLY; he is about 18 years old, slim made, smooth faced, swarthy complexion, speaks much in the Irish dialect, and has a down look: had on and took with him, a blue coat and waistcoat, the waistcoat double-breasted, grey breeches, light worsted stockings, white shirt, good London made shoes, and a fine felt hat, and a yellow flowered silk handkerchief. Whoever apprehends the said servant, and brings him to me, living on Elk-Ridge, or to CHARLES PORTER, overseer on said place, shall receive, as a reward Twenty Shillings if taken twenty miles from home, Thirty Shillings if thirty miles, forty if Forty Miles, and Three Pounds if out of the province, besides what the law allows, and reasonable charges, paid by
JOHN DORSEY.

The Maryland Journal, and the Baltimore Advertiser, From Saturday, November 27, to Thursday, December 9, 1773; From Thursday, December 9, to Saturday, December 18, 1773. See *The Maryland Gazette*, December 16, 1773.

Ten Pounds Reward.

RAN away this morning, from the subscriber, living in Tawny-town, Frederick County, Maryland, an Irish servant man named HUGH M'KAIN, by trade a taylor, about five feet four inches high, small and slender, of a middle age; his forehead almost bald, black hair, a pale visage, a great snuffer, much given to liquor, has a mark or scar under his left nostril; had on and took with him, a half-worn beaver hat, a light-coloured half worn Wilton coat, the hind part and the left fore part of a new green duroy jacket, a white linen and a check shirt, a brown pair of half worn cloth breeches; a green pair, a ribb'd pair, and a plain pair of grey stockings, and old shoes, with buckles. He is known almost all over Maryland, Virginia, Pennsylvania and the Jerseys. Whoever takes up said servant, and secures him in any of his Majesty's gaols, so that his master may get him again, or brings him home, shall have the above reward, and reasonable charges paid by me, CONROD BONER.
Nov 1, 1773.

The Maryland Journal, and the Baltimore Advertiser, From Saturday, November 27, to Thursday, December 9, 1773; From Thursday, December 9, to Saturday, December 18, 1773; From Saturday, December 18, to Thursday, December 30, 1773. See *The Pennsylvania Gazette*, December 1, 1773.

October 22. 1773.
FOUR DOLLARS REWARD.
RAN AWAY from the subscriber, living in Cicel County, an apprentice boy, by trade a tanner, named HALY TOWLAND, about eighteen years of age, about five feet eight or nine inches high; he is a straight well-made fellow, with a bold countenance, coarse voice, short black hair, and is left handed; had on when he went away, a coarse home-made lead coloured cloth jacket not lined, with small metal buttons, a claret coloured broadcloth jacket without sleeves, white drilling breeches, coarse thread stockings, new shoes with double soals, a felt hat almost new, with yellow lining, an old white shirt, a stock, and silver clasps with two large letters in the inside, unknown; he also took with him two oznabrug shirts. Whoever takes up said apprentice, and brings him to his master living on Bohemia Manor, near the Church, or secures him in any of his Majesty's gaols, shall have the above reward, and reasonable charges, paid by
JAMES HUKILL.

Dunlap's Pennsylvania Packet or, the General Advertiser, December 12, 1773, January 24, 1774.

TEN DOLLARS Reward.
RUN away from the subscriber, in Dorchester county, an Irish servant man, named JOSEPH ANDERSON, a Schoolmaster, but it is likely he may change his name, a thin visaged fellow, about 5 feet 10 inches high, near about 30 years of age, wears his own hair tied behind, but short, and very grey headed; had on, when he went away, an old surtout coat, and a very good jean coat, and knit pattern jacket, with buttons covered with the same, an old English hat, cut in the fashion, check shirt, old leather breeches, English ribbed stockings, English shoes, Pinchbeck shoe-buckles, and black Barcelona handkerchief. It is supposed he took with him about 15 or 20 Pounds in cash, that was stolen. Whoever takes up said servant, so that his master may get him again, shall have the above reward, and reasonable charges, paid by
November 27, 1773.   THOMAS ENNALLS, 3d.

The Pennsylvania Gazette, December 15, 1773; January 12, 1774; January 26, 1774. See *The Maryland Gazette*, December 16, 1773 and *The Maryland Gazette*, January 13, 1774.

Carlisle Goal, Cumberland County, November 27, 1773. WERE committed to this Goal, the following persons, viz. Henry Linderman, *a German, house carpenter and joiner by trade, who was advertised in the Maryland Journal, the* 17*th of September last, No.* 5, *by a certain Henry Fraley, of Germantown, in Pennsylvania, as a person who had absconded from his bail, together with a certain* John Housdorf; *therefore I desire the said Henry Fraley to come, and pay reward money and fees, in three weeks after date, or he will then be discharged, on paying his fees. Also* Sarah Cooper, *who confesses she ran away from James White, of Baltimore county,* 14 *miles from Baltimore-town, living on the great road from Baltimore to Carlisle; her master is desired to come, in three weeks after this date. Absconded from his bail last March, a certain Henry Kerr, black hair tied, flat broad face, about* 5 *feet* 6 *inches high,* 28 *years old, is much given to drinking strong liquor. Whoever takes up said Kerr, and secures him in any goal, so as I get him again, shall have THIRTY SHILLINGS reward, and reasonable charges, paid by*
ROBERT SEMPLE, Goaler.
The Pennsylvania Gazette, December 15, 1773.

RAN away from the subscriber's plantation, near Poplar Spring Chapel, in Anne Arundel county, an Irish convict servant, named Lawrence Connolly, about eighteen years old, swarthy complexion, slim made, speaks much in that dialect: had on and took with him, a blue coat and waistcoat double breasted, white shirt, worsted stockings, new shoes, and a Carolina felt hat.—Whoever takes up the said servant, and delivers him to Charles Porter, overseer on said plantation, or the subscriber living on Elk-Ridge, shall receive as a reward twenty shillings if taken twenty miles from home, thirty shillings if thirty miles, forty shillings if forty miles, and three pounds if out of the province, besides what the law allows.
JOHN DORSEY.
The Maryland Gazette, December 16, 1773; December 23, 1773; December 30, 1770; January 6, 1774; January 13, 1774; January 27, 1774; February 3, 1774; February 10, 1774; February 17, 1774; February 24, 1774; March 10, 1774; March 17, 1774; March 24, 1774; March 31, 1774; April 7, 1774; April 14, 1774; April 28, 1774; May 5, 1774. See *The Maryland Journal, and the Baltimore Advertiser*, From Saturday, November 27, to Thursday, December 9, 1773.

Fredericksburg, November 30, 1773.
RAN away from the subscribers on the twenty-second instant, two servant men, the one a barber, an Englishman, named John Cockle, with short

brown curled hair, five feet seven inches high: had on, a coloured coat and jacket, blue cloth breeches, and a small fashionable hat, speaks thick, and stoops a little in the shoulders. The other a tailor, calls himself an Englishman but has the Irish accent, named John Driver, with short bushy hair, five feet five or six inches high: had on, a blue coat, red striped gingham jacket, and wilton breeches. Whoever takes up said servants, and delivers them to us in Fredericksburg, shall have five pounds reward, or in proportion for either of them.
JOHN ATKINSON,   JAMES NEWTON.
The Maryland Gazette, December 16, 1773; December 23, 1773; December 30, 1773; January 13, 1774.

December 14, 1773.
RAN away from the subscriber on Sunday last, a servant man, named Thomas Hall, a carver by trade: had on, a Wilton coat of a redish colour, one frock of dark coloured fustian, waistcoat of the same, new buckskin breeches, ribbed worsted stockings, and silver buckles; he wears his own hair which is curled at the ears and clubbed behind, is about five feet nine inches high, slim made, pitted with the small-pox. The indenture he signed in London was given up to him and a discharge, after which he executed another indenture, by which he was to be allowed in consideration of his former service, wages after the rate of ten shillings per week till the expiration of his time, which would have been in September next: masters of vessels are requested not to carry him out of the country; and whoever takes up and secures the said servant, shall receive five pounds reward, and if brought home reasonable charges.
WILLIAM BUCKLAND.
The Maryland Gazette, December 16, 1773; December 23, 1773; December 30, 1773; January 6, 1774; January 13, 1774; January 20, 1774; January 27, 1774; February 3, 1774; February 10, 1774; February 17, 1774; February 24, 1774; April 3, 1774.

TEN DOLLARS REWARD.

November 27, 1773.
RAN away from the subscriber, in Dorchester county, an Irish servant man, about five feet ten inches high, named Joseph Anderson, schoolmaster, but 'tis like he may change his name, has a thin visage, about thirty years of age, wears his own hair tied behind, but short, gray headed: had on, when he went away, old surtout coat, a thin jeans coat, a knit pattern jacket with buttons covered of the same, old leather breeches, a pair of ribbed worsted stockings, a pair of English shoes, pinchbeck buckles, English hat cut in the fashion, check shirt, and black Barcelona handkerchief: 'tis supposed he has

taken with him about eighteen or twenty pounds in cash that was stolen. Whoever takes up said servant, so that his master may get him again, shall have the above reward, and reasonable charges, paid by
THOMAS ENNALLS, 3d.
The Maryland Gazette, December 16, 1773; December 23, 1773; January 6, 1774; January 13, 1774. See *The Pennsylvania Gazette,* December 15, 1773 and *The Maryland Gazette,* January 13, 1774.

BALTIMORE COUNTY, Dec. 10, 1773.
EIGHT DOLLARS REWARD.
RAN away from the subscriber, living near Deer-Creek, near Mr. Samuel Ashmead's mill, a convict servant man, named RALPH HATELEY, about 25 years of age, 5 feet 3 or 4 inches high, has short brown hair, and a bold daring look. Had on an old blue broadcloth coat, something too long for him, serge jacket, tow trousers, old shoes and stockings, very much addicted to drinking and gaming, and it is supposed he has forged a pass. Whoever secures said servant in any of his Majesty's gaols, or brings him to me the subscriber, shall have the above reward, and reasonable charges, if brought home, paid by
DANIEL PRESTON.
The Maryland Journal, and the Baltimore Advertiser, From Thursday, December 9, to Saturday, December 18, 1773; From Saturday, December 18, to Thursday, December 30, 1773; From Saturday, January 8, to Thursday, January 20, 1774.

Bedford, ss. *December 10, 1773.*
COMMITTED to this prison, the 5th instant, a certain JOHN MILLER, about 18 years of age, who says he is a servant to a certain John Denny, who lives in Maryland, about 30 miles from New-Castle. His master is requested to come, pay charges, and take him away, otherwise he will be sold for his fees. JAMES PIPER, Sheriff.
The Pennsylvania Gazette, December 22, 1773.

RAN away from the subscriber, living in Kent County, last night, being the 30th of this instant, an Irish servant man named EDWARD MURPHY, aged about twenty-three, about five feet four inches high, a well set fellow, round shoulder'd grey eyes, of a fair complexion, talks much on the Irish brogue: had on, and took with him, a green jacket with yellow buttons and small cuffs, an old pair of leather breeches too big for him, a new pair of shoes tied with leather strings, two pair of stockings, one a light blue, the

other mixt grey, two shirts, one an old white one, the other oznaburg, and a black great coat; he may probably change his clothes as he went with a countryman of his, one TOBIAS BURK, five feet eight inches high, with black hair; had on, when he went away, a lightish kersey coat half worn, a new pair of buckskin breeches, two shirts, one an old white one, the other sheeting linen, and a very good hat, the lining of which turns out behind, like a cap, to the back part of his head; his left leg is very sore.—Whoever takes up the two fellows shall have SIX POUNDS reward, or THREE POUNDS for each, paid by
JACOB FORKNER.

N. B. As the said BURK took said servant with him, and it is imagined that they are posses'd of money, it is very probable they may change their clothes.
December 31, 1773.

The Maryland Journal, and the Baltimore Advertiser, From Saturday, December 18, to Thursday, December 30, 1773; From Thursday, December 30, 1773, to Saturday, January 8, 1774; From Thursday, January 20, to Thursday, February 10, 1774; From Thursday, February 10, to Thursday, February 17, 1774; From Thursday, February 17, to Thursday, February 24, 1774.

RUN away from the subscriber, living near Sam's creek, Frederick county, about a mile from Solomon Miller's, on the road that leads from Frederick to Baltimore-town, an indented servant man, named JOHN MARTINGLE, but may change his name; but may change his name; he pretends to be a sadler; he is about 5 feet 5 inches high, well set, round visage, down look, black hair and eyebrows; had on, and took with him, a yellowish wig, half-worn felt hat, a grey coloured waistcoat, with sleeves, old black breeches, grey yarn stockings, old shoes, with silver plated buckles, and an old grey surtout coat, with a hole under the cape. Whoever takes up the said servant, ten miles from home, shall have *Twenty Shillings*, and if 20 miles *Forty Shillings*, and if out of the province *Twenty Dollars* reward, if secured in any of his Majesty's goals, paid by HENRY BAKER.

The Pennsylvania Gazette, January 5, 1774.

Baltimore county, December 24, 1773.
THE following persons are committed to my custody as runaways.

JOHN CLARK, about 36 years of age, 5 feet 6 inches high, well made, a dark complexion, has on a brown cloth coat and jacket, and osnabrig trousers, says he formerly lived with Samuel Kelly, near Newport, in New-Castle county, Pennsylvania.

JAMES BOWERS, about 42 years of age, 5 feet 4 inches high, slim made, a dark complexion, he has on two spotted flannel jackets, and has been a sailor.

JOHN SKYRAM, about 50 years of age, 5 feet 5 inches high, very pale complexion, has on a blue coat, and osnabrig trousers.

JOHN LEAMAN, about 25 years of age, 5 feet 8 inches high, a stout made fellow, but appears to be an idiot.

GEORGE GRAY, 20 years of age, about 5 feet 6 inches high, fresh complexion, has on a blossom coloured coat and waistcoat, and says he formerly lived with Henry Darby, at Newark, in Pensylvania.

HENRY ROBERTSON, who confesses he is a servant to Henry Pomeroy, in Old Town, Frederick county, near to Col. Cresop's.

Their masters, if they have any, are desired to take them away and pay charges to ROBERT CHRISTIE, jun. Sheriff.

The Maryland Gazette, January 6, 1774; January 13, 1774; January 20, 1774; February 3, 1774.

Prince-George's county, December 31, 1773.
COMMITTED to my custody as a runaway, a certain Alexander Bell, who answers in every respect (except his height and the great coat) the description given of Joseph Anderson, by Thomas Ennals the 3d. Bell is very near if not quite six feet high: has on, a new dark coloured knap surtout coat, a jeans jacket without lining, and buttons covered with the same; a clouded knit pattern jacket, buttons covered with the same; country dressed leather breeches, yarn hose, very good shoes, with scolloped Pinchbeck buckles; a very good castor hat almost new, London made, and cocked fashionably; two old white shirts, a new check ditto; his hair is naturally black, but is now about half mixed with gray, and he wears it loose, though it appears just long enough to tie. His master is desired to pay charges and take him from. RALPH FORSTER, sheriff.

The Maryland Gazette, January 13, 1774; January 20, 1774; February 3, 1774. See *The Maryland Gazette*, December 16, 1773 and *The Pennsylvania Gazette*, December 15, 1773.

SIXTEEN DOLLARS REWARD.

RAN AWAY from the subscriber, living in Baltimore county, Maryland, within eight miles of the Lower Ferry, Susquehanna, on Sunday the 31st of October last, two servant men; one an Englishman named WILLIAM SPRINGALL, came into Baltimore Town with Capt. Robertson about the 20th of June 1772; he was born in Middlesex, is about twenty-three years of age, five feet six inches high, a fresh complexion, black beard, and short

brown hair; he professes to be a barber or hairdresser: Had on when he went away, a blue gray suit of cloaths with yellow gilt buttons, the coat has a red cape and button holes worked with red and blue twist mixed; he is much given to liquor. The other an Irishman, named EDWARD MAGINAN, has been in the county about six months, and is five feet eight inches high, a down-looking slow-spoken fellow, with short brown hair, has had the fever and ague lately, and looks very yellow; had on when he went away, a suit of black broadcloth cloaths and a blue surtout; but as they have other cloaths with them they may have changed their dress, and it is supposed they have forged a pass. Whoever secures the said servants in any gaol, so that their master may have them again, shall have the above reward, or THREE POUNDS for each, and reasonable charges, paid by
JAMES GILES.
N. B. All masters of vessels are forbid to carry them off, at their peril.
Dunlap's Pennsylvania Packet or, the General Advertiser, January 24, 1774. See *Dunlap's Pennsylvania Packet or, the General Advertiser*, April 11, 1774.

FORTY SHILLINGS REWARD.
RUN away from the subscriber, living near Vienna, in Dorchester county, Maryland, the 6th of January, 1774, an indented servant man, named *Cornelius Schawn*, a short well set fellow, about 5 feet high, has something of a down look, and when he talks is pretty apt to swear in common, wears his own black hair, much curled about his head; had on, and took with him, a small round castor hat, pretty much worn, a homespun thread and cotton yellow coloured coat, a white cotton waistcoat, and an old blue duffil or plains ditto, an old striped lincey woolsey ditto, long skirted, which he frequently wears under his coat, homespun shirts, one almost new, striped blue and white, the other pretty much worn, old buckskin breeches, very dirty, and two linen trowsers, which it is likely he may wear over them, white yarn stockings, lately footed, very good shoes, with small rimmed copper buckles in them; he says he was born near Dover, in Pennsylvania. Whoever takes up said servant, and confines him in any of his Majesty's goals, or brings him to the subscriber, shall have the above reward, and reasonable charges, paid by
MICHAEL WILLCOX.
All masters of vessels are forbid to harbour or carry him off, at their peril.
The Pennsylvania Gazette, January 26, 1774; March 23, 1774.

Annapolis, Jan. 26, 1774.
RAN away last Sunday night from the subscriber, one William Quelch, an old, tall, slim made fellow, stoops when he walks, and wears his own gray

hair: had on when he went away a whitish coloured kersey jacket, old leather breeches, osnabrig shirt, white stockings, old shoes new soaled, and an old felt hat. He stole and carried away with him a white shirt, a check ditto, a pair of new shoes, four pair of stockings, a vest with the fore parts made of blue hair shag, a small silver watch, maker's name John Roberts, London, No. 7677, a pair of handsome silver buckles carved, a set of stock-buckle marked M B, a set broach, a silver dollar that has been attempted to be cut in two and not done, with other small money not know what, and several other things too tedious to mention. He served the latter part of his time with Capt. John Ireland in Elk-Ridge Whoever will take up said fellow and secure him, so that he may be brought to justice, shall receive three pounds reward, paid by ISAAC M'HARD.

The Maryland Gazette, January 27, 1774; February 3, 1774; February 10, 1774; February 17, 1774; February 24, 1774; March 17, 1774; April 3, 1774.

FIVE POUNDS REWARD.

Dec. 19, 1773.

RAN away last night from the subscriber living on Snowdens manor, Fredrick county, Maryland, an Irish servant man named Timothy Corker, by trade a tailor, about 5 feet 6 inches high, fair complexion, thin yellow hair, talks fast and in the Irish dialect: had on and took with him a felt hat, a light brown kersey jacket with sleeves, a pair of breeches of the same cloth, an Irish linen shirt, a check ditto, a pair of white country yarn stockings, a pair of country made shoes, and his hands are hard occasioned by chopping with the ax; it is probable some evil minded person has furnished him with other cloaths and a pass. Whoever apprehends the said servant and secures him in any jail, so that I may get him again, shall be intitled to above reward, and if brought home reasonable charges paid by
JEREMIAH DUCKER.

The Maryland Gazette, February 10, 1774; February 17, 1774; February 24, 1774.

RAN away, from the subscriber, on Long Green, Baltimore County, the eleventh of January last, an apprentice boy, named JAMES GREEN; had on when he went away, a brown broad cloth coat, buckskin breeches, and a beaver hat.—Whoever takes up said apprentice and brings him to his master, shall have FOUR DOLLARS reward, and all reasonable charges paid by MOSES DILLIN.

N. B. All masters of vessels are forwarned concealing or carrying him off, at their peril.

The Maryland Journal, and the Baltimore Advertiser, From Thursday, January 20, to Thursday, February 10, 1774; From Thursday, February 10, to Thursday, February 17, 1774; From Thursday, February 17, to Thursday, February 24, 1774.

SEVEN POUNDS REWARD.

MADE his escape from me the subscriber, a certain JOHN COPPINGER, a runaway servant, who was advertised in the Pennsylvania Chronicle by Daniel and Samuel Hughes, of Frederick County, Maryland, and was taken up by me; but before he was committed to justice or returned to his master, he stole from me a horse, saddle and bridle, and went off from John Sherrid's, store-keeper in Alexander Township, in the Jerseys; the horse is of a brown colour, about 13 and a half hands high, and 15 years old. Said COPPINGER is about 5 feet 6 inches high, has dark brown hair, short and curled, a fair complexion, and understands working in a forge; was bound to Joseph Morris, of Philadelphia, when a child, and afterwards sold to the aforesaid Daniel and Samuel Hughes. Whoever apprehends said servant, and brings him back, or commits him to any of his Majesty's gaols in this province, Maryland, Carolina, &c. so that I may have him again, shall have the above Reward, by applying to me at Daniel and Samuel Hughes's Iron Works in Frederick County, Maryland, or to Mr. James Cunning in Philadelphia.   JAMES DARRAGH.

Dunlap's Pennsylvania Packet or, the General Advertiser, February 21, 1774; March 14, 1774; March 28, 1774; April 11, 1774; April 18, 1774; May 9, 1774; May 23, 1774. See *The Pennsylvania Chronicle*, From Monday, September 20, to Monday, September 27, 1773

TEN POUNDS REWARD.

FEBRUARY [ ], 1774.

RAN away, last night, from the subscriber, living in Baltimore County, about twelve miles from Baltimore-Town, in Maryland, a convict servant man, named JAMES HICKMAN, straight, well made, and of a fresh complexion; about 23 years of age, five feet 6 or 7 inches high, has short dark hair, dark eyes, a blemish in his left eye; is pitted with the small-pox, and has had his collar bone broke, which makes a bump; had on and took with him, a felt hat about half worn, a blue great coat, the cap to the cape made of the same cloth, white country cloth jacket and breeches, mostly new, the jacket has pieces set on the elbows, and a pocket inside the skirt, the breeches made with a large flap, and buttons to the knee-bands, light coloured fearnought under jacket, coarse white yarn stockings, strong country made shoes, with strings, and well nail'd; the said fellow ran away last June, and was taken up at the mouth of Juniata; he will probably change his name, and perhaps his clothes, and 'tis likely he may have a pass: Whoever takes up said servant, and secures him, so that his master may get him again, shall have FORTY SHILLINGS, if 50 miles from home, FOUR POUNDS, if 100 miles, if 150 miles EIGHT POUNDS, and if 200 miles the above reward, including what the law allows, and reasonable charges if brought home, paid by   THOMAS OWINGS.

The Maryland Journal, and the Baltimore Advertiser, From Thursday, February 24, to Thursday, February March 3, 1774. See *The Pennsylvania* Gazette, July 7, 1773.

FOUR DOLLARS Reward.

RUN away from the Subscriber, living in Kent county, Maryland, a certain WILLIAM LONG, about 5 feet 6 inches high, much marked with the small-pox, wears his own black hair, is a Dutchman, and a turner and joiner by trade; had on, when he went away, a white surtout coat, a Wilton close-bodied coat and waistcoat, black or grey stockings; he also took with him, a black MARE, about 12 ½ hands high, a white spot under the foot lock of her off hind foot; it is supposed he will make towards Long-Island. Whoever takes up and secures said Man and Mare, so that the subscriber may get them again, shall have the above reward, and reasonable charges, paid by me JACOB FALCONER.

The Pennsylvania Gazette, March 9, 1774; March 23, 1774.

Anne-Arundel, Maryland, March 15, 1774.

COMMITTED to my custody as a runaway, a white servant man whose name is WILLIAM WHITE, he says he belongs to William Knight of Frederick county; he is a tall slim young fellow, with short strait brown hair, and appears to be about 25 years of age; his cloaths consist of a coarse crocus shirt, a cotton jacket and breeches, and shoes and stockings which are very much worn. His master is desired to take him away and pay charges to   WILLIAM NOKE, sheriff.

The Maryland Gazette, March 17, 1774.

FIVE POUNDS REWARD.

RAN away from the subscriber, on Sunday the 4th of March, a servant man named THOMAS M'INERHENCY, a joiner by trade, about 24 years of age, wears his own hair which is red, is much freckled, he is a slim made man, and may be known as an Irishman by his talk, and is about 5 feet 10

inches high: had on and took with him a short light coloured bearskin coat and breeches of the same, a pair of redish coloured cloth breeches, double breasted red waistcoat, light gray worsted ribbed stockings, and was imported into the province in June last by Capt. Caldwell Howard. Any person who secures the said servant so that I get him again shall receive the above reward and all reasonable charges.
W. BUCKLAND.

The Maryland Gazette, March 17, 1774; March 24, 1774; March 31, 1774; April 7, 1774.

February 28, 1774.
THREE POUNDS REWARD.
RAN AWAY last night, from the subscriber near Bush Town, Baltimore County, Maryland, a convict Irish servant man, named DARBY DWYER, a lying talkative fellow, stout made, about 35 years of age, 5 feet 9 or 10 inches high, stoops in his shoulders, has short brown hair, one of his upper fore teeth half broke off, a scar in the palm of his right hand, a red beard, and probably may change his name and forge a pass: Had on when he went away, an old castor hat, a flaxen coloured wig with one buckle, an upper grey coarse cloth jacket, two under ditto, one striped lincey, the other brown, coarse home-spun shirt, old buckskin breeches, grey yarn stockings, and good shoes tied with strings. Whoever takes up said servant, and secures him in any of his Majesty's gaols, so that his master may have him again, shall receive the above reward, and reasonable charges if brought him, paid by   JAMES MATHER, or JOSEPH STILES.

Dunlap's Pennsylvania Packet or, the General Advertiser, March 21, 1774; April 11, 1774.

March 22, 1774.
RAN away from the subscriber, on the 11th instant, living near Lyon's creek, Calvert county, a servant man named John Baptist Dilla Franey, born in England, but of French extraction: he went away with a certain Mary Pain, who has with her a young child, they are supposed to have gone to some part of Herring Bay or the river sides, as he professes seine knitting and can cart and plow. The said Franey is well set, broad shouldered, about five feet two inches high, his hair between a sandy and lightish brown, gray eyes, full visaged, and remarkable for stammering in his speech: had on when he went away a lightish coloured jacket and breeches, osnabrig shirt, old yarn stockings, new shoes and buckles, and a felt hat. Whoever takes up the said servant and brings him to the subscriber shall have 20 shillings reward if taken in the county, and if out of the county a pistole, paid by the subscriber, and reasonable charges; and if in any prison to give immediate notice to   HENRY CAMDEN.

The Maryland Gazette, March 24, 1774; March 31, 1774; April 7, 1774; April 14, 1774; April 21, 1774; April 28, 1774; May 5, 1774; May 12, 1774; May 19, 1774; May 26, 1774.

RAN away from the subscriber, living near Pig-Point in Anne-Arundel county, on the 28th day of December last, a stout healthy boy, named JOHN WALSH, 15 years of age: Had on when he went away, a striped country cloth jacket kersey wove, a brown cloth ditto, a pair of full'd country cloth breeches, a check shirt, a pair of new yarn stockings, old shoes, brass buckles, and a fan-tail'd hat. Whoever takes up the said boy, and brings him to his master (the subscriber) shall receive two dollars reward of taken in the county aforesaid, if out of the county three dollars, exclusive of what the law allows, to be paid by
THOMAS SHEELES.
N. B. Let this forewarn all master of vessels and others not to harbour him.
The Maryland Gazette, March 31, 1774; April 7, 1774.

Great Pipe-Creek Bridge, Fred. county, March 12, 1774.
FIFTEEN POUNDS REWARD.
RAN away from his bail the first day of November last at night, a certain Hugh Nujen, but calls himself Hugh M'Can, came into the country a servant, but did not serve out half his time, having passed for a freeman these two years or near there abouts; he is about five feet one or two inches high, one or two and twenty years of age, has a young innocent look, an Irishman, but speaks good English, much pock marked; had on when he went away a suit of light coloured Nankeen, a new furred hat, blue worsted stockings, pumps with pinchbeck buckles and a watch; he had a pass above a year ago, signed by Joseph Wood, in the name of M'Can, by which I understand he has passed since he run away; likewise stole a large iron gray horse, about fifteen hands high, neither branded or ear marked, trimmed, shod before, and has two feathers or roses on each side of his neck, has a large mane and foretop, a large switch tail and carries it a little on one side, he is a natural pacer, but can trot a little, is eight years old this spring. Whoever takes up the said thief, and secures him in any jail, and said horse, so that his owner may get him again, shall have the above reward, and reasonable charges, or eight pounds for the thief, and seven for the horse, by applying to   JOSEPH EVERETT.
The Maryland Gazette, March 31, 1774; April 7, 1774; April 14, 1774.

TEN DOLLARS Reward,

[RA]N away from the subscriber on the night of the 28th of March, an English convict [servant] man, named William Gafford, alias William [ ], about five feet four inches high, very stout [ ] pitted with the small-pox, about 39 years of [age,] short brown hair, a little curled, large grey eyes, [th]e two first letters of his name, marked on his [.] Had on when he went away, an old brown cloth [ ]t, lined with blue flannel, has leather buttons, patched in sundry places , a brown under jacket [ ]t sleeves, the seam strap'd with sail cloth, coarse cloth breeches, yarn stockings, old shoes tied [with] strings, oznabrigs shirt, an old cast hat, covered [with] black oil cloth; he came into Potapsco, a convict, [with] Capt. M'Dugal, of the Thornton, in the year [ ], ran away in a month after he was bought, says [he w]ent in a canoe from Curtesses Creek to the head of [G]reat Choptank, where a certain John Hudson, [ ] him in his pilot boat, and carried him on board [ ] Sewal, with whom he went home by the run, [ ]g a good seaman; he came in again convicted last [ ], and has run away sundry times since.—Whoever [take]s up and secures said servant, in any public gaol, [so th]at his master may have him again, shall be intitled to the above reward, paid by   THOMAS HAWKINS.
Head of Curtesses-Creek, March 29, 1774.

N. B. He had an iron collar and fetter on, when he [went] away, but no doubt he has taken both off.

The Maryland Journal, and the Baltimore Advertiser, From Thursday, March 3, to Thursday, March 31, 1774.

Baltimore, *March* 21, 1774.
EIGHT DOLLARS REWARD.

RUN AWAY, about the 18th (inst.) from the subscriber, an indented servant man, named WILLIAM KNELLERS, born in London, brought up to surgery; about twenty-two years of age, five feet six or seven inches high, wears his own hair tied behind, brown cloaths ruffled shirt, &c. Whoever takes up said servant, and secures him in any goal, so that his master may have him again, shall be entitled to the above reward, and reasonable charges, paid by
MICAJAH JAMES.

N. B. He took with him other cloaths, and a case of surgeon's instruments.—It is supposed he is gone towards New-York.

Dunlap's Pennsylvania Packet or, the General Advertiser, April 4, 1774; April 18, 1774; April 25, 1774; *The Pennsylvania Gazette,* May 4, 1774. Minor differences between the papers. The *Gazette* does not have the last paragraph. See *The New-York Gazette; and the Weekly Mercury,* April 11, 1774.

RUN away, the 26th of March last, at night, out of Baltimore-town, from the subscribers, living near Harford-town, Maryland, two servant men, the one an Englishman, named RICHARD PAYNE, aged about 25 years, of about 5 feet 5 inches high, fair complexion, smooth face, black curled hair, pretty talkative; had on, when he went away, a fur hat, two coarse blue jackets, a pair of coarse canvass trowsers, good shoes, white metal buckles, &c. The other an Irishman, aged about 27 years, thin faced, pitted with the small-pox, sandy beard, brown coloured hair; had on, when he went away, a green coloured cloth coat, black lapelled worsted jacket, blue plush breeches, black ribbed worsted stockings, white metal or plated buckles, good shoes, with long quarters, a good fur hat, scalloped, with a yellow loop and button; he formerly went by the name of JOHN DOON: They had a good deal of cash with them, and each of them a bag with clothes, one about a yard long, the other something longer. Whoever takes up said servants, and secures them, so that the owners may have them again, shall have SIXTEEN DOLLARS reward, and if brought home, reasonable charges, paid by us,
JOHN M'ADOW, HUGH KIRKPATRICK.
The Pennsylvania Gazette, April 6, 1774.

FIFTEEN POUNDS Reward.

RUN away from the subscriber, living near Westminster, Frederick county, Maryland, an Irish servant man, named JAMES DIAR, but perhaps may change his name, and probably may have a discharge with him, by another name, as he has been in the country before; he is a well set fellow, aged about 25 or 30 years, abut 5 feet 4 or 5 inches high, of a dark complexion, much pitted with the small-pox, short black hair, has a down look, if sharp spoken to, black eyes; had on and took with him, an iron collar, one sailor's mermith cap, one fearnought jacket, with white kersey sleeves, one striped flannel ditto, one pair of brown country-made breeches, much patched on the knees with white kersey, and much too long for him, one pair of old grey yarn stockings, and in common ties them over the knees of his breeches, one pair of country-made shoes, with strings in them, one ozenbrigs shirt. Whoever takes up the said servant, and brings him home, shall have, if taken 30 miles off, Two Pounds, 50 miles, Three Pounds, 100 miles, Five Pounds, 150 miles, Seven Pounds Ten Shillings, 200 miles, Ten Pounds, and, if 300 miles, the above reward, including what the law allows, paid by JOSHUA GIST.
The Pennsylvania Gazette, April 6, 1774.

FIFTEEN POUNDS Reward.

RUN away from the Subscriber, living in Baltimore town, on the 28th day of March, early in the morning, a Scotch indented servant man, named WILLIAM CARVER, by profession a Groom, a stout young man, about 26 years of age, 5 feet 8 or 9 inches high, sandy coloured hair, curls a little, long visaged, and much pitted with the small-pox, sharp nose, white eyebrows and white eyelashes, his hair cut close to the top of his head; had on, when he went away, a green coat, lapelled, with white metal buttons, or a whitish coat, broke in the elbows, the green of cloth, and the other of white twilled jean, a white swanskin jacket, with black spots, one white shirt, and two check ones; a surtout coat, of red Bath coating, one pair of new shoes, and a pair of ribbed stockings, a pair of new buckskin breeches, and a pair of old ones, and a small new beaver hat; likewise stole out of the stable, a likely half blooded dark brown horse, belonging to Mr. James Cheston, with a very good saddle and bridle, very gay and full of spirit, about 14 hands and a half high, with a black mane and tail, a little white on his near hind feet, and a lump, occasioned by a kick when young, on the same leg, between his knee and foot lock joint, his eye is remarkably fine, with a good deal of white in it, his hind shoes feathered, to prevent this cutting, and likewise stole another horse, which cannot be rightly described, and sundry clothes belonging to the servants. For the horse, Ten Pounds, and for the Man, Five Pounds, to be paid by
Mr. JAMES CHESTON, *or* DANIEL GRANT.

The Pennsylvania Gazette, April 6, 1774; May 4, 1774; Dunlap's Pennsylvania Packet or, the General Advertiser, April 11, 1774. May 9, 1774. Minor differences between the papers.

Annapolis, April 3d, 1774.
RAN away last night from the subscriber, three servant men, viz. RICHARD SADLER, an Irishman, is a plasterer by trade; he is a stout well made man, about 35 years of age, 5 feet 9 or 10 inches high, wears his own dark coloured hair: had on and took with him, one light coloured short bearskin coat and breeches, one white Russia drill coat and breeches, gray yarn stockings, and single channel pumps. JOHN WAKEFIELD, a plasterer by trade, a square well built man, about 40 years of age, is remarkably flat faced, is about five feet 8 or 9 inches high, wears his own brown hair, was born in the west of England, his dress nearly the same as Sadler's, only his shoes are quite new and country made; the above two went off together, and are supposed to have forged passes: whoever secures them, shall receive five pounds for each, and reasonable charges. CROASDALE SPROTSON, a joiner by trade, about 6 feet high, is a remarkable ill looking fellow, slim made, wears his own hair: had on a light bearskin coat and breeches, yarn

stockings, and country made shoes tied with leather strings; whoever secures him shall receive forty shillings reward.
WILLIAM BUCKLAND.
The Maryland Gazette, April 7, 1774; April 14, 1774; April 21, 1774; April 28, 1774. See *The Pennsylvania Gazette*, April 20, 1774, and See *The Maryland Journal, and the Baltimore Advertiser*, From Saturday, November 27, to Thursday, December 9, 1773.

FORTY SHILLINGS REWARD.

RAN away from Hagar's-town, on the night of the 14th instant, an Irish convict servant man, named Thomas Lake, by trade a barber and hairdresser, about 26 years of age, of a swarthy complexion, much pitted with the small pox, round shouldered, about 5 feet 2 or 3 inches high, is fond of liquor, and when drunk is very impertinent: Had on and took with him, an old castor hat with white lining, an old brown surtout coat, an old blue strait bodied ditto with a dirty crimson velvet cape, a very old red jacket, a pair of good buckskin breeches much too large for him, two white and one check shirt; [*sic*] he came from Ireland last fall in a vessel that put into Antigua, from thence in another vessel to Norfolk in Virginia, and from thence in a boat to Baltimore-town. Whoever takes up said servant and secures him in any public jail, or delivers him to James Kelso at Patapsco ferry, shall be entitled to the above reward, paid by said Kelso, or
JAMES WILSON.

N. B. It is supposed he intends for Baltimore-town, Philadelphia, or Annapolis, in order to get a passage to some of the West-India islands; masters of vessels are requested not to take him away.
The Maryland Gazette, April 7, 1774; April 14, 1774; April 21, 1774; April 28, 1774; May 5, 1774.

SIXTEEN DOLLARS REWARD.

RUN AWAY from the subscriber, living in Hartford county, Maryland, within eight miles of the Lower Ferry, Susquehanna, on Sunday the 27th day of March last, two servant men; one an Englishman, came into the country with Capt. Robertson, to Baltimore-Town, about the 20th of June, 1772; his name is WILLIAM SPRINGALL, was born in Middlesex, about 23 years of age, 5 feet 6 inches high, a fresh complexion, very black beard, and short brown hair; he professes to be a barber or hair-dresser; had on when he went away, a blue suit of cloaths, the button-holes of the coat worked with red and blue twist mix'd, and he took with him a deep blue broadcloth coat: He is much given to liquor. The other named EDWARD MAGIN, an Irishman, has been in the county about six months; he is about

5 feet 8 inches high, a slow spoken fellow, has a down look, short brown hair, has had the fever and ague lately, and looks very yellow; had on when he went away, a suit of black broadcloth cloaths, and a blue surtout, but they have other cloaths with them, and may have change their dress: It is supposed they have forged a pass. Whoever secures the said servants in any of his Majesty's gaols, so that their master may have them again, shall have the above reward, or THREE POUNDS for each, and reasonable charges, paid by   JAMES GILES.
N. B. All masters of vessels are forbid to carry them off, at their peril.

Dunlap's Pennsylvania Packet or, the General Advertiser, April 11, 1774; May 9, 1774. See *Dunlap's Pennsylvania Packet or, the General Advertiser*, January 24, 1774.

SIXTEEN DOLLARS Reward.

RUN-away about the 18th of March, from the subscriber, living in Baltimore town, an indented servant man named William Kneller, born in London, brought up to surgery, and took a case of instruments with him, aged 22 years, about 5 feet 6 or 7 inches high, remarkably smooth faced, bashful look, appears to be younger than he really is, wears his own dark brown hair tied behind; had on when he went away a dark brown suit of cloaths, coating surtout, black stockings, good shoes, with pinchbeck buckles, and took with him a suit of claret coloured cloaths, likewise a scarlet jacket, two pair of breeches, one black, the other light coloured cordery, several pair silk, thread, and worsted stockings, several ruffled and other shirts, three hats, and several other cloaths. Whoever apprehends said servant, and commits him to any of his Majesty's goals so that his master may get him again, shall receive the above reward, and reasonable charges paid by   MICAJAH JAMES.
N. B. It is supposed he will change his name, and pass for a doctor.

The New-York Gazette; and the Weekly Mercury, April 11, 1774; April 18, 1774; April 25, 1774; May 2, 1774. See *Dunlap's Pennsylvania Packet or, the General Advertiser*, April 4, 1774.

Baltimore, April 4, 1774.
FIFTEEN POUNDS Reward.
RUN away from the subscribers, a convict servant man, named HOPKINS HOPKINS, *by trade a shoemaker, a well set fellow, about 25 years of age, pale complexion, grey eyes, and black hair; had on, and took with him, a blue boat, striped silk jacket, cloth breeches, good stockings, and new shoes.—He went off with a servant, belonging to James Perigo, named Robert Read, a Scotchman, a well made man, about 5 feet 9 inches high, 22*

years of age, of a black complexion, very fresh face, full grey eyes, and long black hair, tied behind, has a very flat foot, and is very remarkable in his walk, turning one foot nearly square, occasioned by a hurt in his ancle; he had on a sky blue superfine cloth coat and jacket, with silver buttons, a pair of buckskin breeches, good stockings, and new shoes; he is supposed to have plenty of money, as he kept a store for his master some time.—He took a number of shirts, and 2 or 3 nankeen jackets and breeches, with other clothes unknown; as he can read and write well, it is supposed he will forge a pass; he stole his indentures, and it is supposed has altered the date; and has a letter of recommendation from his former master in London. It is thought hey will either buy or steal a horse. Whoever apprehends said servants, and confines them safe in some goal, shall have the above reward, or one half for each, and reasonable charges, if brought to Baltimore Town, and delivered to WILLIAM and DARBY LUX, or JAMES PERIGO. All masters of vessels are forbid to carry them off.
    The Pennsylvania Gazette, April 13, 1774.

FOUR POUNDS REWARD.

RAN away from his bail, the 10th of March last, from Calvert county, George Young, a shoemaker by trade, about 21 years of age, 6 feet high, well made, talks quick, has a bold walk and brazen look: had on when he went away, a pair of shoe boots with plated spurs, a dark mixed cloth coat faced with shalloon, the back not lined; his other apparel is unknown, but he is well dressed. Whoever apprehends the said Young, and secures him in any jail in this province, so that he may be brought to justice and answer the complaint of the subscriber, shall receive the above reward besides what the law allows.   RICHARD HELLEN, 3d.
    The Maryland Gazette, April 7, 1774; April 21, 1774; April 28, 1774.

SIX DOLLARS REWARD.

RAN away from the subscriber, living in Talbot county, Bay side, on Friday, March 17th, 1774, a servant lad, named Robert Farrow, he is about 4 feet 9 inches high, was born in Sudbury, wears his own hair, brown or sandy, had on, and took with him, an old felt hat patcht on the crown, a blue half thick jacket, a stripe lappelled ditto, country kersey breeches, milled sail stockings, old nailed shoes patch behind; it is likely he has changed his name and cloaths, he has a large scald on the back of his thigh; whoever takes up, and brings home the said boy, shall have the above reward, and reasonable charges, paid by   BENJAMIN SANDS.
    N. B. It is supposed he is carried of [*sic*] by some waterman, as he is a sly young villain.

The Maryland Gazette, April 14, 1774; April 21, 1774; April 28, 1774.

Annapolis, April 3, 1774.
RUN away, last night, from the subscriber, two servant men, viz. RICHARD SADLER, an Irishman, is a stout well made man, about 35 years of age, 5 feet 9 or 10 inches high, wears his own dark coloured hair, and is a plaisterer by trade; had on, and took with him, one light coloured bearskin coat and breeches, one white Russia drilling coat and breeches, grey yarn stockings, and single channel pumps. JOHN WAKEFIELD, a plaisterer by trade, is a square well made man, about 40 years of age, has a broad flat face, pale complexion, and is about 5 feet 8 or 9 inches high; his dress nearly the same as the other, only his shoes are new and country made. The above two men went off together, and carried their tools, such as trowels, hammers, &c. with them. Whoever secures them in any goal, so that I get them, shall receive TEN POUNDS reward, or FIVE POUNDS for either of them, and if brought home, reasonable charges, paid by
WILLIAM BUCKLAND.

Pennsylvania Gazette, April 20, 1774; May 4, 1774. See *The Maryland Gazette*, April 7, 1774, and *The Maryland Journal, and the Baltimore Advertiser*, From Saturday, November 27, to Thursday, December 9, 1773, for Sadler.

Annapolis, April 7, 1774.
TEN POUNDS Reward.
RUN AWAY, last night, from the subscriber, living in Annapolis, the two following servants, viz. JOHN FOGARTHY, an Irishman, a free-willer, about 22 years of age, by trade a bricklayer, about 5 feet 10 inches high, red complexion, wears his own hair, but is short and remarkably red; had on, and took with him, an old blue cloth coat, much worn, an old felt hat, double breasted swanskin jacket, thickset breeches, grey yarn stockings, an ozenbrigs shirt, and has with him a Free-mason's apron. CHARLES SAWYER, an Englishman, a convict, by trade a bricklayer, 5 feet 7 or 8 inches high, about 21 years of age; had on, and took with him, an old felt hat, bearskin coat and breeches, old brown cloth waistcoat, much patched, yarn stockings, new country made shoes; wears his own black short hair, large eyebrows, and looks very sulky. Whoever takes up and secures said servants, so that their master may get them again, shall receive the above reward, besides reasonable charges, if brought home, paid by
THOMAS PRICE.

N. B. They stole, and took with them, a plain SILVER WATCH, maker's name and number unknown.

Pennsylvania Gazette, April 20, 1774; May 4, 1774. See *The Maryland Journal, and the Baltimore Advertiser*, From Saturday, November 27, to Thursday, December 9, 1773.

TEN POUNDS REWARD.

RAN AWAY from the subscribers, living in Funk's Town, two indented English servant men; one named WILLIAM PALMER, about 26 years of age, 5 feet 10 inches high, short black hair, dark complexion, lame in one of his legs, which is a little crooked and bigger than the other; had on and took with him, a pale blue coat with silver twist buttons, a dark brown waistcoat, a pair of drilling breeches, and a pair of breeches and waistcoat of a buff colour, without buttons, three fine shirts, three pair of stockings, and a cocked hat, but it is probable he will change his dress. The other named RICHARD PENDERGAST, about 25 years of age, has short curled hair, a smiling countenance, is very talkative, says he has formerly been a sailor, and walks very much like one; had on when he went away, a short blue coat with white metal buttons, lined with white Scotch plaid, snuff coloured waistcoat about half worn, a pair of good leather breeches, a pair of brown ribbed stockings, a pair of old shoes, odd buckles, one a large brass and the other a steel one, a pretty good hat which he mostly wears cocked, and had an iron collar round his neck, which he may have taken off. Whoever takes up the said servants and secures them, so that their master s may have them again, shall receive a Reward of FIVE POUNDS for each, paid by
THOMAS BROOKE, and WILLIAM LEE.

Dunlap's Pennsylvania Packet or, the General Advertiser, April 25, 1774; May 9, 1774; May 23, 1774. See *The Maryland Journal, and the Baltimore Advertiser*, From Saturday, October 9, to Saturday, October 16, 1773.

April 20, 1774.
FIFTEEN POUNDS REWARD.

RAN away last night, an indented servant man, named Festus Burke; twenty-two years of age, about five feet eight inches high, wears his own light sandy coloured hair, tied; had on when he went away, a half worn blue duffel jacket with sleeves, white linen shirt, leather breeches, a pair of pretty good shoes, old thread stockings, and an old castor hat; he likewise had on an iron collar, but I imagine he will soon get it off: he writes a pretty good hand, may likely forge a pass, and change his apparel. Whoever takes up the said servant, and delivers him to the subscriber in George Town, shall receive three pounds reward; if taken about twenty miles from home, five pounds; if forty miles, ten pounds; and if sixty miles or upwards, the above reward.   WILLIAM DEAKINS, Junior.

The Maryland Gazette, April 28, 1774; May 5, 1774; May 26, 1774; June 2, 1774.

Elk-Ridge, April 22, 1774.
THIS day, I the subscriber took up a young man on suspicion of his being a runaway, who says his name is John Hains, and that he travelled with a waggon from Jersey to Virginia, and is now going home. He rid a black gelding about 14 hands high, with a little narrow white in his forehead, shod all round, his left eye sunk, but no perceivable brand. I had them before major Ridgely, who ordered me to deliver the man to the constable, to be imprisoned; but while I was going, the man made his escape, leaving his horse, saddle, and bridle: which the owner, on proving his property, and paying charges, may have from me, living at Mr. Magill's, near Elk-Ridge church, in Anne Arundel county.
JOHN BRYAN.
N. B. He says he had another horse, which in his way homewards he sold to one John Nodding in Virginia, near the Falls of Patowmack; whose obligation he produces for the payment of 10 pounds, 10 shillings, Maryland currency.
The Maryland Gazette, April 28, 1774; May 5, 1774; May 12, 1774.

Baltimore, April 30, 1774.
FIVE POUNDS Reward.
ABSCONDED from his BAIL, on Tuesday, the 26th instant, a certain Barney Cunningham, an Irishman, who has followed draying in this town for some time, and formerly lived with one Mr. Mathers, Inn-keeper, in Chester, Pennsylvania; he is about 5 feet 9 or 10 inches high, pretty red faced, sandy hair and beard, one leg larger than the other, which has been sore all winter, and probable is now so; had on, and took with him, a blue coat, patched on the elbows and under the arms, with silver washed buttons, an English castor hat, a white HORSE, about 13 or 14 hands high, which has the poll evil [sic] on his head, a silver WATCH, which opens with a pin, four white shirts, two of them are marked B.C. It is imagined he is well acquainted both in Pennsylvania and the Jerseys; it is probable he may change his clothes, and offer the horse for sale. Whoever takes up said Cunningham, and secures him in any goal, so that Notice may be given to JOB GREENE, *in Baltimore-town, shall be entitled to the above reward, and if brought home, reasonable charges will be allowed.*
THOMAS BABB.
The Pennsylvania Gazette, May 4, 1774; June 1, 1774.

TEN POUNDS REWARD.

Anne-Arundel county, Elk Ridge, May 10, 1774.

RAN away last night, an Irish servant man, named Thomas Bready, about 25 years old, 5 feet 6 inches high, has but little beard, and some marks of the small-pox in his face, is a good deal freckled, has long brown hair clubbed, and often nicely curled at the sides; his common dress is a fulled black and white country cloth over jacket, very long, a short under waistcoat unfulled black and white, with breeches of the same, black and white country yarn stockings, old country shoes with strings, one of them patched on the side, a pretty good English fine hat with a black silk band and buckle; he carried with him sundry other cloaths, viz. an old green cassimer coat very much worn and faded, an old striped flannel waistcoat, a pair of mixt cloth breeches made out of an old coat turned, I suppose he has worn these last mentioned cloaths, and carried the others for change, he has a brown dowlas, and two osnabrig shirts, is subject to get drunk, and has had one of his thighs broke, which makes him hop very much in his walk, I expect that he is gone off with a brother of his, a very strong well set fellow, a servant to Mr. Philemon Warfield, as I found the horse at my house this morning which I believe that servant used to ride when he came to visit my servant, his brother. Whoever takes up the said servant and brings him home to me, shall receive the above reward.
REUBEN MERIWETHER.

N. B. I have since discovered that he has stolen a light mixed wilton coat with a red cape, and a light blue broad cloth waistcoat with plain white metal capped buttons, which I suppose was for his brother to wear.

The Maryland Gazette, May 18, 1774; May 26, 1774.

EIGHT DOLLARS REWARD.

RAN AWAY from the subscriber, living in Hereford, alias Baltimore county, Upper Deer-creek Hundred, Maryland, on the 9th[h] of April last, an Irish servant man, named SILVESTER PRISKIL, about twenty-one years of age, five feet five or six inches high, has a down look, black hair, and speaks with a good deal of the brogue: he had on and took with him when he went away, a green sailor jacket, a spotted flannel under jacket, fine linen shirt, new buckskin breeches, worsted stockings, old shoes, and a little felt hat bound with blue tape. Whoever takes up said servant and secures him in any gaol, so that his master may have him again, shall receive the above reward, and if brought home, reasonable charges, paid by
JOHN WHITEFORD.

Dunlap's Pennsylvania Packet or, the General Advertiser, May 23, 1774; June 13, 1774; July 11, 1774.

Wye-Town, May 20, 1774.
RAN away from the subscriber on the 17th instant, a convict servant man, named George Mitchell, he is a well set fellow about 5 feet 8 inches high, of a fair complexion, and brown hair, which is generally clubbed behind and curled at the ears, plays on the french-horn and fife, can beat the drum, has a sore leg, and is very fond of drink: had on and took with him when he went away, a white linen and an osnabrig shirt, a light coloured fearnought waistcoat, white drilling breeches, thread stockings, and a pair of jockey boots. Whoever takes up the said servant, and brings him to the subscriber living at Wye-Town on Wye river, shall receive five pounds reward, paid by   RICHARD GRASON.
The Maryland Gazette, May 26, 1774; June 9, 1774.

FIVE POUNDS REWARD.
RAN AWAY from the subscriber's Iron-Works, situation on the north side of Deer creek, Hartford county, Maryland, an English servant man named JOHN HOLLIS, about 40 years of age 5 feet 8 or 9 inches high, calls himself a stone mason by trade, but was a whipper in Philadelphia gaol some time ago; had on when he went away, an old hat, old green coat, blue jacket and leather breeches, the rest of his clothes not known; said Hollis also stole a brown horse, about 8 or 9 years old, between 13 and 14 hands high, has one white foot on the off side, a natural pacer; he also stole a saddle nearly new, fretted a little on the pommel with a blue housing, double barr'd stirrup irons, one of the bars broke out of the off stirrup, and a single reigned bridle. Whoever takes up the said servant, and delivers the horse, saddle and bridle at the subscriber's Iron-Works, shall have the above reward, and an ENGLISH SHILLING for the man, paid by
JACOB GILES,
N. B. The above servant is the property of a certain Robert Montgomery, taylor, in Chester County.
Dunlap's Pennsylvania Packet or, the General Advertiser, May 30, 1774; June 20, 1774; July 25, 1774.

RAN away from the subscriber living on Fell's Point, an English servant man, named John Foster, by trade a turner and has worked sometimes at the joiners business; is an extraordinary good fidler, about five feet seven inches high, he is much given to liquor, of a light complexion, a long pale face, blue eyes, a high forehead, short brown hair and walks stooping; had on when he went away, a check shirt, an old blue surtout coat much torn, a striped flannel jacket with the stripes across, and a blue ditto under it, a blue

close bodied coat without lining, and yellow buttons on it, leather breeches, brown ribbed stockings and old shoes; he has been 18 months in the country, and formerly belonged to one Richard Button merchant on Fell's Point, and has his old indentures in his pocket, he is a pretty good scholar and perhaps may forge a pass and change his cloaths. Whoever takes up the said servant and brings him home, or secures him in any gaol so that his master may get him again, shall have a rewayd [sic] of thirty shillings if taken within forty miles, if eighty miles three pounds, if a hundred miles four pounds, and reasonable charges if brought home, paid by
SAMUEL BURTUS.

The Maryland Journal, and the Baltimore Advertiser, From Saturday, May 28, to Saturday, June 4, 1774; From Saturday, June 4, to Saturday, June 11, 1774; From Saturday, June 11, to Saturday, June 18, 1774.

Baltimore-Town, May 5th, 1774
TWENTY SHILLINGS Reward,
RAN away last night, between 8 and 9 of the clock, from the subscriber, a servant girl, named Winney Carney, a low likely girl, well built, fresh coloured, has light hair and grey eyes; had, when she went away, a red and white flowered linen gown, a coarse blue and white callicoe ditto, a sheeting shift with ruffles, a new sheet, good aprons and handkerchiefs, a brown stuff peticoat, a white bed gown, a blue and white petticoat, and black everlasting shoes:—Whoever takes up said servant, shall have the above reward,   GEORGE PATTON,

The Maryland Journal, and the Baltimore Advertiser, From Saturday, May 28, to Saturday, June 4, 1774; From Saturday, June 4, to June 11, 1774.

Elk-Ridge Furnace, May 1, 1774.
TWELVE POUNDS Reward,
RAN-away, from the subscriber, the four following English servant men, *viz*. Joseph Jennings, aged twenty four years, five feet one inch high, of a dark complexion, and round visage; has short dark curled hair, and grey eyes; had on a light coloured jacket, bound with black, blue breeches, white shirt, pumps, without inside soals, and a felt hat. John Gough, from Staffordshire, speaks in the Scotch dialect, aged fifty-four years, five feet ten inches high, stalks in his walk, of a fair complexion, has grey eyes, dark curled hair, and a large black beard; took with him a cotton jacket, one black ditto without sleeves, old leather breeches, two white shirts, oznabrigs ditto, grey worsted stockings, old shoes, half worn castor hat and sundry other clothes not known. John Ball, aged twenty-five years, five feet ten inches high, stoops in his walk, of a fair complexion, has black curled hair,

a thin black beard, hazel eyes, and an impediment in his speech; took with him two cotton jackets, cotton breeches, old yarn stockings, oznabrigs shirt, old shoes, marked in the inside of the quarter S, and a coarse felt hat. John Woolferd, twenty-seven years old, five feet seven inches high, of a fair complexion, round full face, short dark hair, has a large beard of a red cast, hazel eyes, and shuts one of them when spoke to; is a thick well set fellow, has a large scar on his left foot, which makes him limp in his walk: He took with him a cotton jacket and a pair of breeches, two oznabrigs shirts, old yarn stockings, new shoes, marked on the inside S. and an old felt hat.— Whoever takes up the said servants shall have, if 20 miles from said furnace, 30 shillings, if 30 miles, 40, and if out of the province, 3 pounds reward for each, and reasonable charges if brought home, paid by
SAMUEL DORSEY, Junior.

The Maryland Journal, and the Baltimore Advertiser, From Saturday, May 28, to Saturday, June 4, 1774; From Saturday, June 4, to June 11, 1774.

Baltimore Town, April 19, 1774.
RAN away last night from the subscriber, living about half a mile from Baltimore-Town, an English convict servant man named John Pedder, alias Peather, five feet seven or eight inches high, about 27 years of age, wears his own short light brown hair, of a thin visage, and darkish complexion; much pock-marked; he is an artful, talkative fellow, writes a tolerable good hand, and may probably forge a pass; he professes the business of a gardener, and has been constantly employed as such these three years past;—had on when he went away, a blue coarse jacket (with sleeves) and breeches, both lined with white flannel, an oznabrig shirt, &c. It is uncertain what dress he may appear in, as he has taken sundry other cloathes with him, particularly a half worn fustian coat, faced with white persian;— Whoever takes up and secures said servant, so that his master may have him again, shall receive (if taken in this county or harford) 6 dollars, (if taken in any other county) 8 dollars, and if out of the province, 10 Dollars, and reasonable charges paid by HENRY STEVENSON.

The Maryland Journal, and the Baltimore Advertiser, From Saturday, May 28, to Saturday, June 4, 1774; From Saturday, June 4, to Saturday, June 11, 1774; From Saturday, June 11, to Saturday, June 18, 1774; From Saturday, June 18, to Saturday, July 2, 1774; From Saturday, July 2, to Saturday, July 9, 1774.

BALTIMORE TOWN, May 23, 1774.
Five Pounds Reward.
RAN away from the subscriber on the 21st instant, an English convict servant man, named William Scrowfield, he is about 23 years of age, 5 feet

3 or 4 inches high, has black eyes, short black hair, and a very good complexion: had on when he went away, a green broad cloth coat, double breasted, trimmed with yellow metal buttons, it is pretty good and hath been turned; likewise a small round hat, an old fine white shirt, black worsted breeches, and black leather shoes; he is a very handy fellow, has been used to waiting in a house, likewise shaving and dressing, and is a very good ostler, but very subject to drink.

Whoever shall take up the said servant within ten miles from town, and shall bring him to me, shall receive the reward of twenty shillings, if twenty miles forty shillings, if thirty miles fifty shillings, and if out of the county and more than forty miles from home five pounds and all reasonable charges, paid by
BENJ. NICHOLSON.

The Maryland Journal, and the Baltimore Advertiser, From Saturday, May 28, to Saturday, June 4, 1774; From Saturday, June 4, to Saturday, June 11, 1774; From Saturday, June 18, to Saturday, July 2, 1774; From Saturday, July 2, to Saturday, July 9, 1774. See *The Maryland Journal, and the Baltimore Advertiser*, From Saturday, September 18, to Saturday, September 25, 1773, and *The Maryland Journal, and Baltimore Advertiser*, November 30, 1774.

Elk, April 22.
SIX DOLLARS Reward,
RAN away from the subscriber, yesterday in the afternoon, an English servant lad, named Thomas Day, about eighteen years of age, 5 feet, two or three inches high, wears his own light coloured hair—Had on a home made light coloured cloth jacket, an under ditto, (either blue or brown) blue cloth trowsers, yarn stockings, old shoes, and an old meally beaver hat. Whoever takes up and secures said servant, so as his master may get him again, shall receive the above reward, paid by
JONATHAN BOOTH,

The Maryland Journal, and the Baltimore Advertiser, From Saturday, May 28, to Saturday, June 4, 1774; From Saturday, June 4, to Saturday, June 11, 1774.

Baltimore. April 7, 1774.
RAN away from the subscriber, on Friday the 25th of March last, an Irish servant man, named Nicholas M'Coy, about 20 years of age, 5 feet 6 or 7 inches high: had an old felt hat, dark hair, brown jacket without sleeves, blue coat the sleeves of which are of a different hue, being somewhat newer, leather breeches long at the knees and something torn in the seat, new strong shoes, may to tye, and a tow linen shirt, but 'tis probable he may change some of his clothes;—Whoever takes up said servant and brings him

home, shall have Five Pounds reward, viz. 40 shillings if taken about town, 3 pounds if out of the county, and 5 pounds if out of the province, paid by
ABRAHAM PATTON.

N. B. He formerly lived with Melcher [Keen]er, tavern-keeper, in this town, and understands the Dutch language. All masters of vessels are warned not to take him [ ] at their peril.

The Maryland Journal, and the Baltimore Advertiser, From Saturday, May 28, to Saturday, June 4, 1774; From Saturday, June 4, to Saturday, June 11, 1774.

May 22, 1774.

RAN away from the subscriber, living on Herring bay, in Anne-Arundel county, an indented servant man, named Henry Reed, about twenty three years of age, five feet seven inches high, has a full face, short black curley hair, little or no beard, has a bold look and speech: had on and took with him a white cotton jacket and waistcoat, two osnabrig shirts, a pair of white cotton trousers, negro shoes with strings, old check handkerchief, and an old hat; but it is supposed that he went with one or two that went away about the same time, and it is possible he might have changed his dress. Whoever takes up the said servant, and brings him home, shall receive forty shillings, and if secured otherways, shall have what the law allows.

N. B. He professes the coach-makers trade.
ISAAC SIMMONS.

The Maryland Gazette, June 9, 1774; June 23, 1774.

Patapsco Ferry, May 17, 1774.
TEN POUNDS Reward.

RUN away from the subscriber, on the 16th instant, an indented servant, named *William Barcley*, 30 years of age, about 5 feet 3 or 4 inches high, speaks in a low voice, he appears very innocent, and has a tolerable good countenance, light brown hat, but not long enough to tie, and is bald on the top of his head, pretends to be a plaisterer, and is a middling good farmer; has lived 13 years of the country, and is so well acquainted with many places, that he will probably deceive the one who takes him up; had on, and took with him, a brown broadcloth coat, thread-bare, good black velvet jacket, good buckskin breeches, a pair of white ribbed and a pair of white plain yarn stockings, fine turned pumps, half-worn, one old and two new ozenbrigs shirts, check trowsers, felt hat, and may have stolen sundry other things as he is a notorious thief. Whoever takes up said servant, and secures him in any public goal, so that his master may have him again, shall receive, if he is taken 40 miles from home, Three Pounds; if above 40 and

under 120 Five Pounds; if more than 120, the above reward, and reasonable charges, paid by JAMES KELSO.
The Pennsylvania Gazette, June 8, 1774; July 27, 1774.

May 30, 1774.
RAN away the 28th instant from the brigantine Stephen, George Brown late master, two indented servant men; William Sanders, a horse-jockey and groom, about five feet four inches high, freckled face, and brown hair, he has a large scar on one of his wrists: had on when he went away a brown coat with white buttons, and a pair of leather breeches. John Nisbett, by trade a brass founder, about five feet five inches high, pale face, and light hair, round shoulders, and much knock-kneed; had on when he went away a blue surtout coat; they took with them other cloaths and their beds and blankets. Whoever takes up the said servants, and secures them in any jail, shall have fifteen shillings for each, besides what the law allows, or if delivered on board the said ship at Lower Marlborough, thirty shillings for each, besides what the law allows.
DAVID CARCAUD.
The Maryland Gazette, June 9, 1774; June 23, 1774; June 30, 1774; July 14, 1774.

May 27, 1774.
RAN away from the subscriber, living on Lyon's Creek, in Calvert county, the two following indented servants; Thomas Gregory, a short well set fellow, about five feet six inches high, dark complexion, by trade a butcher: had on a grey coat, white shirt, dirty leather breeches, black worded [sic] stockings, and London made shoes. Isaac Skipper dressed in a pale green cloth coat, white shirt, trousers, or dark coloured short breeches, and felt hat; they took with them sundry other cloaths in a bundle, and probably may change their dress. Isaac Skipper is a small man, of thin visage, and walks lame from having his leg broke a considerable time ago; they were imported this Spring in Capt. Lane. [sic] Whoever takes up the said servants and brings them to me, or confines them in any jail, so that they be had again, shall receive five pounds currency and reasonable charges, or fifty shillings and charges for either of them.
WILLIAM JOHNSON.
The Maryland Gazette, June 9, 1774; June 23, 1774.

RAN away from the subscriber, living in Anne-Arundel county, near Lyon's Creek, an indented servant man, named John White, about five feet ten inches high, has a dark complexion, and a chearful countenance, grey eyed, has short black hair, and a black beard, he has lost some of his upper fore teeth, speaks in the north country dialect, as he came from Berwick; professes gardening and farming: had on and took with him a light mixed cloth coat and waistcoat, with yellow metal buttons, nankeen breeches, with pale yellow ferret in the knees, old thread stockings footed with linen, and a pair of light worsted ones ribbed, a pair of old channel pumps, and small pinchbeck buckles, two pair of black knit breeches, a fine linen shirt and neckcloth marked I K, two muslin ones marked I W with black silk, a good fashionable hat, three coarse shirts, and three osnabrigs ditto, three pair of osnabrig trousers; it is thought he went away in company with two servants in the neighbourhood, who absconded about the same time. Whoever takes up and secures the said servant, so that his master may get him again, shall have forty shillings reward, and reasonable charges if brought home, paid by   JOHN KILTY.

The Maryland Gazette, June 9, 1774; June 23, 1774; July 7, 1774; July 21, 1774; August 4, 1774.

Baltimore, June 9th, 1774.
RAN AWAY from his Bail, on the 10th Day of May, Alexander Noler, about 24 Years of Age; about five Feet five Inches high, very much Pockmarked, dark color'd Hair: Had on when he went away, a Snuff color'd Coat and Waistcoat, and Leather Breeches, he is by Trade a Carpenter and Joiner:— Whoever secures the said Alexander, and lodges him in the Goal of this Town, shall receive three Dollars reward, and if out of the Country, Thirty Shillings, paid by
ISAAC GORDON.

The Maryland Journal, and the Baltimore Advertiser, From Saturday, June 4, to Saturday, June 11, 1774; From Saturday, June 11, to Saturday, June 18, 1774; From Saturday, June 18, to Saturday, July 2, 1774; From Saturday, July 2, to Saturday, July 11, 1774.

June 10, 1774.
RAN away from the subscriber, at Alexandria ferry, on Sunday night the 5th instant, an indented Irish servant man, named Thomas Breaten, about 22 or 23 years of age, 5 feet 9 or 10 inches high, much pitted with the smallpox, smooth face, has light coloured short hair, thin visage, down look, of a ruddy complexion, has a rupture on one side, and is supposed to be in company with another servant: had on and took with him one blue surtout coat, one light coloured bearskin ditto much worn, one Irish linen shirt, three osnabrig ditto, one pair of buckskin breeches, two or three pair of osnabrig trousers, one pair of black worsted hose, one pair light ditto, an

half worn felt hat, a pair of shoe not fellows, a pair of leather bags, and other things too tedious to mention; he has a forged pass with him which I expect has Mr. John Bayne's and Capt. Alexander Kayn's names signed in it, wrote by himself; he writes a very good hand and speaks very broad. Whoever takes up the said servant shall have three pounds reward if taken thirty miles from home, five pounds in fifty miles, and reasonable charges paid, if brought home.   JOHN CLIFFORD.

The Maryland Gazette, June 16, 1774. See *The Maryland Gazette,* August 11, 1774.

Virginia, Loudon county, May 1, 1774.
RAN away from the subscriber, a servant man, named James Brown, about 5 feet 4 or 5 inches high, had two scars in his forehead, dark eyes, dark short curled hair, speaks much in the Dutch dialect, and it is thought is a tailor by trade: had with him when he went away, a blue [f]lip coat with a velvet cape of a claret colour; tho' pretty much faded, a claret coloured ditto, both without lining, a light blue jacket without sleeves, and a velved [sic] ditto of a claret colour, one check shirt, a pair of trousers, a pair of linen breeches, a pair of white thread stockings, a pair of old shoes, and a scolloped hat. Whoever takes up said servant shall have five pounds reward, and if brought to his master, reasonable charges, paid by
PETER OVERFIELD.

The Maryland Gazette, June 16, 1774; June 30, 1774; July 14, 1774.

May 26, 1774.
FORTY SHILLINGS REWARD.
RAN away yesterday morning from the subscriber, living near Piscataway, Patowmack river; an indented servant man named Thomas Columbine, born in England, brought in this province by Capt. Richard Lane this Spring, about 22 years of age, short well set fellow, about five feet four or five inches high, dark complexion, short black hair: had on and took with him a brown thickset coat, an old red jacket, pale blue ditto, striped blue and white damask ditto, with lappels; one pair of leather breeches very black and greasy, one pair of white drillings ditto, one pair of men's shoes and buckles almost new, thread and worsted stockings, and an old castor hat; he has a watch in his pocket, which I believe does not go, he professes keeping of riding horses, he walks a little lame as he lately sprained one of his ancles; its more than propable he may make towards Patuxent river, and endeavour to get on board some ship for his passage to England again. Whoever takes up the said servant, or secures him so as his master may get

him again, shall receive the above reward of forty shillings and reasonable charges paid if brought home.
WILLIAM LYLES.
The Maryland Gazette, June 16, 1774; June 23, 1774; June 30, 1774; July 14, 1774.

Bladensburgh, June 13, 1774.
EIGHT DOLLARS REWARD.
RAN away from the subscriber, in Bladensburgh, on Sunday the 12th instant, an indented servant man, about 5 feet 5 inches high, aged 19 years, by trade a tailor, named William Wallace; had on when he went away a jean coloured coat and jacket, white yellow gilt buttons, a pair of pompadore coloured breeches, white ribbed stockings, a white holland shirt with a watch in his pocket, came into Patowmack river last month, in the ship [printer's blank] from London, Capt. Broadstreet. Whoever takes up the said runaway, and secures him in any jail, shall receive a reward of 30 shillings if 20 miles from home, 40 shillings if 40 miles, and if out of the province, the above reward of eight dollars and all reasonable charges paid if brought home to the subscriber.
ADAM CRAIG.
N. B. It is supposed he went away with a sailor, who had on a blue coat with yellow metal buttons, striped jacket, and nankeen breeches.
The Maryland Gazette, June 16, 1774; June 30, 1774.

Annapolis, June 13, 1774.
RAN away on Saturday night last, the following servants, viz. Joseph Belong, a convict, aged about 35 years, born in the west of England, by trade a joiner and painter; he is a short thick fellow, wears his own dark hair, his dress is supposed to be a dark grey coat, nankeen waistcoat and breeches, and new shoes. The property of George Steuart.

Thomas King, an indented servant man, imported in the Chance, Capt. Campbell, in March last, a bricklayer by trade, a stout well set fellow, of a swarthy complexion, about 30 years of age, born in England, and has been many years on board a man of war; had on and took with him, a brown bearskin coat, blue cloth waistcoat and breeches, gray yarn stockings, country made shoes and castor hat. The property of Richard Sprigg.

Thomas Easton, by trade a joiner, an indented servant man, imported in the Betsey Richmond, Capt. Nicol, in February last, is a Scotchman, and talks much in that dialect; he is a middle sized man, about 5 feet 6 or 7 inches high, has short black hair, his fore teeth are very irregular, his dress uncertain, though it is supposed he has on and with him a suit of purple broad cloth with twist buttons, a new fine hat, an old brown cloth coat,

black velvet waistcoat, leather breeches, striped holland trousers, a pair of English shoes that have been soled, and sundry white shirts and neckclothes; he has money with him. The property of John Randall. Whoever apprehends the said servants, and delivers them to their masters, or secures them in any jail, so that they may get them again, shall receive for each man five pounds reward, and reasonable charges, paid by the subscribers.
GEORGE STEUART.   RICHARD SPRIGG.   JOHN RANDALL.
The Maryland Gazette, June 16, 1774; June 30, 1774; July 14, 1774; July 28, 1774; August 11, 1774; August 25, 1774; September 8, 1774; September 15, 1774.

June 12, 1774.

RAN away from the subscriber, living near Risteau's-Town in Baltimore county, a convict servant man named JOHN HARRIS, about 5 feet 3 or 4 inches high, thin visaged, pock marked, high nosed, has light brown hair, and is slender made: had on when he went away, an oznabrig shirt and trousers much worn, and old felt hat, old kersey jacket, old shoes with buckles in them: it is probable he may forge a pass and change his name, as he has run away several times before. Whoever takes up the said servant and secures him in any gaol within this province, or brings him to his master, shall have, if 10 miles from home, 20 shillings, if 20 miles 40 shillings, and if out of the province 3 pounds including what the law allows, and reasonable charges paid if brought home.
JOHN WELLS, son of CHARLES,   or   EDWARD WONN.
The Maryland Journal, and the Baltimore Advertiser, From Saturday, June 11, to Saturday, June 18, 1774; From Saturday, June 18, to Saturday, July 2, 1774; From Saturday, July 2, to Saturday, July 9, 1774. See *The Maryland Journal, and Baltimore Advertiser* September 21, 1774.

June 12, 1774.

TEN POUNDS REWARD.

RAN away last night from the Subscriber, living in Bond's forest, Harford county, two convict servant men, viz. JOHN BROWN, about thirty years of age, about five feet eight inches high, has black hair, large temples, narrow chin and thick lips, used to the sea, and a great swearer. .JOHN KNIGHT, a Westcountryman, about 35 years of age, about five feet seven or eight inches high, a thick well set fellow, has black hair, black beard, sour look, subject to drink, and a great swearer. Had on and took with them, a brown jockey coat, a sky blue ditto, blue cloth breeches, spotted flannel jackets, new shoes, oznabrigs shirts, one check ditto, sky blue milled stockings, a pair of thread ditto, a new hat, an old ditto, and took with them a pewter tankard.

Whoever takes up and secures the said servants, shall receive, if taken in the county, fifty shillings for each, and if out of the county five pounds for each (including what the law allows) paid by
BUCKLER BOND.

N. B. All masters of vessels or others, are forbid to carry them off at their peril.

The Maryland Journal, and the Baltimore Advertiser, From Saturday, June 11, to Saturday, June 18, 1774; From Saturday, June 18, to Saturday, July 2, 1774; From Saturday, July 2, to Saturday, July 9, 1774. See *The Pennsylvania Gazette*, January 10, 1771, and *The Pennsylvania Gazette*, May 3, 1775, for Brown.

June 13, 1774.

RAN away from the subscriber, living in Frederick-Town in Frederick county, last night, a servant man named JOHN COOMB, a shoemaker; he is 5 feet 7 or 8 inches high, about 22 years of age, has a pale complexion: he had on and took with him a brown lapelled coat, a jacket of the same cloth with white metal buttons, two dowlas shirts, one black silk neckcloth, on red handkerchief, a hat cut in the fashion, one pair of white drilling breeches, one ditto brown ribbed velvet, a pair of coarse thread stockings, a pair of pumps with yellow buckles; it is supposed the he stole a black mare with a blaze face, and his working tools. Whoever secures the said servant, so that his master may have him again, shall have three pounds reward., if taken up out of the province and brought home, five pounds reward, and fifty shillings for bringing the mare, paid by
BENJ. DULANY.

The Maryland Journal, and the Baltimore Advertiser, From Saturday, June 11, to Saturday, June 18, 1774; From Saturday, June 18, to Saturday, July 2, 1774; From Saturday, July 2, to Saturday, July 9, 1774.

New Castle County, on Delaware, June 13, 1774.
NOW in the goal of this county, a certain John Phillips, who confesseth that he is the person who made an escape from the Sub-sheriff of York county, in the province of Pennsylvania, and that was advertised in the Pennsylvania Gazette, No. 2330. And two runaway servants, and one Negroe slave, namely, *John Nichols....James Linsey*, who confesses himself to be a servant to Messieurs Snowden and Company, of Prince-George's county, in the province of Maryland. A NEGROE LAD, who calls himself ISAAC....The masters, or others interested in the prisoners above named,

are desired to come, pay charges, and take them away, within six weeks from the above date, otherwise the said prisoners will be sold for their fees, and discharged, by   THOMAS PUSEY, Goaler.

N.B. Also in said goal, John Welsh, and Patrick Morgan, who confess themselves to be runaway servants, belonging to James Black, of Kent county, Maryland.

The Pennsylvania Gazette, June 22, 1774; August 3, 1774.

Anne-Arundel county, June 13, 1774.
RAN away from the subscriber, on the 13th instant, a convict servant man, named Thomas Sexton, about twenty-five years of age, about five feet three inches high, of a swarthy complexion, short black hair, has a scar on his upper lip; had on when he went away, one old red duffil jacket, country cloth breeches, Irish linen shirt, and a hat about half worn bound with old binding. Whoever secures said servant in any jail, so that his master may get him again, shall receive a reward of forty shillings, or if brought home, three pounds currency, paid by
SEBORN TUCKER.

The Maryland Gazette, June 23, 1774. See *The Maryland Gazette*, June 30, 1774.

TWENTY DOLLARS REWARD.
Dumfries, Virginia, April 25, 1774.
RAN away last night from my plantation, near this place, two servant men, namely George and John Allen, they were lately imported in the Justitia, and consigned to Mr. Thomas Hodge; George is a likely young fellow, about 25 years of age, 5 feet 10 or 11 inches, stoops much, and is remarkably round shouldered and intoed: had on when he went away, a bearskin jacket and breeches, new shoes, and a small round hat with a black ribbon and buckle. John is about 27 years old, is brother to George, more slender made, and about two inches under the size of his brother; had on the same sort of cloaths, only a pair of old shoes cut at the toes: they may however change their cloaths, as they have carried with them such as they brought from the ship, which were brown sailors jackets and breeches. Whoever will apprehend the said servants, and secure them so that I may get them again, shall be entitled to the above reward. All masters of vessels are forewarned from carrying them off.
THOMAS MONTGOMERIE.

The Maryland Gazette, June 23, 1770; June 30, 1774; July 21, 1774; August 4, 1774.

ON the second of this instant, a young man by the name of Crosby, about 20 years of age, 5 feet 6 inches high, and spare made; had on a light green cloth coat and ruffled shirt, professes to play on instruments of music, has a turn to singing, says he has been well educated, and wants to get into business; he hired of the subscriber a small black mare to ride to the mouth of Patuxent, where he said he had business of great importance with a gentleman on board Capt. Eden's ship; he has returned from thence and has not returned the mare; she paces naturally and very short, stands straight, and runs fast: he showed a letter of recommendation from one Ruggles of Boston: on enquiry I have reason to believe he has made off to Virginia. Whoever will stop the mare and saddle shall have three pounds reward, paid by   WILLIAM EDMONS.

The Maryland Gazette, June 23, 1774; July 7, 1774.

Philadelphia, June 20, 1774

NOW in the Goal of the County of Philadelphia, the following runaway SERVANTS, viz. *James Dempsey*, belonging to James Brown, in Maryland. *James Johnston....Martha Murrey... Ann King...*Their Masters are desired to come, pay Charges, and take them away, in three Weeks, otherwise they will be discharged, on paying their Fees.
PETER ROBESON, Goaler.

The Pennsylvania Gazette, June 29, 1774.

THIRTY POUNDS REWARD.

June 3, 1774.

WENT away from the subscriber, living on Morgan's Run, near Little Pipe-Creek, in Baltimore county, Maryland, two Irish servant men, viz. James Riley, a stout well set fellow, about 30 years old, round shouldered, short strait brownish hair, red beard, grey eyes, down look, and fair complexion, has lost the little finger of his left hand. Patrick Ennis, a chunkey well set fellow, about 25 years old, remarkable red hair and curls, grey eyes, down look, and shews much of the white of his eyes, fair complexion, and has a scar on his chin; they had on and took with them, a blue broad cloth coat, with a small cape to the neck, and silver capped buttons, one ditto of a lightish mixt colour which has been turned, and the pockets moved from the sides to the folds, yellow buttons, one brown broad cloth jacket, with red backs and gold basket buttons, one ditto country spun and striped, much worn, a pair of old velvet breeches, patched in the crotch with blue cloth, one pair of osnabrig trousers, one pair ditto striped linen, three Irish linen shirts marked R O, one osnabrig ditto, three pair of shoes, a pair of plated buckles, and a pair of odd ones, a castor hat, one ditto of felt, bound round the edge with worsted binding; took with them a cane with a sword in it, and a pocket pistol. Whoever takes up the said servants, and brings them to their master, shall have if taken 50 miles from home five pounds, if 100 miles ten pounds, if 200 miles fifteen pounds, if 300 miles twenty pounds, and if 400 miles, the above reward, or in proportion for either, or three pounds for securing them in jail, so that I may get them again, paid by RICHARD OWNINGS, son of Samuel.

The Maryland Gazette, June 30, 1774; July 14, 1774; July 28, 1774; August 11, 1774; August 25, 1774; September 8, 1774; September 15, 1774; September 22, 1774. See *The Maryland Gazette*, August 6, 1772.

Charles county, June 20, 1774.
RAN away from the subscriber, on Saturday night last, an indented servant lad, named Thomas Clifford, from at Rancliff in Yorkshire, and speaks that dialect; he is about 19 or 20 years of age, near 5 feet high, of a fair complexion, sandy coloured hair, whitish eyebrows, and somewhat pitted with the small-pox: took with him, a dark grey coarse broad cloth coat lined with black shalloon, trimmed with black buttons and holes, a black broad cloth waistcoat and breeches, two white Russia linen and one new osnabrig shirts, a pair of new osnabrig trousers, a coarse castor hat lined with yellow linen, and cut after the maccaroni fashion. Whoever takes him up and brings him to my plantation near Brian-Town in the county aforesaid, shall have twenty shillings reward besides what the law allows, from me.
THOMAS THORNTON.

The Maryland Gazette, June 30, 1774; July 14, 1774.

COMMITTED to the jail of Charles county as a runaway, a convict servant man, who calls himself Thomas Sexton, and says he belongs to Seborn Tucker, living in Anne-Arundel county; he is a well set fellow, about 5 feet 9 inches high, has short dark hair, and a remarkable Scar in his upper lip; his cloathing is an old red waistcoat, country cloth breeches, and an Irish linen shirt; his master is desired to pay charges and take him away,
WILLIAM HANSON, deputy sheriff.

The Maryland Gazette, June 30, 1774; August 11, 1774. See *The Maryland Gazette*, June 23, 1774.

TWENTY-FOUR DOLLARS REWARD.

May 24, 1774.

WENT away last night from Patuxent iron-works, the two following servant men, viz. James Lindsey, about 22 years of age, born in Ireland, a lusty well made fellow, about 5 feet 10 inches high, light grey eyes, and black hair; had on and took with him, 2 cotton jackets, 2 osnabrig shirts, a pair of cotton breeches, 1 pair of osnabrig trousers, a felt hat, and old shoes. Thomas Sutton, about 25 years of age, born in England, a lusty well made fellow, about 6 feet high, grey eyes, short brown hair; had on and took with him, an old castor hat, 2 cotton jackets, 2 osnabrig shirts, a pair of brown roll trousers and old shoes: it is supposed there is a negro man named Jacob....Whoever takes up and secures the said servants and negro, so that their masters may have them again, shall receive, if 20 miles from home, 30 shillings, if 30 miles, 40 shillings, and if out of the province, 3 pounds for each, including what the law allows, paid by
SAMUEL, JOHN, and H. SNOWDEN.

The Maryland Gazette, June 30, 1774; July 14, 1774; July 28, 1774.

EIGHT DOLLARS REWARD,

Chaptico, St. Mary's county, June 20, 1774.

RAN away from the subscriber, about the 22d of last month, an indented servant man, named William Bawn, by trade a stone-mason and bricklayer, about 27 or 28 years of age, 5 feet 7 or 8 inches high, well made, short black hair, dark complexion, marked with the small-pox and fond of drink; is an Englishman, and worked principally at Bristol: he served his time with the honourable John Ridout, Esq: of Annapolis, and afterwards worked in Virginia, from thence he came to this county, where he got indebted to Richard Mason, who he indented himself to for three years, and who I since bought him of. Whoever takes up the above servant, and brings him home, shall receive the above reward, and all reasonable charges.
PHILIP KEY.

The Maryland Gazette, June 30, 1774; July 14, 1774; July 28, 1774; August 4, 1774.

EIGHT DOLLARS REWARD .

RAN away from the subscriber, living in West Pennsborough Township, Cumberland County, the 5th inst. an indented Irish servant man, named THOMAS FOWLER, a chunky fellow, about five feet five or six inches high, looks to be upward of thirty years of age, straight black hair, with some grey hairs on the fore part, freckled and pitted with the small-pox, has had his left leg broke, which may be known by examining; had on when he went off, an old felt hat, the loops wore out, a light coloured turn'd fly coat, net hair buttons, and blanket lining, a blue linsey lapell'd jacket with one row of metal buttons, tow shirt and trowsers, old blue worsted stockings, soaled shoes, tied with strings. Whoever secures said servant, so as his master may have him again, shall receive the above reward and reasonable charges paid by   JOHN M'KEEHAN.

N. B. He undoubtedly has a guide with him, otherwise he could not make out, on account he speaks broken English, and it's thought the guide is one THOMAS BOUDREN, a native Irishman, who may pretend to be his master, and came over in the vessel with him.

Pennsylvania, June 20, 1774.

The Maryland Journal, and the Baltimore Advertiser, From Saturday, June 18, to Saturday, July 2, 1774; From Saturday, July 2, to Saturday, July 9, 1774; From Saturday, July 9, to Saturday, July 16, 1774.

THIRTY DOLLARS Reward.

RAN away last Night, from the Subscriber, living on Tom's Creek, Frederick County, Maryland, two indented servants, viz. JOHN M'MAHON, born in Ireland, and speaks with the brogue; he is about 50 years of age, of a thin visage, has black curled hair, is round shouldered, about 5 feet 7 inches high, and has lost all his fore teeth: had on and took with him, an old brown coat, a spotted flannel waistcoat, an old felt hat, half worn buckskin breeches, a pair of good shoes, and plain brass buckles, two shirts, and two pair of trowsers of country made linen.

N. B. He has been in the army 7 years, and gives an account of many places he has been in his travels.

BRIDGET CURLY, an Irish woman, born in the west of Ireland, and speaks a little with the brogue, about 18 years of age, and about 5 feet high, round fac'd, a little pitted with the small-pox, and has light brown hair: had on and took with her, a striped callico gown; a blue camblet petticoat, a white sattin bonnet, with a narrow ribbon round the edge, a black stuff ditto, two linsey petticoats, the one striped and the other plain, a kenting apron and handkerchief, a pair of high heel'd shoes, with sundry other things not known. Whoever takes up said servants, and secures them, so that their master may have them again, shall have, if 10 miles from home, ten dollars, if twenty miles, twenty dollars, and if further, the above reward, and reasonable charges if brought home, and if proportion for either, paid by HENRY WILLIAMS: June 22, 1774.

The Maryland Journal, and the Baltimore Advertiser, From Saturday, June 18, to Saturday, July 2, 1774; From Saturday, July 2, to Saturday, July 9; From Saturday, July 9, to Saturday, July 16, 1774.

June 22, 1774.
TEN POUNDS Reward.
RAN away last Sunday night from us the subscribers, two men, one an English convict servant, named JAMES GODDARD, a lusty well made, full faced man, fair complexion, aged about 28 years, about five feet 9 or 10 inches high; had on and took with him, a felt hat bound round the edge with black ferret, several wigs, two of which were black, one striped and flowered Barcelona handkerchief, a blue cloth coat with metal buttons, one jacket, the fore parts red plush, one country cloth ditto, one white linen shirt, one tow ditto, blue cloth breeches, one pair of tow trowsers, one tow linen waistcoat; a pair of blue worsted stockings, one pair of grey ditto, and country made shoes shod with nails; he likewise took an assignment of William Carpenter, who was free the 14th day of June, 1773, and signed by myself and Mr. Andrew Buchanan, and 'tis supposed he will change his name to William Carpenter.

The other a negro fellow....it is supposed they will change cloaths.

Whoever takes up the said servants, and secures them so as we may get them again, shall receive if taken ten miles from home, *Three Pounds*, if thirty miles, *Six Pounds*, and if out of the province the above reward, or half for each, and reasonable charges paid, if brought home, by us, living near the Soldier's Delight, Baltimore County, Maryland.

WILLIAM CROMWELL.   JOHN EBERT.

N. B. All masters of vessels are forewarned not to take them off at their peril.

The Maryland Journal, and the Baltimore Advertiser, From Saturday, June 18, to Saturday, July 2, 1774; From Saturday, July 2, to Saturday, July 9, 1774; From Saturday, July 9, to Saturday, July 16, 1774. See *Dunlap's Pennsylvania Packet or, the General Advertiser*, July 11, 1774.

June 29, 1774.
TEN DOLLARS Reward.
RAN away last night from the subscriber, living in Mount-Joy township, York county, an Irish servant man, named *Patrick Welsh*, 37 Years of age, 5 feet 8 inches high, with straight black hair, is much marked with the smallpox, blind of the left eye: Had on and took with him, a greenish colour'd fustin coat, one brown ditto, an old red jacket, and brogues with nails in their heels. Whoever takes up said servant, and secures him in any gaol in this province, or brings him to me, shall have the above reward, and reasonable charges paid by   DANIEL M'BRIDE.

N. B. Said servant has been in the country before, and served his time in the Quaker settlement in the Jerseys, and very probably may be gone there now.

The Maryland Journal, and the Baltimore Advertiser, From Saturday, June 11, to Saturday, June 18, 1774; From Saturday, June 18, to Saturday, July 2, 1774; From Saturday, July 2, to Saturday, July 9, 1774; From Saturday, July 9, to Saturday, July 14, 1774.

Baltimore-town, June 25, 1774.
THIRTY POUNDS Reward.
RAN away from his special bail, on Saturday the 18th inst, a certain *Dominick Joseph Keyser*, aged about 28 years age; he came from Germany about two years ago, is of a swarthy complexion, long black hair, black eyes, and is about 5 feet 10 inches high: he took with him a variety of clothes, and will probably wear a gold lac'd waistcoat and hat, it's very likely will may cut off his hair and wear a wig, as he got several made before he left this place; he understands Latin, and can speak the French and Dutch languages, he likewise speaks broken English, is a Roman by profession, and is an artful cunning fellow; it is likely he will change his name to *Joseph Kayser* or *Joseph Dominick*: he took with him a great quantity of goods, to the amount of three hundred pounds and upwards, from different people in this place, likewise a woman, who says she is his wife: she is a French woman, of a dark complexion, is short but very corpulent, and professes great knowledge in physic, and will probably practise; he will perhaps practise himself, but never practised regular: it is thought he went with a certain Capt. Brown to North-Carolina, the said Brown was very intimate with him, and he absconded with all his goods at the time Brown set sail. Whoever takes up that said *Kayser* and brings him to the subscriber, or puts him into the gaol of Baltimore, shall have the above reward, paid by   VOLERIUS DUKEHART.

The Maryland Journal, and the Baltimore Advertiser, From Saturday, June 18, to Saturday, July 2, 1774; From Saturday, July 2, to Saturday, July 9; See *Dunlap's Pennsylvania Packet or, the General Advertiser*, July 11, 1774; August 15, 1774. Minor differences between the papers.

RUN away, on the 27th of June, from the subscriber, living in the borough of Wilmington, New-Castle county, an Irish servant lad, named Thomas Connely, by trade a barber and hair-dresser, about 5 feet 5 or 6 inches high, of a sandy complexion, grey eyed, wears his hair tied, and has the brogue on his tongue; is apt to get drunk, and very quarrelsome when so; took with him some razors and combs; had on, when he went away, a blue cloth short coat, with a red velvet collar, and yellow cording round the edging, a blue cloth jacket let out at the sides, new Russia drilling breeches, cotton stockings, a coarse wool hat, old turned pumps, and brass buckles. As he can write a tolerable hand, and is well acquainted in this country, it is likely he will forge a pass. Whoever takes up said servant, and confines him in any of his Majesty's goals, so that his master may have him again, shall have Ten Dollars reward, and reasonable charges, paid by WILLIAM BROBSON.

N. B. The said servant formerly run away from Robert Wilson, at the Head of Wye river, Maryland, was taken up and put into goal at Philadelphia, and brought from thence in November last.

The Pennsylvania Gazette, July 6, 1774. See *The New-York Gazette; and the Weekly Mercury*, August 15, 1774.

Baltimore, July 5, 1774.
ELEVEN DOLLARS REWARD.
RAN away, last night, from the subscriber at his mills, on the Great Falls of Gunpowder, an Irish servant man named THOMAS WELSH, not a year in the country, about 5 feet 6 or 7 inches high, a thick set fellow, full faced and pretty much freckled, has brown hair, which he commonly wore tied; he took with him, a large black horse, saddle and bridle, with a switch tail and mane, trots, paces, and hand-gallops, has no brand or natural mark, his back is sore on and near his withers; he had with him, a new felt hat, one check, one linen, and one Russia linen shirt, and a pair of trowsers of the latter kind, a light coloured fustian fly coat, a green coat and waistcoat, white cloth breeches, good shoes and stockings, and silver buckles; it is likely he may look for employ in waiting upon a Gentleman, as he has been formerly in that way; it is imagined he is gone in company with a supposed *Cornelius Cummings*, a cooper by trade, about five feet 6 or 7 inches high, has a long brown coat, flannel waistcoat, striped ticken trowsers, a large round hat, sandy complexion and hair, scarce long enough to tie, he has some cooper's tools with him, and 'tis thought they are bent for the West-Indies. All masters of vessels are forbid to carry them off at their peril. Whoever takes up and secures said servant and horse, with the said *Cornelius Cummings*, if found together, so as the subscriber may get them again, shall be entitled to the above reward, or *Five Pounds* for *Welsh*, and *Three Pounds* for the supposed Cornelius Cummings, if he is found in company, by   ROBERT CUMMINS.

The Maryland Journal, and the Baltimore Advertiser, From Saturday, July 2, to Saturday, July 9, 1774; From Saturday, July 9, to Saturday, July 14, 1774; *Dunlap's Pennsylvania Packet or, the General Advertiser*, July 18, 1774. *Dunlap's* shows Welsh as "about 5 feet 5 or 6 inches" in height, and lists a reward of "THREE POUNDS for the horse."

June 22, 1774.
TEN POUNDS REWARD.

RAN AWAY last night, from the subscribers, living near Soldier's Delight, Baltimore county, Maryland, two men, one an English convict servant, named JAMES GODDARD, a lusty, well made, full faced man, of a fair complexion, about 28 years of age, 5 feet 9 or 10 inches high; had on and took with him a felt hat bound round the edge with black ferret, several wigs, two of which were black, one striped and flowered Barcelona silk handkerchief, a blue cloth coat with metal buttons, one jacket, the fore parts red plush, one country cloth ditto, one white linen shirt, one tow ditto, blue cloth breeches, a pair of tow trowsers, a pair of blue worsted stockings, a pair of grey ditto, and a pair of country made shoes shod with nails: He took with him an assignment of one WILLIAM CARPENTER's, who was free the 14th of June, 1773, signed by myself and Andrew Buchanan, and it is supposed he will change his name to William Carpenter.—The other is a negro fellow, about 23 years of age, and about 5 feet 10 inches high, slim made, has a bend in his knees, three scars on each cheek and each breast, and several scars on his back by whipping, talks coarse broken English; he took with him a new fur hat, a blue camblet coat and jacket half worn, a spotted swanskin jacket, a pair of linen trowsers, a new holland shirt, a homespun ditto, two oznabrugs ditto, and country made shoes; it is supposed they will change cloaths: The whiteman forged a pass for the negro, in which he was called Charles Harday, and signed Samuel Owing and Philip Plowman. Whoever takes them up and secures them in any of his Majesty's gaols, shall have the above reward, and reasonable charges if brought home, paid by
  WILLIAM CROMWELL. JOHN EBERT.

N. B. All masters of vessels are forewarned not to take them off at their peril.

Dunlap's Pennsylvania Packet or, the General Advertiser, July 11, 1774; August 1, 1774. See *The Maryland Journal, and the Baltimore Advertiser*, From Saturday, June 18, to Saturday, July 2, 1774.

George-Town, June 29, 1774.

RAN away from George-Town on Patowmack, on Sunday the 26th instant, an indented servant man named John Bryan, by trade a plasterer and tiler; he is a stout well proportioned fellow, about 5 feet 8 or 9 inches high, smooth face and fresh complexion, short black hair, but wore an old wig over it: Had on and carried with him, a blue cloth coat and blue surtout, a striped linsey-woolsey jacket, a white ditto, a pair of leather breeches, a pair of white twill'd ditto, a pair of blue worsted hose, a pair of white thread

ditto, and a good castor hat; he is a native of Ireland and retains much of the accent of that country; he arrived here about two weeks ago in the snow Betty Gray, captain William Scott, belonging to Belfast, but last from Cork. Whoever takes up the said fellow and brings him to the subscriber shall receive five pounds reward   WILLIAM DEAKINS, jun.
The Maryland Gazette, July 14, 1774; August 11, 1774.

TEN POUNDS REWARD.

June 21, 1774.

RAN away from the subscriber living near Port-Tobacco, Charles county, William Murphey, a servant man, was born in Ireland, and is about 5 feet 6 inches high, of a swarthy complexion, pock marked, black hair tied in a club: had on and took with him, a brown surtout coat much worn, black waistcoat and breeches, short cotton jacket, a pair of coarse linen breeches, white shirt, check ditto, a pair of boots almost new, a new pair of shoes, and a new felt hat, with a bed, blanket, and rug. Thomas Stone, an English Servant man, a joiner by trade, short and thick set, of a fair complexion, brown hair lately cut: had on and took with him, a light coloured cloth coat and waistcoat, a pair of blue breeches, check shirt, osnabrig trousers, coarse stockings, a pair of shoes almost new. Whoever delivers them to me or secures them in prison, shall be entitled to the above reward or five pounds for either.   BAKER BROOKE.
The Maryland Gazette, July 14, 1774; July 28, 1774; August 4, 1774.

TEN POUNDS REWARD.

Baltimore, July 6, 1774.

RAN away from the subscriber on the 8th of April last, the two following servant men, viz. Samuel Powis, a tailor and stay-maker, born in the west of England, and speaks broad, is a low small man, about 40 years of age, has short brown hair, a white Welch cotton coat, with a fall down collar and short skirts, a dark wilton jacket, linen breeches, old shoes with nails in the heels, his other cloaths unknown; he took a country made sickle with him, stamped Hew's. Edward Williams, a stout tall down looking fellow, of a brown complexion, born in Wales, and speaks in the Welch dialect, has short brown hair, is about 30 years of age: took with him, a new osnabrig bedtick, a light coloured superfine broad cloth coat, which is too small for him, one old dark coloured cloth coat, trimmed with brass buttons and brown binding, one brown broad cloth jacket, one green bird eyed ditto, several pair of coarse gray stockings, new felt hat, sundry knives and buckles, with some store goods unknown, osnabrig shirts, and a silver watch, the winding chain of which is broke. Whoever secures the said

servants so as their master may get them again, shall have forty shillings for each or either of them, or either of them, if fifty miles off and brought home, shall have five Pounds for each and reasonable charges. paid by ABRAHAM JARRETT.
P. S. It is supposed they will attempt to take shipping.
The Maryland Gazette, July 14, 1774; July 28, 1774; August 11, 1774; August 25, 1774. See *The Maryland Journal, and the Baltimore Advertiser*, May 24, 1775, and July 5, 1775, for Powis/Powes.

Anne-Arundel County, July 11, 1774.
COMMITTED to my custody as runaways, Jane Hall, who says she belongs to Samuel Neale of Baltimore-Town; she is of a small stature and much pitted with the small pox: she hath on and with her an old camblet jacket and quilted petticoat, a white flannel ditto with calico border, and a calico bedgown. Also, Negro Ned.... Their masters are desired to take them away and pay charges to   WILLIAM NOKE, Sheriff.
The Maryland Gazette, July 14, 1774; July 28, 1774.

Patuxent Iron-Works, June 28, 1774.
FIVE POUNDS REWARD.
WENT away last night from the subscriber, an English servant man, named James Cookman, a lusty well made fellow, 5 feet 10 or 11 inches high, round shouldered, and about 26 years of age; had on and took with him an osnabrig shirt, crocus trousers, cotton jacket, old hat, and old shoes. Whoever takes up the said servant, and secures him in any jail, so that he may be had again, shall receive if taken 10 miles from home 20 shillings, if 20 miles 40 shillings, and if fifty miles, or out of the province, the above reward (including what the law allows) and reasonable charges if brought home, paid by   THOMAS SNOWDEN.
N. B. There is missing an old broad cloth coat, waistcoat and breeches, one white linen shirt, and two pair of stockings, which it is probable he may have taken with him.
The Maryland Gazette, July 21, 1774; July 7, 1774. See *The Maryland Gazette*, August 6, 1772, for Cookman.

Annapolis, July 8, 1774.
RAN away from the subscriber, an indented servant man named Thomas Spriggs, by trade a silk weaver, about 23 years of age, 5 feet 4 inches high, of a pale complexion, with light brown short hair: had on and took with him a white flannel jacket trimmed with black buttons and binding, a coarse

check shirt and osnabrig trousers. It is supposed he is gone off with one Benjamin Porter, about 32 years of age, who came here as a Redemptioner with Capt. Charles Ainzell, master of the snow Adventure, and was sold to Thomas Ringgold, Esq; for a coachman. The said Porter is of a brown complexion, about 5 feet 8 inches high, with brown curled hair: had on and took with him a light gray Bath beaver great coat, a thickset frock, a short flannel waistcoat, and a pair of leather breeches. Whoever will apprehend them, so that their masters may get them again, shall receive 40 shillings reward for each if taken within the province, if out of the province five pounds.   W. WHETCROFT.

N. B. Said Porter has fraudulently carried off his indentures, by which means he may impose on the public.

The Maryland Gazette, July 21, 1774; August 4, 1774. See *Dunlap's Pennsylvania Packet or, the General Advertiser*, August 8, 1774, for Porter.

WENT away on Wednesday the 15th of June, from Elk-Ridge Landing, two convicted men, and one indented servant woman, viz. William Byers, about 5 feet 9 inches high, straight black hair, pale complexion: had on, a brown coat and jacket with check trousers. Thomas Baird, about 5 feet 7 or 8 inches high, a square well set fellow, by trade a weaver, the thumb of his right hand is cut off a little above the first joint: had on a blackish coat, jacket and breeches. Margaret Byers, wife to the above William Byers, about 5 feet 3 inches high, ruddy complexion: had on, a dark ground [sic] calico gown, her other cloaths forgot. Whoever brings the above servants to the subscriber, shall receive twenty shillings for each or either of them, besides what the law allows, and reasonable travelling charges, paid by ARCHIBALD MONCREIFF.

The Maryland Gazette, July 28, 1774.

Baltimore, July 25, 1774.
TEN POUNDS REWARD,

RAN AWAY from the subscriber, on Friday the 25th of March last, an Irish servant man named NICHOLAS M'COY, about 20 years old, 5 feet 6 or 7 inches high, dark hair; had on an old felt hat, brown jacket without sleeves, blue coat, the sleeves of which are of a different blue, being somewhat newer, leather breeches, long at the knees and something torn in the seat, new strong shoes made to tye, and a tow linen shirt, but it is probable he may change some of his clothes. Whoever takes up said servant and brings him home, shall have, if out of the country, FIVE POUNDS Reward, and if out of the province, the above Reward, paid by

ABRAHAM PATTON.

N. B. He formerly lived with Melcher Keener, Tavern-keeper, in this town, and can speak and understand Dutch. All masters of vessels are warned not to take off said servant at their peril.

Dunlap's Pennsylvania Packet or, the General Advertiser, August 1, 1774.

THREE POUNDS REWARD.

RAN AWAY the 23d of May last, from the subscriber, living in Harford county, Maryland, two convict servant men; one named JOHN HAWKINS, an Englishman, about 35 years of age, 5 feet 8 inches high, is of a fair complexion, wears his own brown hair, and has a red beard: Had on an old castor hat, old coarse shirt and trowsers, a red jacket with sleeves, old shoes, and plated buckles, and has a large scar on each side of his neck. The other named PETER LYNCH, an Irishman, of a sandy complexion, wears his own red hair, and pitted with the small pox: Had on when he went away, an old fur hat, the crown sewed in, coarse shirt and trowsers, old brown surtout coat, old shoes and brass buckles. Whoever takes up said servants, and secures them again, shall have the above reward, or THIRTY SHILLINGS for either, and reasonable charges if brought home, paid by MANASSEH or JOHN FINNEY.

N. B. They are both good scholars, and it is very likely they will forge passes for themselves, and change their names. Lynch is a hatter by trade.

Dunlap's Pennsylvania Packet or, the General Advertiser, August 1, 1774; August 15, 1774.

SIX POUNDS Reward.

RUN away from the Antietam Forge, in Frederick county, on the 19th of July, 1774, two servant men, viz.

TIMOTHY SHAW, a convict, about 5 feet 5 inches high, dark complexion, very short hair, about 35 years of age; had on, when he went away, an ozenbrigs shirt and trowsers, a small lincey jacket, striped round the body, a new shirt, and old shoes.

CON GELLAHER, an indented servant, about 5 feet 6 inches high, dark complexion, short brown hair, pock marked, about 25 years of age, clothed the same as SHAW; they both came from Ireland about a month ago. Whoever secures them, so as their masters may have them again, shall have the above reward, if taken above 10 miles from home, or half the sum if taken under that distance, paid by
DANIEL and SAMUEL HUGHES.

The Pennsylvania Gazette, August 3, 1774; February 22, 1775.

TWENTY SHILLINGS REWARD.
RAN AWAY on the 21st of July last, from the subscriber, in Cecil county, Maryland, an indented servant man, named BENJAMIN WARRINGTON, about 5 feet 8 inches high, a thick chunky fellow, of a dark complexion, and wears his own brown hair tied behind; had on when he went away, a brown coat, waistcoat and breeches. He is a West-countryman, and may have his old indentures with him. Whoever takes up said fellow and brings him home to the subscriber, shall have the above Reward, and reasonable charges, paid by   WILLIAM CROKER.
  Dunlap's Pennsylvania Packet or, the General Advertiser, August 8, 1774; August 29, 1774; September 19, 1774.

FORTY SHILLINGS REWARD.
RAN AWAY from the subscriber, living on Manokesy, near Frederick Town, Maryland, a convict servant man, born in the west of England and speaks much of that dialect, and likely he will change his name; he is about 35 years of age, 5 feet 8 or 9 inches high, and has lost the fore finger of his right hand; had on and took with him, two shirts of country made linen, one pair of trowsers of the same, a new light coloured lincey jacket lined with striped lincey, a pair of old leather breeches, and an old felt hat. Whoever takes up the said servant and confines him in any gaol, so that his master may have him again, shall receive the above Reward, and reasonable charges if brought home, paid by the subscriber, at his plantation on Manokesy, Frederick County, Maryland, seven miles from Frederick Town. July 11th, 1774.   WILLIAM CRUM.
  Dunlap's Pennsylvania Packet or, the General Advertiser, August 8, 1774; September 5, 1774; September 19, 1774.

Hartford County, August 4, 1774.
ESCAPED from Hartford County gaol, which was broke open on the 3d instant—BENJAMIN PORTER, a coachman; he is about five feet eight inches high, has brown hair curled behind, and is about thirty-two years old; he had on and took with him a thickset frock, a short white flannel waistcoat, leather breeches, one white and one striped shirt.—JOHN SMITH, about thirty years of age, has a fair complexion, smooth face, a small scar under his left eye, short brown curling hair, and is about five feet eight inches high; he had on and took with him, a woollen jacket striped yellow, with sleeves buttoned at the wrist below, check shirt, trowsers of coarse brown linen, and a narrow brimmed hat bound with black binding. Whoever takes up and secures said prisoners, so that the subscriber may have them again, shall receive FORTY SHILLINGS Reward for each of

them, if taken up in this province, and if out of the province, THREE POUNDS, to be paid by
THOMAS MILLER, Sheriff.
> *Dunlap's Pennsylvania Packet or, the General Advertiser*, August 8, 1774; August 15, 1774; September 5, 1774; September 19, 1774. See *The Maryland Gazette*, July 21, 1774, for Porter.

TWENTY POUNDS Reward. RUN away, on the 5th of July last, from the subscriber, living near Northampton furnace, Baltimore county, Maryland, an Irish servant, named DAVID TOOL, about 27 years of age, 5 feet 5 or 6 inches high, is well made, has grey eyes, short black hair, down look, ruddy complexion, his left thigh has been broke, which occasions him to walk lame, though scarcely perceivable, is an artful fellow, has run away several times, and been a great distance back; he is a noted thief and drunkard. He has been taken up since he run away, and made his escape (about the 20th of July) near George Myers, on the road to York, and it is now thought he will go towards the Warm Springs, in Virginia. He had with him two white shirts, checquered cotton jacket, Russia sheeting breeches, country thread stockings, old country made shoes. Whoever takes up said servant, and secures him, so that his master may get him again, shall have 30s. if taken 20 miles from home; 40s. if 30 miles; 3l. if 50 miles; 5l. if 100 miles; 7l. 10s. if 150 miles; 10l. if 200 miles; the above reward, if 300 miles; and reasonable charges, if brought home, paid by
JOHN R. HOLLIDAY.
> *The Pennsylvania Gazette*, August 10, 1774; September 21, 1774; *Dunlap's Pennsylvania Packet or, the General Advertiser*, August 15, 1774; August 29, 1774; October 3, 1774; November 14, 1774. Minor differences. See *The Maryland Gazette*, August 8, 1771, for "David Toole."

RUN away, the 16th of July last, from the subscriber, living near Oxford, in Talbot county, an indented Irish servant man, named Thomas Burn, a shoemaker by trade, about 5 feet high, about 22 years of age, of a fair complexion, pitted with the smallpox, has short dark coloured hair, and sandy beard; had on, when he went away, a coarse felt hat, a pale blew saggathy coat, black and dirty, much worn, coarse shirt and trowsers, old white kersey jacket, mended with striped red and white swanskin on the fore parts of it, thread stockings, old shoes, with large pewter buckles. Whoever takes up said servant, and secures him, so that his master may

have him again, shall receive Thirty Shillings reward, and all reasonable charges, paid by   RICHARD BARNETT.
The Pennsylvania Gazette, August 10, 1774.

Northampton quarter, *Baltimore county, July* 26, 1774.
ONE HUNDRED DOLLARS Reward.

RUN away, on the 15th of June last, from the subscriber, two convict servant men, viz. *Robert Hardey*, an Englishman, 5 feet 9 inches high, round visage, fair complexion, much pitted with the smallpox, fair hair, slim made, he has a scar on the left side of his upper lip, and one on the joint of his left wrist, has hasel eyes, and squints, and is subject to fits; he is a farmer; had on, and took with him, an ozenbrigs shirt, old white thickset coat, much torn in the sleeves, red jacket, a pair of crocus and a pair of old ozenbrigs trowsers, old yarn stockings, country made shoes, and an old felt hat. *James Lamberd*, an Englishman, 5 feet 6 inches high, round visage, fair complexion, black hair, he has a philm or speck in his right eye, which makes him blind of that eye, much pitted with the small-pox, he is thick and well set, 31 years of age, and is a farmer or baker; had on, and took with him, an ozenbrigs shirt, a cotton jacket, crocus trowsers, a pair of old black yarn stockings, country made shoes, and old hat; they took two matchcoat blankets, one of them striped with red and the other with blue. Whoever takes up and brings home the said servants, if 60 miles from home, 4l. for each; if 80 miles from home, 5l. for each; if 100 miles, 6l. for each; if 120 miles from home, 7l. for each; if 150 miles from home, 9l. for each; if 200 miles from home, 11l. for each; if 250 miles from home, 13l. for each; if 300 miles from home, 15l. for each; and if 350 miles from home, the above reward, paid by   CHARLES RIDGELY.

N. B. They talk the West of England dialect. It is possible they may have a forged pass.

The Pennsylvania Gazette, August 10, 1774; September 7, 1774; November 9, 1774; *Dunlap's Pennsylvania Packet or, the General Advertiser*, August 29, 1774; September 12, 1774; September 26, 1774; October 3, 1774. Minor differences between the papers.

July 31, 1774.

RAN away from the subscriber, living at the ferry opposite Alexandria in Prince-George's county Maryland, on Wednesday night the 27th instant, an Irish indented servant man named Thomas Breaton, about 23 years of age, 5 feet 9 or 10 inches high, much pitted with the small-pox, short sandy coloured hair, thin visage, down look, ruddy complexion, and has a rupture in his bowels: had on and took with him, a light coloured Wilton coat, blue broad cloth jacket, a pair of osnabrig trousers, striped holland ditto, buckskin breeches, country made pumps, plated buckles, and felt hat; as he can write a tolerable hand, it is possible he may forge a pass. Whoever takes up the said servant, and secures him again, shall receive three pounds including what the law allows, and reasonable charges paid if brought home, by   JOHN CLIFFORD.

N. B. As the aforesaid servant has made several elopements and forged passes, and after being confined has privately made his escape, whoever apprehends him are desired to take particular care to confine him. He has stolen sundry cloaths.

The Maryland Gazette, August 11, 1774; August 25, 1774; September 8, 1774. See *The Maryland Gazette*, June 16, 1774.

FIFTY DOLLARS REWARD.

Rock-Creek, Frederick county, August 3, 1774.
RAN away last night from the subscriber, a convict servant man named Joseph Barker, an Englishman, about 25 years of age; he is a well looking fellow, of a ruddy complexion, about 5 feet 10 inches high: had on and took with him, a reddish coloured mixed broad-cloth coat with a velvet cape, two white flannel short jackets bound with red, two pair of nankeen breeches, a pair of old leather breeches, a pair of old worsted stockings, a pair of thread ditto, old shoes, and a felt hat. He wears his own dark hair tied behind. It is supposed he is gone in company with some other man unknown to me, as I have missed two horses out of my pasture, one of which is a large sorrel, about 15 hands high, paces naturally, the other a chesnut sorrel, about 14 hands and a half high, paces, trots, and gallops; he is low before, crest fallen, and has a short scanty tail; the horses are both shod before. The man took with him a half worn saddle and curb bridle; one of the staples is gone off the fore part of the saddle on the near side. Whoever takes up said servant and brings him home to the subscriber, shall have, if taken 30 miles from home 10 dollars, and 5 pounds for the other man and the two horses, and so in proportion for a greater distance for the servant and horse, paid by RICHARD CRABB.

The Maryland Gazette, August 11, 1774; August 25, 1774; September 8, 1774; September 15, 1775; September 29, 1775; October 6, 1774; October 20, 1774; November 10; 1774; November 17, 1774; November 24, 1774; December 1, 1774; December 8, 1774; January 5, 1775; January 12, 1775; January 19, 1775; January 26, 1775; February 9, 1775; February 16, 1775; February 22, 1775; March 9, 1775.

Deer Creek, Harford County, Aug. 15, 1774.
FIVE POUNDS REWARD.

RAN AWAY from the subscriber, on the 5th inst. MICHAEL JORDAN, an Irishman, by trade a saddler, has been about one year in the country, is slim, strait, and of a fair complexion, appears to be about 35 years of age, and 5 feet 10 inches high, much pitted with the small-pox, and has a very remarkable scar on his left cheek, much in the shape of a horse shoe, the middle part of the scar extending to his mouth; he says it was occasioned by the kick of a horse: He took with him sundry cloaths, though it is likely he may appear in a nankeen coat and breeches, blue jacket, the fore parts silk; he wears a short wig which seems to have been of one curl, and a beaver hat almost new: As he took sundry cloaths with him it is likely he may change his dress, but the scar is so remarkable he may be discovered in any dress. He is known to have gone towards Philadelphia. Whoever apprehends the said Michael Jordan, and secures him in any of his Majesty's gaols on the continent, on giving information thereof to WILLIAM KENLEY, Deputy Collector of Excise, at the Excise-Office in Philadelphia, or to the subscriber living near Harford town, in Harford county, Maryland, shall be entitled to the above Reward, and reasonable charges if brought to
WILLIAM HOPKINS, Jun.

N. B. As it is supposed that he will attempt to get to some distant part of the continent by water, all masters of vessels are forbid to harbour or carry him off at their peril: And if any such should discover said Jordan, and bring him either to Philadelphia or Baltimore Town, shall, on delivering him up, be entitled to the above Reward, besides being paid for his passage.

Dunlap's Pennsylvania Packet or, the General Advertiser, August 15, 1774; August 29, 1774; September 19, 1774.

RUN away from the subscriber, living in the borough of Wilmington, in New-Castle County, upon Delaware, the 27th ultimo, an Irish servant Lad named THOMAS CONNELY, by trade a barber and hair-dresser, about five feet five or six inches high, of a sandy complexion, grey eyes, reddish hair, which he wears tied; has the brogue in his speech, is apt to get drunk, and is then very quarrelsome; took with him some razors and combs. Had on when he went away a blue cloth short coat, with a red velvet collar, and corded round the edges; a blue cloth jacket let out at the sides, new Russia drilling breeches; and as he can write a tolerable hand, and is acquainted with the country, it is probable he may forge a pass; for he formerly lived at New-York, from whence he went about five years ago to Maryland, and after some time became a valet to Colonel Richard Tilghman, of Queen Ann's County, with whom he went in that character to New-York. He afterwards indented to Robert Wilson, at the Head of Wye River, in

Maryland, from whom he ran away, and was put into gaol at Philadelphia, soon after which the subscriber purchased him. He was apprehended the 2d instant at Elizabeth-Town-Point, and brought back to Princeton, from whence he made his escape next morning; he had taken off the collar from his coat, and sold his jacket. Whoever secures said servant in any of his Majesty's goals so that his master may have him again, shall receive TEN DOLLARS reward, besides reasonable charges, paid by
Wilmington, July, 29, 1774.   WILLIAM BROBSON.
The New-York Gazette; and the Weekly Mercury, August 15, 1774; August 22, 1774; September 5, 1774. See *The Pennsylvania Gazette*, July 6, 1774.

RUN away from the subscriber, living in Kent county, Maryland, on the 8th day of August, 1774, two English servant lads, named George Thomas and William Thomas; GEORGE is about 19 years of age, a thick well set lad, about 5 feet 1 inch high, wears short black hair, and is somewhat deaf; had on, and took with him, a fustian coat, a brown camblet surtout, lined with red flannel, a pair of black silk breeches, about half-worn, a yellow striped silk waistcoat, about half-worn, rufled shirt, and white silk ribbed stockings. WILLIAM is about 17 years of age, near the same heighth, slim made, wears short black hair; had a white broadcloth coat, with a red collar, a yellow silk waistcoat striped, black silk breeches, shoes and stockings indifferent. Any person who secures them in any goal, or brings them to the subscriber, if taken out of the county, shall receive a reward of Twelve Dollars; if taken in the county, Thirty Shillings for each, and reasonable charges, if brought home.
WILLIAM CARMICHAEL.
The Pennsylvania Gazette, August 17, 1774.

TWENTY DOLLARS REWARD.

August 8, 1774.

RAN away last night from the subscriber, living on Elk-Ridge, in Anne-Arundel county, Maryland, a convict servant man named Stephen Steuart, lately arrived in the ship Aston Hall, capt. Parker, from London, a likely fellow about 30 years of age, about 5 feet 7 inches high, middling slender made, fair complexion, short red or sandy coloured hair, freckled fact, speaks good English, and pretends to understand farming: had on and took with him, a new osnabrig shirt, new coarse country linen trousers, new felt hat, an old lightish coloured full'd country cloth coat without cuffs, the fore parts and sleeves much patched, and is considerably too long for him, a pair of old shoes lately soaled, and iron buckles without tongues, which he

fastens on with nails. Whoever takes up the said servant and secures him in any jail, so that his master gets him again, shall receive, if taken 10 miles from home 30 shillings, if 20 miles 3 pounds, if 50 miles 5 pounds, and if out of the province the above reward, including what the law allows, and reasonable charges if brought home.
JOHN HOOD.

The Maryland Gazette, August 18, 1774; August 25, 1774; September 1, 1774.

EIGHT DOLLARS Reward.

RAN away from the subscriber living in York County, Hopewell Township, an English servant man, of the name of George Otley, about 6 feet high, with long black hair tied behind; had on when he went away, a home made kersey jacket, the backs not just the same, with metal buttons, a striped linen shirt, and trousers, a pair of old ribb'd stockings homespun worsted, a pair of new pumps with carved pinchbeck buckles, he is long visaged, and pock-marked in the face, very talkative, and a good scholar, was keeping school when he went away; he understands book-keeping very well; he took with him a fine shirt; he sings a song very well. Whoever takes up or secures said servant, so that his master may have him again, shall have the above reward, and reasonable charges, paid by
DAVID WILEY.

The Maryland Journal, and the Baltimore Advertiser, August 24, 1774.

August 1, 1774.
TEN POUNDS Reward.

RAN away from the subscriber, (living in Alexandria) on Monday night the 25th of July past, an Irish servant man named MICHAEL CONNER: He is about 26 years of age, and about 5 feet 6 inches high, a thick well made fellow, very much pitted with the small-pox, black curled hair, thick lips, heavy eye brows, hollow eyes, can talk very good French; had on when he went away, a brown cloth coat, white jacket with blue glass buttons, white cord duroy breeches, one drillen ditto, several pair of stockings, white, black and mixture, a pair of silver shoe-buckles, a pair of channel pumps not much worn, and an old Carolina hat cut in the fashion; he was seen last Saturday the 30th of July, 6 miles from Bladensburgh, on the road leading to Baltimore, with his apparel changed, his dress being then a red and white striped holland jacket, black velvet breeches, a pair of white cotton stockings, with a bundle in his hand tied up with a handkerchief, the pumps and silver buckles, he had as before mentioned: its probable he will change his name, as he has got a forged pass, and passes for a free man. Whoever

secures said servant, and lodges him in any of his majesty's jails, shall have the above reward and reasonable charges, paid by
PATRICK MURRAY.
N. B. All masters of vessels are forwarned not to take him off at their peril.
The Maryland Journal, and the Baltimore Advertiser, August 24, 1774. See *The Maryland Gazette*, September 1, 1774.

August 15, 1774.
TEN POUNDS Reward.
RAN away from *Fort-Frederick* Furnace, two convict servants, viz. ROBERT BEES, born in *Gloucestershire*, [28] years of age, five feet 5 or 6 inches high, of a fair complexion, has blue eyes, brown hair and eye-brows, talks much in the West Country dialect, and is by trade a miner; had on, a good felt hat, Irish line shirt, light-coloured coarse broad-cloth jacket, without sleeves, very broad check trousers, good shoes, and a pair of large plated carved buckles. STEPHEN RICHARDS, born in *Cornwall*, 30 years of age, about 5 feet 2 or 3 inches high, of a ruddy complexion, is pitted with the small-pox, has short red hair, talks much in the West Country dialect, and is by trade a miner; had on, a red broad cloth jacket without sleeves, blue shag breeches, Irish linen shirt, a good felt hat, and good shoes, with plain metal buckles: It is supposed they have sundry other clothes with them, such as oznabrigs shirts, trousers, &c. Whoever takes up the said servants, and secures them, so as the subscriber may get them again, shall receive, if 20 miles from home, 40 shillings for each, if 40 miles 4 pounds, and if 50 miles, the above reward, and reasonable charges, if brought home, paid by   JAMES JOHNSON.
The Maryland Journal, and Baltimore Advertiser, August 24, 1774; September 7, 1774. See *The Maryland Gazette*, June 8, 1775, for Bees.

Baltimore County, July 25, 1774.
RAN away from the subscriber, living about 16 miles from Baltimore-Town, near Mr. Samuel Worthington's, a convict servant man, named HENRY BOSWELL; he is a half East-India Indian, about 30 years of age, 6 feet high, very well made, has high cheek bones, long sharp nose, wide mouth, short black hair, and small dark eyes, with a remarkable cast in them; his arms and fingers are rather shorter than common, and he has been much whipp'd on his back—he chews tobacco, and talks in the West of England dialect:—Had on, when he went away, an old check shirt, patched on the shoulders with coarse white linen, and a pair of good oznabrigs

trousers, Whoever shall secure the said servant, so that I may get him again, shall receive a reward of FIVE POUNDS.

N. B. I judge he will make for Philadelphia and New-York, by way of Lancaster.   BENJAMIN NICHOLSON.

The Maryland Journal, and Baltimore Advertiser, August 24, 1774; September 7, 1774. See *The Maryland Journal, and the Baltimore Advertiser*, From Friday, August 20, to Saturday, August 28, 1773, and *The Pennsylvania Chronicle*, From Monday, September 27, to Monday, October 4, 1773, and *Dunlap's Pennsylvania Packet or, the General Advertiser*, August 29, 1774, for Henry Boswell.

ANNE-ARUNDEL COUNTY, August 11, 1774.
RAN away from the subscriber, on Wednesday, the 10th Instant, a convict servant man, named JAMES M'GINLEY, (a Printer) about 5 Feet 8 inches high; had on, when he went away, a Drab-coloured Broadcloth Coat, Buckskin Breeches, white Thread Stockings: He stole and carried off upwards of One Hundred Pounds in Cash, a small sorrel Horse, and an indifferent Saddle. Whoever takes up said Fellow, and secures him, so that his Master may have him again, shall have a Reward of Three Pounds for the Fellow only, with reasonable Charges, and Ten Pounds if the Money and Horse are also recovered, paid by
THOMAS PERIMON.

N. B. It is thought said Fellow will make for Philadelphia or New-York, in order to take Passage to foreign Parts, all Masters of Vessels and others are therefore cautioned against harbouring, concealing, or carrying him off.

The Maryland Journal, and Baltimore Advertiser, August 24, 1774; September 7, 1774.

Baltimore, July 25, 1774.
NINE POUNDS Reward.
RAN away, last night, from the subscribers, living in the lower part of Frederick County, Maryland, the three following Irish servants, viz Darby Linnaham, an indented servant, has been about 12 months in the country, a square built fellow, about 5 feet 7 or 8 inches high, about 21 years of age; has short black hair, cut close on the top of his head, dark complexion, and a down look: Had on and took with him, an old castor hat, old dark brown bearskin surtout coat, leather breeches, one white shirt, one brown holland jacket, one pair of worsted stockings, and a pair of country made shoes, which are rather too large for him. Nicholas Walch, an indented servant; a straight well made fellow, about 20 years of age, has short brown curled hair, dark complexion, and down look: had on and took with him, an old

felt hat, [d]eep pea-blue jacket, one white linen ditto, one pair of reddish colour'd broadcloth breeches, one check shirt, one pair of oznabrigs trousers patched on the right knee, one pair of yarn stockings, and old country made shoes. Michael Hays, a convict, has been about two months in the country, a spare slim fellow, about 5 feet 6 or 7 inches high, about 18 years of age, long yellow hair: Had on and took with him, an old blue Scotch bonnet, a striped linsey jacket with sleeves, check shirt, crocus trousers, yarn stockings, and a pair of old turn'd pumps. As there are two other Irish servants gone from the neighbourhood, 'tis supposed they are gone together: one is a lusty fellow, and the other a small slim lad. Whoever takes up and secures the above servants, in any jail, so that they may be had again, shall receive, if 20 miles from home, 30 shillings; if 30 miles, 40 shillings; if 40 miles, 50 shillings; if out of the province, Three Pounds for each, including what the law allows, paid by
RICHARD THOMAS, JOHN THOMAS, and SHADRICK CASE.

The Maryland Journal, and Baltimore Advertiser, August 24, 1774.
See *The Pennsylvania Gazette*, September 14, 1774, for Darby Linnaham/Lehan and Welch/Walch.

RAN away from the Sea-Flower, capt. Thomas Smith, commander, an indented servant man called Owen Riley, about 30 years of age, 5 feet 4 or 5 inches high, round visaged, wears his own black hair thin before and generally tied behind, has been formerly a marine, and has been lately seen on board the boats or flats of the ship Chance, capt. Campbell, and calls himself Williams. Whoever takes up and secures the said servant, or brings him to me, shall receive two dollars reward over and what the law allows.
E. JOHNSON.

The Maryland Gazette, August 25, 1774.

WENT away from the subscriber, in Dumfries, Virginia, some time in May last, a servant man who appears to be both deaf and dumb, but is suspected to hear a little; convicted under the name of Thomas Jones, and transported in the Justitia, capt. Gray, last spring. He is a genteel tall fellow, about six feet high, with dark hair hanging down a little inclinable to curl, and has dark piercing eyes: he had on when he went away, a deep blue broadcloth coat and vest, with leather breeches and good stockings and shoes; his natural misfortunes render a more particular description unnecessary. I will give six dollars for apprehending and securing him, and all reasonable expences for bringing him either to Mr. James Stewart at Alexandria, or to me in Dumfries.   ANDREW LEITCH.

The Maryland Gazette, August 25, 1774; September 15, 1774.

Caecil County, August 21, 1774.
FOUR DOLLARS REWARD.
ESCAPED from the subscriber, on Monday the 8th instant, a certain JOHN YORKE, by trade a carpenter, about 43 years old, 5 feet 6 inches high, well set, of a sandy complexion, and red eyes. Whoever will apprehend him, and secure him in any of his Majesty's goals, so that the subscriber may have him again, shall receive the above Reward, from
JOHN HAMILTON, Sheriff.
Dunlap's Pennsylvania Packet or, the General Advertiser, August 29, 1774; September 12, 1774; October 3, 1774.

TWENTY-FIVE POUNDS
REWARD.
RAN AWAY from the subscriber, living near Mr. .Samuel Worthington's, about sixteen miles from Baltimore Town, three servant men, viz. .HENRY BOSWELL, an half East-Indian, about 6 feet high, very well made, has high cheek-bones, a long sharp nose, a wide mouth, short black hair and dark eyes, with a cast in them, his arms and fingers are rather shorter than common, he hath a scald between his shoulders near his neck, he chews tobacco, and talks in the west of England dialect: had on when he went away, an oznabrigs shirt, crocus trowsers, and an iron collar round his neck. TIMOTHY SHANE, . a stone mason and bricklayer, about 25 years of age, and an Irishman, he is about 5 feet 5 or 6 inches high, a trunchey well set fellow, has a fair complexion, (but much sun-burnt) short light brown hair, and grey eyes, his arms hang in a particular manner, and he is thicker through the jole than common: had on and took with him a good felt hat, an old brown coat much tarr'd, a brown jacket with white [yarn] stocking sleeves, two old white linen shirts, two check ditto, patched on the shoulders with coarse white linen, two pair of new oznabrigs trowsers, one pair of Welsh cotton drawers, and sundry other cloaths not known. WILLIAM EASUN, . an Englishman about 35 years of age, a house joiner by trade, is about 5 feet 3 inches high, of a dark complexion with black eyes, and a large hanging under lip, he is left handed but works at the bench with his right hand: had on and took with him an old brown cloth coat tarr'd, two nankeen jackets, one of them with sleeves, two pair of new oznabrigs trowsers, one pair of Welsh cotton drawers, one check shirt patched on the belly and in other places with white coarse linen, one striped linen ditto, patched in the same manner, with new striped linen of a different kind, one pair of speckled worsted stockings, with black leather shoes, and plain steel buckles, a pretty good castor hat, a short dark bob wig, and blue studs in his sleeves, his breath smells very offensive; hath taken with him some files, and it is supposed will get off HENRY

BOSWELL'S collar; he and the mason can both write very good hands, and very probably will forge passes. Whoever shall secure the two servants, TIMOTHY SHANE, and WILLIAM EASUN, so that I may get them again, shall receive the reward of TEN POUNDS for each of them, and for the other, HENRY BOSWELL, the reward of FIVE POUNDS.
BENJAMIN NICHOLSON.

N. B. 'Tis judged they will make for Philadelphia, by the way of York town, and Lancaster.

Dunlap's Pennsylvania Packet or, the General Advertiser, August 29, 1774. See *The Maryland Journal, and the Baltimore Advertiser*, From Friday, August 20, to Saturday, August 28, 1773; *The Pennsylvania Chronicle*, From Monday, September 27, to Monday, October 4, 1773, and *The Maryland Journal, and Baltimore Advertiser*, August 24, 1774, for Boswell.

Queen Ann's county, Maryland, August 22, 1774.
TWENTY DOLLARS Reward.

RUN away from the subscriber, on the 18th instant, an indented servant man, named RALPH ADAMS, a joiner by trade, born in England, a short well set fellow, with light brown hair, and very thick lips, he stoops in the neck when walking, and steps quick, is very talkative and stammers something in his speech, is an artful fellow, fond of drink, and will both swear and lie; went away meanly clad with only a country linen shirt and trowsers, old hat, and a brown jacket with sleeves. Whoever takes up and secures him in any goal, so as he may be had again, if taken in this province, TEN DOLLARS, if out, the above reward, paid by
JOHN MECONEKIN.

The Pennsylvania Gazette, August 31, 1774.

THE following persons are committed to my custody as runaways: Mary Seedhouse, who says she is a servant to Anthony Cummings.—Negro Jack....Robert Bell, a sailor belonging to the Minerva, Capt. Robinson, lying in the Ferry branch, Patapsco river.—Michael Conner, a servant to Patrick Murphy of Alexandria.—Nicholas Petercoster, a servant to Thomas Tilbury, in Sixth-street, Philadelphia.—Thomas Parks, about 22 years old, 5 feet 9 inches high, well made, brown hair, full faced, and much pitted with the small-pox: had no other cloathing but a pair of breeches.—Thomas Perry, a slim fellow, about 22 years of age, 5 feet 6 inches high, blue eyes, brown hair, pale complexion, and has no cloathing except a blanket.—Their masters are desired to take them away and pay charges to

ROBERT CHRISTIE, jun.   sheriff of Baltimore county.
The Maryland Gazette, September 1, 1774; September 8, 1774; September 15, 1774. See *The Maryland Journal, and Baltimore Advertiser,* August 24, 1774.

THREE POUNDS REWARD.

RAN AWAY from near the Lower Cross Roads, in Harford County, a certain JOHN WILSON, a schoolmaster, and shoemaker by trade; he is a stout made young fellow, about 5 feet 7 or 8 inches high, pock marked, with small seams about his chin, and hair almost black; had on a cross barred silk and cotton jacket, a good white shirt, check trowsers, and turned pumps; he is very fond of liquor, and is a noisy fellow in a tavern; took with him a little sorrel mare, heavy with colt, with a whitish mane and tail, hurt with the collar, has a running sore on her shoulder; also a bridle that looks ragged, and a saddle with a hogskin seat and a piece on the hind part: He was seen in Wilmington on the 21st ult. and there parted with his jacket and rode off in his shirt, and took the road towards New Garden in Chester county. Any person that will apprehend the said Wilson, and lodge him in any of his Majesty's goals, so that the owners may get the mare, bridle and saddle again, shall have the above Reward, or FORTY SHILLINGS for the fellow alone, paid by
JACOB LEMMON, NICHOLAS BAKER.

Dunlap's Pennsylvania Packet or, the General Advertiser, September 5, 1774; September 19, 1774.

August 1, 1774.
FIVE POUNDS REWARD.

RAN AWAY from the subscriber, living near Deer Creek, Hartford county, Maryland, the 29th of June last, an English convict servant man, named ROBERT BARTLEY, about twenty-five years of age, a well set fellow, with dark curled hair, has a large scar under his left knee on the shin bone: Had on and took with him, a half wore country made castor hat, one old blue straight bodied coat and jacket, one old yellow surtout coat, one pair lead coloured sagathy breeches, too large for him, one pair shoes, two large for him, with old fashioned cross barred brass buckles, a check shirt, pieced at the sleeves, a red spotted silk handkerchief, and an old oznabrugs trowsers and shirt. Whoever takes up and secures him in any of his Majesty's goals, so that his master may have him again, shall have the above reward, paid by   JOB KEY.

N. B. All masters of vessels are forbid to harbour or carry him off at their peril.

Dunlap's Pennsylvania Packet or, the General Advertiser, September 5, 1774; September 19, 1774.

August 29, 1774.
TWELVE POUNDS Reward.

RAN away, last night, from the subscriber, living in Baltimore County, Maryland, near the Falls of Gunpowder, two convict servant men, lately imported to Baltimore, in the ship Aston Hall, John Parker, master. Mark Coe, an Englishman, about 22 years of age, 5 feet 8 or 9 inches high, a middling full face, straight bony fellow, with short brown hair; had on and took with him when he went away, a hat, cut small in the brim and tarred or oiled, two white linen shirts, one red cloth jacket with sleeves, a light coloured ditto, without sleeves, one pair of crocus trousers, one pair of leather breeches, a pair of grey yarn or worsted stockings ribbed, a pair of old shoes nailed round the heels. John Paxman, an Englishman, a weaver by trade, but has been used to go by water, about 25 years of age, 5 feet 6 inches high, a well set fellow, dark eyes, has short hair, quick spoken, has lost part of one of his little fingers, and has lately had a cut over one of his eyes, is a little knock-kneed, and his toes turns very much out; had on and took with him when he went away, a hat much as the above described, osnabrigs shirt, old brown cloth coat, with tar on it, crocus trousers, black ribbed stockings, and old shoes. Whoever takes up said servants, and brings them to the subscriber, or secures them so as the owner may get them again, if 20 miles from home, shall have, Forty Shillings for each, if 40 miles, Four Pounds each, and if 80 miles, the above reward, including what the law allows, paid by   NICHOLAS MERRYMAN.

N. B. It is supposed that both the above servants have forged passes. All masters of vessels are forbid carrying them off at their peril.

The Maryland Journal, and Baltimore Advertiser, September 7, 1774; *The Maryland Gazette*, September 8, 1774. Minor differences between the papers. The *Gazette* shows a reward of Forty Shillings at a distance of 20 miles.

FIVE POUNDS REWARD.

RAN AWAY in July last, from the subscriber's plantation near North Point, Patapsco Neck, Maryland, a convict servant man, named JOHN DAVIS, a Welshman, and talks very much in that dialect; was imported in the Restoration, Capt. James Thomas, in March last, to Baltimore Town; he is about five feet ten inches high, something slim made, and stoops much in his shoulders, had on when he went away, an old oznabrigs shirt, crocus trowsers, and an old felt hat; has lately had his hair cut off. Whoever takes up said servant and returns him to his master, or secures him so that he may be had again, shall, if taken out of the county, receive THIRTY SHILLINGS, if out of the province THREE POUNDS, and if 100 miles from home, the above Reward, and reasonable charges if brought home, paid by   THOMAS TODD.

Dunlap's Pennsylvania Packet or, the General Advertiser, September 12, 1774; October 3, 1774; October 17, 1774.

Chester, September 5, 1774.
WAS committed into my custody, on suspicion of being runaway servants, the following people, viz. *Patrick Dunn*, 18 or 19 years old, about 5 feet 3 inches high, some freckles; confesses he is a servant to Thomas Dalton, of Red-creek, in Baltimore county, Maryland. *Darby Lehan*, about 20 years of age, 5 feet 4 or 5 inches high, darkish hair, and pitted with the smallpox. *Nicholas Welch*, 19 or 20 years of age, 5 feet 6 or 7 inches high, brownish hair; they confess to be servants to Richard Thomas and John Thomas, in Frederick county, Maryland. *John David*, about 20 years of age, 5 feet 3 or 4 inches high, pretty much pitted with the smallpox; confesses to be a servant to Philip Renshaw. *John M'Daniel*, alias *M'Conel*, about 19 or 20 years of age, 5 feet 7 inches high, lightish hair; confesses to be a servant to James Moorehead, of Lancaster county. *John Woods*, about 25 years of age, 6 feet high, red hair. *Robert Irwin*, confesses he run away from on board a the ship Renown, [*sic*] a Carpenter by trade, and is advertised by John Pringle, of Philadelphia. A Negroe, named *Cato*....Their masters are desired to come, pay charges, and take them away, in three weeks from this date, or they will be discharged, paying their fees.   JOEL WILLIS, Goaler.

The Pennsylvania Gazette, September 14, 1774. See *The Maryland Journal, and Baltimore Advertiser*, August 24, 1774, for Darby Lehan/Linnaham and Walch/Welch.

Harford county, Joppa, August 15, 1774.
THREE POUNDS REWARD.
RAN away last night from the subscriber, an English servant man, named Thomas Painter, about 30 years of age, 5 feet 6 or 7 inches high, of a sandy complexion, very short hair a good deal on the reddish cast; it is thought he took a light coloured wig with him, which in all probability he will wear; hath sore lips, his hands very much freckled, stoops in his shoulders, his legs are a good deal swelled, owing (he says) to his being confined on ship-board, and is battle-hamm'ed; had on and took with him, a light coloured cloth coat, with a velvet cape much worn, a black cloth jacket without sleeves, buckskin breeches, and coarse linen ditto, very greasy, Irish linen shirt, ozenbrigs ditto, grey ribb'd worsted stockings, good shoes and plated

buckles, castor hat half worn. Whoever takes up and brings home said servant, if five miles or under, from home twenty shillings; if ten miles thirty thillings; if twenty miles, forty shillings; if thirty miles, fifty shillings; and if fifty miles, the above reward paid by
ALEXANDER COWAN.
The Maryland Gazette, September 15, 1774; September 29, 1774. See *The Pennsylvania Gazette,* September 21, 1774.

FOUR POUNDS REWARD.

July 30, 1774.
RAN away from the subscriber, (living in Dorchester county, in Maryland), an indented [ ]servant man, named Samuel Trayner, about 26 or 28 years of age, is about five feet ten or eleven inches high, much burned with the sun in the face, and on his shoulders, has light blue eyes, and a very simple look when in liquor, which he will always be if he can get it: he is a ditcher and flax-dresser by trade, but very handy at many other things; he had on when he went away, a deep blue broad cloth coat and waistcoat, with white raised metal buttons, a pair of plush breeches, an osnabrig shirt, a pair of thread stockings, and half worn shoes. Whoever secures the said servant, that I may get him again, shall have the above reward, paid by
THOMAS HILL AIREY.
The Maryland Gazette, September 15, 1774.

Alexandria, 27th July 1774.
RAN away, on Sunday evening last, an Irish servant boy, named Daniel Kennedy, about 16 years old, fresh complexion, light brown hair, inclining to curl, small of his age; had on and took with him, one wilton and one brown holland coat, one nankeen, one striped holland, and one brown holland waistcoat, two pair of nankeen, and one pair of drilling breeches, a blue duffil great coat, silver shoe, knee, and hat buckles, (nearly all new) beaver hat, with shirts, stockings, trowsers, &c. It is supposed he went away with his uncle, who lives on or near Choptank, on the eastern shore, who is master of a small bay-craft. As the boy has been very ungrateful in going away, and the uncle very wrong in assisting him, I do promise the uncle if he brings home the boy in a reasonable time, not to take that advantage the law has given me over him; and if he does not, I will give a reward of five pounds to any person that will secure the boy, that I may get him, and give such information that will be sufficient to bring the uncle to justice; or three pounds for the boy only. JAMES HENDRICKS.
The Maryland Gazette, September 15, 1774.

EIGHT DOLLARS REWARD.

RAN AWAY from the subscriber, living near Harford county, Maryland, an indented servant man, named JAMES MURRAY, born in Ireland, speaks on the North country dialect, about five feet five inches high, forty years old, swarthy complexion, grey hairs mostly on the fore part of his head, thick lips; he took a tow shirt, and a pair of trowsers, old English castor hat with holes in the brim, no shoes or stockings, but perhaps may have got some from some person. He came from Ireland in August 1773, with Captain Morrison, from Newry, and consigned to Joseph Carson, in Philadelphia, says he has been a Pedlar and Flax-dresser in the Jerseys and New-England. Whoever takes up and secures said servant, so that his master may have him again, shall have the above reward, and reasonable charges, if brought home, paid by
HUGH JEFFERY.

N. B. it is thought he will go off by water, therefore, all masters of vessels are foprbid to harbour or carry him off at their peril. He took two jackets, one a brown lapelled ratteen, without sleeves, the other contry cloth of a lightish colour, with sleeves. Perhaps he may change his cloathing as it is thought he has more cloaths than what is mentioned.

Dunlap's Pennsylvania Packet or, the General Advertiser, September 19, 1774; October 3, 1774. See *The Pennsylvania Gazette,* September 21, 1774, and *The Maryland Journal, and Baltimore Advertiser*, October 26, 1774.

THREE POUNDS REWARD.

MADE his escape from the subscriber, on Sunday the 28th of August last, WILLIAM HOLLIS, this country born, about 33 years of age, 5 feet 8 inches high, well set, of a swarthy complexion, and has lost two of his fore teeth; he is very fond of strong liquor, and a remarkable gambler; had on and took with him, a straw coloured velvet suit of cloaths, a new castor hat, thread stockings, and old shoes. Whoever apprehends said HOLLIS, and brings him to the subscriber, shall receive the above reward.
JOHN HAMILTON,   Sheriff of Caecil County.

Dunlap's Pennsylvania Packet or, the General Advertiser, September 19, 1774; October 3, 1774; October 24, 1774.

SIX POUNDS REWARD.

September 19, 1774.

RAN away from the subscribers, living near Westminister town, in Frederick county, an indented servant men, the one named *Charles Justice*, about 5 feet 6 inches high, slender made, yellow hair tied behind: had on

when he went away, a tow linen shirt, with flax linen sleeves, a black silk handkerchief, a pair of two trousers, a striped linsey jacket with sleeves, and a short blue jacket with sleeves, a pair of new shoes, with iron buckles in them, and an old felt hat, has a scar on his upper lip, and born in Ireland. The other named *Ralph Lawson*, a stout well set fellow, born in England, about 5 feet 3 inches high, has short yellow curled hair: had on when he went away, an old flax shirt, a yellow striped silk handkerchief, something worn, tow trousers, a short blue jacket with sleeves and leather buttons, a pair of old shoes, with one brass and one iron buckle, and a new felt hat. Whoever takes up said servants, and secures them, so that their masters may have them again, shall have, if 10 miles from home, 20 shillings; if 20 miles, 30 shillings, if 40 miles, 50 shillings for each, and if out of the province the above reward, including what the law allows, and reasonable charges paid, if brought home, by
PHILIP WERHLE, & JACOB GRAMER.
N. B. All masters of vessels are forewarned carrying them off at their peril.
The Maryland Journal, and Baltimore Advertiser, September 21, 1774.

September 12, 1774.
RAN away, on the 12th of June, from the subscriber, living near Risteau's-Town in Baltimore county, a convict servant man named *John Harris*, about 5 feet 3 or 4 inches high, thin visaged, pock marked, high nosed, has light brown hair, and is slender made: had on when he went away, an oznabrigs shirt and trousers much worn, and old felt hat, old kersey jacket, old shoes with buckles in them: it is probable he may forge a pass and change his name, as he has run away several times before. Whoever takes up the said servant and secures him in any gaol within this province, or brings him to his master, shall have, if 10 miles from home, 20 shillings, if 20 miles 40 shillings, and if out of the province 3 pounds including what the law allows, and reasonable charges paid if brought home.
JOHN WELLS, son of CHARLES,
 or
EDWARD WONN.
The Maryland Journal, and Baltimore Advertiser September 21, 1774.
See *The Maryland Journal, and the Baltimore Advertiser*, From Saturday, June 11, to Saturday, June 18, 1774.

September 5, 1774.
SIX POUNDS Reward.
RAN away from the subscriber, living in Harford county, near the blue rocks, two English convict servant men, viz, *James Wilkes*, about 22 years of age, 5 feet 7 inches high, short black hair, straight and well made, but has

a halt in his walk; had on a blue sailor's jacket, beaver hat bound with black velvet, with two holes burnt in it, dirty flax shirt, a pair of tow trousers, and a silk handkerchief.

Richard M'Boise 28 years of age, 5 feet 8 inches high; had on when he went off, a white flannel jacket, one brown under ditto, short tow trousers, a small hat bound round with back binding, old shoes with plated buckles in them, and he has the palsy. Whoever takes up said servants, and brings them to Mr. *George M'Candles*, living in Baltimore, or to the subscriber, shall have 3 pounds for either, or 6 pounds for both, paid by
PATRICK ROCK.

The Maryland Journal, and Baltimore Advertiser, September 21, 1774. See *Dunlap's Pennsylvania Packet or, the General Advertiser*, October 10, 1774.

FIVE POUNDS REWARD.

September 12, 1774.
RAN away from the subscriber, living in Cumberland Township, York county, a Scotch servant man, named *John M'Donald*, about 5 feet 6 inches high, of a dark complexion, has black curled hair, speaks in the Scotch dialect, and is a miller by trade: Had on and took with him, when he went away, a felt hat, blue camblet coat, 2 new linen shirts, check trousers, blue stockings, blue velvet jacket, new shoes and plated buckles, a silver watch, and a good fiddle.

Whoever takes up said servant and secures him, so that his master may have him again, shall be entitled to the above reward, and reasonable charges, paid by   JOHN FLEMING.

The Maryland Journal, and Baltimore Advertiser, September 21, 1774.

EIGHT DOLLARS Reward.

RUN away from the subscriber, living near Harford town, in Harford county, Maryland, an indented servant man, named James Murray, born in Ireland, speaks on the North country dialect, about 5 feet 5 inches high, 40 years old, swarthy complexion, grey hairs, mostly on the fore part of his head, thick lips; he took a tow shirt, and a pair of trowsers, old English castor hat, with two holes in the brim, no shoes or stockings, but perhaps may have got some from some person. He came from Ireland, in August 1773, with Captain Morrison, from Newry, and consigned to Joseph Carson, in Philadelphia, says he has been a pedlar and flax dresser in the Jerseys and New England. Whoever takes up and secures said servant, so that his master may have him again, shall have the above reward, and reasonable charges, if brought home, paid by HUGH JEFFERY.

N.B. It is thought he will go off by water, therefore, all masters of vessels are forbid to harbour or carry him off at their peril. He took two jackets, one a brown lappelled ratteen, without sleeves, the other country cloth, of a lightish colour, with sleeves; perhaps he may change his clothes, as it is thought he has more clothes than what are mentioned.
September 13, 1774.

The Pennsylvania Gazette, September 21, 1774. See *Dunlap's Pennsylvania Packet or, the General Advertiser*, September 19, 1774, *The Maryland Journal, and Baltimore Advertiser*, October 26, 1774.

Harford county, August 15, 1774.
THREE POUNDS Reward.

RUN away from the subscriber, an English servant man, named *Thomas Painter*, alias *Robert Harvey*, about 30 years of age, 5 feet 6 or 7 inches high, of a sandy complexion, very light coloured wig with him, which in all probability he will wear; hath sore lips, his hands very much freckled, stoops in his shoulders, his legs are a good deal swelled, owing (he says) to his being confined on ship-board, and is battle-hammed; had on, and took with him, a light-coloured cloth coat, with a velvet cape, much worn, a black cloth jacket, without sleeves, buckskin breeches, and coarse linen ditto, very greasy, Irish linen shirt, ozenbrigs ditto, grey ribbed worsted stockings, good shoes, plated buckles, and a half worn castor hat. Whoever takes up and secures said servant, so as his master may get him again, shall have, if 5 miles or under from home, Twenty Shillings; if 10 miles, Thirty Shillings; if 20 miles, Forty Shillings; if 30 miles, Fifty Shillings; and if 50 miles, the above reward, paid by ALEXANDER COWAN. *The Pennsylvania Gazette,* September 21, 1774. See *The Maryland Gazette*, September 15, 1774.

TEN POUNDS Reward.

RUN away, the 6th day of August, from the subscriber, living in Riestertown, Baltimore county, Maryland, a servant man, named MARK O'BRION, an Irishman, by trade a shoemaker, about 25 years of age, about 5 feet high, red hair, freckled face, full eyed, has a scar over his left eye, round shouldered, stoops pretty much as he walks, speaks very bold, and is a great lover of drink; had on, when he went away, an old grey surtout coat, claret coloured jacket, with a new piece set in the left side of the breast, and old shoes; it is supposed he might steal other clothes, and alter his dress. His wife, Mary O'Brion, went away with him, and took sundry other clothes unknown. All masters of vessels are forewarned not to harbour them. Whoever secures the said servant, in any of his Majesty's goals, so that his master may have him again, if taken 20 miles from home, Twenty Shillings; if 40 miles, Forty Shillings; if our of the province, Five Pounds; and if brought home, the above reward, and reasonable charges, paid by ALEXANDER DAVIS.

The Pennsylvania Gazette, September 21, 1774.

[ ] 9, 1774.
TEN POUNDS REWARD.
RAN away from his bail, living in Dorchester county, Maryland, a servant man named Edwin Bean, about twenty years of age, five feet six or seven inches high, well set, full faced down look, dark hair tied behind: had on a brown surtout with gilt buttons and claret coloured binding, a light coloured brown cloth coat and a pair of thickset breeches, he is a tailor by trade; he took with him a dark bay mare, about fourteen hands high, paces very well, and had some white saddle spots on her back. Whoever takes up the said runaway, or mare, and secures them, so that the owner may get them again, shall receive twenty dollars reward, or five pounds for either of them, and if brought home, the above reward and all reasonable charges, paid by me JAMES CONNEY.

The Maryland Gazette, September 22, 1774.

September 19, 1774.
TEN POUNDS REWARD.
RAN away last night, from the subscriber living in Baltimore county, in the fork of Gunpowder, a convict servant man, named John Rice, has lost one of his eyes, has been in the country about two months, about five feet seven inches high, middle aged, had on and took with him a small hat with the brim bound, a brown coat, blue jacket, one striped ditto, a pair of light coloured breeches, white cotton stockings, white worsted and brown thread ditto, white linen shirt, oznabrigs ditto and trousers, a pair of double soled shoes stitched round the quarters, a silk handkerchief. He took with him a bay mare about 13 hands high, and old saddle. Whoever takes up and secures the said servant and mare, so that I may get them again, shall have if 10 miles from home three pounds, if out of the country five pounds, and if 100 miles the above reward, and reasonable charges if brought home, and two thirds of the above reward for the servant alone, paid by
JOHN STEVENSON, son of Edward.
N. B. All masters of vessels are forbid to carry him off at their peril.

The Maryland Gazette, September 22, 1774; September 29, 1774; October 13, 1774; October 27, 1774; November 7, 1774; *Dunlap's Pennsylvania Packet or, the General Advertiser*, October 3, 1774; October 24, 1774; November 7, 1774. Minor differences between the papers. In *Dunlap's* the ad is headlined with the date September 17, 1774.

RAN away from the subscriber on the 11th of this instant, an Irish convict servant man, named Michael Conray, about five feet eight inches high, about twenty-one or two years of age, pitted with the small-pox and freckled, full faced and pale complexion, light grey eyes, brown hair tied behind; had on and took with him an old castor hat of the new fashion, cocked up behind, an old dark coloured bearskin coat with long skirts and turned down cape, a jacket with blue foreparts, the back dark bearskin with short skirts, old black breeches much patched, a pair of crocus trousers, two old check shirts, a pair of old thread stockings, a pair of old pumps or brougs, a sensible fellow of few words, smooth tongue, and on the Irish dialect. Whoever shall take up the said runaway, and bring him to the subscriber, living about seven miles from Snowden's iron-works on the Point Branch, near the new chapel Prince George's county, shall receive a reward of twenty shillings if ten miles from home, forty shillings if more than ten, and three pounds if out of the province, besides what the law allows, or brings him to Otho French, near the head of South River, Anne-Arundel county, shall receive the reward abovesaid.
ISAAC SHORT.
The Maryland Gazette, September 22, 1774; October 6, 1774; October 13, 1774.

RAN away from the ship Patty, laying at Lower Marlborough, two servants, the one a hair dresser and barber, of low stature, with his own short strait hair; had on a remarkable short coat and sailors blue drawers, white stockings, his shoes out at the toes, and wants a tooth in the front of his mouth, his hat is cut round, named John Willson. The other a cabinet maker, middle stature, with his own curled flaxen hair, fresh coloured; had on a blue coat with metal buttons, black waistcoat, and breeches, speaks Scotch, aged about 22 years, named John Smith. Whoever takes up the said servants, and secures them, so as they may be received again by the said master, shall receive a reward of 20 shillings each, over and above what the law allows, with all charges.
THOMAS AYRE, at Lower Marlborough.
The Maryland Gazette, September 22, 1774.

FIFTEEN POUNDS REWARD.
RAN AWAY from the subscriber, living on Elkridge, near Caroll's Manor, in Ann Arundle county, on the 16th of this inst. (September) two convict

servant men, viz. THOMAS FRANKLIN, an Englishman, about 5 feet 8 or 9 inches high, about 23 years old, with short light hair, has been lately sick, and is weakly at present.—TIMOTHY COLLINS, an Irishman, well set, chunky, well looking fellow, about 5 feet 6 or 7 inches high, about 26 years old, has short black hair inclining to be grey: Perhaps they may change their names. They took with them sundry cloaths, viz. one light blue broadcloth coat patched on the right arm, much worn, and split in the left elbow, one purple coloured broadcloth coat and waistcoat much faded, two striped gingham jackets, one redish coloured Bath coating surtout coat, two pair of Russia drab breeches, four or five Irish linen shirts, three or four pair of thread stockings, one old castor hat without loops or band, one or two pair of English shoes, one pair of pinchbeck buckles, one pair of leather spatterdashes, and perhaps other things not known.—It is supposed they took two horses, bridles and saddles, as they were missing on the 19th inst. viz. one bay horse about thirteen and a half hands high, branded on the near shoulder R. B. shod all round, has a star in his forehead, thick bushy mane that hangs chiefly on the near side. The other a dark brown horse, about fourteen hands high, branded on the near shoulder or buttock G. has a remarkable knot near as big as a hen's egg on the inside of one of his hind legs, and is unshod. Whoever takes up the said servants, and secures them, and gives notice so that their master may get them again, shall have Forty Shillings for each man, and Fifteen Shillings for each horse; if taken up and brought home, if about 40 miles from home, Fifty Shillings for each man and Twenty Shillings for each horse; if out of the province and above an hundred miles, Four Pounds for each man and Twenty-five Shillings for each horse; and if above 150 miles from home, Six Pounds for each man and Thirty Shillings for each horse, including what the law allows, paid by NICHOLAS WATKINS.

Dunlap's Pennsylvania Packet or, the General Advertiser, September 26, 1774; October 17, 1774. See *The Maryland Gazette*, October 13, 1774.

Baltimore, September 13, 1774.
EIGHT DOLLARS REWARD.
RAN AWAY yesterday morning, from the subscriber, living in Gay-street, Baltimore, a servant man, named WILLIAM PIERS, a printer, about 20 years of age, near 6 feet high, pale complexion, thin visage, a simple look, has large grey eyes, stoop shouldered, his chin is remarkable, which turns up and forms a dent; he is remarkably slim and tall, has long hands and fingers; he has but little courage, and is easily scared: he takes a good deal of snuff, is fond of liquor and a great liar: Had on and took with him, 2 check shirts, one old, the other new, a pair of striped linen trowsers and oznabrugs ditto, a short purple jean coat much faded and linen with brown

holland, blue beaver coating jacket bound, a pair of new calf-skin shoes with one of the straps pieced; had a black silk stock and a spotted pocket handkerchief, a coarse hat bound with worsted binding. I believe he has other cloathes than those described, and has some cash with him. Whoever takes up the said fellow, and brings him to the subscriber, or secures him in any goal, so that I get him again, shall have the above reward and reasonable charges, paid by
ENOCH STORY.

N. B. He writes an extraordinary hand and very likely will forge a pass. It is thought he will make towards Philadelphia. All masters of vessels are forbid to harbour or carry him off at their peril.

Dunlap's Pennsylvania Packet or, the General Advertiser, September 26, 1774.

THREE POUNDS Reward.
RUN away from the subscriber, living in Frederick county, Maryland, an indented Irish servant man, named Richard O'Donovan, 22 years old, 5 feet 11 inches high, of a sandy complexion, red beard, and light brown hair, which he wears tied in a club, he is freckled; he came in the brig Mermaid, Richard Briscoe, master, from Limerick, Sept. 19, 1772. Had on, and took with him, an old lightish coloured coat, mended on the breast, with large metal buttons, and lined with lincey, two town shirts, tow trowsers, tow drawers, thick Indian dressed leather breeches, made very long, an old felt hat, scolloped in the brim, coarse mixed yarn stockings, black and white wool, coarse shoes, tied, besides several books, some of them Latin, and one Dutch grammar; it is likely he may pass for a schoolmaster, having some Latin, and a middling share of arithmetic, and can do something at the taylor's trade, and at the slight of hand. Whoever takes up said servant, and secures him in any goal, shall have the above reward and reasonable charges, paid by
July 5, 1774.   W. YATES.

The Pennsylvania Gazette, September 28, 1774.

RUN away, on the 26th of August last, from the subscriber, living in Caecil county, in the province of Maryland, near Elk Forge, an indented servant man, named James Munks, by trade a Collier, about 5 feet 2 inches high, has short black hair, about 25 years of age, is very much given to liquor; had on, and took with him, a cloth coloured jacket, without sleeves, with a metal button to each corner of the flap, a red flannel ditto, 2 shirts, one of tow the other ozenbrigs, and two pair of trowsers, one ticklenburgh, pretty much patched, the other ozenbrigs, old shoes, tied with strings, and an old felt hat, without lining. It is likely that he may pass for an ostler, and may possibly give a tolerable good description of the country to New York, having inlisted into a regiment which laid there in 1771, from which he got his discharge for being under size. Whoever apprehends the said runaway, and secure him in any goal, shall have the reward of FOUR DOLLARS, and reasonable charges, paid by ROBERT MILLS.

The Pennsylvania Gazette, September 28, 1774

September 26th, 1774.
TEN POUNDS REWARD.
RAN away yesterday morning from the subscribers in Annapolis, two indented servant men, the one named Thomas Salisbury, a coachman, is about 5 feet 8 inches high, short yellow coloured hair, a very impudent fellow, with an indifferent sour countenance: Had on, and took with him, a white drilling coat and breeches, with white metal buttons, several white shirts, brown worsted stockings, a pair of new thin pumps, and a gold laced hat. The property of Richard Lee. The other an Englishman, named John Rhodes, born in London, a carpenter by trade, is about 25 years of age, five feet 7 inches high, bow-legged, of a swarthy complexion, and short black hair. Had on a suit of superfine broad mixed coloured cloth that had been lately turned, white metal buttons, two or three white shirts and an old beaver hat. The property of Philip Thomas Lee.

Whoever takes up said servants, and secures them in any jail within this province, so that their masters may get them again, shall receive six pounds reward, or three pounds for either; and if taken out of the province ten pounds for both, or in proportion, and reasonable charges if brought to Annapolis.   RICHARD LEE   PHILIP THOMAS LEE.

The Maryland Gazette, September 29, 1774.

SIX POUNDS REWARD.

September 22, 1774.
RAN away from the subscriber, living near Baltimore-town, a convict servant man, named John Baver, about 24 years of age, 5 feet 7 inches high, has short brown hair, and brown skin much burnt with the sun: had on and took with him, a reddish coloured cloth coat and jacket, lined with white, a pair of linen twilled breeches, osnabrig trousers, osnabrig shirt, white Irish linen ditto, a pair of old grey worsted stockings, a pair of country made black and white coarse ditto, a pair of country made coarse shoes, tied with strings, an old felt hat, some cash, a wallet, and some other trifles. Whoever takes up the said servant, and secures him, so as I may get him again, shall receive if taken 10 miles from home 40 shillings, if 20 miles 3 pounds, if

100 miles 5 pounds, if 200 miles the above reward, and reasonable charges if brought home, paid by
HENRY STEVENSON, son of Edward.
The Maryland Gazette, September 29, 1774.

MADE their escape from the subscriber, on Sunday, the 3d of October instant, two convict servants, as he was taking them from Philadelphia to Maryland, near Chester, one named JAMES WELKIS, an Englishman, about 5 feet 9 inches, with a blue jacket, coarse shirt and trowsers; the other named RICHARD DARROCTT, having a line jacket, coarse shirt and breeches, all very bad, no hat, a new pair of shoes, one tied with a string, the other buckled. They are both dirty fellows. Whoever takes up said runaways, and delivers them to any of his Majesty's goals, so as their masters may get them again, shall receive FIVE POUNDS reward, paid by Doctor DAVID BENFIELD, in Harford county, Maryland.
The Pennsylvania Gazette, October 5, 1774.

FIVE POUNDS REWARD.

RUN away from the subscriber, in Baltimore county, the 18th of September last, a servant man, named John Coughlen, *about 5 feet 6 or 8 inches high, his apparel uncertain, as I have heard he has changed them since he went away; he is a lusty well looking man, has short black hair, muddy coloured grey eyes, large legs, stands and walks straight, has a good address, and is a smooth artful fellow in his discourse, speaks good English, but may be known to be an Irishman by his discourse and behaviours, Whoever takes up said servant, and brings him home, shall have the above reward (including what the law allows) and reasonable charges, paid by*
JAMES WELSH.
*** He was seen in Baltimore town the day he went away.
The Pennsylvania Gazette, October 5, 1774. See *The Maryland Journal, and Baltimore Advertiser*, December 26, 1774.

SIX POUNDS Reward.

RUN away from the Antietam Forge, Frederick county, Maryland, on the 19th of September 1774, *two servant men, viz.* William Miller, *an indented servant, about 5 feet 10 inches high, about 30 years of age, a stout well set fellow, round visage, of a swarthy complexion, is pitted with the smallpox, and has short brown hair; has been in the country before, and is well acquainted with it; had on, and took with him, two ozenbrigs, shirts and trowsers, a coarse fearnought jacket, a new felt hat, and a pair of country made shoes.* John Wilcox, *a convict servant, from England, 5 feet 10 inches high, about 27 years of age, a tall slim fellow, round visage, smooth face, of a swarthy complexion, and has short brown hair; had on and took with him the same kind of clothes, as Miller's; it is likely they may change their apparel, as they stole two and half yards of mixed broadcloth, two white shirts, two silk handkerchiefs, a pair of white stockings, a brown jacket, a bearskin coat, and a blue coat with metal buttons, and several other things unknown. Whoever secures the said servants, so as their masters may have them again, shall have the above reward, paid by* DANIEL *and* SAMUEL HUGHES.

The Pennsylvania Gazette, October 5, 1774. *The* New-York Gazette; and the Weekly Mercury, October 10, 1774; October 17, 1774. Minor differences between the papers. *The* New-York Gazette *spells the second man's name as* Willcox.

TEN POUNDS Reward.

RUN away, on the 25th of September 1774, an indented servant man, named Marsh Sowerbutts, *an Englishman, a sawyer by trade, about 5 feet 9 or 10 inches high, of a dark complexion, dark brown hair, cut short; walks stooping, a great lover of liquor, has a blackguard way of expressing himself, when he should say yes, he says 'Tis all That; he had on, and took with him, a dark bearskin surtout coat, a thickset under ditto, white flannel jacket, greasy leather breeches, old ribbed stockings, old shoes, odd buckles, an old felt hat, one white shirt, and one ozenbrigs ditto. Whoever takes up said servant, and secures him, so that his master may get him again, shall have, if taken 20 miles from home, 30s. if 40 miles 50s. if 60 miles 3l. if 100 miles 5l. and if 200 miles 10l. paid by* DAVID BENFIELD, *living in Harford county, Maryland, near the Upper Cross Roads.*

The Pennsylvania Gazette, October 5, 1774.

TEN POUNDS REWARD.

RAN away on the 18th of July from the subscriber, living near Elk-Ridge landing, Anne-Arundel county, Maryland, two convict servant men, viz. Thomas Boucher, an Englishman, born in West-Chester, by trade a blacksmith, about 30 years of age, 5 feet 4 or 5 inches high, short curled red hair, freckled face and pock-marked, with a blemish in one of his eyes: had on and took with him gray fearnought jacket, gray cloth lappelled ditto without sleeves, two osnabrig shirt and trousers, country made shoes, and felt hat.

Laurance Fisher, born in the west of England, and speaks in that dialect, about 5 feet 2 or 3 inches high, short red hair, red beard, wide mouth, and thick red lips; had on a cotton jacket, osnabrig shirt and

trousers, country made shoes and felt hat, supposed to have a forest cloth jacket faced and turned up with red. Whoever takes up the said runaways, and secures them, so that they may be had again, shall receive the above reward, or five pounds for either, and reasonable charges paid if brought home, by   CALEB OWINGS.
The Maryland Gazette, October 6, 1774; October 20, 1774; October 27, 1774; November 7, 1774; December 1, 1774.

September 28, 1774.
COMMITTED to my custody as a runaway, a white servant man, who says he belongs to Edward Garrett, of Frederick county, he is a thin spare man, has on an old osnabrig shirt and an old jacket and breeches, has a pair of stockings on without feet, no shoes. Likewise a small negro man who appears to be old....Their masters are desired to take then away, and pay charge to   WILLIAM NOKE, sheriff.
The Maryland Gazette, October 6, 1774; October 20, 1774.

Maryland, September 25, 1774.
FIFTEEN POUNDS REWARD.
RAN away last night from Dorsey's forge, 3 servant men, viz. William George, born in England, about 34 years old, about 5 feet 7 inches high; he has a down look, light coloured short hair, pock marked, round shouldered, and has had his left wrist broke, which occasions it to be much larger than his right; he is a carpenter and joiner by trade: had on and took with him, one check shirt, one osnabrig ditto, old leather breeches, light blue jacket without sleeves, small round hat bound with black worsted binding, and has a small piece of crape tied round the crown, a pair of ribbed worsted stockings and a pair of pumps with steel buckles. Had on an iron collar.

Solomon Burnham, born in Yorkshire and speaks in that dialect; he is about 26 years of age, about 5 feet 10 inches high, swarthy complexion, down look, short black curled hair: had on and took with him, one osnabrig shirt, blue grey jacket without sleeves, leather breeches, a coarse hat about half worn, a pair of yarn stockings, and one pair of shoes and buckles; he professes himself to be a compleat farmer. Had on an iron collar.

Samuel Chapman, an Englishman, 28 years of age, 5 feet 7 inches high, a lusty well made fellow, a little round shouldered, he is of a swarthy complexion, has a large boney face, thick lips, and a very full set of teeth: had on and took with him a cloth jacket, an osnabrig shirt, a check ditto, osnabrig trousers, 2 pair of stockings, new shoes with buckles, and a new felt hat.

Whoever takes up said servants, and brings them to the subscribers, shall have if 20 miles from home thirty shillings, if 30 miles forty shillings, and if 60 miles five pounds for each (including what the law allows) and reasonable charges.

SAMUEL DORSEY, jun.   EDWARD NORWOOD.

The Maryland Gazette, October 6, 1774; October 27, 1774; November 10, 1774; November 17, 1774; December 1, 1774; *Dunlap's Pennsylvania Packet or, the General Advertiser,* October 10, 1774; October 31, 1774; November 7, 1774; November 13, 1774; December 12, 1774; January 9, 1775. Minor differences between the papers.

SIXTEEN DOLLARS REWARD.

RAN AWAY on the 4th of September last, from the subscribers living near the Blue Rocks, in Baltimore county, two English convict servant men; one named JAMES WILKS, about 28 years of age, a well looking man, about 5 feet 8 inches high, has short black hair, and little of the palsy which is discernable when he stands; had on when he went away, a coarse white shirt, short blue jacket made sailors fashion, tow trowsers, and a felt hat bound with tape. The other named RICHARD DAROUGH, but may change his name to BOYES, about 5 feet 6 or 7 inches high, has short curled black hair, and talks fast; had on a white flannel jacket made sailors fashion, a short pair of tow trowsers, a hat bound with tape, and a pair of pumps with plated buckles. Whoever takes up and secures said servants, so that their masters may have them again, shall have the above Reward, and reasonable charges, paid by

PATRICK ROCK.   JAMES M'BOYES.

N. B. All masters of vessels are forbid to carry them off at their peril.

Dunlap's Pennsylvania Packet or, the General Advertiser, October 10, 1774; November 7, 1774; November 28, 1774. See *The Maryland Journal, and Baltimore Advertiser,* September 21, 1774.

Caecil County, September 22, 1774.
THREE POUNDS REWARD,

ESCAPED from the subscriber, a certain JAMES PEN, alias WINHAM, an Englishman, he is about 5 feet 8 inches high, well made, dark complexion, short brown hair, one of his arms is a little crooked, and he chiefly uses his left hand, had on and took with him an oznabrigs shirt, a linen ditto, a pair of nankeen breeches, a pair of old leather ditto, a pair of oznabrigs trowsers, dark coloured mix'd wilton coat, nankeen waistcoat, yellow striped silk handkerchief, boy's new felt hat, new pumps, and sundry other things now known. Whoever takes up said run-away, and secures him in any of his

Majesty's gaols so that the subscriber may have him again, shall receive the above reward, paid by JOHN HAMILTON, Sheriff.

Dunlap's Pennsylvania Packet or, the General Advertiser, October 10, 1774; November 7, 1774; November 14, 1774.

July 6, 1774.
TEN POUNDS REWARD.

RAN away from the subscriber, living in Baltimore county, near Joseph Scott's mill, in Gunpowder Barrens, Maryland, an English convict servant man, named Allis Ashworth, a weaver by trade, born in Yorkshire, about 30 years of age, 5 feet 10 inches high, he is a very lusty man and stoop shouldered, sandy coloured hair, red eyes and beard, he talks slow and much on the brogue, had on and took when he went away, a blue double breasted jacket with sleeves, an old white under ditto, an old osnabrig shirt, a pair of new tow trousers, a new felt, [*sic*] and a pair of new shoes. Whoever brings the said fellow to the subscriber, or secures him so that his master may get him again, shall have the above reward, and reasonable charges if brought home, paid by MATTHIAS WISNOR.

N. B. It is supposed he may change his name to Thomas Owen, and probably may have other cloaths than what he ran away with.

The Maryland Gazette, October 13, 1774; October 27, 1774; November 10, 1774.

September 29, 1774.

COMMITTED to the jail of Charles county, as a runaway, a convict servant man, who calls himself by the name of Thomas Franklin, and says he belongs to Nicholas Watkins, on Elk-Ridge; there was a printed advertisement found with him, signed by the name of said Watkins, in which Franklin is truly described as to his person and cloathing, so that I think there can be no doubt but he is the same person mentioned in the said advertisement. Timothy Collins, who is also named in the same advertisement, Franklin says he parted with him near Piscataway, with an intention to proceed downward, in order to get on board some ship. The owner of said Franklin, is desired to take them [*sic*] away, and pay charges to WILLIAM HANSON, sheriff.

The Maryland Gazette, October 13, 1774; October 20, 1774. See *Dunlap's Pennsylvania Packet or, the General Advertiser,* September 26, 1774.

FORTY SHILLINGS REWARD.
RAN AWAY on the night of the 5th inst. (October) from the subscriber, near the Lower Cross Roads, Harford county, Maryland, an indented native

Irishman, who has been in this country but a few months, is from the west of Ireland and has the brogue much upon his tongue, about 24 years old, and about five feet eleven inches high, strong made, has short red hair, sandy complexion, is blind of his right eye, marked with the small-pox, his face remarkably ordinary, and does not commonly look at a person when speaking to him: Had on an old black frize coat much worn, a pepper and salt wilton jacket, both of which are too little for him, an oznabrig shirt, new buckskin breeches, milled country-made blue stockings, and a pair of half worn seal-skin shoes. It is supposed he took with him some buck or doe-skins to sell, as he had no money, Whoever brings him to the subscriber, or lodges him in gaol so that he may get him again, shall have the above Reward, from   JACOB LEMMON.

The New-York Gazette; and the Weekly Mercury, October 17, 1774; October 31, 1774; November 7, 1774; *Dunlap's Pennsylvania Packet or, the General Advertiser*, October 17, 1774; *The Pennsylvania Gazette*, October 19, 1774.

SIXTEEN DOLLARS REWARD.

RAN AWAY the eleventh inst. (October) from the subscriber, living in Baltimore county, Maryland, near the falls of Gun-Powder, an English convict servant man, named WILLIAM TRAVERS, has been about three months in the country, twenty-two or twenty-three years of age; five feet five or six inches high, middling full and red faced, a well set fellow, has short light hair, grey eyes, has a large scar on the back of one of his hands, occasioned by a burn;—Had on and took with him, a hat bound with black binding, three oznabrug shirts, cross-barred swanskin jacket with sleeves, blue ditto much patched, four pair of oznabrug trowsers, a pair of leather breeches, a striped silk handkerchief, a pair of old shoes nailed and a pair of plated buckles. Whoever takes up said servant and secures him, so that his master may have him again, shall have, if twenty miles from home FORTY SHILLINGS, if forty miles, FOUR POUNDS; if eighty miles the above reward; including what the law allows and reasonable charges if brought home, paid by   NICHOLAS MERRYMAN, jun.

N. B. All masters of vessels and others are forewarned not to harbour or carry off said servant, at their peril.

Dunlap's Pennsylvania Packet or, the General Advertiser, October 24, 1774; November 14, 1774; November 21, 1774; November 28, 1774; *The New-York Gazette; and the Weekly Mercury*, November 7, 1774; November 14, 1774. Minor differences between the papers.

FIFTEEN POUNDS REWARD.

RAN AWAY from the subscriber, living on North Point, Patapsco River, near Baltimore town, Maryland, on the first of July, 1773, an Irish servant man named THOMAS DOYL, about 22 years of age, 5 feet 8 or 9 inches, a likely well made fellow, pitted with the small-pox, lisps in his speech, and has light brown hair; had on when he went away, a white country cloth kersey fulled jacket, and a short red under one without sleeves, a pair of white kersey breeches, oznabrug shirt, and an old castor hat much worn. He was since taken and put into York gaol, and made his escape from Conrad Miller, of York county, on his way home, about the first of August, 1773; it is probable that he passes for a freeman, as I have heard that he was some time between York and Susquehannah Ferry. Whoever secures said the servant, so that he may be had again, shall receive if 100 miles from home, SIX POUNDS, if 150 miles SEVEN POUNDS TEN SHILLINGS, if 200 miles TEN POUNDS, if 250 miles TWELVE POUNDS, and if 300 miles the above Reward, and reasonable charges if brought home, paid by
THOMAS TODD.

Dunlap's Pennsylvania Packet or, the General Advertiser, October 24, 1774; October 31, 1774; November 7, 1774. See *The Maryland Journal, and the Baltimore Advertiser*, From Saturday, October 16, to Saturday, October 23, 1773.

TWELVE DOLLARS Reward.

Harford County, September 11, 1774.

RAN away from the subscriber, living near Harford town, Maryland, an Irish indented servant man, named *James Murray*, about 40 years of age, about 5 feet 5 inches high, of a swarthy complexion, a down look when spoken to, speaks in the north country dialect, has thick lips, and is addicted to strong liquor; he formerly practised peddling, and understands the dressing of flax: had on a whitish Country cloth jacket with sleeves, a brown lapelled under ditto, the back parts white, an old castor hat with 2 holes in the brim, and was without shoes or stockings. 'Tis supposed he went off with a certain *Thomas Joyce*, who is about 5 feet 10 or 11 inches high, has brown hair and a bashful look: had on a blue broad-cloth coat and waistcoat, white russia drab breeches, he rode a small reddish roan gelding, and 'tis supposed they will make for Holstein, in Virginia or Carolina. Whoever takes up the said indented servant man, and secures him so that his master may have him again, shall have the above reward, and reasonable charges if brought home, paid by
HUGH JEFFERY.

The Maryland Journal, and Baltimore Advertiser, October 26, 1774; November 7, 1774, November 16, 1774. See *The Pennsylvania*

Gazette, September 21, 1774, and *Dunlap's Pennsylvania Packet or, the General Advertiser,* September 19, 1774.

THREE POUNDS Reward.

October 8, 1774.

RAN away from the subscriber, living in Carlisle, on the 8th inst. an English servant man, named John Smith, born in Bath, a carpenter by trade, has been two years in the country, is a short well made fellow, about 30 years of age, stoop shouldered, sandy complexion, his hair tied behind, grey eyes, and has a rock in his walk like a sailor: had on a wainstone coloured coat, lined with black linsey, clear metal buttons, a short double breasted jacket with blue fore parts, very coarse, with grey backs, and clear metal buttons, a country linen shirt, tow trousers half worn, shoes with metal buckles in them, a half worn fur hat, cut in the fashion; he has been in the army in Ireland, and took the shipping from Dublin, and landed in Philadelphia. Whoever takes up said servant, and secures him in any Gaol, so that his master may have him again, shall have the above reward, and reasonable charges if brought home, paid by
WILLIAM BROWN.

The Maryland Journal, and Baltimore Advertiser, October 26, 1774; November 7, 1774; November 16, 1774.

TEN POUNDS Reward.

Louden-County, October 5, 1774.

RAN away from the subscriber, on the 3d inst. a convict servant man, named Francis Irwin, a stout well made fellow, about 5 feet 10 inches high, of a sandy complexion, has light short brown hair, two large upper foreteeth, a remarkable hoarse voice, by trade a blacksmith, though he pretends to be a whitesmith: had on a brown cloth coat, white linen jacket, brown or claret coloured breeches, white thread stockings, bound shoes, and a new castor hat. It's propable [sic] he may have an indenture with him, and a pass, under the name of Peter Diglan. Any person who will secure the said servant, so as his master may have him again, shall have the above reward, with charges, paid by   SAMUEL CANBY.

N. B. All masters of vessels are desired not to permit any such person on board.

The Maryland Journal, and Baltimore Advertiser, October 26, 1774; November 7, 1774; November 16, 1774; November 30, 1774.

Chester, October 25, 1774.

WAS committed to my custody, on the 17th instant, a certain *John Kealing*, alias *Wilcocks*, an Englishman, about 25 years old, 5 feet 9 or 10 inches high, of a brown complexion, short brownish hair; says he came from Antietam forge, in Maryland. Also *John Humphreys* and *Elizabeth*, his wife.... JOEL WILLIS, Goaler.

The Pennsylvania Gazette, October 26, 1774; November 16, 1774.

THREE POUNDS Reward.

WENT away from me, the subscriber, living in the upper end of Anne-Arundel county, in the province of Maryland, in the night of the 27th of August 1774, a certain *Thomas Brady,* an indented Irish servant man, about 24 or 25 years of age, about 5 feet 8 or 9 inches high, thin body, pale face, with a good many freckles; has but little beard, of a light sandy colour, almost white, long brown hair, grey eyes, pitted with the smallpox, has had his right thigh broke, which causes him to have a little hitch in his walking, scarce perceivable unless narrowly inspected; he is very talkative, pert and impudent, unless detected in his villainy, and then very abject, with a wonderous pitious look; he also is very subject to get drunk, and much given to swearing; he carried with him a variety of clothes; but has been seen a small distance from the town of Carlisle, in the province of Pennsylvania, about the 13th day of September last, enquiring his way to the Mountains (where his brother was taken up, who ran away with him) he was then dressed in a blue Bath coating coat, and a waistcoat with blue fore parts, and the backs of a brown cloth, a pair of old black everlasting breeches, a new castor hat, fine Irish linen shirt, with an old set broach in the bosom, white thread stockings, two old odd shoes, which have been half soaled, one with five rows of hob nails in the soal, the other without, except in the heel, a pair of plated silver knee buckles, a pair of four-square plain new copper shoe ditto; he had with him a pair of new country made turned pumps, two old ozenbrigs shirts, a pair of new brown roll trowsers, and a pair of old black and white country yarn stockings, in a small wallet on his shoulder; he stole an old indenture of Nicholas Macnamara, assigned to William Gardner, with an assignment on the back to Richard Dorsey, and a discharge from said Richard Dorsey, dated the 25th of July last, also indorsed on the back; also a pass to the said Nicholas Macnamara, wrote on a small slip of paper, dated July 26th last, and signed by Mr. Jonathan Plowman, of Baltimoretown.—The said *Thomas Brady* now passes by the name of Nicholas *Macnamara,* agreeable to the pass and indenture, and says he came from Baltimore-town. Whoever takes up the said servant, and secures him in any goal, so that I get him again, shall receive a reward of Three Pounds, including what the law allows.

October 25, 1774.   REUBEN MERIWETHER.
The Pennsylvania Gazette, October 26, 1774.

TWENTY DOLLARS Reward.
RUN away, on the 29th ult. from the subscribers, living in Hartford county, Maryland, near the Bald Fryer Ferry, on Sasquehanna river, two Irish convict servant men, viz. *John Dudgen*, by trade a shoemaker, about 25 years of age, 5 feet 4 inches high, fair complexion, short brown hair, somewhat pitted with the small-pox; had on, and took with him, a chocolate coloured half-worn broadcloth coat, a striped silk waistcoat, one blue broadcloth ditto, two pair of breeches, one of Russia drab, the other of black sergedenim, [*sic*] two fine and one coarse shirts, 3 pair of stockings, one of ribbed grey worsted, one light blue ditto, and one white thread, two castor hats, one new, the other half-worn, a black silk handkerchief, 3 pair of new shoes, a pair of round broad rimmed silver buckles, and a sett of shoemakers tools. *Joseph Dudgen*, brother to the above, a shoemaker likewise, much of the same complexion, hair partly of the same colour, curls very much, much pitted with the small-pox; had on a brown broadcloth coat, half-worn; it is supposed, as they are brothers, they will divide the clothes between them, to appear as well as they can; it is likely they will change their names, and forge passes, as they are middling good scholars. Whoever takes up said servants, and secures them in any goal, so that their masters may get them again, shall have the above reward, or Ten Dollars for either, and reasonable charges, if brought home, paid by
JAMES MOORE, and JAMES FISHER.
The Pennsylvania Gazette, October 26, 1774; November 23, 1774.

October 26, 1774.
COMMITTED to the jail of Charles county, as a runaway, a white servant man, who, when he first came, called himself James Brown, but since says his name is James Buckinhorne, and that he belongs to George Moore, near Bladensburgh; he is a lusty fellow, appears to be about forty years of age, much pitted with the small-pox; his cloathing two osnabrig shirts, an osnabrig frock and trousers, old shoes, and an old hat. His master is desired to pay charges, and take him away.
W. HANSON, sheriff.
The Maryland Gazette, November 3, 1774; December 1, 1774; December 8, 1774; December 21, 1774; January 5, 1775.

FIFTEEN POUNDS REWARD.

RAN away from the subscribers, living at Annapolis, on the night of the 22d instant, October, three servent men, viz. John Johnson, a Scotchman, by trade a baker, about 33 years of age, a seeming orderly fellow, speaks deliberately, but not much on the Scotch dialect, is 5 feet near 6 or 7 inches high, of a dark complexion, and strait black hair: had on and is supposed to have taken with him, a light coloured cloth coat with metal buttons, a fustian waistcoat, two dowlais and two linen shirts, a pair of leather breeches and osnabrig trousers; has a silver watch in his pocket with a silver dial p[e] to it. Mathew Driscol, an Irishman, about twenty years of age, by trade a baker, five feet near six inches high, of a pale yellow complexion, his face a little pimpled, short light brown hair much inclined to curl, and round shouldered: had on and took with him, a blue coat and jacket, with yellow metal buttons, a crimson flannel waistcoat, check shirt, leather breeches, and osnabrig trousers. Charles Blundell, an Englishman, about 19 years of age, by trade a rope-maker, 5 feet 8 or 9 inches high, a very slender made fellow, much knock kneed, with light brown hair very short: had on and took with him, a dark brown jacket, osnabrig shirt and trousers. The above servants are supposed to have gone in a small boat with a black bottom, and tarred on her gunwales, is no way painted, has rings in her to be occasionally hoisted on deck by, rows very light and goes well, has a step in her keelson for a mast. Whoever takes up and secures said servants so as their masters may get them again, shall be paid forty shillings for each if taken in the province, and if out of this province £15 paid by
WHETCROFT and HIGGINSON.

N. B. Whoever brings back the boat and delivers her to the owners, shall be entitled to forty shillings reward.
W. and H.

The Maryland Gazette, November 3, 1774.

FIFTEEN POUNDS REWARD.

RAN away from Alexander Henderson, of Colchester, in Virginia, on the 28th of last month, a convict servant man, named Pooling Horne, but calls himself John Herne, he came into Potowmack in the ship Tayloe, last September, is an Englishman, about 24 years of age, 5 feet 8 or 9 inches high, with short black hair, a smooth face, and a scar under his left eye; had on and took with him, a new light grey jacket and breeches of coarse cloth, with white metal buttons, the jacket lined with striped plaiding, a black waistcoat, brown striped corderoy breeches, light marled stockings and old shoes, two new osnabrig shirts, several other shirts, silk handkerchiefs and other things. He took away a likely black blooded mare, about 14 hands high, old, a star on her forehead, branded on the near shoulder H, and M on

the near buttock. The above reward will be paid by me for the delivery of the servant and mare at Bladensburgh, or ten pounds for the mare only, and five pounds for the servant when committed to any jail in this province.
RICHARD HENDERSON.

The Maryland Gazette, November 7, 1774; December 1, 1774; December 8, 1774. See *The Maryland Journal, and Baltimore Advertiser*, November 7, 1774, and *The Pennsylvania Gazette*, November 16, 1774.

TEN POUNDS REWARD.

October 28, 1774.

RAN away from the subscriber's plantation, on Bull Run, a convict servant man, who says his name is John Hurn, but was convicted by the name of Pooling Horne, imported into Potowmack last month in the ship Tayloe; he is an Englishman, about 24 years of age, 5 feet 8 or 9 inches high, with short black hair, a smooth face, and a scar under his left eye: had on and took with him, an old blue sailors jacket, very short, with small black buttons set on thick, on both sides, a black waistcoat, brown striped cordduroy breeches, light marled stockings, and old shoes; also new light grey jacket and breeches of coarse cloth, with white metal buttons, the jacket lined with striped plaid, and 2 new osnabrig shirts, with several other shirts, silk handkerchief, and other things; he took with him, a very likely black blooded mare, about 14 hands high, old, with a star on her forehead, branded on the near shoulder H, and on the near buttock M.—I will give ten pounds, Virginia currency, reward for the servant and the mare delivered to me at Colchester, in Virginia. ALEXANDER HENDERSON.

The Maryland Journal, and Baltimore Advertiser, November 7, 1774; November 16, 1774; November 30, 1774. See *The Pennsylvania Gazette*, November 16, 1774.

Great-Pipe-Creek, Nov. 8, 1774.

RAN away last night from the subscriber, a German servant man, named *George Fell*, about five feet high, of a fresh complexion, has blue eyes, small wiskers on both sides of his cheeks, a high forehead, speaks bad English, and has lost his foreteeth: had on a whitish coat, red waistcoat, a large hat, and silver buckles. Whoever takes up said servant, and secures him so that his master may have his again, shall receive the above reward.
JACOB FERVER.

N. B. All masters of vessels and others, are forbid harbouring or carrying him off at their peril.

The Maryland Journal, and Baltimore Advertiser, November 8, 1774; November 16, 1774; December 19, 1774.

FIVE POUNDS REWARD.
October 16, 1774.

RAN away from Richard Graves, living in Kent County, Maryland, a servant man, named Thomas Mags, by trade a ship-carpenter; he has a thin visage, and is pock pitted: Any person securing the said servant, so that his master may have him again, shall receive the above reward, paid by RICHARD GRAVES.

The Maryland Journal, and the Baltimore Advertiser, November 8, 1774; December 19, 1774.

THIRTY DOLLARS REWARD.

WENT away from the subscriber, living in Dumfries, Virginia, the night of the 21st of October last, in a small boat, three servant men, viz. Joseph Fisher, a tailor, about 5 feet 5 or 6 inches high, dark complexion and hair, down look, wore blue broadcloth cloaths, good stockings, shoes, hat, and white shirt. Patrick [*sic*], a tailor, about the same size, but stouter and young, wore bearskin cloaths and otherwise well dressed. William Booth, a sailor, with a wooden leg, about five feet 7 or 8 inches high, dark complexion, and black hair, he has sundry cloaths which cannot now be recollected—I will give the above reward to any person who will deliver them to me here, and twenty dollars if secured in and gaol, or in proportion for any one of them,   ANDREW LEITCH.

The Maryland Gazette, November 10, 1774. See *The Maryland Gazette,* November 24, 1774.

Charles County, Maryland, Nov. 7, 1774.

RUN away, from the subscriber, two indented servants, imported by Capt. Joseph Street last September, one named *Robert Mills,* a Gardener; he is an Irishman, about 22 years old, a likely fresh coloured man; he had on, and took with him, a snuff coloured cloth coat and breeches, a red jacket, two white shirts, one check ditto, shoes, stockings, hat, and silk handkerchief. The other a Yorkshire man, named *James Bell,* a Miner, about 40 years old; took with him a dark blue coat, a brown jacket, snuff coloured breeches, hat, shoes, stockings, and a number of small bells. Whoever takes up the

said servants, or either of them, and brings them home, shall receive Three Pounds for each, besides what the law allows, from
SAMUEL HANSON.

The Pennsylvania Gazette, November 16, 1774; November 30, 1774; December 14, 1774; *The Maryland Gazette*, November 17, 1774; December 1, 1774; December 8, 1774. Minor differences between the papers. *The Maryland Gazette* refers to Bell as "a minor." See *The Maryland Gazette*, December 1, 1774.

TWENTY POUNDS Reward.

RAN away from the subscriber, on the 28th of last month, a convict servant man, who says his name is JOHN HERN, but was convicted by the name of POOLING HORNE, imported into Potowmack in the ship Tayloe in September last: He is an Englishman, about 24 years of age, 5 feet 8 or 9 inches high, with short black straight hair, a smooth face, has a scar under his left eye, and a down look: Had on and took with him sundry clothes, among which are a new light grey over jacket and breeches, of coarse cloth, with white metal buttons, the jacket lined with striped Scotch plaiding, a black waistcoat, and brown striped corderoy breeches. He took with him a very likely and valuable black blooded MARE, about 14 hands high, 8 years old, with a star in her forehead, branded on the near shoulder H, and on the near buttock M, has a long body, and is of a clear and beautiful colour. I will give the above reward of Twenty Pounds, Pennsylvania currency, for the Servant and the Mare, delivered to me in Colchester, Virginia.   ALEXANDER HENDERSON.

N. B. A reward of *Five Pounds* will be given to any person, who commits the servant to prison, so as his master may have him again, and of *Ten Pounds* for the mare, delivered in Bladensburg, Maryland, to RICHARD HENDERSON, or to the Printers, in Philadelphia. Nov. 10, 1774.

The Pennsylvania Gazette, November 16, 1774. See *The Maryland Gazette* Noveber 7, 1774, and The *Maryland Journal, and Baltimore Advertiser*, November 7, 1774.

November 9, 1774.

RAN away from the subscriber, living in George town, on Potowmack, the 25th day of last month, an indented servant man, named John Wilson, by trade a barber, about five feet six inches high: had on when he went away, a London brown cloth coat, red waistcoat, nankeen breeches, shoes and stockings, and a castor hat; wears his own short black hair, he is very talkative, and will endeavour to pass for a freeman, as I am told he has forged a pass; he was seen at Elk-Ridge landing, and went in a boat from

thence to Baltimore. Whoever takes up said servant, and delivers him to the subscriber at George town, shall receive if taken up twenty miles from home forty shillings, if above twenty miles and under forty, three pounds, and if above forty and under sixty miles, five pounds, and so in proportion for a greater distance, paid by   WILLIAM BELT.
The Maryland Gazette, November 17, 1774; December 1, 1774; December 8, 1774.

FORTY SHILLINGS REWARD.

RAN AWAY on Thursday the 3d instant, (November) from the schooner Endeavour, lying in Langfoot's Bay Creek, Kent County, Maryland, a convict servant man named RICHARD COE; had on when he went away, a white flannel jacket, a pair of long canvas trowsers, a check shirt, a pair of shoes and buckles but no stockings: he is a tall man, of a fair complexion, wears his own hair, and is a little pitted with the small-pox: Perhaps he may attempt to pass for a sailor, and may forge a discharge. Whoever takes up said servant and secures him in any gaol, and gives notice to his master, shall receive TWENTY SHILLINGS Reward, and if brought to Deep-water Point, Mills River, Maryland, the above Reward, besides what the law allows, paid by
JAMES BRADDOCK, or   RICHARD HARDING.
Dunlap's Pennsylvania Packet or, the General Advertiser, November 21, 1774; December 1, 1774; December 12, 1774; December 19, 1774. See *The Pennsylvania Gazette*, November 23, 1774, and *The Maryland Gazette*, December 1, 1774.

Baltimore County, Maryland. Oct. 22, 1774.
TEN POUNDS REWARD.

RAN AWAY from the subscribers, at Northampton Furnace, an Irish indented servant man, named THOMAS HARNETT, about twenty-five years of age, five feet five or six inches high, long visage, fair complexion, grey eyes, short dark brown hair, much pitted with the small pox, a thick square-made fellow, has some stoppage in his speech, is well acquainted in and about Philadelphia, and from that down about Newcastle; he has been a butcher, but has worked with a tanner in Philadelphia, also at ditching and grubbing, and has lived in and about Chestnut Level: He says he has two brothers, William and James Harnett, one of whom lives about five miles from Philadelphia, as an overseer for some gentleman, and the other about nine miles. He says he has formerly lived with one Hugh Steal, in Hance's Neck, near Newcastle, with whom he left a bond of one of his brothers to him for 60l. Pennsylvania currency, when he went home to Ireland about

twelve or eighteen months ago. He had on when he went away an oznabrug shirt and trowsers, upper jacket of white kersey with leather buttons, an under lappelled ditto of red striped gingham with sleeves, and white horn buttons with brass shanks, coarse country made shoes nailed in the heels, and an old felt hat bound round the brim. Whoever takes up the said servant, and secures him, so that his masters may get him again, shall have the above reward, paid by
CHARLES RIDGELY and HOWARD.

Dunlap's Pennsylvania Packet or, the General Advertiser, November 21, 1774; December 19, 1774; January 5, 1775; January 9, 1775; *The Pennsylvania Gazette*, November 23, 1774; December 7, 1774; January 18, 1775. Minor differences between the papers. The *Gazette* spells the names "Harnet" and "Steel."

RUN away, on Wednesday, the 2d of November, 1774, from the schooner Endeavour, when lying in Langford's Bay, Kent county, Maryland, a certain Richard Coe, a convict, was brought into this country in February last: had on, when he went away, an old flannel jacket, a check shirt and canvass trowsers, and took a dirty ozenbrigs shirt along with him, also a brown coloured coat and jacket, about half-worn, with plain plaited buttons; he is about 6 feet high, and stoops or hangs forwards as he walks, speaks much in the Lancashire or West of England dialect, and expresses himself very bad, is of a fair redish complexion, but of a down look, and pitted with the smallpox. Whoever takes up the aforesaid runaway, and secures him in any goal in this province or Pennsylvania, and gives notice thereof in the public papers, shall receive Six Dollars reward, or if brought to Deep water point, Miles River, Maryland, shall receive the said reward, and reasonable charges, from JAMES BRADDOCK.

The Pennsylvania Gazette, November 23, 1774. See *Dunlap's Pennsylvania Packet or, the General Advertiser*, November 21, 1774, and *The Maryland Gazette*, December 1, 1774.

Dumfries, October 22, 1774.
RAN away from the subscriber in Dumfries last night, three servant men, viz. Joseph Fisher, a convict and tailor, about 5 feet 6 or 7 inches high, dark visage, down look, and has a scar on his upper lip; had on when he went away, a blue coat and jacket with metal buttons, white fustian breeches and pinchbeck buckles. William Booth, a convict and [s]ailor, about 5 feet 5 or 6 inches high, has a wooden leg which he endeavours to hide with trousers, he is pitted with the small pox, dark complexion, and very black hair, he has sundry cloaths with him. Patrick Creamer, a tailor, about 21 years of age;

had on when he went away, a bearskin coat, jacket and breeches, about 5 feet 5 or 6 inches high. Whoever takes up the said runaways and delivers them to me in Dumfries, shall receive eighteen dollars reward.
ANDREW LEITCH.
The Maryland Gazette, November 24, 1774. See *The Maryland Gazette*, November 10, 1774.

FIVE POUNDS REWARD.

RANAWAY from the subscriber, near Choptank Bridge, the 15th of November, a convict servant man, named Henry Williams, was born in North Wales, speaks pretty good broken English,, wears his own hair not tied, of a yellow cast, has one strait finger on his right hand, is about 5 feet 4 inches high, stole and took with him a whitish frize short coat, with metal buttons, two [sic] large for him, old buckskin breeches, country linen trousers over them, milled stockings lately footed, good shoes &c. Whoever takes up said servant, and secures him, so that his master may get him again, shall have the above reward, or 20 shillings if 20 miles from home, and so on to 50, by me,   WILLIAM CHIPLEY.
The Maryland Gazette, November 24, 1774.

THREE POUNDS REWARD.

RAN AWAY from the subscriber, living near Ellicott's Mill, in Ann Arundle county, an indented Irish servant man named EDWARD HAYES, about twenty years of age, five feet seven or eight inches high, well set, swarthy complexion, has dark hair tied behind, and is a pert, talkative fellow; he took with him a new felt hat, a white shirt, a green casimir coat lined with green silk in the fore skirts, a pair of pale blue breeches with black knee-bands and button-holes, a pair of grey yarn hose with white tops, and a pair of old shoes lately mended. Whoever takes up and secures said servant, so that his master may get him again, shall have TWENTY SHILLINGS Reward, besides what the law allows, or if brought home, the above Reward and reasonable charges, paid by
JOSEPH HAWKINS.
Dunlap's Pennsylvania Packet or, the General Advertiser, November 28, 1774; , December 19, 1774; January 16, 1775.

EIGHT DOLLARS Reward.
November 25, 1774.

RAN away from the subscriber, living near Mr Samuel Worthington's, in the Garrison-Forest, a servant man, named WILLIAM SCROWFIELD, he is an Englishman, about 22 years of age, 5 feet 3 or 4 inches high, has short black hair, black eyes, and is very likely: had on when he went away, an old grey bath coating surtout, a middling good green cassimer coat, a striped blue and white cotton and thread waistcoat, a pair of old patched nankeen breeches, ribbed worsted stockings, a pair of black leather pumps, osnabrig shirt, and a small round hat; he is very handy in waiting in a house and taking care of horses: He likewise combs hair, and shaves. Whoever shall secure the said servant, so that I may get him again, shall have the above reward, and reasonable charges. BENJAMIN NICHOLSON.

The Maryland Journal, and Baltimore Advertiser, November 30, 1774; December 19, 1774. See *The Maryland Journal, and the Baltimore Advertiser*, From Saturday, September 18, to Saturday, September 25, 1773, and *The Maryland Journal, and the Baltimore Advertiser*, From Saturday, May 28, to Saturday, June 4, 1774.

TEN DOLLARS Reward.
Baltimore, November 28, 1774.
RAN away, last night, from the subscriber, living near the Blue Ball, a convict servant man, named Matthew Bailey, (though perhaps he may change his name) he is a stout well made fellow, about 45 years of age, 5 feet 7 or 8 inches high, of a fresh complexion, has grey eyes, and straight yellow hair: Had on and took with him, a light coloured coat, a claret coloured jacket, which buttons at the wrist with a leather button, dirty leather breeches, brown yarn ribbed stockings, old shoes, with nails in the heels, steel buckles, a large brim felt hat, one osnabrig shirt, Russia sheeting ditto, and a match-coat blanket.—Whoever takes up the said servant man, and secures him, so that his Master may have him again, shall receive if taken 20 miles from home, 5 dollars; if [3]0, 8 dollars; and if out of the province, the above reward, and reasonable charges if brought home, paid by John Bacon, in My Lady's Manor, near the Chapel, or
SAMUEL MORRIS.

The Maryland Journal, and Baltimore Advertiser, November 30, 1774; December 19, 1774.

RUN away from the subscriber, living in Caroline county (being part of Queen-Anne and Dorset counties) three servant lads, viz. *John Toothill*, aged about 22 years, about 5 feet 4 or 5 inches high; had on a kersey jacket, coarse homespun shirt, and homespun trowsers, with old breeches under them; is of a pale complexion, thin visaged, marked with the smallpox, and has lost one of his fore teeth in the under row. *John Holder*, aged about 16 or 17; had on a lappelled striped jacket; is about 5 feet high, thin countenance, high nose, and light coloured hair. *John Norman*, aged about 16 or 17; had on, when he went away, a check shirt, jacket the same as *John Toothill*, a pair of trowsers over an old pair of breeches; is of a very dark yellowish complexion, black hair, and his under lip turns down very much. Whoever takes up said runaways, and secures them in any of his Majesty's goals, shall have *Six Pounds* reward, or in proportion for either of them, paid by THOMAS STEDHAM, living near Parson Kean's, in the county aforesaid.

The Pennsylvania Gazette, November 30, 1774; December 14, 1774.
See *The Pennsylvania Gazette*, April 26, 1775.

Charles county, Nov. 25, 1774.
RAN away from the subscriber, about three weeks ago, two indented servants, Robert Mills and James Bell; the first a gardener, a healthy likely young Irishman, the other a Yorkshireman, about forty years old, by trade a mason; their apparel I do not remember, but they are pretty well dressed. Six pounds currency reward will be given for each, when brought home.
SAMUEL HANSON.

The Maryland Gazette, December 1, 1774; December 8, 1774; December 15, 1774. See *The Pennsylvania Gazette*, November 16, 1774.

Maryland, Talbot county.
RAN away, on Wednesday, the 2d of November, 1774, from on board the schooner Endeavour, when lying in Langford's-Bay, Kent county, Maryland, a certain Richard Coe, a convict; he was brought into this country in February last: had on, when he went away, an old flannel jacket, a check shirt, and canvas trousers, and took a dirty osnabrig shirt along with him, also a brown coloured coat and jacket about half worn, with plain plated buttons; a pair of white stockings, and plain plated buckles; he is about six feet high, and stoops or hangs forward as he walks, speaks much in the Lancashire or west of England dialect, and expresses himself very badly; he is of a fair reddish complexion, but of a down look, and pitted with the small-pox. Whoever takes up the aforesaid runaway, and secures him in any jail on this continent, and gives notice thereof in the public papers, shall receive six dollars reward; or. if brought to Deep-Water-Point, Miles-River, Maryland, shall receive the said reward, and reasonable charges, from   JAMES BRADDOCK.

The Maryland Gazette, December 1, 1774; December 8, 1774; December 15, 1774. See *Dunlap's Pennsylvania Packet or, the General Advertiser,* November 21, 1774, and *The Pennsylvania Gazette,* November 23, 1774.

Caecil County, December 1, 1774.
RUN away from the subscriber, living within 5 miles of Charlestown, or within 3 miles of Stevenson's Ferry, on Sasquehanna, an Irish servant man, named *Michael M'Daniel,* but is supposed to change his name; he had on, when he went away, a dark brown coat, without lining, and chewed all in the skirts by the cows, an old blue jacket, with grey back, buckskin breeches, ripped in the crotch, blue ribbed stockings, old shoes, newly mended, brass buckles, not fellows, a coarse dirty shirt, a narrow brim wool hat, with two cocks, and an iron collar on him; he is about 5 feet 5 inches high, with short black hair, black eyebrows, and is of a swarthy black complexion, marked a little with the smallpox, a straight cut on his cheek, aside his left eye, and is about 22 or 23 years of age, speaks middling good English, but a little broad; he ran away once before, and was taken and put into York goal. Whoever takes up said servant, and secures him, so as his master may get him again, shall have EIGHT DOLLARS reward, and reasonable charges, paid by   ROBERT ACKIN.
The Pennsylvania Gazette, December 14, 1774; January 25, 1775.

December 12, 1774.
EIGHT DOLLARS REWARD.
RAN AWAY on Saturday night last, from the subscriber, living in Tuckahoe, Queen Ann's County, Maryland, an Irish servant man, named THOMAS TOLBERT, about 18 or 19 years of age, 5 feet 6 inches high, well made, somewhat pitted with the small-pox, and has short black hair: Had on and took with him, a fine beaver hat bound with black velvet round the brim, an old fashioned surtout, and a redish sagathy coat, a white cotton jacket, two pair of white drilled breeches, one pair of nankeen dittio, striped holland trowsers, three pair of coarse yarn stockings, one pair of county thread ditto, four white shirts, one silk handkerchief, and a pair of shoes with double rimmed pinchbeck buckles: He also took off with him, a bay Mare, with a white star in her forehead, branded on the buttock with an I. Whoever apprehends the said servant so that his master may have him again, if taken in the county shall have FOUR DOLLARS Reward, and if out of it and in the province, the above Reward, besides what the law allows, paid by   ANDREW LEVINGTON.
Dunlap's Pennsylvania Packet or, the General Advertiser, December 19, 1774, January 2, 1775; January 30, 1775.

Baltimore, December 12, 1774. THREE POUNDS REWARD.
WENT off from the subscriber yesterday, a servant man named WILLIAM FINLEY, about 26 years of age, came from London in the Dulany, Capt. Jarrold, about twelve months ago, was bred in London, by trade a looking-glass frame maker, but since his arrival in Baltimore he has been chiefly employed at cabinet work, more particularly in making desks and dining tables; he is a tall slim fellow, has a stoop in his shoulders, thin pale visage, sharp eyes, lightish brown hair, and is an artful, soft spoken, insinuating fellow: Had on and took with him when he absconded, a darkish coloured bearskin surtout coat, a light brown tight coat with a small red collar, a striped gingham jacket with loops, black stocking breeches, new yarn stockings, and old shoes: Whoever apprehends said servant, and confines him in any of his Majesty's gaols, so that his master may have him again, shall receive, if taken twenty miles from Baltimore, TWENTY SHILLINGS; if thirty miles, THIRTY SHILLINGS; if forty miles, FORTY SHILLINGS; and if out of the province, the above Reward, paid by
ROBERT MOORE,   Cabinet-maker, in Baltimore.
Dunlap's Pennsylvania Packet or, the General Advertiser, December 19, 1774; January 9, 1775.

Queen-Anne's County, November 21, 1774.
COMMITTED to my custody, Andrew Thompson, who says he belongs to Matthew Gaud, in Baltimore County, on Chesnut Ridge, about 45 miles from Baltimore-Town—His master is desired to come and pay charges, and take him away—Said Thompson was committed by the name of Thomas Wright.   JAMES BUTLER, Gaoler
The Maryland Journal, and Baltimore Advertiser, December 19, 1774; December 26, 1774; January 9, 1775.

Elk hundred, in Caecil county, December 10, 1774.
TWENTY SHILLINGS REWARD.
RUN away from ELIZABETH KINKEY'S, an Irishman, named EDWARD TAYLOR, 21 years of age, very fair complexion, about 6 feet high, stoop shouldered; had on, when he went away, a felt hat half cocked, a blue jacket, a swanskin under blue ditto, Russia sheeting shirt, old breeches, patched with white cloth, yarn stockings, and had one buckle and one string in his shoes, when he went off, he took a new axe, branded with Benjamin Rickitt's name on it. Whoever will apprehend the said Edward Taylor, and secure him in any of his Majesty's goals, and give notice thereof to the

subscriber, so that he may bring him to justice, shall have the above reward, and reasonable charges, paid by   PATRICK LYNCH.

The Pennsylvania Gazette, December 21, 1774.

FOUR POUNDS REWARD.

Harford County, November 29, 1774.

RAN away from the subscriber, living in Harford County, Maryland, an Irish indented servant man, named Thomas Callagan, about 22 years of age, 5 feet 6 inches high, has fair hair, red beard, is pitted with the small-pox, and is a weaver by trade: Had on and took with him, a brown suit of clothes, with broad metal buttons, one pair of ticking breeches, patched with linen, three pair of stockings, check shirt, black silk handkerchief, and an old wool hat.

Whoever takes up and secures the said servant, so that his master may have him again, shall receive the above reward, paid by
JOSEPH DOWLER, or JOHN BRYEELY.

The Maryland Journal, and Baltimore Advertiser, December 26, 1774; January 2, 1775; January 9, 1775.

FIVE POUNDS REWARD.

December 26, 1774.

RAN away from the subscriber, living in Baltimore County, the 18th of September last, a servant man, named John Coughlen, 30 years of age, about 5 feet 6 or 8 inches high, black curled hair, muddy coloured gray eyes, high cheek bones, large legs, stands and walks straight, his apparel uncertain, as he has changed them since he went away; he is a lusty well made man, speaks good English, but may be known to be an Irishman by his discourse and behaviour; he pretends to be a strict Roman Catholic, but is in fact a hypocrite; he took an Indenture belonging to one Thomas Holton, with a discharge on the same from Mr. Jonathan Hanson; it is supposed he will pass by that indenture, or a pass of his own forging, as he can write a good hand; it is supposed he will make for the lower counties, and that by water if he can get a passage. Whoever takes up said servant, and secures him in any gaol on the continent, and gives notice, so that I get him again, shall have the above reward, and reasonable charges, including what the law allows, paid by   JAMES WELSH.

N. B. All masters of vessels and others, are warned not to entertain or harbor said servant at their peril.

The Maryland Journal, and Baltimore Advertiser, December 26, 1774; January 9, 1775. See *The Pennsylvania Gazette*, October 5, 1774.

Chester, December 26, 1774.

NOW in the goal of Chester, and county of Chester, John Welch, belonging to James Black, in Kent county, Maryland; John Eagan...Peter Brown, a Mulattoe....Their masters are desired to come, pay charges, and take them away in three weeks from this date, otherwise they will be discharged, paying their fees.   JOEL WILLIS, Goaler.

The Pennsylvania Gazette, December 28, 1774.

Lancaster, December 20, 1774.
EIGHT DOLLARS Reward.

RUN away from the subscriber, on Sunday night, the 18th inst. an indented servant man, named Jared Ervin....

Was committed to my custody, the following servants, viz. Charles M'Null...William Wagham....Michael M'Daniel, *a servant to Robert Aitkin, in Maryland; was committed the 3d day of December.* Daniel Hearly....*Their masters are desired to come, pay charges, and take them away in three weeks, otherwise they will be discharged, on paying their fees, by*   GEORGE EBERLY, Goaler.

The Pennsylvania Gazette, December 28, 1774. See *The Pennsylvania Gazette*, January 25, 1775.

Erratum page to Index

Shane, Timothy, 304
Shaw, James, 72
Shaw, Timothy, 293
Sheeles, Thomas, 259
Sheldon, John, 180
Shepperd, William, 120
Sheridan, Thomas, 179
Sherrid, John, 256
Shields, James, 208
Shields, John, 43
Shipley, John, 176
Short, Isaac, 315
Silcocke, Jacob, 62, 63, 72
Simmins, Edward, 22
Simmons, Isaac, 274
Simon, Joseph, 20
Simpson, Matthew, 193
Skees, Richard, 136
Skellton, Standiford, 113
Skipper, Isaac, 275
Skyram, John, 253
Skyrme, John, 214
Slacum, Captain, 201
Slacum, Job, 185
Slade, Richard, 219
Small, Mr., 25
Smally, Timothy, 147
Smart, William, 109
Smith, James, 142, 150
Smith, John, 7, 294, 315, 326
Smith, John Adam, 191
Smith, Stephen, 57
Smith, Thomas, 82, 303
Smith, William, 72, 210
Smyth, Thomas, 137, 227, 234
Snow, Willam, 4
Snowden, H., 284
Snowden, Henry, 213
Snowden, John, 178, 183, 225, 284
Snowden, Mr., 120, 280
Snowden, Samuel, 178, 183, 225, 284

Snowden, Thomas, 154, 212, 213, 225, 291
Socea, Anthony, 91
Somervell, Alexander, 90, 99
Sowerbutts, Marsh, 320
Sparrow, James, 139
Spencer, Captain, 178
Spencer, Thomas, 228
Sprague, John, 159
Sprigg, Richard, 278
Spriggs, Thomas, 291
Springall, William, 253, 263
Springate, William, 95, 99
Sprotson, Croasdale, 262
Squires, Daniel, 37
Stackabout, William, 210
Stanton, Adam, 68
Stanton, John, 132
Steal, Hugh, 333
Stectham, Thomas, 141
Stedham, Thomas, 337
Steele, John, 165
Stephens, Olivers, 102
Stephens, William, 119, 215
Steuart, George, 179, 278
Steuart, Stephen, 299
Stevens, Edward, 138
Stevenson, Edward, 134, 314, 319
Stevenson, Henry, 272, 319
Stevenson, John, 314
Steward, Stephen, 121, 148, 190, 238
Stewart, James, 303
Stewart, Mr., 4, 6
Stewart, Stephen, 105
Stiles, Joseph, 258
Stillin, John, 24
Stoakes, Francis, 153
Stone, Frederick, 31
Stone, T., 31
Stone, Thomas, 290
Story, Enoch, 317

These names follow page 361 and were inadvertently left out of the Index.

INDEX

Abair, Joseph, 138
Abbot, William, 155, 158
Abbott, William, 208
Ackin, Robert, 338
Adams, George, 23, 46
Adams, James, 209
Adams, Ralph, 305
Adamson, George, 25
Addams, John, 231
Addison, John, 7, 81
Adley, Joseph, 140
Agan, Roger, 246
Ager, Thomas, 20, 22, 207
Agnew, Thomas, 40
Aikens, John, 9
Aile, Boston, 97
Ainzell, Charles, 292
Airey, Thomas Hill, 309
Aisquith, William, 199
Aitkin, Robert, 341
Aldworth, Joseph, 74
Alexander, Arthur, 155
Alexander, Mark, 38, 66, 73, 106
Allan, William, 138
Allen, Charles, 90, 164
Allen, George, 281
Allen, John, 281
Allen, William, 176
Allmerry, John, 220
Allsworth, Samuel, 14
Ambler, Samuel, 67
Amies, Edward, 127
Anderson, Captain, 52
Anderson, John, 227
Anderson, Joseph, 248, 250, 253
Andrew, William, 286
Angess, William Daniel, 129, 130, 141
Armstrong, George, 223
Armstrong, Robert, 209
Arnett, William, 137

Ashburner, John, 76
Ashmore, Tobias, 55
Ashworth, Allis, 323
Atkinson, John, 250
Attix, George, 10
Ayre, Thomas, 315
Ayres, Abraham, 39
Ayres, Robert, 120
Babb, Thomas, 268
Backster, George, 13
Bacon, John, 336
Baggott, John, 146
Bagnall, John, 223
Bagnell, John, 128
Bailey, Anne, 79
Bailey, Matthew, 336
Bailey, Thomas, 154
Baird, Thomas, 292
Baker, Charles, Jr., 65
Baker, Henry, 252
Baker, James, 216, 217
Baker, John, 67, 152
Baker, Nicholas, 306
Ball, Henry, 27
Ball, John, 271
Ballandine, John, 57
Barber, James, 91
Barclay, David, 144
Barclay, William, 274
Barker, James, 231
Barker, Joseph, 297
Barker, William, 41
Barkush, John, 231
Barnes, James, 181
Barnet/Barnett, William, 25, 26
Barnett, Richard, 296
Barney, William, 188
Barnhold, John, 148
Barr, Robert, 205
Barrell, William, 114

Barris, James, 99
Barrot, Andrew, 155
Barrowcliff, John, 153
Barry, Bernard, 195, 200
Barset, John, 90
Bartham, George, 71
Bartlett, John, 90
Bartley, Robert, 306
Bass, Robert, 159
Bate, John, 91
Bateman, Michael, 189
Bates, John, 91
Bathum, George, 152
Baver, John, 318
Bawden, William Henry, 68
Bawn, William, 284
Baxter, George, 81
Bayley, Henry, 151
Bayne, John, 277
Baynes, John, 2
Beakes, William, 205
Beall, Benjamin, 226
Beall, Ninian, 118
Beall, Rinian, 121
Bean Edwin, 314
Bees, Robert, 301
Bell, Alexander, 253
Bell, David, 36
Bell, George, 40
Bell, James, 331, 337
Bell, Robert, 305
Belong, Joseph, 278
Belt, William, 333
Benfield, David, 319, 320
Bennett, Hooper, 214, 233
Bennett, Joseph, 80
Bentley, Thomas, 43
Bently, John, 6
Berkley, Samuel, 84
Berns, Thomas, 122
Berry, Benjamin, Jr., 161

Berry, Zachariah, 161
Besson, Nicholas, 172
Bevan, Thomas, 57, 58
Bevers, Thomas, 153
Biddle, Thomas, 134
Bigham, Robert, 1
Bishop, John, 1
Bissey, John, 133
Bitting, Henry, 128
Bivens, Thomas, 152
Black, James, 281, 341
Black, Richard, 241
Blackall, John, 53
Blair, Mr., 132
Blake, William, 27
Bleany, Thomas, 74, 87
Blincoe, Thomas, 3
Blundell, Charles, 329
Boardman, James, 63
Bocker, John, 138
Bollard, Samuel, 230
Bollord, Samuel, 182, 202
Bond, Buckler, 65, 280
Bond, Charles, 112
Boner, Conrod/Conrad, 244, 247
Booth, Jonathan, 273
Booth, William, 331, 334
Bordley, Stephen, Jr., 101
Bordley, William, 101
Bordman, James, 50
Bosman, Edward, 40, 41, 139
Boswell, Henry, 220, 234, 301, 304
Boswell, Timothy, 220, 234
Bottin, John, 126, 127
Boucher, Captain, 219
Boucher, Mr., 2
Boucher, Rev. Mr., 168, 169
Boucher, Thomas, 320
Boudren, Thomas, 285
Bowen, William, 155
Bower, Daniel, 158

Bowers, James, 253
Bowers, William, 202
Bowie, Allen, Jr., 30
Bowie, Fielder, 128
Bowling, Thomas, 173
Bowlls, George, 30
Boyd, James, 208
Boyes, Richard, 322
Boythroid, Jeremiah, 156
Braddock, James, 333, 334, 337
Bradshaw, William, 93
Brady, Thomas, 327
Brand, John, 148
Brassup, Joseph, 93
Bravard, Benjamin, 133
Bready, Thomas, 269
Breaten, Thomas, 276
Breaton, Thomas, 296
Breckinridge, Captain, 21
Brellossic, John, 117
Brian, John, 101
Briscoe, Richard, 317
Britten, Abraham, 166
Britton, Nicholas, 23, 46, 220, 234
Broadstreet, Captain, 278
Brobson, William, 288, 299
Brooke, Baker, 290
Brooke, Basil, 152
Brooke, Clement, 61, 169
Brooke, James, 143
Brooke, Rev. Mr., 169
Brooke, Richard, 169
Brooke, Thomas, 267
Brooker, Dr., 170
Brooks, Benjamin, 159
Brooks, Humphrey, 18
Brooks, John, 150
Brown, Captain, 167, 287
Brown, David, 128
Brown, George, 129, 275
Brown, Hugh, 197

Brown, James, 145, 277, 282, 328
Brown, John, 65, 108, 110, 128, 129, 279
Brown, Joshua, 108
Brown, Noah, 196
Brown, Peter, 341
Brown, Richard, 108
Brown, William, 29, 30, 133, 326
Browning, George, 107, 109
Bruce, David, 156
Bruce, Normand, 70
Bruscup, Joseph, 110
Bryan, George, 289
Bryan, John, 268
Bryan, Thomas, 59, 92
Bryant, Robert, 237
Bryarly, Hugh, 223
Bryeely, John, 340
Buchanan, Andrew, 103, 289
Buchanan, Mr., 236
Buchannan, James, 157
Buck, John, 148
Buckinhorne, James, 328
Buckland, W., 258
Buckland, William, 230, 246, 250, 263, 266
Bull, Constantine, 171
Bull, John, 8, 9
Bullin, Luke, 95, 178
Bulmore, George, 225
Burgess, Caleb, 49
Burgess, Charles, 71
Burk, Tobias, 186, 252
Burke, Festus, 267
Burn, Bartholomew, 164
Burn, George, 150
Burn, Thomas, 59, 295
Burnes, John, 64
Burney, Jane, 5
Burnham, Solomon, 321
Burns, Hugh, 103

Burrell, Thomas, 5
Burten, William, 186
Burtus, Samuel, 271
Butler, James, 108, 339
Butler, Peter, 26, 41
Buttler, John, 214
Button, Richard, 271
Byers, Margaret, 292
Byers, William, 292
Cail, Moses Rankin, 75
Calender, Philip, 39
Callagan, Thomas, 340
Callahan, Thomas, 191
Camden, Henry, 258
Campbell, Captain, 278, 303
Campbell, Charles, 58
Campbell, Robert, 143, 150, 164
Canby, Samuel, 326
Cannon, Patrick, 151
Canter, William, 80
Carcaud, David, 275
Carmichael, William, 299
Carnan, Charles, 243
Carney, Winney, 271
Carpenter, William, 286, 289
Carr, George, 83
Carr, John, 28, 89
Carrol, John, 204
Carroll, Charles, 16, 37, 191
Carroll, William, 184
Carson, Humphrey, 83
Carson, Joseph, 310, 312
Carter, Jeremiah, 68
Carter, Timothy, 81, 85
Carver, William, 262
Case, Shadrick, 303
Caswell, William, 39
Cather, William, 24
Catling, James, 34
Caton, John, 148
Cattell, John, 75

Causin, Gerard B., 125
Chaddock, Thomas, 222
Chaffy, John, 111
Chambers, James, 192
Chamier, Daniel, 5, 96, 99
Chance, Jeremiah, 110
Chapman, Samuel, 321
Chauncey, George, 190
Cheston, James, 262
Chew, Mr., 188
Chipley, William, 335
Christie, Robert, Jr., 253, 306
Christopher, John, 106
Church, Wait Still Singellton, 226
Clapham, John, 7, 11, 31, 41, 57, 81,
    85, 90, 121, 124, 128, 145, 162, 165,
    169
Clark, David, 99
Clark, Donald, 99, 147
Clark, John, 17, 252
Clark, Mary, 146
Clarke, James, 184
Clayton, John, 222
Cleary, Caleb, 10
Clement, John, 224
Clements, John, 231
Clements, Walter, 173
Clemmisson, Amburst, 40
Clemons, John, 231
Clifford, John, 146, 277, 297
Clifford, Thomas, 283
Clingan, William, 207
Coady, William, 197, 205
Cochran, John, 117
Cockey, John, 51, 205
Cockey, Thomas, 221
Cockle, John, 249
Coe, Mark, 307
Coe, Richard, 333, 334, 337
Cole, John, 162, 163, 165
Coleman, James, 205

Collerd, Thomas, 29, 30
Collier, John, 207
Collings, William, 8
Collins, Timothy, 316, 323
Collins, William, 69, 186
Colloquher, William, 162
Columbine, Thomas, 277
Compton, Stephen, 11
Condon, John, 5
Cone, Rebecca, 221
Conn, William, 177
Connelly, Charles, 103
Connelly, Henry, 214
Connelly/Connolly, Lawrence, 247, 249
Connely, Thomas, 287, 298
Conner, Michael, 300, 305
Conner, Thomas, 118
Conner, Timothy, 107, 109, 129
Conney, James, 314
Conray, Michael, 315
Conwan, Evan, 220, 234
Conway, James, 231
Conway, Thomas, 54
Cookman, James, 153, 291
Cooksey, John, 33
Coomb, John, 280
Cooper, Sarah, 249
Copland, Captain, 170
Coppinger, John, 229, 256
Corbin, Thomas, 127
Corker, Timothy, 255
Corman, Joseph, 136
Cormick, Thomas, 213
Corner, Thomas, 124
Cornish, Charles, 4
Cornthwait, John, 241
Costolow, Edward, 229
Coughlen, John, 319, 340
Coulson, Thomas, 18
Cowan, Alexander, 222, 309, 313
Cowan, Samuel, 181, 202, 230

Cowell, Francis, 86
Cox, James, 82
Cox, John, 11
Cox, William, 111
Coyl, Owen, 201
Crabb, Richard, 154, 156, 297
Crafford, David, 231
Craig, Adam, 278
Craighill, William, 131
Crain, John, 83
Crandell, William, 45
Cravan, Laurence, 51
Crawford, David, 128
Crawley, John, 79
Creamer, Patrick, 331, 334
Cresap, Colonel, 206
Cresop, Colonel, 253
Croker, William, 294
Cromwell, William, 286, 289
Crosby, Mr., 282
Cross, Thomas, 163
Crouch, Richard, 75
Crowley, Cornelius, 17
Crowly, Cornelius, 48
Crowly/Crowley, John, 60, 61
Crum, William, 294
Cullen, Joan [sic], 14
Cumming, David, 101
Cumming, Robert, 101
Cummings, Anthony, 305
Cummings, Cornelius, 288
Cummings, John, 91
Cummins, Robert, 144, 288
Cunning, James, 256
Cunningham, Barney, 268
Curly, Bridget, 285
Dale, Samuel, 66
Dallam, Richard, 132
Dalrymple, Colonel, 143
Dalton, Michael, 195
Dalton, Thomas, 308

Dangerfield, Samuel, 226
Daniel, Benjamin, 15
Danks, John, 216
Darby, Henry, 253
Darough, Richard, 322
Darragh, James, 256
Darroctt, Richard, 319
Dashiell, George, 216
Daughadey, James, 96
Dautistel, Jacob, 187
Davey, Edward, 170
David, John, 308
David, William, 54
Davidson, Sarah, 197
Davidson, William, 197
Davie, Michael, 229
Davis, Alexander, 314
Davis, Edward, 89
Davis, John, 307
Davis, John Forrest, 135
Dawson, James, 71
Dawson, John, 223
Dawson, William, 176
Day, Thomas, 273
Day, William, 125
Dayly, Charles, 3
Deaken, William, 236
Deakins, William, Jr., 267, 290
Deale, Samuel, 73, 105
Delany, Walter, Jr., 131
Delany, William, 144
Dempsey, James, 282
Dennis, John, 6
Denny, John, 251
Denny, Peter, 43
Devall, William, 195
Dew, Henry, 53
Diar, James, 261
Dick, James, 4, 6
Dickerson, William, 15
Dickinson, James, 242

Dickson, James, 162, 163, 165
Digges, William, 103
Diglan, Peter, 326
Dillin, Moses, 255
Dilling, Thomas, 4
Ditto, William, 110
Dixon, Christopher, 104
Dobbins, Joseph, 33
Dobbs, John, 51
Dodd, Charles, 16
Dodson, William, 174
Dogood, Charles, 88
Dominick, Joseph, 287
Donaboo, John, 236
Donovan, James, 76
Doon, John, 261
Dorcias, Erasmus, 117
Dorrovan, Daniel, 11
Dorsey, Benjamin, 35, 47
Dorsey, Caleb, 10
Dorsey, Flora, 2
Dorsey, John, 44, 57, 149, 247, 249
Dorsey, Joshua, Jr., 241
Dorsey, Richard, 327
Dorsey, Samuel, 210
Dorsey, Samuel, Jr., 272, 322
Dougherty, Archibald, 129
Dougherty, Thomas, 215
Dowden, Widow, 217
Dowler, Joseph, 340
Dowling, Patrick, 49
Downey, Alexander, 151
Downs, John, 36
Doyl, John, 142
Doyl, Thomas, 325
Doyle, Thomas, 239
Driscol, Mathew, 329
Driver, John, 212, 250
Driver, John/Windsor, 119
Drury, Mr., 15
Drybrow, Thomas, 138

Ducker, Jeremiah, 255
Dudgen, John, 328
Dudgen, Joseph, 328
Duff, Thomas, 233
Duffee, Patrick, 152
Duffey, Nill, 111
Duffey, Robert, 202
Duffey, Solomon, 49
Duffield, Jacob, 21
Duke, James, 145
Dukehart, Volerius, 287
Dukemart, Volarius, 9
Dulany, Benj., 280
Dulany, D., 196, 200
Dulany, Walter, 32, 164
Duncannson, James, 138
Dunlap, William, 243
Dunlop, Andrew, 117, 139
Dunn, Daniel, 52
Dunn, Patrick, 308
Dunn, Thomas, 81
Duoneilly, Daniel, 194
Duvall, Charles, 136
Duvall, Cornelius, 35
Duvall, Howard, 39
Duvall, Joseph, 119, 120
Duvall, William, 106, 116, 120
Dwyer, Darby, 258
Dyer, Thomas, 75, 78, 93
Eagan, John, 341
Earls, Daniel, 214
Earls, John, 150
Eason, John, 34
East, Charles, 3, 5, 123
Easton, Thomas, 278
Easun, William, 304
Eberly, George, 42, 49, 69, 129, 206, 341
Ebert, John, 286, 289
Eden, Captain, 282
Edmons, William, 282

Edwards, Joseph, 6
Edwards, William, 205
Egleston, Charles, 244
Ellingsworth, Richard, 212
Elliott, Edward, 177
Elliott, Thomas, 174
Ellis, Daniel, 239
Ellis, John Joyner, 103
Ellison, Alexander, 139
Elton, Thomas, 136
Enman/Eaman, Thomas Henry, 131
Ennalls, Thomas, 3rd., 248, 251, 253
Ennis, Patrick, 282
Ensey, John/Joseph, 86
Ensor, Mrs., 111
Etherington, Benjamin, 11
Evans, Arthur, 35
Evans, Rachel, 57
Everett, Joseph, 259
Evin, Jared, 341
Evins, Joseph, 113
Ewel, Richard, 167
Fagan, William, 164
Falconer, Jacob, 257
Faris, John, 200
Farrow, Robert, 265
Fell, George, 330
Fendall, Philip R., 17
Ferguson, James, 5
Ferver, Jacob, 330
Field, James, 176
Field, Matthew, 174
Fields, Roger, 125
Finley, William, 7, 339
Finney, John, 293
Finney, Manasseh, 293
Fisher, James, 328
Fisher, Joseph, 331, 334
Fisher, Laurance, 320
Fitzgarrel, Nicholas, 233
Fitzpatrick, Barnard, 236, 240

Fitzpatrick, Bryan, 191, 194
Fleming, John, 207, 312
Flemings, Henry, 15
Flemming, Richard, 190
Fletcher, John, 52
Flint, William, 203
Floyed, James, 136
Foard, William, 178
Fogarthy/Fogaty, John, 245, 266
Footman, Richard, 53
Ford, Taylor, 128
Foreman, Charles, 92
Forkner, Jacob, 252
Forster, Joseph, 139
Forster, Ralph, 143, 150, 160, 162, 175, 177, 208, 239, 245, 253
Forwood, John, 25, 26, 52, 53, 180
Fossett, John, 12
Foster, John, 270
Founder, Conrad, 187
Fowler, John, 2
Fowler, Thomas, 284
Fraley, Henry, 249
Francis, Barsel, 9
Francis, James, 101
Francis, John, 129, 130, 142, 192, 194
Franey, John Baptist Dilla, 258
Franklin, James, 28, 61, 77, 89
Franklin, Thomas, 316, 323
Franks, David, 132
Fraser, Hugh, 35
Fraugher, Reuben, 138
Frazer, Andrew, 54, 66
Frazer, Henry, 209
Freeman, William, 242
French, James, 92, 124
French, Otho, 183, 315
French, Thomas, 59
Frost, Captain, 7
Gafford, William, 260
Gaither, John, Sr., 156

Gale, George, 168
Galloway, Samuel, 18, 238
Galloway, Thomas, 150
Gambol, John, 219
Gardener, John, 217
Gardner, John, 217
Gardner, William, 327
Garland, James, 240
Garretson, Job, 95, 98
Garrett, Amos, 132
Garrett, Edward, 321
Gasford, Samuel, 168, 170
Gatrill, Stephen, 81
Gaud, Matthew, 339
Gearn, Thomas, 59
Geddes, William, 148
Gellaher, Con, 293
Gents, James, 166
George, William, 321
German, Hugh, 35
Gibbons, Thomas, 5
Giles, Jacob, 270
Giles, James, 254, 264
Gilmer, Daniel, 232
Gilpin, Samuel, 87, 96
Gilsom, John, 120
Gist, Joshua, 261
Gist, Mordecai, 117, 140
Glanding, John, 71
Glass, John, 128
Gleen, Johannes, 51
Glowen, John, 214
Glynn, Elizabeth, 238
Glynn, Thomas, 238
Goddard, James, 286, 289
Godman, Humphry, 128, 169, 239
Golden, Richard, 72
Golding, Peter, 16
Goldsborough, Charles, 209, 222
Good, John, 205
Goodwin, John, 3, 4

Gordon, Isaac, 276
Gordon, James, 213, 214
Gordon, John, 172
Gorman, John, 70
Gorsuch, David, 122, 123
Gorsuch, John, 95, 98
Gott, Richard, 67
Gough, John, 271
Gouldsboury, Michael, 107, 109
Graham, Richard, Jr., 145
Graham, Riginald, 174
Graham, William, 145
Grahame, Patrick, 32
Gramer, Jacob, 311
Grant, Daniel, 262
Grant, John, 10
Grant, Thomas, 61
Grason, Richard, 270
Graves, John, 90
Graves, Richard, 331
Gray, Captain, 303
Gray, George, 253
Graybil, Michael, 187, 197
Graybill, Jacob, 79
Grayham, John, 103
Greaves, Richard, 214
Green, James, 255
Green, John, 12, 33, 116
Green, Richard, 62
Greene, Job, 268
Gregory, Thomas, 275
Gresham, Richard, 111
Grey, John, 116
Gribbine/Gribin, James, 167, 169
Griffin, George, 121
Griffis, Philip, 85
Griffith, Greenberry, 217
Griffith, Greenbury/Greenberry, 217
Griffith, Henry, Jr., 147
Griffith, Joshua, 168
Griffith, Nathan, 112

Griffith, Phillip, 55
Guffey, John, 133
Gullokey, William, 145
Guthrie, James, 229, 239
Guttrey, John, 205
Gwynn, Mansfield Lewis, 37, 41
Hackit, John, 181
Hackman, James, 143, 166
Hagget, John, 147
Hail, George, 94
Haines, Anthony, 238, 239
Hains, John, 268
Hall, Aquila, 115
Hall, George, 10
Hall, James, 77
Hall, Jane, 291
Hall, Philip, 186
Hall, Sarah, 166
Hall, Thomas, 62, 250
Hambleton, John, 209
Hamersley, John, 128
Hamilton, Alexander, 103
Hamilton, Charles, 215
Hamilton, John, 197, 304, 310, 323
Hamilton, John, Jr., 167
Hamilton, Nicholas, 141
Hamilton/Hamlon, William, 173
Hammond, Charles, Jr., 14
Hammond, Denton, 32, 80
Hammond, Mr., 241
Hammond, William, 118
Hamond, Thoma, 177
Hand, Ann, 1
Handlen, Thomas, 235
Handley, Richard, 117
Hannon, Joseph, 176
Hanson, George, 19
Hanson, Jonathan, 340
Hanson, Samuel, 332, 337
Hanson, W., 328
Hanson, William, 194, 283, 323

Hanway, Thomas, 54
Harbett, William, 68
Harday, Charles, 289
Hardey, Robert, 296
Harding, Richard, 333
Harmon, Edward, 4
Harnett, James, 333
Harnett, Thomas, 333
Harnett, William, 333
Harper, William, 76, 78
Harris, Alexander, 124
Harris, John, 42, 53, 58, 279, 311
Harris, Samuel, 36
Harrison, Robert, 4
Harrison, William, 17
Hart, George, 103
Harvey, Robert, 313
Harvey, Thomas, 202
Hastings, Oliver, 90
Hateley, Ralph, 251
Hawk, William, 176
Hawkins, John, 293
Hawkins, Joseph, 335
Hawkins, Thomas, 260
Hayes, Edward, 335
Hayes, William, 242
Hays, Benjamin, 75
Hays, Michael, 303
Hayward, Joseph, 12, 116
Hearly, Daniel, 341
Heavey, Daniel, 56
Heeston, John, 122, 123
Hellen, Richard, 3rd., 265
Henderson, Alexander, 329, 330, 332
Henderson, James, 107
Henderson, John, 13
Henderson, Richard, 330, 332
Hendricks, James, 309
Henry, William, 207
Henwood, Robert, 214
Hepburn, Francis, 175

Herkins, Daniel, 38
Hern, John, 332
Herne John, 329
Heslop, Mr., 132
Hewes, William, 42
Hewitt, Thomas, 27
Hewitt, William, 20
Hickey, John, 32, 80
Hickins, James, 212
Hickman, Andrew, 85
Hickman, James, 207, 256
Higginson, Mr., 329
Higton, Paul, 95, 98
Hill, John, 45
Hill, Sarah, 106
Hill, William, 185, 223, 244
Hilyear, John, 126
Hindman, Richard, 139
Hinson, Richard, 78
Hinton, John, 124
Hipit, William, 99
Hitchcock, Josiah, 163
Hobbs, Joseph, Jr., 198
Hodge, Thomas, 281
Hodges, William, 31
Hogan, James, 69
Hogg, Thomas, 212, 225
Holaway, James, 24
Holder, Edward, 53
Holder, John, 336
Holladay, James, 135
Holliday, James, 145
Holliday, John R., 94, 104, 295
Holliday, John Robert, 64, 86, 88, 109, 214, 219, 238
Hollingsworth, Henry, 155, 158, 208
Hollingsworth, John, 221
Hollis, John, 270
Hollis, William, 310
Holloway, John, 230
Holmes, John, 177

Holmes, William, 80
Holton, Thomas, 340
Hood, John, 44, 47, 300
Hood, John, Jr., 44, 47, 198, 201
Hooke, Andrew, 239
Hoolbrooke, Jacob, 2
Hooliday, John Robert, 103
Hooper, Edward, 1
Hopkins, Hopkins, 264
Hopkins, William, Jr., 298
Horn, William, 31
Horne, Pooling, 329, 330, 332
Hoskins, Thomas, 230
Householder, Henry, 55
Houston, William, 52
Howard, Benjamin, 92
Howard, Caldwell, 258
Howard, Charles, 21, 22, 208
Howard, Collwell, 230
Howard, Ephraim, 14, 50, 118, 212, 214
Howard, Henry, 14, 50, 111
Howard, James, 15, 147, 168, 181
Howard, Mr., 334
Howard, Mrs., 102
Howard, Samuel, 71, 153
Howell, Nicholas, 224
Hudson, James, 260
Hughes, Daniel, 229, 256, 293, 320
Hughes, Elisha, 60
Hughes, Peter, 54, 66
Hughes, Samuel, 229, 256, 293, 320
Hughs, John, 14, 50
Hughs, William, 136
Hukill, James, 248
Humphreys, Edward, 215, 216
Humphreys, Elizabeth, 327
Humphreys, Frances, 40
Humphreys, John, 327
Humphries, John, 13
Humphries, Martha, 72
Hunt, James, 236, 241

Hunt, William, 178
Hunter, James, 131
Hunter, Peter, 27, 200
Hunter, Richard, 103
Hurn, John, 330
Husband, Joseph, 233
Hutchings, James, Jr., 163, 165
Hutchings, Thomas Elliott, 131
Hutchinson, James, 19
Hymon, Richard, 76
Hynson, John Carvill, 93
Hynson, Nath., 28
Hynson, Richard, 93
Hytch, Christopher, 154
Iiams, John, Jr., 174
Iiams, William, 23
Inch, Ann, 46
Inch, John, 41
Inkley, William, 16
Inman, John, 189
Insellow, James, 231
Insheek, Benjamin, 69
Inskeep, Benjamin, 70, 97
Ireland, John, 255
Irvin, Thomas, 82
Irwin, Francis, 326
Irwin, Robert, 308
Jacks, Edward, 165
Jackson, Anthony, 44, 47, 198, 201
Jackson, Captain, 173
Jackson, Daniel, 152
Jackson, James, 123
Jackson, William, 50
Jacobs, Joseph, 84
Jacques, Mr., 188
James, Daniel, 159
James, Joseph, 118
James, Micajah, 260, 264
James, William, 92, 223
Jarrett, Abraham, 110, 291
Jarrold, Captain, 339

Jarvis, John, 26, 40
Jeffery, Hugh, 310, 312, 325
Jefferys, Samuel, 88
Jeffries, William, 205
Jenkins, William, 157
Jennings, John, 217
Jennings, Joseph, 271
Jevins, John, 7
Jewel, Robert, 33
Jewell, William, 159
Joe, Margaret, 146
Johns, William, 243
Johnson, Barnett, 219
Johnson, E., 303
Johnson, James, 188, 301
Johnson, John, 16, 122, 329
Johnson, Joseph, 79
Johnson, Richard, 141
Johnson, Robert, 193
Johnson, William, 65, 66, 73, 106, 133, 219, 275
Johnston, James, 282
Johnston, John, 64
Johnston, Robert, 173
Jolly, John, 100
Jones, Jehu, 6
Jones, John, 28, 46, 135, 198
Jones, Lewis, 146
Jones, Nancy, 214
Jones, Richard, 144
Jones, Robert, 188
Jones, Thomas, 51, 303
Jones, Will, 100
Jones, William, 29, 30
Jordan, Michael, 298
Joseph, Henry, 18
Joyce, Thomas, 325
Jurey, Thomas, 148
Justice, Charles, 310
Kamp, Hercules, 65
Kayn, Alexander, 277

Kayser, Dominick Joseph/Joseph, 287
Kayton, John, 122, 123
Keaine, Dennis, 24
Kealing, John, 327
Kean, Parson, 337
Keener, Melcher, 274, 293
Kees, Thomas, 41
Keith, Andrew, 30
Kelly, John, 79
Kelly, Michael, 19
Kelly, Peter, 62
Kelly, Samuel, 252
Kelly, Thomas, 20
Kelso, Anthony, 82
Kelso, James, 263, 275
Kenally, Henry, 214
Kenley, William, 298
Kennedy, Daniel, 309
Kennedy, Henry, 36
Kennelly, Henry, 48
Kess, Henry, 249
Key, Job, 306
Key, Philip, 284
Keyser, John, 232
Kidd, Captain, 160
Kidd, John, 209
Kilty, John, 276
King, Ann, 282
King, John, 90
King, Thomas, 278
Kinkey, Elizabeth, 339
Kinnard, Mary, 25
Kinsiner, John, 180
Kinsiner, John Balser, 244
Kipp, Benjamin, 5
Kirk, Thomas, Sr., 46
Kirkpatrick, Hugh, 261
Kitchen, George, 110
Kneller, William, 264
Knellers, William, 260
Knight, Charles, 83

Knight, John, 279
Knight, William, 257
Kraner, Michael, 205
Lacey, Thomas, 166
Lacland, John, 30
Lacy, Hugh, 14, 50
Lacy, Thomas, 13
Lake, Thomas, 263
Lamb, Joseph, 176
Lamberd, James, 296
Lane, Captain, 275
Lane, Hardage, 3
Lane, Richard, 277
Lane, William Carr, 13
Langley, William, 64, 93, 98, 119, 127
Lappen, Cormack, 121
Lathim, James, 108
Lathim, John, 114
Laughley, John, 70
Laughley, Philip, 66
Lavely, William, 180
Lawrence, John, 34
Lawrence, Levin, 219
Lawrence, Richard, 214
Lawson, Ralph, 311
Lawson, Thomas, 184
Leaman, John, 253
Leary, Bartholomew, 210
Leary, Jeremiah, 219
Lee, Corbin, 142
Lee, George, 149
Lee, Mr., 159
Lee, Philip Ludwell, 43
Lee, Philip Thomas, 318
Lee, Richard, 104, 211, 215, 224, 234, 318
Lee, Richard, Jr., 57, 119
Lee, William, 81, 127, 162, 237, 267
Leetch, Solomon, 122
Lehan, Darby, 308
Leitch, Andrew, 303, 331, 335

Lemmon, Jacob, 60, 306, 324
Levely, William, 99
Levey, Michael, 229
Levington, Andrew, 338
Lewis, Curtis, 185
Lewis, James, 234
Lewis, John, 142, 189
Lewis, Robert, 172
Lidick, Philip, 13
Lidig, Philip, 167
Life, Robert, 34
Lightfoot, Thomas, 97
Lightfoot, William, 97
Linch, John, 87
Linderman, Henry, 249
Lindsey, James, 284
Linnaham, Darby, 302
Linsey, James, 280
Liston, John Tom, 91
Little, Adam, 193
Loftis, Ralph, 166
Logan, John, 33
Loney, Edward, 3, 4
Long, James, 186
Long, Martin, 42
Long, Richard, 69
Long, William, 257
Loveday, Joseph, 183
Lovely, Thomas, 149
Lowe, William, 212
Lowed, William, 113
Lowry, Jacob, 231
Lucas, George, 85
Lusby, James, 42
Lutts, Philip, 102
Lux, Darby, 265
Lux, Mr., 188
Lux, William, 265
Lyles, William, 278
Lynch, James, 66
Lynch, Patrick, 340

Lynch, Peter, 293
Lyon, William, 227
Lytle, George, 86
Maccubbin, James, 57
MacDonald, Daniel, 30
Mack, Robert, 193, 213, 231
Mackelfresh, John, 226
Mackie, Ebenezer, 124
Mackie, William, 210
Macmin, Nathaniel, 181
MacNabb, John, 10, 70
Macnamara, Nicholas, 327
Maddin, Nathaniel, 192
Magergy, Patrick, 83
Magill, Mr., 268
Magin, Edward, 263
Maginan, Edward, 254
Magrath, William, 232
Magruder, Rector, 48
Mags, Thomas, 331
Main, John, 78
Maine, John, 75
Manning, John, 179
Manyfold, Joseph, 189
Mara, John, 87, 96
Marr, Ms., 92
Marsh, Catherine, 43
Marsh, John, 86, 88
Marshall, Captain, 206, 218
Marshall, James, 180
Marshall, John, 112
Marshall, Joseph, 19
Marsham, James, 161
Marshman, James, 161
Martin, Bartholomew, 175
Martin, James, 184
Martin, John, 230
Martin, Thomas, 152
Martingle, John, 252
Mason, Richard, 284
Mason, Thomas, 112

Master, Legh, 115
Master/Masters, Legh, 77
Mather, James, 258
Mathers, Mr., 268
Mathews, William, 243
Matilda, Susanna Carolina, 194
Matthews, John, 146
Maw, Edmond, 37, 42
Mawe, James, 196, 200
May, Anthony, 219
Mayfield, Thomas, 197
Maynard, William, 144
McAdow, John, 261
McBoise, Richard, 312
McBoyes, James, 322
McBride, Daniel, 286
McCabe, William, 72
McCaddem, Barney, 23
McCan, Hugh, 259
McCandles, George, 312
McCandless, George, 219
McCann, Thomas, 53, 58
McCarty, David, 110
McCarty, George, 124
McCarty, James, 3, 4
McCarty, Owen, 222
McCarty, Peter, 81, 85
McCason, George, 214
McCausland, Captain, 66
McClusky, Patrick, 213
McCollister, Richard, 207
McComos, William, 34
McConel, John, 308
McCormick, Edward, 110
McCoy, Angus, 82
McCoy, Nicholas, 273, 292
McCubbin, James, 59
McCullen, William, 69
McCullum, William, 97
McDaniel, Ann, 145
McDaniel, John, 308

McDaniel, Michael, 338, 341
McDaniel, Patrick, 193
McDonald, Angus, 198, 206
McDonald, John, 82, 184, 312
McDonald, Patrick, 197
McDonall, Ann, 135
McDougall, Captain, 34, 44, 45, 47, 51, 99, 114
McDougall, William, 51
McDugal, Captain, 260
McEvoy, Roger, 18
McFading, Dennis, 157
McFall, John, 5
McFarland, Daniel, 42
McGachen, Mr., 173
McGinley, James, 302
McGlaskey, Patrick, 214
McGowen, Thomas, 54
McGuier, Daniel, 232
McGuire, Michael, 180
McGuire, Michael, Jr., 245
McHard, Isaac, 255
McInerhency, Thomas, 257
McKain, Hugh, 244, 247
McKeehan, John, 285
McKenzie, John, 93
McLachland, Neal, 132
McLane, James, 183
McLaughlin, John, 205
McMahan, Hugh, 205
McMahon, James, 179
McMahon, John, 285
McNull, Charles, 341
McVaven, Benjamin, 205
Meahan, John, 60
Mealy, Roger, 92
Meavis, John, 156
Meconekin, John, 305
Meek, Andrew, 149
Meeke, John, 7
Meriwether, Reuben, 269, 328

Merryman, Nicholas, 307
Merryman, Nicholas, Jr., 324
Meve, Benjamin, 181
Middleton, Anne, 75
Middleton, Mr., 17
Miller, Captain, 143, 145
Miller, Catherine, 112
Miller, Conrad, 239, 325
Miller, Jacob, 221
Miller, James, 57, 59
Miller, John, 13, 251
Miller, Joseph, 12
Miller, Samuel, 60, 62, 79
Miller, Solomon, 218, 252
Miller, Thomas, 157, 295
Miller, William, 319
Milligan, George, 130
Mills, Robert, 318, 331, 337
Milner, Edward, 102
Milson, Abraham, 94
Milson, Susanna, 94
Mitchell, George, 270
Moalson, James, 177
Moncreiff, Archibald, 292
Monroe, Spence, 131
Montgomerie, Thomas, 281
Montgomery, Robert, 270
Moody, Betty, 13
Mooneys, James, 231
Moor, Joseph, 20
Moor, William, 132
Moore, George, 328
Moore, James, 25, 108, 328
Moore, John, 42
Moore, Risdon, 3, 5, 123
Moore, Robert, 100, 199, 339
Moore, Thomas, 82
Moorehead, James, 308
Moran, John, 117
More/Moore, Alexander, 137
Morgan, Charles, 76, 78

Morgan, John, 187
Morgan, Lydia, 74
Morgan, Mr., 99
Morgan, Patrick, 281
Morgan, Thomas, 205
Morphey, John, 141
Morris, Joseph, 256
Morris, Samuel, 336
Morris, Thomas, 219
Morrison, Captain, 242, 310, 312
Mummy, Samuel, 21
Munks, James, 317
Murdock, John, 31
Murien, John, 167
Murphey, William, 290
Murphy, Edward, 3, 4, 55, 251
Murphy, Morgan, 129
Murphy, Nicholas, 305
Murray, Edward, 4
Murray, James, 310, 312, 325
Murray, Patrick, 301
Murrey, Martha, 282
Myers, George, 295
Myers, Jacob, 62, 64, 73, 199
Nabb, Joseph, 194
Nagel, George, 51
Neal, Dennis, 199
Neale, Samuel, 291
Neavers, John, 3
Negroes, Abram, 41; Berkshire, 243; Boston, 160; Cato, 308; Dick, 231; George, 231; Gilbert, 166; Harry, 64; Isaac, 280; Jack, 165, 305; Jacob, 284; Jem, 64; Joas, 64; Joe, 121; John Jones, 100; John Nichols, 280; Moses, 64; Ned, 41, 291; Pero, 231; Peter, 231; Pompey, 193; Prince, 143; Sarah, 28; Samuel Harday, 289; Toney, 108; Whitehaven, 121
Neilson, John, 157
Nevin, James, 20

Nevin, Patrick, 206
Newton, James, 119, 250
Nesbitt, James, 153
Newton, Thomas, 31
Nicholson, Benj., 273
Nicholson, Benjamin, 221, 232, 235, 302, 305, 336
Nickolson, James, 160
Nicol, Captain, 278
Nicolls, Isaac, 3, 123
Niness, William, 3, 4
Nisbett, John, 275
Noble, William, 184
Nodding, John, 268
Noke, Samuel, 291
Noke, William, 184, 187, 210, 257, 321
Noler, Alexander, 276
Norman, John, 337
Norrington, Thomas, 215
Norris, William, 133
Norton, John, 32
Norwood, Edward, 11, 126, 127, 322
Norwood, Samuel, 189
Nower, Janus, 115
Nujen, Hugh, 259
Nunar, James, 209
Nunn, Edmund, 216
O'Brien, John, 115
O'Donovan, Richard, 317
O'Hara, Arthur, 33
O'Brion, Mark, 313
O'Brion, Mary, 313
Oakly, George, 32
Obriant, John, 210
Offord, James, 210
Ogle, Joseph, 178
Oliver, John, 153
O'Neal, Lawrence, 233, 246
Orme, John, 79
Osborn, Walter, 130
Osborne, William, 160

Otley, George, 300
Overfield, Peter, 277
Owen, Thomas, 323
Owing, Samuel, 289
Owings, Caleb, 321
Owings, John, 188, 235
Owings, Richard, 153, 188, 235, 283
Owings, Samuel, 153, 283
Owings, Samuel, Jr., 182, 203, 230
Owings, Thomas, 21, 22, 208, 257
Pain, Mary, 258
Painter, Thomas, 308, 313
Palmer, William, 267
Pancoast, Adin, 209
Pancoast, William, 209
Pardon, Catharine, 170
Parker, Captain, 28, 53, 299
Parker, John, 307
Parker, Mary, 179
Parks, Richard, 53
Parks, Thomas, 305
Parrish, William, Jr., 55
Parson, Richard, 78
Parsons, John, 237
Patrick, John, 109
Patrick, Robert, 128
Patterson, Samuel, 70
Patton, Abraham, 94, 98, 119, 128, 293
Patton, Abraham, 274
Patton, George, 271
Patton, John, 241
Paul, William, 157
Paxman, John, 307
Payne, Richard, 261
Payne, Thomas, 166
Pearce, Henry Ward, 6
Pedder/Peather, John, 272
Pell, John, 86, 88
Pen, James, 322
Pendergast, Richard, 237, 267
Pendergest, Richard, 160, 175

Pendergrass, Richard, 197
Penny, Benjamin, 142
Perigo, James, 264
Perimon, Thomas, 302
Perkins, Isaac, 151
Perry, Charles, 151
Perry, Thomas, 305
Perry, William, 126
Petercoster, Nicholas, 305
Peters, Abraham, 65
Peterson, John, 193
Philips, John, 234
Philips, Mary, 234
Philips, Thomas, 115, 119
Philips, William, 108
Phillips, John, 280
Phillips, Thomas, 106
Philpot, Benjamin, 221
Phipps, Stephen, 89
Piers, William, 316
Pindelbury, Marmaduke, 147
Pinkeney, Isaac, 122, 123
Pinkney, Robert, 67
Piper, James, 251
Pitt, John, 99
Pitt, William, 211, 213
Plain, William, 16
Plovey, Thomas, 84
Plowman, Jonathan, 201, 327
Plowman, Mr., 41
Plowman, Philip, 289
Plummer, John, 203
Pollard, John, 133
Pollingbrook, Jeremiah, 154
Pomeroy, Henry, 253
Pool, Joseph, 74, 86
Poole, Samuel, 14, 168
Poor, Daniel, 214
Porter, Benjamin, 292, 294
Porter, Charles, 173, 247, 249
Porter, Collin, 19

Poteet, Thomas, 33
Powel, John, 228
Powel, William, 39
Powell, John, 174, 239
Powis, Samuel, 290
Prat, John, 2
Pratt, Francis, 224
Preston, Bernard, 8
Preston, Daniel, 251
Preston, Thomas, 108
Price, Aquila, 171, 172
Price, Thomas, 49, 55, 56, 63, 207, 246, 266
Prince, Hubbard, 87
Pringle, John, 308
Priskil, Silvester, 269
Pritchard, James, 193
Pugh, Thomas, 49
Purviance, Samuel, Jr., 81
Pusey, Thomas, 281
Putrell, Thomas, 223
Puttrell, Thomas, 210
Quelch, John, 60
Quelch, William, 254
Quiegly, Thomas, 76
Quima, John, 236
Quinn, Patrick, 182, 203
Raften, Daniel, 158
Ragan, Timothy, 187
Ragon, Morris, 5
Raison, Captain, 210, 223
Ramsay, Alexandria, 100
Randall, Bale, 84
Randall, John, 279
Randall, Larkin, 50, 56, 63
Randall, Thomas, 92
Randall, William, 84
Randell, George, 1
Rankin, John, 12
Ranson, Willian, 112
Ratcliff, Stephen, 228

Read, John, 77, 96
Read, Nathaniel, 84
Read, Robert, 264
Ready, Thomas, 135
Redford, William, 38
Redmond, Andrew, 114
Reed, Henry, 274
Reed, John, 227
Rees, Daniel, 196, 246
Reese, Daniel, 99
Reeves, William, 26
Reid, Captain, 210, 223
Reid, James, 150
Reily, Barnard, 222
Reily, John, 8, 9
Renshaw, Philip, 308
Rew, Joshua, 142
Reynolds, James, 8, 9
Reynolds, John, 132
Reynolds, William, 71, 130
Rhodes, John, 318
Rice, John, 314
Richard, Thomas, 70
Richards, Stephen, 301
Richardson, Awbray, 100
Richardson, John, 161
Richardson, Robert, 16
Richardson, Sarah, 76
Rickets, William, 174
Rickitt, Benjamin, 339
Riddick, Josiah, 161
Ridgely, Charles, 27, 42, 296, 334
Ridgely, Charles G., 94
Ridgely, Charles, Jr., 58
Ridgely, Henry, 203, 207
Ridgely, Major, 268
Ridgely, Nicholas Greenbury, 168
Ridley, Matthew, 45
Ridout, John, 284
Ridrom, Joseph, 117
Rigden, Edward, 24

361

Rigden, Thomas, 236
Riggs, Samuel, 143
Riley, Bell, 30
Riley, James, 153, 282
Riley, Owen, 303
Riley, Patrick, 14
Ring, Thomas, 134
Ringgold, Thomas, 292
Robe/Robin, Robert, 205
Roberson, John, 104
Roberts, John, 117, 216, 241, 255
Roberts, Levin, 66
Roberts, Mr., 1
Roberts, William, 95, 98
Robertson, Captain, 253, 263
Robertson, Henry, 253
Robertson, John, 166
Robertson, Lawrence, 149
Robeson, John, 54
Robeson, Peter, 282
Robinson, Abraham, 55
Robinson, Captain, 305
Robinson, George, 192
Robinson, John, 19
Robinson, William, 16, 205
Rock, Patrick, 312, 322
Rodgers, John, 114
Rogers, Benjamin, 210, 246
Rogers, Edward, 162, 163, 165
Rogers, Hugh, 235
Roper, James, 191
Ross, John, 28, 29, 57, 59
Routlidge, James, 92
Rowe, Mary, 218
Roynane, Dennis, 38
Royston, James, 130
Ruckman, Thomas, 74
Rudge, William, 124
Rue, Joshua, 189
Ruff, Richard, 211
Rufner, Peter, 149

Ruggles, Mr., 282
Rupum, Winlock, 68
Russell, Mr., 188
Russell, Thomas, 155
Russell, William, 45
Rutland, Thomas, 25, 95, 162, 178
Ryan, Thomas, 201
Rylot, Edward, 133
Sadler, Richard, 245, 262, 266
Salisbury, Thomas, 318
Salmon, Francis John, 208
Salter, Thomas, 180
Sanders, William, 275
Sandford, William, 5
Sands, Benjamin, 265
Sapleton, Thomas, 11
Sappington, Thomas, 216
Sawyer, Charles, 245, 266
Scanian, Edward, 164
Scarran, John, 214
Schawn, Cornelius, 254
Scott, George, 2
Scott, Henry, 104
Scott, James, 228
Scott, John, 50
Scott, Joseph, 323
Scott, Upton, 196
Scott, William, 290
Scrowfield, William, 231, 272, 335
Scully, Thomas, 228
Sedgwick, Matthew, 155
Seedhouse, Mary, 305
Self, Stephen, 159
Sellars, Francis, 187
Sellers, Francis, 167
Selman, William, 176
Semple, Henry, 249
Semple, Robert, 128
Sexton, Thomas, 281, 283
Shane, Arthur, 198
Shane, Cornelius, 210

Street, John, 41
Street, Joseph, 331
Sudler, Emory, 69
Sullivan, Dennis, 229
Sullivan, Patrick, 128
Sutton, Thomas, 212, 284
Sweeny, Bernard, 197
Symonds, William, 45
Talbey, William, 204
Tandy, John Merry, 8
Tankard, William, 195, 199
Tayloe, Colonel, 90
Taylor, Edward, 339
Taylor, James, 2
Taylor, Jenifer, 138
Taylor, John, 11, 180, 183
Taylor, Robert, 84
Tharp, Jacob, 245
Thomas, Captain, 124, 188
Thomas, George, 299
Thomas, James, 192, 307
Thomas, John, 303, 308
Thomas, Joseph, 25
Thomas, Meredith, 206, 218
Thomas, Richard, 19, 36, 48, 66, 67, 69, 70, 80, 103, 137, 193, 303, 308
Thomas, Willam, 299
Thompson, Andrew, 339
Thompson, Benjamin, 123
Thompson, James, 83
Thompson, Mr., 172, 242
Thompson, Richard, 212
Thompson, Samuel, 17
Thompson, William, 11, 179
Thomson, Lawrance, 114
Thomson/Thompson, Isaiah, 48
Thornton, Captain, 168
Thornton, Thomas, 283
Tilbury, Thomas, 305
Tilghman, Richard, 298
Tink, John, 146

Tipins, George, 101
Tipping, Thomas, 34, 47
Tittle, John, 154
Todd, Thomas, 240, 308, 325
Tofft/Toft, Thomas, 167, 169
Tolbert, Thomas, 338
Tool, David, 295
Tool, Thomas, 7
Toole, David, 104, 238
Toothill, John, 336
Towland, Haly, 248
Townsend, Thomas, 100
Travers, William, 324
Trayner, Samuel, 309
Trevers, Thomas, 26
Tucker, Seborn, 281, 283
Tuff, Betty, 13
Tuff, Thomas, 233
Turberville, Mr., 159
Tutle, John, 141
Ullas, Mr., 35
Unrick, Rosannah, 246
Unsworth, John, 46
Unthank, Daniel, 171
Valliant, Robert, 243
Vancleave, John, 206
Vickers, William, 151
Wagham, William, 341
Wakefield, John, 262, 266
Walch, Nicholas, 302
Walker, Charles, 125
Walker, John, 86
Walker, Thomas, 147
Walker, William, 210, 223
Wall, Edward, 111
Wallace, William, 278
Wallis, Hector, 226
Walsh, John, 259
Ward, Joseph, 140
Ward, Thomas, 186
Ward, William, 143

Warfield, Philemon, 269
Warfield, Seth, 33
Warle, Joseph, 108
Warren, Richard, 37
Warricker, William, 47
Warriker, William, 44
Warrington, Benjamin, 294
Watkins, Nicholas, 316, 323
Watts, Robert, 45
Watts, William, 36
Weatherall, Philip, 16
Weathers, William, 39
Weaver, Henry, 180
Weaver, Thomas, 8
Webb, Sarah, 7
Webb, William, 202
Weeden, Robert, 170
Welch, John, 341
Welch, Joseph, 164
Welch, Nicholas, 308
Welch, Richard, 45
Weldon, William, 190
Weles, William, 15
Welkis, James, 319
Wells, Alexander, 21, 22, 208, 233
Wells, Benjamin, 50, 63
Wells, Charles, 279, 311
Wells, Christopher, 75
Wells, John, 54, 279, 311
Welsh, James, 319, 340
Welsh, John, 54, 281
Welsh, Patrick, 286
Welsh, Thomas, 288
Welsh, William, 25
Werhle, Philip, 311
West, Edward, 75
Wharton, Robert, 183
Wheatley, Thomas, 171
Wheeler, Jacob, 38
Wheeler, Nathan, 196
Whetcroft, Mr., 329

Whetcroft, W., 292
Whitaker, Abraham, 38
White, James, 249
White, John, 18, 185, 208, 237, 275
White, Thomas, 1
White, William, 257
Whiteford, John, 269
Whitehead, James, 51
Whitelock, Charles, 79
Wiffen, Joseph, 226
Wilcocks, John, 327
Wilcox/Willcox, John, 320
Wiley, David, 300
Wilkes, James, 311
Wilkin, Thomas, 192
Wilkins, Mary, 192
Wilks, James, 322
Willard, Edward, 182
Willcox, Michael, 254
Willett, Ninian, Jr., 50
Williams, Andrew, 94, 103
Williams, Edward, 211, 213, 290
Williams, George, 11, 72
Williams, Henry, 285, 335
Williams, John, 14, 64
Williams, Owen, 303
Williams, Thomas, 84
Williams, William, 157
Williamson, John, 161
Williamson, William, 162
Willis, Joel, 308, 327
Willis, Thomas, 32
Willlis, Joel, 341
Willmott, Robert, 27
Willson, John, 80, 315
Wilson, Captain, 76
Wilson, George, Sr., 114
Wilson, James, 263
Wilson, John, 43, 214, 306, 332
Wilson, Robert, 288, 298
Wilson, Sarah, 194

Wilson, Thomas, 166
Wilson, William, 69, 97
Windrode, Jacob, 119, 125
Winham, James, 322
Winters, John, 118
Wiseman, John, 7
Wisnor, Matthias, 323
Withers, William, 59
Witmore, Henry, 133
Wonn, Edward, 279, 311
Wood, Joseph, 259
Wood, Thomas, 69
Wood, William, 128, 169, 239
Woods, John, 308
Woodward, Abraham, 140
Woolferd, John, 272
Woolridge, Stephen, 188
Worgar, John, 92, 105, 121

Worthington, Brice, 164
Worthington, Brice T. B., 77, 240
Worthington, Charles, 177, 207
Worthington, John, Jr., 49
Worthington, Samuel, 204, 220, 225, 301, 304, 335
Wright, Archibald, 91
Wright, Thomas, 339
Yates, W., 317
Yealdhall, Gilbert, 140
Yeates, Richard, 184
Yetts, Frances, 96
Yorke, John, 304
Young, Charles, 206, 218
Young, George, 265
Young, Mr., 213
Young, Samuel, 66
Young, William, Jr., 211
Zimmerman, Frederick, 138

www.ingramcontent.com/pod-product-compliance
Lightning Source LLC
Chambersburg PA
CBHW071147300426
44113CB00009B/1108